THE COIN COLLECTOR'S SURVIVAL MANUAL®

FIFTH EDITION

SCOTT A. TRAVERS

House of Collectibles
New York Toronto London Sydney Auckland

 Published in the United States by House of Collectibles, an imprint of The Random House Information Group, a division of Random House, Inc., New York, and simultaneously in Canada by Random House of Canada Limited, Toronto.

House of Collectibles and colophon are registered trademarks of Random House, Inc.

RANDOM HOUSE is a registered trademark of Random House, Inc.

Coin Collector's Survival Manual® and *Coin Collector's Survival*®are registered trademarks of Scott A. Travers.

Some of the material in this book appeared previously in *How to Make Money in Coins Right Now*, by Scott A. Travers.

The author holds or has previously held positions in various for-profit and non-profit hobby organizations. The views reflected in this book are his own and do not reflect the views of any such organization. The author also may have a financial or other interest in some or all of the products or organizations featured or reviewed in this book.

Coin photographs are for educational purposes and are not necessarily reproduced to scale.

ON THE COVER:

1909-S V.D.B. Lincoln cent, PCGS MS-66 RED. *(Photograph courtesy Superior Galleries)*

1898 Morgan dollar, NGC Proof-69, ex Jenks. Designated "finest known U.S. silver dollar (1794–1935)" in 1992 by the National Silver Dollar Roundtable. *(Photograph courtesy Terry J. Popkin, www.popkinphoto.com)*

1933 Saint-Gaudens double eagle, sold at auction by Sotheby's and Stack's in July 2002 for the world record price of $7,590,020. *(Photograph courtesy Sotheby's)*

ON THE SPINE: 1898 Morgan dollar, NGC Proof-69, ex Jenks.

This book is available for special discounts for bulk purchases for sales promotions or premiums. Special editions, including personalized covers, excerpts of existing books, and corporate imprints, can be created in large quantities for special needs. For more information, write to Special Markets/Premium Sales, 1745 Broadway, MD 6-2, New York, NY, 10019 or e-mail *specialmarkets@randomhouse.com*

Please address inquiries about electronic licensing of any products for use on a network, in software, or on CD-ROM to the Subsidiary Rights Department, Random House Information Group, fax 212-572-6003.

Visit the House of Collectibles Web site: www.houseofcollectibles.com

Printed in the United States of America

10 9 8 7 6 5 4 3 2

Library of Congress Control Number: 2002116864

ISBN-10: 0-375-72127-4

ISBN-13: 978-0-375-72127-4

CONTENTS

To my parents

ACKNOWLEDGMENTS

The author extends credit to the following individuals who lent expertise, knowledge and ability in the preparation of the text:

John Albanese; Ed Aleo; David T. Alexander; Charles Anastasio; Susan Anderson; Richard A. Bagg; Jon Bahner; Dennis Baker; Gail Baker; Doug Baliko; Tom Bilotta; Q. David Bowers; Kenneth E. Bressett; Robert Brueggeman; Chris Bush; Tom Caldwell; David Camire; Bob Campbell; Randy Campbell; Michael A. Chipman; Christopher Cipoletti; Simon Codrington; Pedro Collazo-Oliver; William L. Corsa, Sr.; D. Larry Crumbley; Barry Cutler; John W. Dannreuther; Frederick W. Daily; Steve Deeds; Beth Deisher; Thomas K. DeLorey; Silvano DiGenova; Shane Downing; Steve Eichenbaum; Michael S. Fey; William Fivaz; Harry J. Forman; Les Fox; Leo P. Frese; Michael Fuljenz; David L. Ganz; Jody Garver; Salvatore Germano; Larry Gentile, Sr; Marcy Gibbel; William T. Gibbs; Richard Giedroyc; Ira Goldberg; Larry Goldberg; Barbara Gregory; Mike Gumpel; Cathy Hadd; David G. Hall; Kenneth Hallenbeck, Jr.; James L. Halperin; Cary B. Hardy; David C. Harper; Sarri R. Harper; Dorothy Harris; Reed Hawn; Michael R. Haynes; Brian Hendelson; Alan Herbert; John Highfill; Ed Hipps; William H. Horton, Jr.; Erin Hughes; Robert L. Hughes; Steve Ivy; Jay W. Johnson; Robert W. Julian; Donald H. Kagin; Christine Karstedt; Melissa Karstedt; Christopher Kirkpatrick; George Klabin; Charles H. Knull; Timothy J. Kochuba; Robert Korver; Chester L. Krause; Randy Ladenheim-Gil; Ron M. Howard; Mark LaFlaur; David W. Lange; Julian M. Leidman; Robert J. Leuver; Gary E. Lewis; Jesse Lipka; Kevin J. Lipton, Sr.; David Lisot; Denis W. Loring; Andrew P. Lustig; Susan Maltby; Dwight N. Manley; Steve Mayer; John McDonough; Robert F. McLaughlin; Raymond N. Merena; Bob Merrill; Lee S. Minshull; Richard S. Montgomery; Phoebe D. Morse; Bernard Nagengast; William J. Nagle; Paul Nugget; John Pack; Jay Parrino; John Pasciuti; Martin B. Paul; Robert Paul; William P. Paul; Donn Pearlman; Douglas Plasencia; Arnold I. Rady; Henry Rasof; Ed Reiter; Robert S. Riemer; Steven Ritter; Greg Roberts; Edward C. Rochette; Gregory J. Rohan; Maurice H. Rosen; Deborah G. Rosenthal; Will Rossman; Margo Russell; Mark Salzberg; Florence M. Schook; Rick Sear; Thomas W. Sharpless; Larry Shepherd; Michael W. Sherman; James C. Sherwood; Jeffrey Shoop; Rick Snow;

Stephen H. Spahn; Harvey G. Stack; Michael J. Standish; Sheryl Stebbins; Jeffrey A. Stern; Barry Stuppler; David Sundman; Anthony J. Swiatek; James Taylor; Sol Taylor; Barbara J. Travers; Harvey C. Travers; Julius Turoff; Armen R. Vartian; Simon Vukelj; Matthew Weigman; Fred Weinberg; Michael White; John Wilson; Nancy Wilson; Mark Yaffe; Marc D. Zand and Keith M. Zaner.

Credit is also due the following companies and institutions:

American Numismatic Association; American Numismatic Rarities, LLC; Amos Press, Inc.; ANACS; Auctions by Bowers and Merena, Inc.; Bausch & Lomb Optical Company; Coin Dealer Newsletter, Inc.; E&T Kointainer Co.; First American Numismatics, Inc.; Heritage Galleries & Auctioneers; Industry Council for Tangible Assets; Intercept Shield LLC; Krause Publications, Inc.; Miller Magazines, Inc.; Numismatic Conservation Services, LLC; Numismatic Guaranty Corporation of America, Inc.; Professional Coin Grading Service; Professional Numismatists Guild, Inc.; Sotheby's; Superior Galleries; Universal Coin & Bullion, Inc.; U.S. Mint; and Whitman Publishing, LLC.

The following individuals are due credit and special thanks for their generous contributions of photographs and other materials, time and advice, and support ("original manuscript" refers to the raw material before it was first submitted in 1984):

John Albanese, who candidly explained subtle tactics used by unscrupulous dealers to rip off consumers and who offered courageous and controversial opinions on grading standards.

Q. David Bowers, who carefully selected Morgan dollar color photographs from the American Numismatic Rarities image archive in order to illustrate grading from AG-3 to MS-68 and who, over the years, wrote me many pages of suggestions for previous editions.

Kenneth E. Bressett, editor of *A Guide Book of United States Coins*, who carefully reviewed the grading chapter in earlier editions and made invaluable suggestions, and who provided the most explicit photographs of hairlines on a Proof I've ever seen.

David Camire, president of Numismatic Conservation Services LLC, who provided exceptionally crisp color digital images that skillfully educate in the area of conservation and curation.

Pedro Collazo-Oliver, a former ANACS authenticator/grader, who provided most of the photographs for the chapter concerning altered and counterfeit coins, and who closely read the original manuscript for this chapter and made some sensible revisions.

D. Larry Crumbley, KPMG Endowed Professor at Louisiana State University and the author of many books and articles on taxes and collectibles, who offered opinions about coins and retirement plans.

Frederick W. Daily, renowned tax lawyer and author of critically acclaimed books on taxes, who spent much time helping to review, update and offer opinions on the sections throughout the book that relate to taxes.

Thomas K. Delorey, former senior authenticator of the ANA Certification Service, who spent endless weeks and many tiring hours examining the original manuscript and making important revisions in the coin grading areas.

Shane Downing, publisher of the *Coin Dealer Newsletter*, who reviewed the major portions of the book that refer to wholesale values and candidly shared with me important information about how the teletype systems work.

William Fivaz, authority on cherrypicking and an ANA seminar instructor, who provided me with outstanding photographs of coin striking characteristics, first points of wear, and Proof and non-Proof coins and who made valuable suggestions about grading at the time of his reading the original manuscript.

David L. Ganz, top coin lawyer and a former president of the American Numismatic Association, who wrote important sections on taxes, securities laws, and grading standards.

Dorothy Harris, director of antiques and collectibles for Random House Information Group, who provided extraordinary inspiration and guidance in making this work of tremendous scope and magnitude the ultimate consumer protection tool.

James L. Halperin, co-chairman of the board of Heritage Capital Corporation and the Bill Gates of the coin industry, who revealed how he makes a mint by cracking coins out of their certified holders and upgrading them; who shared various anecdotes and fascinating experiences in 68 e-mail communications; and who spent hours personally searching through his archives for appropriate photographs to illustrate grading nuances.

Charles H. Knull, one of the nation's leading intellectual property lawyers, who was instrumental in making this new edition—a complicated blending of two books—a working reality.

Mark LaFlaur, editor for the Random House Information Group, who tirelessly and conscientiously fine-tuned important details of the manuscript.

Susan Maltby, highly regarded conservator, preservation authority, and *Coin World* columnist, who spent considerable time reviewing the chapters for earlier editions on cleaning, storage, preservation and safety; who updated information for earlier editions in her specialty area with painstaking accuracy; and who shared information about preservation for earlier editions that should prove to be a public service to numismatics for generations.

Phoebe D. Morse, former Boston regional director of the Federal Trade Commission (FTC), who, for an earlier edition, and in her FTC capacity, provided me with FTC documentation of cases brought against coin dealers.

Ed Reiter, *COINage* senior editor and author of *The New York Times Guide to Coin Collecting*, for his close review of virtually every area of the book; for his time-consuming careful check of historical facts and figures; and for his support of the book and me from Day One in his articles for *The New York Times*.

Maurice H. Rosen, editor/publisher of the *Rosen Numismatic Advisory*, who reviewed many of the survival strategies suggested in this book and, on a cumulative basis over the years since the first edition, spent many weeks devoted totally to writing various sections.

Deborah G. Rosenthal, one of the most talented contract lawyers I know, who reviewed important areas of my agreement with Random House and also offered opinions on sections of the book that deal with the law.

Anthony J. Swiatek, editor/publisher of the *Swiatek Numismatic Report*, who spent countless hours reviewing the original manuscript; who gave me photographs illustrating the effects of "dipping"; and who allowed me to reprint the results of his study concerning artificial toning.

Armen R. Vartian, leading numismatic attorney, who provided opinions about doctored coins; who served as the source of information about donating coins to charity, and who wrote an excellent synopsis about coins and the Internet.

Marc D. Zand, certified public accountant, who offered his professional opinions about the general tax implications of certain coin transactions.

The following individuals, now deceased, were important contributors to earlier editions:

Stanley Apfelbaum; Morris Bram; Walter Breen; Clarence Clarkson; Ron Downing; John J. Ford, Jr; Thomas V. Haney; Allen Harriman; George D. Hatie; Arthur M. Kagin; Helen Carmody Lebo; Leon Lindheim; James L. Miller; Bob Rose; Joseph H. Rose and Michael Keith Ruben.

Special recognition is given to David Hall and the Professional Coin Grading Service for providing extraordinary color photographs of artificially toned, doctored, altered and counterfeit coins.

John W. Dannreuther, senior grader for PCGS and one of the finest grading minds and most brilliant numismatists our industry has to offer, devoted much time to assist in describing some of the digital images provided by PCGS for the color section.

Michael W. Sherman, senior vice president of Collectors Universe, was instrumental in seeing that PCGS provided digital images for the color section, and he painstakingly reviewed and edited some of the detailed information in chapter 13. He also made many suggestions to improve the text and provided a comprehensive list of suggested words to be added to the glossary.

PREFACE TO THE FIFTH EDITION

The rare coin market has changed considerably since 1984, when *The Coin Collector's Survival Manual* appeared in its first edition. This new fifth edition reflects those changes with extensive additions and enhancements. It is, in fact, far and away the most comprehensive makeover this book has ever undergone.

Amid all these revisions, though, my basic message to readers remains very much the same: Profiting from rare coins takes knowledge, shrewdness, and a high degree of healthy skepticism. Today, as in 1984, the coin market is a perilous place for the unwary—an ocean filled with hungry sharks just looking for a chance to feast on a powerless victim. Now as then, *The Coin Collector's Survival Manual* gives you the equipment—the survival kit—you need to emerge from those waters unscathed . . . not just to survive, but to thrive. It is the ultimate consumer protection resource.

From beginning to end, this is by far the largest and most sophisticated edition ever published. This is in response to a coin market that is larger and more sophisticated now than ever before.

The original edition demystified coin grading by revealing the thought process of the American Numismatic Association Certification Service, then the leading service in the field. Since then, the ANA has sold its grading service, and new coin grading companies have come to the fore. With those new companies come new concerns—grading standards apparently not remaining completely constant is one of them.

In some respects, the advent of independent third-party certification services addressed the grading problem that was undermining the marketplace in 1984. Expert grading backed by a guarantee restored a high degree of confidence and significantly reduced the threat that had been posed by rampant and flagrant overgrading at the time of this book's first edition. But grading-related abuses persist in less obvious forms, and these remain the greatest source of potential financial losses for consumers. This new edition identifies these abuses and tells you how to avoid being victimized. You will find many words of updated advice on changes in grading standard methodologies.

In addition to mere words, sharp, enlarged photographs show the subtle nuances of coin grading today. This edition features magnificent new digitized images—exceptional color pictures that are the products of the finest technology in the business. The beefed-up color section has surprising photos of the same coin given different grades by leading services, examples of difficult-to-detect doctored and altered coins, and illustrations of endangered coins rescued from harm's way.

In one of the most extensive and significant updates of all, the chapter on mail-order abuses has been expanded to address in detail the hazards of buying rare coins on the Internet. Here, you will find the very latest state-of-the-art advice about state-of-the-art technology—in particular, vital caveats on bidding in online auctions and how you're most likely to get ripped off by sellers if you do.

There has been a perceptible deviation in the direction of looser interpretation or enforcement of some grading guidelines. You will find valuable tips on how to turn these grading nuances into sizable profits by capitalizing on these apparent changes in the standards of some certification services. This is an area where even a very small edge might mean a difference—plus or minus—of hundreds, even thousands, of dollars.

Many thousands of dollars can be lost, too, if you let Uncle Sam pick your pocket. Up-to-date and expanded tax-slashing strategies from seasoned tax experts could help you to keep money in *your* pocket.

You also must avoid purchasing coins from Uncle Sam that are losers—and despite all the hoopla surrounding America's 50 State Quarters Program, a number of U.S. Mint products rank high on that list. This book will explain why. It also will tell you how to maximize your return by targeting your purchases at coins that will make you money right now.

Speaking of "right now," also incorporated is a treasure trove of invaluable advice and information from my highly popular book, *How to Make Money in Coins Right Now*, which has been blended into the present volume.

Making money quickly in this fiercely competitive marketplace requires recognition of opportunities. This new edition goes into great detail on how to recognize—and capitalize upon—these situations. It tells you, for example, how to make money from short-term increases in the price of gold—how to buy certain gold coins now and possibly sell them later for a profit. It identifies the coins that are winners, coins that have some potential to go up in value.

Most importantly, it examines grading arbitrage—the technique of enhancing a certified coin's value by resubmitting it to a major certification service and getting it regraded at a higher level. Grading arbitrage secrets and strategies are revealed by the most financially successful coin dealer of all time, Jim Halperin. His masterful advice is explored and explained in simple terms, so that you can play this game yourself and increase the chance of surviving and maybe even turning a profit.

Some of the information in the first edition of *The Coin Collector's Survival Manual* is just as true and useful today as in 1984. How to look at a coin . . . how to negotiate with a coin dealer . . . how to profit from coin conventions . . . how to choose holders that won't damage your coins—the basic dos and don'ts remain much the same as they were when the book first appeared. Refinements have been made; this is, after all, a highly dynamic marketplace, and even basic truths need to be put in perspective as time goes by. But the insights I provided in 1984 have stood the test of time and will help today's readers and collectors prosper as well.

In some cases, the changes since 1984—while seemingly small—have been quite significant. That's true, for instance, in the sections on lighting and coin preservation. Since the first edition, the use of halogen lighting has become widespread among dealers and other knowledgeable coin buyers and sellers. This intense source of light makes it far easier to spot imperfections on coins' surfaces, particularly hairlines on proofs. At the same time, halogen lighting can be dangerous if it isn't used with proper care. All of this is spelled out in this new, revised edition. Coin preservation, on the other hand, has become more difficult in recent years since the U.S. government banned new production of trichlorotrifluoroethane, a substance which had proven extremely useful in this process. Scientists have determined that this chemical, when released into the air, can damage the earth's ozone layer and thus contribute to various forms of skin cancer. Given this important development, the chapter on coin preservation has been updated substantially and provides alternative substances that can help prevent your coins from deteriorating and, at the same time, keep all of us in good health.

There is change, too, in the information about choosing coin holders that won't damage your coins, and in the advice about safekeeping and insurance. The art of coin conservation has been converted into a professional service. The horrific attacks on September 11, 2001, and the ravages of Hurricane Katrina have served as wake-up calls for newer and higher-level protection of coins. In the wake of these terror attacks and natural disaster, the ground rules for insurance changed, and these changes are explained.

In this war-on-terrorism era, gold has begun to glitter. So an appendix that explains how gold coins can be used as a hedge against calamity has been expanded.

As I said in the original preface, whether you're a casual collector or a serious student of the hobby or someone in between, I'm certain you'll find the advice contained in the following pages to be useful and valuable in your quest for coins, whether you buy those coins through the mail or with the click of a mouse.

This is *your* survival manual. Enjoy it, and use it well!

Scott A. Travers
travers@pocketchangelottery.com
February 2006

INTRODUCTION

Rare coins are a mirror of our civilization, and have captured mankind's imagination for many centuries. Coins reflect political and social turmoil, artistic and cultural triumph, and both obstructed and unobstructed societal evolution. Ionian merchants collected the first coins in the fifth century B.C., when coins were first made.

The coinage of America is the coinage of a special people. The beauty of rare coins is appreciated by connoisseurs, just as works of art are treasured by art lovers. Coin collecting, once termed "the hobby of kings," has been a source of pleasure and profit to king and commoner alike. For many years, though, the acquisition of high-quality rare coins was dominated by the elite: King Farouk of Egypt, Baron de Rothschild, and the DuPont and Lilly families, for example. The proliferation of educational materials and, thus, of artistic appreciation has caused a surge of interest in rare coins from people in all walks of life.

The notion of making money from coins—turning a profit from buying, holding, and selling them—is of recent origin, at least as a primary objective of those who covet and collect them. Frustration with the performance of paper assets such as stocks, bonds, and commodities has encouraged an increasingly greater number of people to buy rare coins, a tangible asset with a sparkling performance record.

Coins came of age as a vehicle for investment during the 1960s. Up to then, the coin field had been dominated by traditional-style collectors who pursued rare coins primarily for pleasure, rather than profit. The emphasis changed dramatically in the early 1960s when uncirculated rolls of modern U.S. coins—coins that were still brand-new—became the objects of widespread speculation nationwide.

It was during that decade that coin collecting—and investing—experienced the single biggest boom in the hobby's history. Coin prices soared to unprecedented heights; an uncirculated roll of Jefferson nickels struck at the Denver Mint in 1950, for example, was selling for as much as $1,200—an average of $30 for each of the 40 nickels in the roll. U.S. government proof sets of newly minted coins were snapped up by the public in staggering numbers each year, hitting an all-time high of more than 4 million sets in 1964, when the Kennedy half dollar first appeared on the scene. Major new coin periodicals sprouted up, and hobby publications reached circulation and advertising levels never approached since. In short, it was a time of tremendous excitement and growth.

The End of Silver Coins

The roll boom sputtered in the mid-1960s, and late-date coin rolls have never regained the prominence they enjoyed prior to that. In part, this reflected the growing realization that coins which could be obtained in roll or bag quantities weren't likely to be scarce and desirable. Thereafter, the emphasis shifted to individual coins that possessed low mintage, high quality, or both. The market's decline involved more than rolls, however; interest and prices diminished across the board. A major reason for this was the U.S. government's action in eliminating, or greatly reducing, the silver content of circulating coinage.

In 1965, silver was removed entirely from the quarter dollar and dime, giving way to a "sandwich-type" base-metal composition consisting of an outer layer of copper-nickel bonded to a core of pure copper. The half dollar's silver content was reduced from 90 percent to 40 percent from 1965 through 1970, and then, in 1971, it joined the quarter and dime as a silver-less coin. When these newfangled "clad" coins first appeared, President Lyndon B. Johnson asserted that silver dimes, quarters, and halves would never bring a premium simply because of their precious-metal content and that they would circulate side-by-side with the new coins for many years to come. He proved to be a prophet without honor: Almost overnight, silver coins vanished from circulation, for they were correctly perceived as stores of value. This greatly reduced the chances of finding worthwhile coins in pocket change, and that, in turn, dampened Americans' interest in coin collecting, for circulation finds had been a major factor in the hobby's rapid growth.

It took the introduction of the U.S. Mint's 50 State Quarters Program in 1999 to breathe new life into the coin market. From the very outset of the program, millions of Americans started searching their pocket change. Through good times and bad, the notion of using coins as a way to turn a profit—of making big money from collectible small change—has remained an important factor in many people's involvement with the hobby and the marketplace. And the hope of quick profit—of making money right now—has proven to be a particularly powerful lure.

A New Golden Era

After the roll boom faded, the coin market drifted aimlessly for the next decade or so before getting a boost in 1974 when Uncle Sam restored the right to private gold ownership. That awakened millions of Americans to the investment possibilities of precious metals, and rare coins went along for the ride. Around the same time, astute coin dealers began promoting coins' investment potential through aggressive and sophisticated marketing campaigns, attracting a new breed of buyer—typically, well-heeled professional men or women with limited knowledge of coins but substantial financial resources. A company called First Coinvestors, Inc. of Albertson, New York, and its founder, the late Stanley Apfelbaum, played pivotal roles in this process, and although they came under fire for the relatively high markups they charged, they deserve recognition for increasing public awareness that coins might indeed be a good investment.

Fueled by rampant inflation, gold and silver soared in price in 1979 and 1980, and again, rare coins boomed right along with them. Price guides could hardly keep up with the non-stop increases in value: Seemingly overnight, desirable coins were doubling and tripling in price. Within weeks, coins that had been worth $500 were trading for $5,000. In the inefficient marketplace of 1979 and 1980, a keen-witted young numismatist could go to a coin show and make a profit of $25,000 just by trading coins over a weekend. Many young collectors who got their start at that time went on to become professional numismatists—full-time coin dealers—and virtually all of them look back on the experience with wistful recognition that those were truly the good old days.

At the start of the 1980s, coin investing was really a shot in the dark. Prices were rising dramatically, to be sure, and some investors did fare very well—notably those who caught the wave on the rise and jumped off before it hit the shoals. But many ill-informed coin buyers lost their shirts, often because unscrupulous coin dealers took unfair advantage of their lack of expertise. It wasn't at all unusual for a well-heeled non-collector to visit a local coin shop in 1979, put $10,000 on the counter (and often much more), and tell the dealer, "Buy me something pretty." Big Brother wasn't watching the coin market then, wasn't looking over the shoulder of the coin merchant and saying, "You need to disclose this and you need to disclose that." The buyer was on his or her own, and "caveat emptor" was an understatement. Many of the people who purchased coins in 1979 and 1980 received much less than what they paid for: They got coins that were grossly overgraded—described as being in a much higher level of preservation than they really were—and just as grossly overpriced.

The Grading Revolution

As word of such abuses reached Washington, D.C., the Federal Trade Commission entered the picture in the mid-1980s and started bringing suit against some of the bigger offenders, charging them with engaging in false, deceptive, and misleading practices in trade and commerce. In 1986, the industry itself launched a major counterattack with the founding of the Professional Coin Grading Service (PCGS), a company that offered independent certification of rare coins' authenticity and grade by seasoned coin dealers, plus encapsulation—or "slabbing"—of each coin in a sonically sealed, hard plastic holder. (Sonic sealing is accomplished by using high-pitched sounds to convert energy into heat, and then using that heat to fuse together the hard plastic holder's two halves.) The Grading Revolution had begun.

PCGS claimed to provide an expert, arm's-length opinion regarding the grade of each coin submitted for its review, using a 1-to-70 scale in which 1 represents a coin barely identifiable as to its type—a coin so worn it could hardly be identified—and 70 represents a perfect coin, a coin with no nicks, no scratches, no flaws, and no imperfections. PCGS was soon joined by the Numismatic Guaranty Corporation of America (NGC), another skilled coin-grading service which—like PCGS—encapsulated coins in sonically sealed, tamper-resistant holders. Together, these two companies instilled a sense of confidence in coin buyers—and especially in investors with limited knowledge (or no knowledge at all) about coins. Rip-offs were far less likely with certified coins, for the grades of those coins had been independently verified by experts.

Before long, the coin market's faith in NGC and PCGS was so great that many certified coins were trading "sight-unseen." Buyers and sellers accepted the accuracy of the companies' grades without even seeing and examining the coins. This caught the attention of Wall Street financiers, who reasoned that certified coins could readily be traded in much the same way that investors trade stocks and bonds. Several large brokerage houses began to test the waters by setting up multimillion-dollar funds based upon investments in rare coins. As the decade neared a close, Merrill Lynch and Kidder, Peabody both had established such funds, and coin prices were soaring in expectation that this was just the beginning.

The Bubble Bursts

Unfortunately, the end of the 1980s also marked the end of Wall Street's brief flirtation with rare coins. The coin market proved to be just too small—just too thin a market—to sustain the types of price gains that were taking place in 1989.

Merrill Lynch was the subject of a highly publicized class-action lawsuit over its Athena Funds—limited partnerships in coins and antiquities. I remember these tumultuous times well, as I was the only coin expert retained by any of the four law firms that litigated the case and helped consumers get refunds for the money they had invested. (Armen R. Vartian, general counsel to the Professional Numismatists Guild, said in print that I "made a significant contribution" in getting Athena participants their "excellent settlement.")

Bruce McNall, former owner of the L.A. Kings hockey team, was later convicted in this well-publicized scandal—and even wrote a book about it (*Fun While It Lasted: My Rise and Fall in the Land of Fame and Fortune*, Hyperion, 2003) which was published after his release from prison.

Rare coins plummeted in value just as quickly as they had gone up. Merrill Lynch and Kidder, Peabody both beat a hasty retreat, and the rest of the Wall Street crowd went out the exit with them. This had the effect of exacerbating the downturn in the market, driving prices even lower—and the slump even deeper—than would have been the case under normal circumstances.

The coin market has witnessed few rallies that rivaled that last major peak in May of 1989. And as this brand-new edition is written in 2005, and gold is beginning to show life and stability over $400 an ounce, many people are gun-shy about recommending coins for people to buy and hold as a safe, long-term investment. Conventional wisdom simply doesn't seem all that wise anymore. In the old days, investment advisers had a tried-and-true formula: "Buy this coin today for $2,500, or buy this coin investment portfolio today for $25,000, and hold on to it for ten years and you'll be able to cash out at 20 percent a year." That kind of advice is now a fallacy; what's more, it has become politically incorrect. In fact, it has become so politically incorrect that even Salomon Brothers, the respected Wall Street brokerage house, has discontinued its once-ballyhooed survey of investment vehicles, which perennially ranked rare coins as the number one investment from the standpoint of long-term performance. Rare coins are simply not viewed as a long-term investment today, although many believe the climate is changing to one that favors tangible assets. Despite the fact that rare coin prices are strong and 19,000 lots were sold by one auction firm at a single convention in January 2005 for over $60 million, coins are viewed merely as a fun and profitable diversion and—in the case of certain gold coins—a hedge against calamity in an uncertain world.

A New Ball Game

It's a different kind of marketplace today. The advent of online auctions and the introduction of the 50 State Quarters, the Sacagawea dollar, and the Lewis and Clark nickels have changed the look and feel of the rare coin marketplace. That doesn't mean you can't make money in coins; it means that you have to be smarter than smart, you have to exercise more caution, you have to be more careful with your funds, and you have to act more quickly than in the past.

To make money in the coin market today, you have to think and act like a dealer and you have to seek—and heed—advice from extremely smart dealers who are also honest. *The Coin Collector's Survival Manual, Fifth Edition*, will show you how to do all this. Among other things, it will level the playing field and give you the knowledge you need to minimize—and even totally neutralize—the marketplace's most worrisome hazards. From grading to trading—and from storage to tax-slashing strategies, this ultimate consumer protection resource will enable you to fortify your defenses in every area of the hobby.

One of the best ways to make money in coins is to sell off investments that are losing money, then put the proceeds into something productive. This is a common practice among successful coin dealers. You need to cash out your non-performers and free up your funds for coins that are winners. *The Coin Collector's Survival Manual, Fifth Edition* will tell you how to do this and thereby obtain capital for profit-making purchases.

This is also a book that tells you how successful coin dealers play the game. It takes you behind the scenes and puts you in the experts' shoes, and shows you how you, too, can make the same kinds of profits. But don't think this is an area you can explore without risks; on the contrary, the coin market is a high-risk area. If you're merely curious about collectibles, you'll still find this book highly informative. But it's really aimed at somebody who is willing to take some big chances—somebody who lives by the motto, "No guts, no glory!"

It's the collecting instinct that encourages all of us to set aside something we can hold, touch, and feel. There are three basic types of individuals who buy coins: the collector, the collector/investor, and the investor. Even the unknowledgeable investor is touched, sooner or later, by the collecting instinct.

Collectors buy coins for their artistic, cultural, and historic significance. They are not overly concerned with price, just with having a particular coin to complete a particular set. They want each and every date for that set, and they would sell their houses or cars or clothing to get that coin. If a collector buys a coin for $50 which increases in value to $500 a year later, chances are he or she won't sell it.

Collector/investors also appreciate the artistic, cultural, and historic significance that coins have to offer. But they buy coins to make a profit. It's like the doctor who invests in rare paintings but hangs them on his or her wall for their beauty. While collector/investors own the coins, they look at them and admire their breathtaking magnificence. But if the value increases substantially in a short period of time, chances are those coins will get sold.

Unknowledgeable investors buy coins to make a profit. They are interested in only one thing: the bottom line. Ironically, many unknowledgeable investors become dedicated collectors. Just holding a rare coin is a thrill; and many unknowledgeable of these investors are educated and culture-oriented individuals to begin with, seeking to diversify their holdings.

In short, almost everyone who buys coins learns to appreciate them sooner or later. *The Coin Collector's Survival Manual, Fifth Edition* will intensify this appreciation by showing you how to protect yourself when you enter the market. Whether you're a collector, collector/investor, or unknowledgeable investor, be careful when you buy or sell coins. Be very careful. One wrong step could spoil your appreciation for the world's greatest avocation.

– 1 –
COLLECTING COINS PROFITABLY

What is a collector? Are collectors born or made? Why do collectors have an inherent advantage over others who acquire rare coins?

These are basic questions that need to be considered by anyone who's thinking of spending time and money on valuable coins. Whether a person's ultimate goal is financial profit, psychic income, or both, he or she needs to approach this pursuit with the proper frame of mind in order to achieve the best results—and the biggest returns.

The Nature of a Collector

In a broad sense, anyone who assembles related items of interest as a hobby is a collector, whether those items are coins, stamps, matchbook covers, beer cans, or just about any other objects you might name. Over the years, however, the term collector has come to have a more specific meaning in the coin hobby—it designates someone who acquires and arranges coins in a systematic way (unlike a mere accumulator, who gets and keeps coins haphazardly, with little or no regard to their organization). It also denotes someone who is motivated primarily by intangible rewards such as the enjoyment of art, beauty, and history (unlike an investor, who tends to be preoccupied, even obsessed, with financial gain).

Time and again, experience has shown that dedicated collectors gain the most from coin collecting, including the biggest monetary rewards. Their discriminating taste and attention to detail result in the acquisition of coins with unusual appeal, and those kinds of coins tend to have greater value when they are sold, even though profit may not have been a motive when they were purchased in the first place. Clearly, then, the most fundamental way to make money in coins—right now or whenever you choose to sell them—is to view them and go after them with the mindset of a dyed-in-the-wool collector.

The Lure of Coins

All collectibles hold a special fascination for those who pursue and peruse them. But the positive features of coins are particularly appealing:

- They are small and portable, easily stored in large numbers, and easily hidden in times of emergency.
- They are durable, sometimes surviving for centuries—or even millennia—in much the same condition as when they were made.
- They record the panorama of human history—and human hopes and dreams—as few other collectibles ever have. A silver denarius of Julius Caesar . . . a shekel of the Jewish revolts against Rome . . . a denier of the Crusaders . . . silver shillings of Britain's King Charles I and his enemy Oliver Cromwell—to possess one of these is to hold a piece of history in your hand.
- They are hand-held works of art, sometimes bearing portraiture as breathtaking in its way as a masterpiece by Rembrandt or da Vinci.
- They can represent significant stores of value just from the standpoint of the metal they contain (in cases where that metal is precious and rare), as with coins made of gold or platinum.
- In addition, coins have historically offered the bonus of rising in value substantially over time, provided that their owners have chosen items that are genuinely scarce and preserve them carefully.

The Collector Mentality

In a very real sense, collectors are builders. First, they lay a solid foundation for their collections, much as a contractor does when erecting a large building. Then, as they go forward, they follow a definite plan, much like an architect's blueprint, and they implement this plan carefully over months and years and sometimes decades. In some instances, where an entire family is involved in assembling and maintaining a collection, the process may continue for generations—possibly as long as a century or more.

Collectors have very specific goals. Some of these may be short-term in nature—perhaps the acquisition of one example of every U.S. gold Type coin with a portrait of Miss Liberty on the obverse, or front, of the coin. Other goals may be long-range and more complex, such as the completion of a set of Bust dimes from every single year, or a set that includes every recognized variety of a particular coin. In each case, however, people who are collectors—truly solid collectors—have a mindset that entails completing a project. And when a collector does complete a set, the whole can be worth much more than the sum of the parts, for it then has heightened appeal—and tangible value-to other collectors.

The Early Days of Collecting

Coin collecting first became an avocation of consequence during the Renaissance. For centuries, however, it was limited almost exclusively to bluebloods and other men of wealth, leading people to dub it "the hobby of kings." Not until modern times did it take root with the masses and come to be known instead as "the king of hobbies." U.S. coinage first appeared in 1793, but collecting of that coinage didn't begin in earnest until the mid-1800s.

One of the first serious numismatists in the United States, Joseph J. Mickley of Philadelphia, became attracted to coins when a casual whim launched him on a virtual treasure hunt. As he neared the age of 20 in 1819, Mickley decided to look for a copper cent from his birth year, not realizing that 1799 cents were rare and elusive even then, a time when the large, heavy cents of the nation's early years were being encountered routinely in circulation. Mickley's search for this birth-year coin escalated into a wider quest: He sought to obtain copper cents from every date the U.S. Mint had made them. Soon, he expanded his interest to other U.S. coin series as well, blazing a trail for future collectors of series such as early silver dollars, quarters, and half cents.

Mickley, a maker of musical instruments, had an ideal location in which to pursue his new hobby: He lived within walking distance of the Philadelphia Mint and went there frequently to purchase new coins at face value. On one such visit, in 1827, he bought four newly struck quarters bearing that date—an acquisition that cost him just a dollar. The coins proved to be extremely rare, and after passing through several great collections, one of them changed hands at a 1980 auction for $190,000. A quarter-century later, in 2005, an original 1827 quarter had a potential value of close to half a million dollars, according to John Albanese of Far Hills, New Jersey, a preeminent professional numismatist.

Mickley also owned an 1804 silver dollar, one of just 15 examples known to exist today of this famous rarity. He got the coin, he said, for little more than face value from a teller at the Bank of Philadelphia. When Mickley's coins were sold in 1867, this dollar fetched $750—a record price at the time for any U.S. coin. By 1993, the coin belonged to prominent Texas numismatist Reed Hawn, and when he chose to sell it in October of that year at an auction sale conducted by Stack's of New York, the winning bid was an eye-popping $475,000. Since then, several specimens of the 1804 dollar have changed hands at auction sales for prices in excess of $1 million. In August 1999, one of them sold for $4.14 million at a New York auction conducted by Auctions by Bowers and Merena, Inc., then of Wolfeboro, New Hampshire—an all-time auction record at the time. [Note: The actual persons, Bowers and Merena, are no longer at the firm named "Bowers and Merena." The namesake company formed by Q. David Bowers and Raymond N. Merena—and managed by Christine Karstedt—was acquired by Collectors Universe, Inc., a publicly traded company. Collectors Universe later sold "Bowers and Merena" to Greg Manning Auctions, Inc., another publicly traded company. Bowers himself and Karstedt, along with most of the staff, left Bowers and Merena before it was sold to Greg Manning. Karstedt then formed American Numismatic Rarities, LLC, in Wolfeboro, NH. Merena is retired. The Bowers and Merena entity, under its Greg Manning ownership, continues to thrive as a top coin auction house. The new firm, American Numismatic Rarities, LLC, quickly established itself as a market leader under the auspices of Karstedt. A short time later, Bowers joined the firm as its numismatic director and editor.]

1804 Stickney Specimen Class I "original" silver dollar. This coin, from the collection of Louis E. Eliasberg, Sr., was sold at auction for $1.815 million in April 1997. The highest price realized for an 1804 dollar was $4.14 million in August 1999 for a near-perfect specimen. *Photo courtesy Bowers and Merena*

Major American Collectors

Joseph Mickley blazed a trail that millions of others have followed. Most have been people of modest means, but the hobby has also attracted men and women of wealth—and some of these have assembled collections of almost legendary stature. Here are a few examples:

- In the late 1800s, Baltimore & Ohio Railroad executive T. Harrison Garrett formed an important collection of U.S. coins. His sons, Robert and John Work Garrett, expanded the collection. When it came up for sale at a four-part series of Bowers and Ruddy auctions from 1979 through 1981, it realized a total of more than $25 million, a record that stood for nearly two decades.
- Before his death in 1926, Chicago beer baron Virgil M. Brand amassed a collection containing more than 350,000 pieces, including a large number of stunning rarities. Many of the coins were later dispersed piecemeal, but when a small segment belonging to Brand's niece came up for sale at a series of public auctions in the early and mid-1980s, they still brought a total of close to $10 million.
- Baltimore banker Louis Eliasberg startled the numismatic community in the early 1950s by announcing that he had formed a complete collection of all U.S. coins, including major varieties, by date and mint mark. The gold coins from the collection brought more than $11 million when sold at public auction by Bowers and Ruddy Galleries in 1982. The remaining coins were sold at auction in 1996 and 1997 and realized an additional $32.4 million, bringing the overall total to more than $44 million, a record that still stands.

Collecting Reaches the Masses

Coin collecting remained a somewhat exclusive pastime for more than a hundred years after Joseph Mickley's entrance on the scene. Ironically, it took hold with Americans at

1933 Saint-Gaudens double eagle sold at auction for a world record price of $7,590,020 in July 2002 by Sotheby's and Stack's. These firms conducted a historic and incredible auction. *Photo courtesy Sotheby's*

large in the depths of the Great Depression, primarily due to a simple yet ingenious new invention. In the early 1930s, an enterprising Wisconsin man named J.K. Post devised a series of inexpensive boards to house and display U.S. coins by date and mint mark. These boards had die-cut holes where people could place each coin as they found it in their everyday pocket change. The Whitman Publishing Company of Racine, Wisconsin, acquired the rights to make and market these boards, and soon they were turning up in 5-and-10-cent stores across the country.

Low-cost forms of amusement and entertainment enjoyed great popularity during the Depression years. Movies, miniature golf, jigsaw puzzles—all of these flourished as Americans looked for ways to inexpensively escape from their worries. "Penny boards" fit this pattern perfectly: Filling a board with Lincoln cents plucked from circulation was well within the budgets of most Americans, even in those brutally hard times, and searching for those coins provided long hours of pleasure. As a bonus, completed boards could be sold for well over face value; many dealers advertised their interest in purchasing these from the public.

Yet another stimulus to coin collecting's growth was the enterprising ad campaign of Fort Worth, Texas, coin dealer B. Max Mehl. During the 1930s and 1940s, the flamboyant Mehl placed ads in newspaper Sunday supplements almost non-stop offering to pay $50 apiece for any 1913 Liberty Head nickel—and also offering, not just incidentally, to send his company's price list and other coin literature to those who would remit a small fee. Mehl was well aware that only five examples of the rare 1913 nickel were known to exist, but the offer got people's attention, and the literature he sent helped cultivate untold thousands of new collectors.

Those 1913 nickels are a story in themselves. Official Mint records make no mention of Liberty nickels of that date; all the five-cent pieces struck in that year are supposed

1913 Liberty head nickel. One of five known, this nickel sold for $1,485,000 in May 1996. This specimen was from the collection of Louis E. Eliasberg, Sr. *Photos courtesy Bowers and Merena*

to have been of the then-new Indian/bison design (commonly referred to as the Buffalo nickel type). Evidently, someone at the Philadelphia Mint surreptitiously made a few Liberty nickels with the 1913 date, using dies that the Mint had prepared as a contingency.

At one point, all five of these nickels belonged to the eccentric Edward H.R. Green, son of reclusive financial genius Hetty Green, who was known as "the witch of Wall Street." The coins were dispersed following Edward Green's death in 1936, and over the years they rose in value astoundingly. In 1993, one of these nickels changed hands at a public auction conducted by Stack's of New York for $962,500—then the highest price ever paid at auction for a single U.S. coin. The seller, Texas numismatist Reed Hawn, had bought the coin in 1985 for $385,000. Then, in 1996, the Eliasberg specimen brought $1,485,000, becoming the first coin to realize more than $1 million at a public sale. In 2003, prominent New Hampshire coin dealer Ed Lee reportedly paid about $3 million to acquire the same nickel in a private transaction.

A Dealer's-Eye View of Collectors

I sat down recently with Julian M. Leidman of Silver Spring, Maryland, one of the nation's most prominent and respected coin dealers. Leidman represents many important collectors at public auction sales, helping them decide which coins they should pursue and executing bids on their behalf. Based on his perspective as a longtime dealer who has been an active participant in hundreds of major auctions, Leidman is convinced that collectors almost always derive the greatest rewards—both financial and emotional—from buying and selling rare coins, even though the monetary aspect of these transactions may be of limited concern to them.

During our conversation, Leidman spoke of one particular client who had been collecting coins for more than 50 years before he sold his collection—at a very handsome profit—at an auction sale conducted by Bowers and Merena. This client, Leidman said, was one of the most enthusiastic collectors he ever dealt with and, throughout the client's half-century of pursuing rare coins, he maintained a simple mindset: He was working on a project that he wanted to complete. Money was never the driving force behind this man's project; in buying coins, his first priority wasn't dollars and cents, but whether a given coin would enhance his collection. He didn't want to pay ludicrously high prices, to be sure—but, on the other hand, if something he needed and wanted was worth $1,000 in the marketplace, and he was presented with an opportunity to buy it for $1,200 or $1,300, he would seriously consider doing so and almost always gave Leidman carte blanche to buy on his behalf in such situations. He enjoyed coins' intangible qualities and never failed to project the pride of ownership. Furthermore, when he reaped a windfall upon his collection's sale, that was merely frosting on the cake.

Collectors Versus Investors

It's really the pride of ownership—of knowing they possess something scarce and desirable—that inspires many collectors to continue acquiring coins as time goes by. Collectors understand that the sets they are assembling have lasting—and perhaps significant—value, but they simply aren't obsessed with making a profit. They view their collections as long-term projects and pay little heed to the day-to-day peaks and valleys in the marketplace. Investors, by contrast, get jittery whenever prices fall and look to unload their holdings at the first sign of clouds on the economic horizon; they feel no long-term commitment to the hobby or attachment to the coins they have acquired.

The contrast between collectors and investors is evident in the way both groups regard "slabs"—the hard plastic holders in which coins are encapsulated after being graded by a third-party certification service. (Detailed discussions of grading and certification will appear in later chapters.) Investors look upon slabs, and the guarantee that accompanies them, as a vital security blanket to protect them against overgrading. Collectors, on the other hand, often remove slabbed coins from their holders because they want to be able to hold, feel, and touch them and examine every detail without obstruction.

Dealers have a special incentive to treat collectors fairly; unlike investors, who tend to come and go, collectors stick around for the long haul and develop a sense of loyalty to the sellers with whom they establish a good relationship. Similarly, collectors are well advised to patronize dealers who are likely to be around for many years to come—dealers with proven track records. These dealers will take pains to give good value and select nice coins if they feel those coins are going to clients who will buy from them again. They also will want to ingratiate themselves with hobbyists who are forming important collections in hopes that those clients will bring the coins back to them when

***LIFE* magazine cover, April 27, 1953.** *Photos courtesy Bowers and Merena*

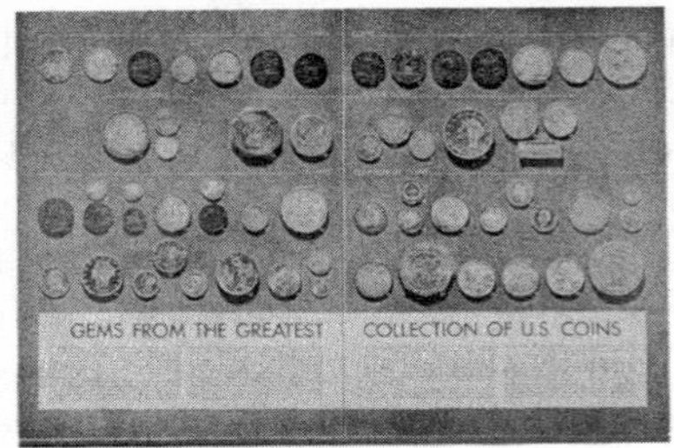

Q. David Bowers reports that this *Life* magazine article about Eliasberg's sensational coin collection generated thousands of letters from readers. *Photo courtesy Bowers and Merena*

they are ready to sell. I can vouch from my own experience that this is a powerful incentive. Some of the greatest collectors of our time have commissioned my firm to acquire rare coins on their behalf. Some of these same people have also subsequently engaged me to help them disperse their holdings, either through a lightning sale (a special kind of quick-turnaround auction my firm conducts), or by assisting them in selling their coins at public auction.

– 2 –
READING A COIN LIKE A BOOK

The rows of plastic holders filled the glass display cases, their neutral color contrasting with the lush blue velvet of the elegant trays that housed them. The holders themselves served as palm-size showcases, their purposely muted white or clear plastic allowing viewers' eyes to concentrate completely on the gold and silver treasures and copper and nickel rarities they contained. This was not a jewelry store, yet the merchandise sparkling in some of these modest holders might easily be compared in value and allure with exquisite diamonds. This was a coin shop, and like many such establishments today its inventory consisted to a great extent of "certified" coins—collectible coins that had been examined by experts, found to be authentic, assigned numerical grades based on their condition, then sealed in these plastic holders for protection and to preserve their marketplace liquidity.

A middle-aged man in a dark business suit leaned over one of the cases, studying a row of glittering silver dollars, mesmerized by their beauty and the shimmering silver luster they emitted. They seemed uniformly pristine, arrayed in meticulous rows. The man had only recently begun collecting coins, his interest having been piqued by the U.S. quarter dollars honoring the 50 states of the Union. As those turned up in pocket change, he had started saving them, and now he was in the coin shop to purchase special holders to store and display these quarters in a permanent, organized way for himself and his two young children. He had found himself drawn irresistibly, though, to the rows of plastic holders and their brightly gleaming contents. The large silver coins—more than a century old, yet newly struck in appearance—especially caught his eye and stirred his still—emerging collector instinct. He motioned to the woman behind the display cases, standing discreetly a few feet away, and asked if he could see one of the coins. She unlocked the case, removed the coin in question and handed it to him.

The man was about to learn the first of many lessons about collectible coins. His Washington quarter albums had cost him less than $20 apiece, but when he asked the young woman how much the silver dollar would cost, he was startled by her response: "We're asking $2,000 for that coin." The coin, it turned out, was a scarce Morgan dollar graded by the Professional Coin Grading Service, one of the major firms engaged in the authentication, grading and encapsulation of rare coins. A coin's "grade" refers to its rating on a scale classifying it according to quality.

Clearly, this hobby was more than just a penny-ante pursuit. The budding collector inquired about several other "cartwheels" from the same row of coins, and each time the price was hundreds, even thousands, of dollars. He began to notice a pattern: The higher the grade on the holder, the higher the price of the coin. And though he wasn't yet adept enough to pinpoint the differences, he recognized that the higher-numbered coins were perceptibly sharper and more pleasing to the eye than the others. Without realizing it, this neophyte numismatist was being introduced to one of the most important—and one of the most complex—aspects of the marketplace he was entering: the grading of coins and, by extension, the relationship between grading and pricing.

Before long, the man became aware of something else that sets some coins apart: While most of the silver dollars were bright and lustrous, others here and there had subtle pastel colors around the periphery; a few were tinted even more extensively, and one seemed almost ablaze with vivid bluish-red hues. As he studied these coins more closely, his fascination turned to total captivation. Like many collectors before him, he was quickly being hooked by toned coins.

(*Toning* is the slow, natural, and regular process by which a coin turns color over a period of months and years. Many collectors pay more for coins with beautiful toning because the colors are so attractive and make the coin stand out from others which are not toned. However, toning often covers up imperfections.)

With coins as with people, first impressions are extremely important. That's why coin dealers sometimes provide attractive settings for their merchandise—plush velvet trays, special lighting, and other devices that highlight the coins' positive features and minimize or mask their deficiencies. With this in mind, prospective buyers, whether they be collectors, investors, or both, need to approach the viewing of coins not only with enthusiasm but also with vigilance and even a touch of skepticism.

Furthermore, if the coin has any overwhelmingly positive characteristics, some prospective purchasers may overlook rather obvious detractions.

Love at first sight is wonderful and sometimes fully justified by the object of one's affection, but you can't let your attraction to any particular coin be guided by blind emotion. You need to step back, take a second look, and temper your emotion with cold, hard logic and analytical reasoning.

It can be a jungle out there; becoming too enamored of a flashy but flawed coin can be a costly mistake, and guarding against such traps is one of the basic components of a coin collector's survival kit. The process begins with learning the proper way to view and evaluate a coin. Even experienced hobbyists sometimes are badly deficient in this regard. All would-be coin buyers need to refine their coin-viewing techniques so that they can recognize and readily evaluate a coin's negative characteristics as well as its positive features. They also need to know how to handle a coin during the viewing process so that its level of preservation isn't compromised. These skills may be less crucial with certified coins, since those already possess two forms of protection: grades determined by independent experts and holders that safeguard their contents from mishandling. On the other hand, certification is not a perfect process; even experts can be wrong, and it's up to you to double-check their assessments. Furthermore, the hard plastic holder (or slab, as it's commonly known)—while it protects the coin—also restricts a viewer's ability to scrutinize the coin in minute detail.

In this chapter, drawing upon my more than twenty-five years of experience as a coin buyer and seller, I will show you the proper way to look at coins so that you become aware of, and familiar with, all their intricacies. I strongly suggest that you systematize this process, so as not to be overwhelmed by any single characteristic. This chapter will also explain how to protect a coin while you are examining it.

Coin-Viewing Attitudes and Techniques

There are four basic coin-viewing attitudes:

1. Looking for beauty and admiring a coin as a work of art.
2. Looking for strengths.
3. Looking for imperfections or detractions.
4. Looking for both strengths and imperfections, while saving your appreciation for the coins you own.

Some rare-coin enthusiasts may have the ability to combine all four of these attitudes successfully. However, for practical purposes, attitude 4 is the best to adopt.

Coins have many aspects and can be appreciated on a number of levels. People who pursue them as collectibles may find them appealing for aesthetic reasons, for example, or because they embody cultural or historical significance. But when coins are being viewed with an eye to possible purchase and money is involved—sometimes substantial sums—the only thing that matters is their physical condition. It has been said that when a coin is offered for sale, the seller sees only the positive characteristics, while the buyer sees only the negative ones. Undoubtedly, there is considerable truth to this. When purchasing a coin, you must make a concerted effort to be totally objective and look at the entire coin—each and every part of it, including the obverse (or "heads" side), the reverse, and the edge.

Looking at a coin is like proofreading a letter. You may not find any mistakes if you just skim the contents of the letter. But if you scrutinize it word by word, you stand a much greater chance of discovering an error. The same principle applies to coins. A quick glance at a coin won't necessarily reveal its detracting characteristics. A coin must be studied closely. However, unlike a letter, a coin can't be read line by line, from left to right. You have to develop a method of "reading" coins for strengths and detractions. You can choose one method you feel most comfortable with—or combine techniques in order to form an effective approach.

Coins and the Clock

In order to facilitate mutual understanding and promote uniformity in descriptions, people who buy and sell coins have established a system whereby each coin's characteristics are described by referring to the corresponding position on a clock. For example, if a coin has a scratch on the obverse near the top, this imperfection may be described as being an "obverse scratch at 12:00." (Some individuals, particularly left-handed ones, may feel more comfortable scanning in a counterclockwise direction.)

Note: The coin-viewing methods presented here are for study purposes. Before taking a coin out of its holder, read the explanation at the end of this chapter on how to protect coins during the viewing process.

The Basic Clockwise Scan

- Scan the obverse in a clockwise direction.
- Repeat the process on the reverse.
- Carefully tilt and rotate the coin while looking at the obverse so that it can be viewed from more than one angle; repeat this for the reverse.
- Scrutinize the rims from the obverse, reverse, and side.
- View the coin in its entirety.

The Clockwise Fields and Devices Scan

- Scan the obverse fields, or plain background areas, in a clockwise direction.
- Scan the obverse devices, or raised portions showing the design and inscriptions, in a clockwise direction.
- Repeat this scanning of both fields and devices on the reverse.
- Carefully tilt and rotate the coin while looking at the obverse so that it can be viewed from more than one angle; repeat this for the reverse.
- Scrutinize the rims from the obverse, reverse, and side.
- View the coin in its entirety.

The Division Scan

- Divide the coin into equal, imaginary sections as you would slice a pie into pieces of the same size. You can choose as many or as few sections as you desire—two, three, or, preferably, four.
- Choose a section, and scan it in a clockwise direction. Move to the next section in a clockwise direction, repeating the viewing action.

- Repeat the obverse viewing action on the reverse.
- Carefully tilt and rotate the coin while looking at the obverse so that it can be viewed from more than one angle; repeat this for the reverse.
- Scrutinize the rims from the obverse, reverse, and side.
- View the coin in its entirety.

The Divisional Fields and Devices Scan

- Divide the coin into equal, imaginary "pie" sections of the same size. You can choose as many or as few sections as you desire—two, three, or, preferably, four.
- Choose an obverse section, and scan its fields in a clockwise direction. Then scan the devices of that obverse section. Move to the next section in a clockwise direction, repeating the viewing action.
- Repeat the process for the reverse.
- Carefully tilt and rotate the coin while looking at the obverse so that it can be viewed from more than one angle; repeat this for the reverse.
- Scrutinize the rims from the obverse, reverse, and side.
- View the coin in its entirety.

These viewing methods embody the basic elements of examining coins. Practice these methods so that you can decide which technique is most effective for you. The methods described can be used with or without magnification.

Unless you conduct a thorough examination, you may miss detracting elements. It is not uncommon for collectors to overlook such deficiencies; in fact, they may go unnoticed for an extended period, once they have escaped initial detection at the time of the coin's acquisition.

Quick Viewing Action

Dealers are human, and they buy coins in much the same way collectors do, for there isn't a single wholesale coin source. At one coin convention, a dealer friend rushed over to show me a coin he called a "terrific buy." It was a Mint State Peace dollar—brilliant and fully struck. (A Mint State coin is one that was produced as a standard business strike, the kind normally minted for general circulation, but which never saw actual use and thus doesn't have any wear.) I scanned the reverse and noticed a large planchet crack. (The planchet is the blank circular piece of metal on which a coin is struck. Sometimes, planchets are imperfect before the coin is struck, causing the coin itself to be imperfect.) The dealer said that he had looked at the coin for hours and never noticed the imperfection. Many dealers, too, need to refine their coin-viewing methods.

Some professional numismatists can look at a coin in a matter of seconds and see both its negative and positive attributes. Extensive experience has made these individuals practiced coin viewers, who use no methods other than the ones described herein (or variations of

The devices, parts that stand out from the coin (e.g. lettering), are highlighted as part of an animated scan of a coin's quadrants. These are still shots from *The Coin Collector's Survival Manual®, Fifth Edition* CD-ROM version of this book, available for $34.95 at www.carlisledevelopment.com, tel. 800-219-0257. *Photos courtesy Carlisle Development Corp.*

them). However, their viewing action is performed with split-second timing. These professionals develop this skill out of necessity, for when they view hundreds of lots during an auction presale viewing session, they can't spend a great deal of time with each coin.

How to Handle Coins

The average collector would be amazed at the number of once-exceptional rare coins that have been ruined through improper removal from holders. Seeing such a coin is disconcerting. Picture a silver Proof coin minted more than a hundred years ago but which still possesses dazzling mirror fields and frosted devices. (A Proof is a coin made especially for collectors; it is struck by a special process and possesses a chromium-like brilliance.) Such a coin immediately captures the viewer's attention. But delight turns quickly to dismay if, when you look upon its nearly perfect surfaces, scratch marks from a staple can be seen. Typically, such marks can be traced back to a collector who wanted to look at the coin outside the holder and didn't first remove all of the staples. Both the premium and the aesthetic value of the coin are lowered considerably by such damage. And future generations of collectors are deprived of a coin whose high level of preservation could have been maintained. So don't try to save not-so-precious seconds and run the risk of ruining a truly precious collectible: Remove every staple before taking a coin out of its holder.

Whenever possible, you should remove a coin from its holder in order to examine the rims. This may not be allowed, however, during viewing sessions prior to an auction—and it may not be feasible with certified coins, which are permanently sealed within their plastic slabs. This should not deter you from buying such coins. If a coin is housed in a clear plastic holder, such as a polished vinyl flip, you should be able to see and examine the rims. In such a situation, you should study the holder to determine whether any apparent imperfections are on the coin itself or on the plastic. In most cases, you should be able to do so without removing the coin. The same viewing technique can be used in assessing coins housed in grading-service slabs. *Coins encapsulated in holders by reputable grading services cannot be removed prior to purchase*. In these cases, the integrity of the service has to be relied upon.

Here are some other techniques you can use to minimize the risk of damaging coins while you are examining them:

- If a coin is in an acrylic sandwich-type holder, you will need to remove it in order to examine the rims. To do this, first tap the holder lightly, obverse downward, to loosen the coin. Next, remove all screws, but keep the holder together. Place the screwless holder, obverse downward, on a flat surface, cushioned by some type of fabric. Remove the top piece of plastic and ease the coin out of the holder by applying light pressure to the coin's reverse with a piece of soft plastic, such as a polished vinyl-flip coin holder. (Perform this procedure with the utmost caution. Each coin has a light oxide coating on its surfaces, and this coating can be easily disturbed. Applying too much pressure to a coin's reverse with the pliable plastic can disrupt this coating. Such injury has the potential of healing unevenly, thus lowering the coin's aesthetic appeal.) Remove the second layer of plastic, and the coin will be resting, reverse upward, on the bottom acrylic piece. Further instructions concerning the removal of coins from holders are provided in chapter 19.
- Make sure there is a piece of soft fabric, such as velvet, under a coin during viewing. However, be certain the color is not distracting, as red velvet might be, for example. Either black or blue would be a more satisfactory, neutral color.
- Hold a coin firmly by the rim, gripping it between your thumb and forefinger. It's an interesting phenomenon that collectors and dealers both tend to drop valuable coins and not their less valuable counterparts. There's a simple explanation for this: People get nervous holding expensive coins. Either their hands shake or they handle the coins so gingerly that they come loose and fall.
- Quite a few collectors have asked me whether holding a coin by the edge may cause fingerprints. It may. If that concerns you, wear cloth or sulfur-free gloves while you are holding the coin. Most collectors like the thrill of actually holding a coin. And if you are like most collectors, you will want to experience this same excitement. Keep in mind, too, that the dealer from whom you purchased the coin probably held it without gloves, and in years to come you may see his or her fingerprints on the edge.
- Don't talk while your coins are out of their holders and anywhere near your mouth or within "spitting" distance. Small drops of saliva can land on the coin and cause "carbon" spots. Such spots really aren't carbon, but rather just toning areas which result from mishandling.

When you look at a coin, look closely. Handle it carefully, but firmly. Don't talk over the coin. These sound viewing methods will furnish a solid foundation for your future collecting pursuits, and help you to appreciate coins and profit from numismatics—both financially and aesthetically.

– 3 –
BIGGER AND BRIGHTER

Beauty is in the eye of the beholder, so they say. The same can be said for blemishes. But the eye of the beholder will see a great deal more—for better or for worse—if it's aided by strong magnification and ideal lighting. Magnification and lighting can have a significant impact on the grade a coin is given. If you grade coins under unusually high-power magnification, you're likely to lower their grades. And you're likely to do so unnecessarily, because small imperfections will appear large and be blown out of proportion. And if you grade coins under less-than-ideal lighting conditions—conditions favorable to a seller, not a buyer—you're likely to raise their grades considerably, because you won't see every imperfection. These guidelines are particularly applicable to Mint State or Uncirculated coins (coins that have never seen use or been passed from hand to hand). The grades of these coins are affected by minute imperfections, and they are often graded according to the quality with which they reflect light. Furthermore, a coin which has light but almost unnoticeable wear on its highest points—an About or Almost Uncirculated coin—can appear Mint State if viewed under too little magnification or if viewed under certain types of lighting.

Magnification has two primary numismatic uses: as an aid in grading and as an aid in authenticating.

Magnification for Grading

In grading, the purpose of magnification is to be able to view an entire side of a coin, not to look at small sections of it under high-power magnification. I recommend a 5-power [5x] or 10-power [10x] glass for grading. (Magnification "power" refers to the number of times a coin is magnified. For example, 1-power [1x] refers to the coin without magnification; 2-power [2x] refers to the coin appearing twice as large as its actual size, and so on.) If you use, say, a 20x glass, you will be tempted to downgrade a coin for having some trivial imperfection that you can't see with the naked eye. As you can see from the Bausch & Lomb chart, the greater the magnification, the smaller your field of vision. If

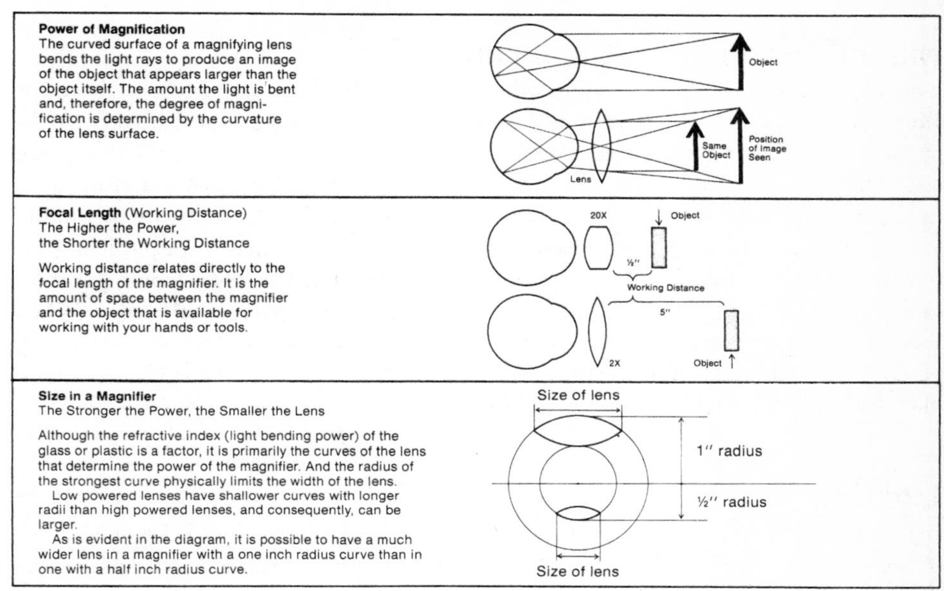

Magnification chart. *Courtesy Bausch & Lomb Optical Company*

you're buying a magnifying glass for grading, buy one large enough for you to be able to look at one side of whatever kind of coin you collect.

Although I recommend against using a stereoscope or high-power magnifier to grade, the most advanced numismatists do use these tools as grading aids. I look for things that would normally go unnoticed under low-power magnification, such as large hidden scratches and artificial re-engraving of certain details done to make the coin appear better than it is. When this approach is used, it's important to discount the appearance of minute imperfections. No coin is perfect. And even the best of the best have tiny nicks that do not count in grade determination. The most important aspect of using magnification is consistency in the power you use. Don't use a 5x glass to grade one coin and a 10x glass to grade another.

Magnification for Authentication

The magnification used to determine whether a coin is real or counterfeit, unaltered or altered, is significantly different from the magnification used for grading. If you're looking at Mint-marks, a 20x glass is recommended. This power glass just about allows you to see the Mint-mark (the letter on a coin which indicates where it was minted) and a little surrounding area. If you want to check out a coin overall for authenticity by gaining a sense of its surface, a stereomicroscope is necessary. A stereomicroscope has lenses for both eyes, rather than just one. The depth and quality of what you are looking at is remarkably improved by the use of two sets of lenses. Quality varies considerably. When shopping for a stereoscope, select one that gives you a feeling of unlimited view, as opposed to one that makes you feel as if you're looking through two tubes. The most popular stereoscopes for coins are made by Nikon.

Lighting

Lighting is the most important environmental variable that affects how coins are graded. It's no longer a secret that lighting can be arranged so that an About Uncirculated coin will appear Mint State. This is startling when you consider that the difference in price between an About Uncirculated coin and its Mint State counterpart can be hundreds or even thousands of dollars.

A Mint State coin reflects light in a fully circular pattern as you rotate it under a pinpoint light source. This circular pattern must be complete for the coin to be Mint State. Imagine a circle. A coin that is About Uncirculated reflects light in an incomplete or disturbed pattern. Imagine a pencil-drawn circle with a few small sections erased. A cleaned coin reflects light in a uniform pattern, all at once, with no trace of a circular pattern.

From this, it sounds as if it might be easy to differentiate About Uncirculated from Mint State. It isn't. If viewed under certain types of lighting conditions, a coin with a grade of About Uncirculated might appear to be Mint State to every expert who looks at it. For example, floodlights increase the brilliance yet decrease your ability to identify detracting marks and wear. If viewed under floodlights (popular at coin conventions), a coin of About Uncirculated grade would reflect light in that almost complete circle but would *appear* to reflect light in a complete circle and, thus, appear to be Mint State. To further complicate matters, chandeliers can create a delightful glowing effect by means of glass and bare filaments. If certain About Uncirculated coins were looked at under both floodlights and chandeliers, they not only would look Mint State, but also would look MS-63, MS-64, or MS-65. (MS-63, MS-64, and MS-65 are numbers which refer to the grade a coin is in: how many nicks, marks, scratches, and abrasions it acquired since leaving the Mint. The Mint State grades range from 60 through 70, with coins grading 70 having no imperfections and coins grading 60 having many. As discussed in chapter 4, the difference in price between a coin that grades MS-63 and its counterpart that grades MS-65 can be hundreds or thousands of dollars.)

The solution is to view coins under a tensor-type lamp, with fluorescent lighting as a background light. Tensor provides a high-intensity pinpoint light satisfactory for grading. Fluorescent light spreads illumination evenly. Make certain that you are consistent in using the same type of light whenever you grade. If you go to a dealer's store or a coin show, don't be afraid to ask the dealer to allow you to examine the coin under a pinpoint light source. If one isn't available, ask to borrow the coin so that you can bring it to your own light source. If you're not granted permission, don't buy the coin.

EFFECTS OF LIGHTING TYPES ON COINS

Light Source	Actual Grade	Apparent Grade Under Light
Sun, halogen	MS-65	AU-55, scratches
Fluorescent	MS-65	MS-60 with scratches
Incandescent light bulb	MS-65	MS-65 with "identity loss" —some details overlooked
Diffused (floodlight)	AU-55	MS-60
Bare filament	MS-60 (and ugly)	MS-65 and attractive
Floodlight and bare filament	AU-55	MS-65

Circulated Coins and Lighting

Although the previous chart refers primarily to coins with high grades, circulated coins are also affected by light. Dull circulated coins often display an attractive glisten when viewed under floodlights and chandeliers. And they are subject to having their defects hidden by the same types of light which hide the defects of Mint State coins.

Remember, magnification and lighting problems can be minimized if each is used consistently. Use the same type of magnification under the same type of lighting to view all of your coins.

Halogen Lamps

In recent years, many coin dealers and a number of collectors, as well, have made halogen lamps their preferred lighting source for examining coins. These lamps provide sharp, pinpoint clarity and are particularly useful in revealing hairlines on Proof coins. Robert S. Riemer of Westport, Conn., a coin dealer who also is a major distributor of halogen lamps, reports that these have become increasingly popular.

A word of caution: Halogen lamps can become extremely hot and therefore must be handled with great care. Several years ago, a halogen lamp was blamed for touching off a fire that caused extensive damage in the midtown Manhattan apartment of musician Lionel Hampton.

Furthermore, some halogen lamps emit large amounts of electromagnetic radiation—the same type of microwave radiation that some say may have caused brain tumors in cell phone users. Until definitive tests are conducted and a determination is made as to the safety of low-level magnetic fields, it might be wise to use halogen lamps with caution.

Handy and relatively safe sources of halogen light are halogen Xenon flashlights manufactured by a number of different companies. I always have one of these flashlights handy at coin conventions. These need to be handled with caution, too, as the light is bright and can cause permanent eye injury if looked at directly.

– 4 –
THE GRADING OF U.S. COINS

> As the system for grading has been refined to include more levels of grading, there is more latitude for misrepresentation of specimens. This practice is not only harmful to the collector, but serves to degradate the efforts of reliable coin dealers who are attempting to compete in the coin market on an equitable basis. Secondarily, as coins have become more valuable in all categories, small discriminations, which at one time might not have seriously affected the value of the coin, are today important in assessing its value. The highest quality coins have appreciated the most and at this point in time, minute differences among these high quality coins are crucial in terms of competitive value. The science of grading coins has not kept pace with the growing need for finite and highly specific valuation.
>
> —Dr. Richard Bagg and James J. Jelinski,
> *The Numismatist*

Grading. It sounds like a simple word and a description of a simple process. The word itself may be simple, but the process it describes in the field of coins couldn't be more complex. The variables related to grading are endless. The debate among knowledgeable numismatists about what affects grade or why coins are graded remains unsettled. The country's foremost numismatists are undecided as to what grading really is. In my attempts here to simplify a complex art and state why coins are graded, I must apologize to some of my professional colleagues in the coin field. About a third will agree with what I have to say, singing my praises and hailing me as a numismatic prophet and savior of the industry. Another third will give my presentation a lukewarm reception, pointing to areas with which they agree and other areas with which they do not. The last third will harshly criticize my explanations, pointing out that I have oversimplified a complex process that must remain complex.

What Grading Is and Why Coins Are Graded

Grading is the universal language which numismatists use to describe coins. Coins are graded on a 1–70 scale, on which 1 is the lowest and 70 is the best. The amount of wear

An astute grader examining a coin under a light in order to scrutinize crucial surface characteristics.

and tear a coin has endured will to a large degree determine its grade. A grade, then, is a description, a numismatic shorthand for what a coin looks like. The best way someone can draw a mental picture of what a coin looks like is for a coin to be graded without regard to imperfections, then for the imperfections to be described separately. In other words, if a well-worn coin has a scratch, grade the coin as if it didn't have a scratch—then describe the scratch. This concept itself is controversial, for most professionals tend to price coins first, then grade them. Students of grading grade coins first, then price them; it's far easier to learn grading without paying attention to price. When learning grading this way, though, it's important to realize that the grade you assign a coin will not immediately let you price the coin if the coin has any imperfections.

Coins are graded so that they can be sold through the mails or over the Internet to people who don't see the coins before ordering; so people who do see the coins they are buying will have an idea of the value of the coins by looking up their values in price guides; so buyers can compare dealers' offerings; and so you can describe your collection and be able to draw a mental image of what it looks like when it's sitting safely in a bank safety deposit box. It all comes down to one thing: money. In general, the higher the grade, the higher the price.

Certification Services and Grading

Precise coin grading is a relatively new phenomenon. Up until the mid–20th century, coin dealers and collectors got by with just a handful of grade designations, and Mint State coins were all lumped together as Uncirculated. Gradually, descriptive adjectives came into use to call attention to coins of exceptional quality; these would be designated as brilliant, gem, or choice, for example. At that point, there was no urgency for more specific language, since prices were relatively modest and didn't increase dramatically, in most instances, from one broad grade level to the next.

The need for precision grading began to become apparent during the 1970s, as large numbers of well-to-do outsiders started buying coins as an investment. These investors placed heavy emphasis on quality, limiting their purchases almost exclusively to Mint State coins—and this, in turn, drove up the prices of these coins, breaking the long-standing pattern whereby values had increased in a steady and consistent manner from one grade level to the next. Suddenly, Mint State coins were commanding far higher premiums than their circulated counterparts.

In the absence of industry-wide standards, abuses developed, or rather, existing abuses became greatly magnified, because so much more money was at stake. Unscrupulous dealers could and did use very creative language in describing the grades of their coins, and proving them wrong was difficult at best. Demand arose for action to remedy the problem, specifically for the establishment of official grading standards that could be applied in a uniform way nationwide.

The logical choice to oversee this project was the national coin club, the American Numismatic Association. The ANA was already deeply involved in *authenticating* coins—certifying them to be genuine. In response to earlier concerns regarding the sale of fake and altered coins, it had set up the ANA Certification Service (ANACS) in 1972, and this agency had taken major strides toward exorcising that demon. Now, responsible dealers and collectors turned to the ANA again, and it responded by drawing up official grading standards and expanding the role of ANACS to encompass not only coin authentication but grading as well.

ANACS started grading coins in March 1979, at just about the peak of the coin market's greatest boom. In contrast to the unalloyed success the service had enjoyed with authentication, though, its assumption of this new role turned out to be a mixed blessing. ANACS grading was wildly successful from a commercial standpoint, attracting many thousands of submissions and generating enormous revenue for the ANA.

ANACS's grading philosophy was to grade coins without regard to imperfections, but to describe the imperfections separately. ANA sold ANACS to Ohio-based Amos Press, Inc. in 1989; Amos sold it to Anderson Press, Inc. in 2005. The new ANACS was able to successfully adapt to the commercial marketplace, while maintaining an emphasis on educating collectors. The new ANACS emerged as a highly respected independent grading service whose coins enjoy relative liquidity—something the ANA strived for, but was never able to fully achieve.

Strike, which refers to the degree of detail appearing on a coin at its manufacture by the Mint (e.g., a "weakly struck" Uncirculated coin is one that has never been circulated but that was manufactured missing much of its usual detail), was not taken into consideration by the ANA's service when the numerical grade was assigned. But you can be absolutely certain that two identically graded Uncirculated coins, one sharply struck and the other weakly struck, do not carry the same value. The ANA's service was criticized initially because even when it followed its own parameters, its assigned grades didn't always relate to price. Again, the "old ANACS" or ANA's ANACS, which issued photocertificates, should not be confused with today's ANACS—a modern, market-sensitive grading and encapsulation service.

A number of other competent certification and grading services have been established, but at the time of this writing, in June 2005, only four such services have emerged as major market forces: the Professional Coin Grading Service (PCGS), the Numismatic Guaranty Corporation of America (NGC), ANACS, and the Independent Coin Grading Company (ICG). PCGS and NGC have emerged as the clear market leaders.

PCGS is an extraordinary market force and seems to have developed its reputation by being the first widely accepted commercial "slabbing" service. Coins are encapsulated and can be traded sight-unseen (although there are some drawbacks to this system). Coins are given a marketplace grade, not a technical or academic one.

NGC has established itself as a relatively consistent, supremely reliable service. NGC, like PCGS, grades coins and encapsulates them in sonically sealed, tamper-resistant, hard plastic holders or "slabs." NGC, as of this writing, is the "official grading service" of both the American Numismatic Association and the Professional Numismatists Guild—honors for which it pays a fee or royalty.

Today's ANACS also authenticates and grades coins and encapsulates them in sonically sealed, tamper-resistant holders. ANACS offers the unique service of encapsulating coins with major imperfections or which have been harshly cleaned. A definition of the problem can serve to educate collectors and investors. Remember: the new ANACS "slabs" coins and assigns one overall grade. In contrast, the ANA's ANACS issued photocertificates from 1979–1989 and assigned split grades—one grade for the front or obverse; another grade for the back or reverse. You might even come across an old ANACS photocertificate: at its height, ANA's ANACS was issuing about 12,000 per month.

The Independent Coin Grading Company (ICG) is a relative newcomer to the ranks of the nation's coin-grading services, having been founded in 1998. However, the company has already carved out an important niche for itself and is competing aggressively with the established leaders in the field. In fact, ICG's volume of business compares favorably with the Big Three that existed when it entered the field. In large part, that's because ICG apparently handles large numbers of high-grade modern U.S. coins—considerably more, percentagewise, than the other leading services. In fact, its encouragement of these submissions has been a significant factor in the rapid growth that sector of the marketplace has enjoyed.

Grading services, their methods of grading, and changes in their standards are explored fully in chapter 5.

What Constitutes Grade

A coin's grade depends upon its level of preservation and its beauty. However, the amount of emphasis that each factor is given during the grading process is the subject of debate.

Level of preservation refers to how well a coin has been preserved since it was minted. A coin that has had a hole drilled in it, that has many scratches, and that is well worn with no detail left is in a low level of preservation. A coin that has been carefully stored and looks as new as when it was minted is said to be in a high level of preservation. There is wide agreement that level of preservation constitutes the major percentage of a coin's grade.

Many dealers consider "beauty" of immense importance and weight when considering what grade to give a coin; the ANA and its certification service took an academic approach and gave little weight to beauty with some exceptions. In my use of the word "beauty," I'm not referring to a coin's design. Rather, I'm referring to factors such as toning, the slow, regular, natural process through which a coin acquires patina or color. The commercial segment of the coin-collecting hobby and business weights the quality of this color heavily; the academic segment discounts the importance of this color.

Coins Made for Circulation

A coin is most valuable if it has been well preserved and, thus, looks the same as it did the day it left the Mint, with the exception of toning. Collectors call these coins Mint State (MS) or Uncirculated (Unc.). Coins that are Brilliant Uncirculated are often referred to as BU. After a business-strike coin—one made for general circulation—is minted, it is distributed to the Federal Reserve System, which distributes it to the banks; the banks then distribute the coin to the public. This distribution system has been in effect since 1913. As a coin passes from person to person or circulates, it becomes worn from being handled. Such coins are called "circulated" coins by collectors and are far less desirable than coins that are Mint State, for wear causes the loss of a great deal of luster and detail from the coins, which can never again be recovered. There are numerous distinctions within both the MS and circulated grade categories.

A coin's grade is an indirect statement of value. It is, therefore, imperative that you be familiar with coin grading or be able to trust someone who is. But even if you are a scholar, able to grade every coin meticulously and accurately, that doesn't mean you can necessarily know a coin's value, as will be explained in chapter 9. Grading habits of dealers change according to the mood of the coin market.

How the Certification Services View Eye Appeal

Although coin grading is a subjective process of evaluation, the most subjective element of a coin's appearance, its overall beauty, was not always incorporated into the grade. The very thought that beauty is not part of a coin's grade seems senseless today with grading services such as PCGS, NGC, ANACS, and ICG routinely incorporating eye appeal into one overall numerical grade. But until its sale to Amos Press, Inc. in 1989, the American Numismatic Association Certification Service (ANACS) graded on an academic basis. Theoretically, if the coin was manufactured with a gaping hole, the old ANACS could still have graded it MS-70.

ANACS used to be an arm of the world's largest nonprofit rare coin organization, the American Numismatic Association. The service issued photocertificates (1979–1989) which carried its opinions of coins' authenticity and grades. Grading standards have tightened since then, and consumers, therefore, should be wary of the old certificates which are reflective of looser standards than those employed by leading grading services today.

If all of the dealers all of the time strongly believed that a particular type of toning on a particular coin was awesome, phenomenal, and overwhelmingly attractive, PCGS would feel justified in raising its grade by half of a grade (high-end 64 raised to MS-65). The trouble is, this concept is one that can only be written about, because not all dealers agree that any particular type of toning is always attractive. Consequently, PCGS has assigned a slightly higher grade to some coins for their beauty, despite the fact that many dealers considered the coin ugly with terribly unattractive toning.

Subjectivity and Self-Certified Coins

Grading is subjective, but not as subjective as some dealers would like you to think. There are a few bad apples in every field, and the coin field is no exception. These bad-apple dealers might sell you an uncertified or "self-certified" coin, give it a high Mint State grade, then refuse to take it back when you find out it isn't Mint State, but has slight wear, claiming that grading is subjective and that there are legitimate differences of opinion. Beware of disreputable dealers who "certify" their own coins—however, not all dealers who certify their own coins are disreputable.

The Federal Trade Commission (FTC) makes available on its website (www.ftc.gov/bcp/conline/pubs/alerts/coinalrt.htm) a consumer alert it issued some years back and advises consumers, in part:

> Grading is not an exact science, and a certificate or slab represents no more than the opinion of the certification or grading service. Find out if the grading service is indeed independent of the dealer, what grading standards the service used, and what is the service's reputation in the industry. . . . Weekly periodicals or sight-unseen trading networks list prices for coins that have been certified by various services. Check the prices for those coins you are considering.

Most dealers, even those few bad apples, know what makes a coin universally beautiful or universally ugly. The "grading is subjective" argument carried to extremes is a defense of unethical grading practices.

Many would agree that *the purpose of grading is more to communicate how well a coin has been preserved than how nice it looks*. The fact remains, though, that in most cases the higher the grade, the better the appearance. A universally ugly coin doesn't deserve a high grade, no matter how high its "technical level of preservation."

Proof—A Method of Manufacture, Not a Grade

When coins were first assigned grades, only a few grades existed: Unc., Fine, Good, Fair, Poor, and mutilated or basal state. Of course, these grades refer to business strikes. The term Proof was also used. But Proof doesn't refer to a grade; rather, it refers to a method of manufacture. A Proof is a coin struck at least twice with specially polished dies on specially selected planchets to assure a chromium-like brilliance. (1982-S, and possibly later-date, commemorative Proof coins were struck three times because of the higher-relief design; virtually every other Proof coin was struck twice.) Proofs are sold to collectors during the year of issue at a premium—a price above the face value of the coin. Brilliant Proof coins are among the most beautiful, for there is often a cameo contrast between the reflective fields and the frosted devices. The Matte Proof has a different appearance and is produced by a different process. For example, some Proof coins struck during 1908–1916 by the Philadelphia Mint appear grainy because either the dies or the coins were sandblasted. This is explored fully in chapter 6.

Grading Guides

As the coin business has become more sophisticated, so have grading philosophies. More and more grades have been added. A good review of these philosophies, some of which are still adhered to today, is provided in *Grading Coins: A Collection of Readings*, edited by Richard Bagg and James J. Jelinski (Essex Publications, 1977). The first major grading guide to gain universal acceptance was *The Guide to the Grading of United States Coins*, by Martin R. Brown and John W. Dunn, which became known as the "Brown & Dunn" method of grading. The authors allowed the reader to grade coins by looking at line drawings and comparing the representations to the coins. The authors stressed that graders familiarize themselves with coin design by closely examining well-struck Mint State coins. This would allow for better understanding of what parts of a coin's design were missing from circulated specimens, thus allowing ease of grading for circulated coins.

The Brown & Dunn method was a good start in promoting standardized grading practices, but it is far from adequate today.

In 1970, *Photograde*, by James F. Ruddy, made its mark on the numismatic community. This was a truly revolutionary book. In it, every major United States coin design is illustrated with black-and-white photographs. The book is still popular and useful today.

In 1986, *The NCI Grading Guide*, by James L. Halperin, was released to much critical acclaim. Although NCI, the Numismatic Certification Institute, wasn't as conservative as some other certification services of the era, the book was hailed as a landmark work in the grading and trading of Uncirculated coins. It was later revised and released as *How to Grade U.S. Coins*. Every collector and investor should read Halperin's work.

Official ANA Grading Standards for United States Coins, Sixth Edition, by the American Numismatic Association (Whitman Publishing, LLC, 2005), is both useful and nicely done. The descriptive terms are deliberately ambiguous, allowing for interpretation. The book contains over 1,200 photographs—an extremely helpful aid. Assistance is offered for persons interested in grading Uncirculated coins. This book is essential to collectors of circulated coins, for circulated grades are illustrated in an understandable manner, with black-and-white photos for all major United States coin types. The latest edition includes a 16-page color section. I am listed in the historical credits.

In 1997, the most impressive and massive grading guide ever produced was launched when Random House published *The Official Guide to Coin Grading and Counterfeit Detection*, by PCGS; edited by Scott A. Travers; text by John W. Dannreuther. The first edition, a 372-page book, is coffee-table size, printed on coated stock, and contains hundreds of exceptional color and black & white photographs. The second edition, published in 2004, is a handier, more compact size and is priced at $19.95. I strongly urge every coin enthusiast to carefully study the PCGS guide. In 1997, former American Numismatic Association president David L. Ganz wrote in *Numismatic News* that it "relegated to historical interest" the other grading guides, including the ANA's own.

The Official Guide to Coin Grading and Counterfeit Detection was named "Book of the Year" and "Best U.S. Coin Book" by the prestigious Numismatic Literary Guild in 1998. Its text's author, John W. Dannreuther, was recognized with the Professional Numismatists Guild's highly important Friedberg award for his work on that book.

In 2004, Whitman Publishing, LLC unveiled the 144-page spiral-bound *NGC Grading Guide for Modern U.S. Coins, 1st* Edition, by Richard S. Montgomery and David W. Lange. This is a basic book that contains some good, helpful pointers for the beginner.

Amos Hobby Publishing unveiled *Coin World*'s landmark milestone color grading guide, *Making the Grade: A Grading Guide to the Top 25 Most Widely Collected U.S. Coins,* in 2005. Many of the photographs were previously published in *Coin Values* magazine and are the best coin grading pictures ever published. This book receives my highest recommendation.

Numerical Grading Standards

In 1977, the American Numismatic Association introduced its *Official ANA Grading Standards for United States Coins*. In it, every United States coin was illustrated by line drawings. Finally, it was thought, the numismatic industry would have a set of uniform, agreed-upon standards. The guide grades coins based on a scale of 1–70, in which 1 is poor or basal state and 70 is perfect. The official ANA grading system scale, as revised in 1991, is as follows:

Adjectival Designation	Numerical Grade	Adjectival Qualifier(s)
Mint State	60-70	—
About Uncirculated	58	Very Choice
About Uncirculated	55	Choice
About Uncirculated	50	Typical
Extremely Fine	45	Choice
Extremely Fine	40	Typical

Adjectival Designation	Numerical Grade	Adjectival Qualifier(s)
Very Fine	30	Choice
Very Fine	20	Typical
Fine	12	—
Very Good	8	—
Good	4	—
About Good	3	—

This numerical system is based on a grading formula devised by the late Dr. William Sheldon for his book *Penny Whimsy*—an authoritative text on large cents. Dr. Sheldon introduced this scale in the late 1940s and early 1950s as an algebraic pricing formula for large cents:

Book Value = Basal Value x Numerical Designation

In other words, by multiplying the value of a particular specimen in its basal state ("basal" means barely identifiable as to type of coin) by its assigned numerical grade, the book value could be computed. For example, if coin X, an Extremely Fine–40, was valued at $2 in Basal State–1, its book value would have been $80:

$80	=	$2	x	40
Book Value		**Basal Value**		**Numerical Designation**

Theoretically, the correct grade of a large cent could have been found if just the book value were stated. As in any algebraic formula, you can always solve for the unknown with two knowns. This formula is outdated today, however, for minute differences in a particular coin's grade can mean a considerable difference in price.

The sixth edition of *Official ANA Grading Standards for United States Coins* is helpful for grading all United States coins. If the seller uses what he or she calls "my own standards," then he or she might claim not to be legally bound to use any system and be free to overgrade. As stated previously, this book is useful and nicely done. I recommend it.

How the Marketplace Defines the Grades AU-58 Through MS-70

From your perspective as a buyer or seller, the most important part of the grading spectrum is the grading of Mint-State coins—coins that have not passed from hand to hand, have not circulated, and have no wear on their very highest points. The difference in price in these "upper-end" coins is tremendous. You literally can't afford not to know how to grade these coins.

Grading services furnish invaluable assistance to buyers and sellers of coins, particularly to those who lack in-depth knowledge of grading. But to maximize your potential for making money from coins, you need to become familiar with how to grade coins yourself—particularly how to grade coins in the 11 Mint State levels—and those grades approaching them.

The grading of coins at grading services, as is explained in chapter 5, has been fine-tooled over months and years and is subject to change.

PCGS Coin-Grading Standards

The following is an excerpt, reprinted with permission, from PCGS's grading standards book, *The Official Guide to Coin Grading and Counterfeit Detection, Second Edition*, by the Professional Coin Grading Service (House of Collectibles/Random House, Inc., 2004), incorporating the basic PCGS coin-grading standards in force when the book was published. Some large gold coin dealers expressed the opinion that after the second edition of the book was published in 2004 they saw PCGS-certified generic gold coins that were certified less conservatively. These standards are subject to wide interpretation, so even if there were any change in interpretations the wording is still completely accurate and authoritative.

"The standards as expressed in the PCGS grading guide have remained constant, but the parameters as described in the book leave some latitude for interpretation," said David Hall, president of PCGS. "There is a subjective nature to coin grading," Hall pointed out. "There is a high end and low end in all grades, and fluctuations in the application of the standard *can and do occur*. Sometimes different batches get out that are too tight or too loose."

Business Strikes—Mint State Standards

MS-70: PERFECT UNCIRCULATED

Marks: An MS-70 coin has no defects of any kind visible with a 5X (5-power) glass. Note: Minor die polish, light die breaks, and so on are not considered defects on business-strike coins.

Strike: The strike is razor-sharp and will show 99 percent of the detail intended.

Luster: The luster is vibrant and undisturbed in any way. Any toning will be attractive. Only the slightest mellowing of color is acceptable for red copper.

Eye Appeal: The eye appeal is spectacular—the ultimate grade!

MS-69: SUPERB GEM UNCIRCULATED

Marks: A virtually perfect coin. It usually takes an intense study of the surfaces to ascertain why the coin will not grade MS-70. Only the slightest contact marks, nearly invisi-

***The Official® Guide to Coin Grading and Counterfeit Detection, 2nd Edition,* authored by PCGS and published by Random House, contains definitive standards for grading coins.**

ble hairlines, the tiniest planchet flaws, and so on are allowable for this grade. Note: Slight die polish, medium die breaks, or slight incomplete striking are not defects.

Strike: The strike is extremely sharp and will show 99 percent of the detail intended.

Luster: The luster will be full and unbroken. Any toning must be attractive. Only the slightest mellowing of color is acceptable for red copper, and only the slightest unevenness of color for red-brown and brown copper.

Eye Appeal: Superb!

MS-68: SUPERB GEM UNCIRCULATED

Marks: A nearly perfect coin, with only slight imperfections visible to the unaided eye. The imperfections (tiny contact marks, minuscule hairlines, a small lint mark, etc.) will almost always be out of the range of the coin's focal points.

Strike: The strike will be exceptionally sharp.

Luster: The luster will be full (or virtually so) and "glowing." Any luster breaks will be extremely minor and usually restricted to the high points. Slight unevenness in toning is acceptable, as long as it is still attractive. Red copper may show some mellowing, and there may be some unevenness of color for red-brown and brown copper.

Eye Appeal: Exceptional, with no major detractions.

MS-67: SUPERB GEM UNCIRCULATED

Marks: Any abrasions on the coin are extremely light and/or well hidden in the design and do not detract from the coin's beauty in any way. As with MS-68 coins, the fields on smaller coins are usually nearly flawless, especially on the obverse. On large silver coins with smooth devices (Morgan dollars, for instance), the flaws will usually be found in the fields; on large gold coins (such as Liberty Head $20s), the fields will usually be superb in this grade, with only minor flaws in the devices.

Strike: The strike will be very sharp and almost always full.

Luster: The luster will be outstanding. Any toning (even if slightly uneven) must be attractive and not impede the luster in any way. Red copper can have mellowing of color, and there can be unevenness of color for red-brown and brown copper. Minute spotting, if present, should be virtually unnoticeable.

Eye Appeal: In almost all cases, the eye appeal will be superb. Any negativity will be compensated for by another area that is spectacular.

MS-66: GEM UNCIRCULATED

Marks: There may be several noticeable, but very minor, defects. If marks or hairlines are in an important focal area, they must be minimal and compensated for by the rest of the coin's superbness.

Strike: The coin will be well-struck.

Luster: The luster will be above average (usually far above average), and any toning should be attractive and should only minimally impede the luster. Red copper can have mellowing of color, and there can be unevenness of color for red-brown and brown copper. Very minor spotting may be present, although it should be noticed only upon close examination. A dipped coin must be "fresh" in appearance and never give the impression of having been cleaned.

Eye Appeal: The eye appeal will almost always be above average for a gem-quality coin, and many MS-66 coins will be superb in this category. Any negative factors must be compensated for in another area.

MS-65: GEM UNCIRCULATED

Marks: There may be scattered marks, hairlines, or other minor defects. If the flaws are in a main focal area, they must be minor and few. Hidden marks and hairlines can be larger. On dime-type and smaller, they almost always must be in the devices or must be very minor if they are in the fields. On larger coins, there can be marks/hairlines in the fields and in the devices, but no major ones.

Strike: The coin will be well-struck.

Luster: The luster will be at least average (almost always above average), and any toning can only slightly impede the luster. Copper coins can have mellowing of color for red and unevenness of color for red-brown or brown coins: Note: There can be a little minor spotting for copper coins.

Eye Appeal: The eye appeal will be average or above. This is a very nice coin. However, there are many ways a coin can grade MS-65. This grade (or MS/Proof-64) may have the largest range of eye appeal. A coin may grade MS-65 with scattered light marks, but with great luster and strike—or a coin with virtually no marks but a slightly impeded luster also could be MS-65. The overall eye appeal still must be positive or the coin does not merit MS-65.

MS-64: CHOICE UNCIRCULATED

Marks: There may be numerous minor marks/hairlines, several significant marks/hairlines, or other defects. There may be a few minor or one or two significant marks/

hairlines in the main focal areas. On minor coinage (dime coinage and lesser), there may be several marks/hairlines in the fields or main focal areas, but none should be too severe. On larger coins, these marks/hairlines may be more severe in the fields or main focal areas. However, a severe mark/hairline would have to be of a size that would preclude grading the coin MS-65, though not so severe as to reduce the coin to MS-63. If there are several fairly heavy marks/hairlines in obvious areas, the coin would grade MS-63.

Strike: The strike will range from average to full.

Luster: The luster can be slightly below average to full, and toning can impede the luster. On brilliant coins, there may be breaks in the luster caused by marks or hairlines. Red copper can be considerably mellowed. There may be noticeable spotting for this grade, although heavy or large spotting would reduce the grade to MS-63 or below.

Eye Appeal: The eye appeal can range from slightly negative to very positive. This is a nice coin, so anything too negative would preclude the MS-64 grade. Balance is key. A coin with marks/hairlines in obvious focal areas would have to have great luster or some other positive factor to attain MS-64. A coin with less severe marks/hairlines hidden in devices could have impaired luster or some other problem and still be graded MS-64. Coins with deficiencies and no redeeming characteristics are graded MS-63 or lower.

MS-63: CHOICE UNCIRCULATED

Marks: There may be numerous marks/hairlines, including several major marks/hairlines in main focal areas. If there are distracting marks/hairlines on the major devices, the fields should be relatively clean. If there are distracting marks/hairlines in the fields, the devices should have less disturbance.

Strike: The strike will range from slightly below average to full.

Luster: The luster can be below average to full. The toning can seriously impede the luster. On brilliant coins, there can be significant breaks in the luster. Red copper can be considerably mellowed. There can be noticeable spotting, including several large spots or a group of small ones. Note: If the luster is poor, then the coin would not be graded MS-63, even if the strike were full and the marks/hairlines were acceptable for the grade.

Eye Appeal: The eye can be slightly negative to very positive. The "average" MS-63 will have neutral eye appeal (noticeable marks/hairlines, average to above-average strike, and average luster). However, quite a few coins are graded MS-63 because of their negative appearance. If either the luster, strike, or marks/hairlines are below the standards set forth here, then one of the other criteria must be exceptional for the coin to attain MS-63.

MS-62: UNCIRCULATED

Marks: The marks/hairlines may cover most of the coin. If the marks/hairlines are light, they may be scattered across the entire coin. If there are several severe marks/hairlines, the rest of the coin should be relatively clean.

Strike: The strike can range from very weak (some New Orleans Mint Morgan dollars, for example) to full.

Luster: The luster can range from poor to vibrant.

Eye Appeal: The eye appeal will be negative to slightly positive. The negativity in this grade usually involves excessive marks/hairlines and/or the strike and/or lack of luster and/or unattractive toning. There can be one to three of the major criteria that contribute to negative eye appeal. Even coins with overall positive eye appeal usually have one or two areas that are negative. Thus, a coin with numerous marks/hairlines but with average strike and luster may grade MS-62, while a coin with just a few marks (probably in the wrong places) and weak strike and luster also may grade MS-62.

MS-61: UNCIRCULATED

Marks: There may be marks/hairlines across the entire coin. There may be several severe contact marks/hairlines. If there are numerous large marks/hairlines in the main focal areas, the fields should be cleaner, although they still could have contact marks/hairlines. On larger coins (half dollars and larger), there may be areas with almost no marks/hairlines.

Strike: The strike can range from very weak to full.

Luster: The luster may be poor, average, or full.

Eye Appeal: The eye appeal will be very negative to very slightly positive.

MS-60: UNCIRCULATED

Marks: Numerous. The marks/hairlines will probably cover all of the coin's surface. On larger coins (half dollars and higher), there may be some areas that have few or no marks/hairlines. The marks/hairlines can be large and in prime focal areas. Note: Sometimes the mark is not from "normal" contact with other coins or from circulation, thus would be considered damage and the coin might not be graded.

Strike: The strike can range from very weak to full.

Luster: The luster may be poor, average, or full.

Eye Appeal: The eye appeal can be very negative to neutral.

Business Strikes—Circulated Standards

AU-58: CHOICE ABOUT UNCIRCULATED

Wear: There will be slight wear on the highest points of the coin. In some cases, 5X magnification is needed to notice this wear, and sometimes it can be noticed by slowly tilting the coin in the light source. This method often may show the slight friction as discoloration. Very often, the obverse will have slight friction and the reverse will be full Mint State (often MS-63 or higher).

Marks: There are usually very few marks for this grade. Instead of marks, the principal detractions on the typical AU-58 coin are rub or hairlines. The few marks should not be major or in prime focal areas. A coin that would grade AU-58 from a wear standpoint, but has numerous marks, would be graded AU-55 or lower.

Strike: The strike can range from below average to full. Note: A very weak strike would be downgraded to AU-55 or lower.

Luster: The luster can range from poor to full. There will be noticeable breaks in the luster on the high points. These areas will be visible to the unaided eye, but should be less than 10 percent of the surface area.

Eye Appeal: The eye appeal is usually very good. Since marks are usually very minor, the eye appeal will be determined mainly by strike, luster, and originality. Many AU-58 coins are lightly cleaned or dipped uncirculated coins that are no longer considered uncirculated because of the light cleaning or rubbing that is now present. These coins can be just as attractive as coins that are graded AU-58 because of slight circulation—and sometimes even more so. Often these coins will have fewer marks than low-grade uncirculated coins.

Note: An AU-58 coin must appear Mint State at first glance. Upon close examination, light friction will be visible on the highest points. (Imagine a perspiration-soaked thumb rubbing the coin; and envision the aftermath.) The AU-58 would ordinarily qualify for the MS-63 grade. However, the light rubbing would remove it from technically being classified as "Mint State." Sometimes, these coins trade among dealers at the MS-63 price (or close to it) because of the overall aesthetic quality of the coin. —Author.

AU-55: CHOICE ABOUT UNCIRCULATED

Wear: There will be slight wear on the high points and some friction in the fields. The reverse will now usually show wear similar to that on the obverse. In a few instances (coins stored face up that have acquired friction), the reverse will still be uncirculated.

Marks: There usually will be several minor marks/hairlines and a couple of major ones. These should be scattered between the devices and fields, with nothing too severe on the prime focal areas.

Strike: The strike will range from slightly weak to full.

Luster: The luster can range from poor to full, although the areas of wear will not show full luster. There will be breaks in the luster covering 10 to 25 percent of the surface.

Eye Appeal: The eye appeal is usually good. The main criteria will be surface preservation, lack of and placement of marks/hairlines, the luster remaining, and originality.

Proofs

PROOF-70: PERFECT PROOF

Marks: There can be no defects visible with a 5X glass. A Proof-70 coin is 100 percent free of hairlines, planchet flaws, lint marks, and any other mint-caused or post-striking defects.

Strike: The strike is full, showing all of the intended detail.

Luster: The surfaces are fully reflective (if applicable) and undisturbed in any way. Any toning must be attractive. Red copper must have no breaks in the color, and only the slightest mellowing is acceptable.

Eye Appeal: Nothing short of spectacular.

PROOF-69: SUPERB GEM PROOF

Marks: This coin will appear perfect to the unaided eye. Upon magnification, one or two minute imperfections (extremely minor hairlines, a previously hidden lint mark, a flake from the planchet, etc.) will be evident. Note: Slight die polish, very minor die breaks, or incomplete striking will not preclude a coin from attaining this grade.

Strike: The strike will be full, showing all of the detail intended.

Luster: The surfaces must be fully reflective (if applicable) and not negatively affected by toning or patina. Any toning must be attractive. Slight mellowing of color is allowed for red copper and only the slightest unevenness of color for red-brown and brown copper.

Eye Appeal: Superb! Note: Darkly toned proof coins will not grade Proof-69.

PROOF-68: SUPERB GEM PROOF

Marks: A Proof-68 coin will have minor defects barely visible to the unaided eye-defects that usually go unnoticed at first look. These will usually include one of the following: virtually undetectable hairlines, a small planchet flaw, or an unobtrusive lint mark. Such defects, no matter how minor, should not be in a conspicuous place such as Liberty's cheek or the obverse field.

Strike: The strike will be full, showing virtually all of the detail intended.

Luster: The coin must be fully reflective (if applicable) or virtually so. Any toning must be attractive, but slight unevenness is allowable. Some mellowing of color is allowed for red copper and some unevenness of color for red-brown and brown copper.

Eye Appeal: The eye appeal will be exceptional. Any hint of negativity will be compensated for in another area.

PROOF-67: SUPERB GEM PROOF

Marks: Any defects visible to the unaided eye will be minor. These could include unobtrusive hairlines, one or more very minor contact marks, a stray lint mark or two, a well-hidden planchet flaw, and so on. If the eye is immediately drawn to a defect, that will almost always preclude the coin from grading Proof-67.

Strike: The strike will be full or exceptionally sharp.

Luster: The reflectivity must be nearly full (if applicable). Toning may be dark or uneven, but not both. Red copper can have mellowing of color, and there can be unevenness of color for red-brown and brown copper. Minute spotting, if present, should be virtually unnoticeable.

Eye Appeal: Superb, or nearly so. Any negativity must be compensated for in another area. Darkly toned coins are almost always penalized at least one grade point at this level-for example, a Proof-67 coin that is dark would grade at least Proof-68 if the toning were attractive or nonexistent.

PROOF-66: GEM PROOF

Marks: A Proof-66 coin can have a few light contact lines/hairlines, but nothing detracting or concentrated in one area. It may have small lint marks or planchet flaws, but any defects must be minor. If the eye is drawn to a flaw, the rest of the coin must be superb to compensate for it.

Strike: The strike must be sharp and will almost always be exceptionally sharp.

Luster: The reflectivity will usually be excellent (if applicable). Any toning must be positive, and reflectivity must be good (if applicable). A Proof-66 coin may have some extremely positive attributes that offset slightly too much negativity in another area. For instance, Coin X has two or three too many hairlines to qualify as Proof-66, but the toning is fantastic, the devices are heavily frosted, and the eye appeal is outstanding, so the coin is graded Proof-66 anyway. Red copper can have mellowing of color, and there can be unevenness of color of red-brown and brown copper. Very minor spotting may be present.

Eye Appeal: Overall eye appeal for this grade is great, since this coin just misses Proof-67. Any deficiency in toning (too dark for Proof-67 because of impeded reflectivity, "splotchy" almost to the point of being negative, etc.) will be slight. If the coin is brilliant, the deficiency usually will be minuscule—contact/hairline/slide marks that preclude a higher grade.

PROOF-65: GEM PROOF

Marks: There may be several minor problems. These may include light contact, hairlines, lint marks, planchet flaws, or other minor defects. Since there may be several minor problems, there are many ways to attain the grade of Proof-65. For example, a coin with virtually no hairlines may have slight contact/slide marks on the high points and still grade Proof-65. In another case, a coin with no contact/slide marks might still grade no higher than Proof-65 because of minor but noticeable hairlines. Any other minor defects, such as lint marks or planchet flaws, should be unobtrusive.

Strike: The coin will be well-struck and, in most cases, very sharp.

Luster: The reflectivity will be average or above. Any toning present can impede the reflectivity only slightly. On untoned coins, the reflectivity can be moderately subdued, but coins with "washed-out" surfaces cannot be graded Proof-65. Red copper can have mellowing of color; color coins can have minor spotting.

Eye Appeal: The eye appeal will be average or above. This is a coin almost everyone finds attractive. The comments for eye appeal under MS-65 are just as relevant for Proof-65. There is a wide range in the appearance of Proof-65 coins. Any slightly negative factors must be compensated for in another area.

PROOF-64: CHOICE PROOF

Marks: There may be numerous minor problems. These may include contact marks, many small hairlines, or several large hairlines. Other defects—such as lint marks or planchet flaws in focal areas—may be allowed.

Strike: There can be some weakness in strike. Note: This is the highest Proof grade where some distracting weakness of strike in the major devices is allowable. Weakness in stars and other minor devices is not usually enough to reduce the grade.

Luster: The reflectivity can be impeded. If the coin is toned, the reflectivity can be noticeably subdued. On untoned coins, there can be dullness or a "washed-out" appearance, but these coins should have fewer contact lines/hairlines than a coin with more of the mirror surface intact. Red copper can be considerably mellowed. There may be noticeable spotting for this grade, although large or numerous spots would reduce the grade to Proof-63 or lower.

Eye Appeal: The eye appeal can range from slightly negative to very positive. This is an attractive coin. However, there can be some negativity in toning (too dark, hazy, splotchy, etc.)—or, with untoned coins, there can be dullness in the mirrored surface.

The amount of hairlines acceptable for this grade is directly proportional to the eye appeal. If a coin has great contrast (frosted devices), the hairlines or other defects can be quite noticeable. On a coin that has less contrast and is either darkly toned or dull brilliant, the hairlines must be minor.

PROOF-63: CHOICE PROOF

Marks: There may be immediately noticeable defects. There may be quite a few contact marks/hairlines or a group of concentrated hairlines, lint marks in prime focal areas, medium-to-large planchet flaws, or a combination of these or other defects. Obvious "slide marks," which usually result from an album's plastic sliding across the devices, will almost always result in a grade of no higher than Proof-63.

Strike: The strike can range from average to full. This is the highest Proof grade where considerable weakness of strike is allowed. If the coin is poorly struck, a grade of Proof-62 or below would be appropriate.

Luster: The reflectivity can be below average to full. On untoned coins, the surfaces are often dull—and on toned coins, there can be dark or uneven toning that will seriously impede the amount of reflectivity. Red copper can be considerably mellowed. There can be noticeable spotting, with several large spots or numerous small ones. Note: If the mirrored surface is almost totally obscured, the grade of Proof-63 will not be attained and a grade of Proof-62 or lower is warranted.

Eye Appeal: The eye appeal can be slightly negative to very positive. The "average" Proof-63 coin will have neutral eye appeal (noticeable hairlines, well-struck, slightly dulled surfaces). Some coins can still grade Proof-63, even if one or more of the major criteria are negative, but that must be compensated for by strength in another area.

PROOF 62: PROOF

Marks: There may be some light contact marks, numerous light hairlines, medium-to-heavy hairlines, or a combination of the above covering most of the coin's surface. There also may be concentrated patches of hairlines, with some areas remaining relatively free of contact marks/hairlines.

Strike: The strike can range from extremely weak to full.

Luster: The reflectivity can range from below average to nearly full. On toned coins, there may be very little of the mirrored surface left, and with brilliant coins the reflectivity may be almost completely impaired by hairlines.

Eye Appeal: The eye appeal will be negative to slightly positive.

PROOF-61: PROOF

Marks: The surfaces may have some contact marks and numerous light-to-heavy hairlines. There may be several small marks hidden in the devices. The entire surface may be covered with contact marks/hairlines, or there may be several areas with concentrated hairlines and some others relatively free of them.

Strike: The strike can range from very weak to full.

Luster: The reflectivity will range from poor to slightly impaired.

Eye Appeal: The eye appeal will be very negative to very slightly positive.

PROOF 60: PROOF

Marks: The surface may have quite a few contact lines or myriad medium-to-heavy hairlines and may have several marks. There should be no large marks for this grade. If there are large marks, the grade would be Proof-58 or lower.

Strike: The strike can range from very weak to full.

Luster: The reflectivity may range from poor to slightly impaired.

Eye Appeal: The eye appeal can be very negative to neutral.

Proofs-Circulated Standards

PROOF 58: CIRCULATED PROOF

Wear: There usually is very little wear on the high points. With Proof coins, wear usually takes the form of slight friction in the fields. Since the mirrored surfaces of Proof coins are so delicate, any minor circulation or mishandling will cause marks and hairlines to become immediately apparent. In some cases, the reverse may have no impairment and will grade Proof-60 or higher. Note: It is much easier to discern wear on a Proof than on a business strike. Proofs and prooflike business strikes reveal marks/hairlines much more easily because of the mirrored surface.

Marks: There could be a few major marks. There can be scattered contact marks, with a few allowed on the devices and in the fields. If there are more than a few marks, a Proof coin would be graded Proof-55 or lower.

Strike: The strike can range from average to full. Note: A weak strike would be downgraded to Proof-55 or lower.

Luster: The reflectivity will be somewhat impaired. This is not always true with Proof-58 coins, since many coins in this grade will have full reflectivity, which is disturbed only by hairlines, marks, or minor wear.

Eye Appeal: The eye appeal is usually very good. There usually is nothing other than slight contact marks/friction on Proof-58 coins. Appearance is usually not the problem with this coin.

PROOF-55: CIRCULATED PROOF

Wear: There will be slight wear on the high points and up to half of the fields will have friction. The reverse will now be impaired in most cases.

Marks: There may be several marks and quite a few contact marks/hairlines. These should be scattered about and should not be concentrated on prime focal areas.

Strike: The strike will range from slightly weak to full.

Luster: The reflectivity may be severely impaired. Up to 50 percent of the mirrored surface is now slightly to fairly severely impaired. There can be a few areas that have lost complete reflectivity.

Eye Appeal: The eye appeal is usually good. The main criteria will be surface preservation, lack of and placement of marks/hairlines, reflectivity remaining, and originality.

PROOF 53: CIRCULATED PROOF

Wear: There will be obvious wear to high points. Friction will cover 50 to 75 percent of the fields.

Marks: There may be several minor and major marks/hairlines. There can be scattered marks/hairlines in all areas of the coin, including prime focal areas, but a severe disturbance in those prime areas will result in a lower grade. Some small areas may have heavy concentrations of hairlines.

Strike: The strike will range from below average to full.

Luster: The reflectivity may be severely impaired. The amount of "mirror" still visible will depend on the original depth of the mirrored surface.

Eye Appeal: The eye appeal now is a function of surface preservation, lack of and placement of marks/hairlines, reflectivity remaining, and originality.

PROOF-50: CIRCULATED PROOF

Wear: Wear is evident. There can be friction in the fields ranging from half to all of the unprotected areas. The high points will have wear that is very obvious to the unaided eye.

Marks: There may be many marks/hairlines. Many times, hairlines and small marks will now start to "blend" into the surfaces. These will appear as discolored areas.

Strike: The strike will range from below average to full.

Luster: The reflectivity may be completely impaired. There may be parts of the surface with no mirror at all. The Proof surface may be visible only around protected devices.

Eye Appeal: The eye appeal is now a function of surface preservation, lack of and placement of marks/hairlines, reflectivity remaining, and originality.

Note: Coins that grade PR-45 and below are graded essentially the same as regular strikes. Since the criteria for determining the overall grade will mostly be the same for both mint state and proof coins, these grades are listed only under the mint state standards mentioned earlier, with any exceptions noted. —Author.

The Coin Grading Spectrum

To a mathematician or scientist, numbers are absolute: 65 is always 65, because numbers don't lie. In the coin industry, numbers may not lie, but they don't always represent exactly what you think they represent.

A coin that grades or rates 65 on this 1-to-70 scale could be worth thousands of dollars more than a coin of the same type grading 64. As a consumer, you might think that all 65s are alike and that all 64s are alike, but you would be wrong.

Low-end Mint State-65 Morgan dollar. The cheek, a grade-sensitive area, is marred by various nicks and marks. If this coin were resubmitted for certification, a grade of MS-64 might be assigned. *Photo courtesy Professional Coin Grading Service*

High-end or "premium-quality" Mint State-65 Morgan dollar. Notice the freedom from flaws on the cheek, as well as the satin-like luster. This coin is so close to the MS-66 grade that if it were resubmitted for certification, a grade of MS-66 might be assigned. *Photo courtesy Professional Coin Grading Service*

This 1887-P Morgan silver dollar grades or rates Mint State-65. It was given this impartial, arm's-length-distance rating by one of the largest independent coin grading services in the world, the Professional Coin Grading Service (PCGS). PCGS rates coins using a consensus approach, then encapsulates the coins in sonically sealed, tamper-resistant holders. This 1879-S Morgan dollar was also was graded Mint State-65 by PCGS. It's obvious, however, that these two coins have significant differences. The 1887 has a number of nicks and scratches on the cheek of Miss Liberty, and the cheek is an important, grade-sensitive area. By contrast, the 1879-S has beautiful, satin-like luster on the cheek. Numbers don't lie, you say? Well, in the coin field, they may not lie—but they can mislead.

Coin grading is performed on a spectrum, or a continuum. Not all coins graded 65, or graded 64-or graded any number on the 1-to-70 scale—are necessarily equal. Coins are like snowflakes; each one is different from every other. Some coins grading 65 might be high-end 65s-almost 66s. An example of this is the 1879-S Morgan dollar shown on the right in the previous set of photos. Some coins grading 65 might be low-end 65s—barely better than 64s—like the 1887-P Morgan dollar on the left.

For people who earn a living as traders of coins—who buy and sell coins on a regular basis to make money—much of the money-making activity centers around the seemingly small detail of whether a coin is high-end or low-end for its grade. If you were to take a rare-date coin grading 65—but high-end 65—and send it back to the grading service and get it recertified as a 66, you might make thousands of dollars. On the other hand, you would have downside risk, rather than upside potential, if you were to purchase a coin such as the one shown on the left, with scratches all over the

MS-65 (overall) Franklin half dollar obverse and reverse. Beautiful toning enhances the obverse (left), which is MS-66. The reverse is just as beautifully toned as the obverse, but a scratch on the bell, indicated by the arrow, causes the reverse to grade MS-64. *ANA photograph*

cheek—an attractive, Mint State-65 coin, yes, but not high-end for its grade. If you were to take that coin, crack it out of its holder, and resubmit it to a leading grading service such as PCGS, it might end up being regraded as a 64.

Weak, Solid, and Strong Grades

I worked as a part-time grader for the Numismatic Guaranty Corporation of America (NGC), another of the nation's preeminent grading services, during its formative years in the late 1980's. Even at that time, we were cognizant of the differences among coins with the same numerical grade in the spectrum. For internal purposes only, we graded coins using the letter suffixes A, B, and C, with A signifying a coin that was at the high end of the spectrum for its grade, C denoting a coin at the low end, and B representing a coin right in the middle. As a high-end Mint State-65 coin, the 1879-S Morgan dollar pictured would have been graded 65-A. As a low-end coin, the 1887-P Morgan dollar would have been graded 65-C.

Coin grading is a process of subjective evaluation. However, it becomes somewhat more objective when a group of experts examines coins and achieves a consensus. It is common practice at the leading grading services for three expert graders to examine each coin. In most cases, they concur in their assessments. On borderline coins, however, they sometimes split—and this is where shrewd submitters sometimes make big money.

Let's say three graders examined the 1879-S dollar previously shown and two of them concluded it was Mint State-65-A, while the third grader decided it was Mint State-66-C. In that event, the coin would probably be graded Mint State-65. (The grading services don't indicate A, B, or C on their holders.)

Now let's suppose that the coin were resubmitted and a different team of graders were to look at it—and instead of two graders rating it 65-A and one rating it 66-C, two were to grade it 66-C and one 65-A. In that case, the coin would probably be regraded as a 66. Thus, for the submitter, wealth would be created—perhaps many thousands of dollars. Small differences in grade can have big implications for the price of a coin, and learning to recognize—and capitalize upon—these subtle but critical differences is one of the central themes of this book.

The 1956 Franklin half dollar shown is worth an MS-65 price, but the technical grade is actually MS-66/64: The obverse grades MS-66, and the reverse grades MS-64. The overall 65 rating is appropriate because of the incredible toning which everyone agrees is stunning: Hues of golden-russet, sky-blue, and olive-green emanate from spotless surfaces. The reverse, however, has a visible scratch on the left side of the bell.

Sometimes a strong obverse can "carry" the grade. This 1956 Franklin half is such a coin.

Overgrading and Undergrading

Overgrading is the describing of a coin as being in a higher level of preservation than it actually is. *Undergrading* is the describing of a coin as being in a lower level of preservation than it actually is. Although both can be used to take advantage of you, market fluctuations can lead to both. Just because a dealer doesn't overgrade doesn't mean that he or she is honest. The dealer may undergrade to try and catch you off guard—then grossly overprice.

These practices have become far less common with the advent of independent grading services.

Impact of Market Fluctuations on Grading Standards

In a boom market, grading standards become very liberal. In a depressed market, grading standards become tight and potential buyers become highly selective: People tend to believe a coin is in a lower grade than is in fact the case. During a business-as-usual market, coins tend to be graded more accurately than during a boom or a bust phase.

It is a disconcerting reality that sometimes even leading grading services can get caught up in bull market frenzies and in an effort to reflect the market become slightly less conservative in their grading.

During a boom market, desirable coins are in short supply because so many people want them and are paying top dollar to get them. Let's use an accurately graded 1880 Liberty Seated quarter (Proof-64) as an example. During a boom market, dealers would call this coin a Proof-65 or better because there are so few actual Proof-65s around to satisfy demand.

During a depressed market, grading standards become very tight because it is difficult to sell coins. So everyone scrutinizes each coin closely. The Proof-64 quarter becomes a Proof-62 quarter. Suddenly that light, almost unnoticeable nick on the knee becomes a gi-

Blowup of a whizzed half cent. The appearance is granular and unnatural, indicating the coin was brushed. *ANA photograph*

gantic gouge, blamed for almost eliminating Miss Liberty. Everyone is looking for a reason not to buy, so trivialities become major imperfections. Furthermore, grading standards have had the general tendency to become stricter over time. Many coins that were graded as MS-65 or MS-67 in 1980 or 1981 are no longer viewed as being deserving of a grade of even MS-63. This phenomenon is explained in chapter 5.

As you can well imagine, these fluctuations have a disruptive effect on value guide accuracy. This is explored in chapter 9.

PCGS and NGC have assembled grading sets to help prevent their standards from shifting, but you should nonetheless learn how to grade on your own to protect yourself so that you buy the coin and not the holder.

How Some Dealers Rip Off Their Customers by Overgrading

There are three basic categories of overgrading: vindictive, blue-collar, and white-collar.

Vindictive Overgrading. This refers to a coin being sold which has little or no premium value (the amount of money a coin is worth above its face value) and has, for all practical purposes, no chance of ever gaining a premium value. Most vindictively overgraded coins are either grossly overgraded or whizzed.

Whizzing is a process used to simulate mint luster on a circulated coin through use of a wire brush (perhaps a rotary electric one) and/or an abrasive chemical. The top layer of metal is modified so that high-point wear is not visible. Whizzed coins can often be spotted because the cleaning is often crude, the surface is highly porous, and the coin often appears with loss of detail. A whizzed 1832 half cent displays a peculiar graininess and surface porosity. A closeup of the "LIBERTY" on that same coin as shown points up the unnatural rippled effect. A genuine Mint State coin would be smooth, with the natural luster beaming from the surfaces if viewed with the naked eye. If viewed under a microscope, the Mint State coin would be smooth, with the natural luster beaming from the surfaces if viewed with the naked eye. If viewed under a microscope, the Mint State coin would exhibit "flow lines" (lines that result from the minting process and spread out from the center to the rim, where they are most prominent). The word "whiz" is used to describe the process because of the noise it was originally associated with.

The whizzed coin is relatively easy to spot and has received so much publicity that it has been virtually eliminated from the marketplace. But watch out for whizzed coins in places such as flea markets where reputable dealers are not the primary sellers. In general, whizzed coins are very difficult to sell, and when they do trade hands, they sell for a significant discount. The current ANACS will grade whizzed coins and add "whizzed" to the description. PCGS will not grade whizzed coins, nor will NGC or ICG—nor many of the other grading services.

Blue-Collar Overgrading. Blue-collar overgrading, the gross overgrading of coins with value, comes in two types. The most common involves circulated coins; the other, less common type concerns subtler, but still gross, overgrading of Extremely Fine and low-grade About Uncirculated coins.

The first type of blue-collar overgrading is the overgrading of circulated coins and of coins in which very little money is made by overgrading. An example of this kind of blue-collar overgrading would be a dealer's grading a particular Buffalo nickel "Choice Extremely Fine–45," even though it is actually a Very Good–8. And the dealer might charge $15 instead of $2, even though a real EF-45 should be, let's say, $35. It's the bargain-hunter instinct in the beginning collector that leads him or her to buy an overgraded, overpriced coin.

A few bad apples might engage in this practice, which is rampant at flea markets or other places where part-time dealers and unknowledgeable collectors meet.

The other kind of blue-collar overgrading involves the sale of coins as "Mint State" which clearly are not. Dealers who engage in this type of overgrading can be identified by their mail-order advertisements, which offer "GEM BRILLIANT UNCIRCULATED COINS AT A FRACTION OF THE GOING PRICE." Despite their claims, the rule still is, you get what you pay for. As the late Lee Hewitt, former editor of the *Numismatic Scrapbook* (which merged with *Coin World*), once said, "There is no Santa Claus in numismatics." Nobody is going to offer you any coins (especially not Gems) at a fraction of the going price. Those "Gems" usually turn out to be either Extremely Fine or About Uncirculated (no higher than 50 on the 1-70 scale) or somewhere in between. Occasionally, United States gold pieces will be graded "Gem" or "MS-65" and be no better than Very Fine. Gold coins retain their original mint luster almost indefinitely, and sometimes even heavily circulated gold coins will have mint luster. Although these coins are collectible and have value, their value is a fraction of the original price paid. To avoid being a victim of blue-collar overgrading, deal with reputable dealers.

White-Collar Overgrading. White-collar overgrading is subtle, sometimes almost unnoticeable, overgrading, and it is what gave the coin industry a black eye. It was of potential harm not only to collectors and investors, but to dealers, too, who also bought coins. This is another practice that is no longer commonplace, after the advent of independent grading services.

White-collar overgraders used to make money by selling strong, no-question Mint State–60s and 63s as "MS-65s," "MS-67s," and sometimes even as higher-grade coins. They also made a habit of selling borderline Uncirculated coins (AU-55 or AU-58) as Mint State, sometimes calling these ever-so-lightly circulated coins "MS-65s." The important factor concerning white-collar overgrading is that it was so subtle. A few unscrupulous individuals engaged in this practice frequently.

Today, in order to squeeze out more money from a retail customer, a dealer can overstate the grade of a coin that has already been certified. Since it is now widely known that a certified coin can be high-end, solid, or low-end for the grade, a dealer can represent a solid or low-end coin to be high-end and charge an unjustified premium.

So, again, the lesson is to deal with reputable and knowledgeable dealers—and to *look at the coins*.

Differences of Opinion and Overgrading

It is important to remember that differences of opinion do exist. Let's say that a Barber quarter graded MS-65 by a leading grading service is brought to twelve top dealers for confirmation of grade. If six dealers believe the coin is MS-65, four believe it is MS-64, and two believe it to be MS-63+, there obviously is a legitimate, and totally expected, difference of opinion. (For the purpose of discussion, we have to assume that these dealers are competent graders, but more about that later.) The subjective element of grading cannot be removed.

But imagine another coin: a common-date Barber half-dollar graded MS-67 by a leading grading service, complete with a spectacular digital image in some dealer's Internet catalog. The coin is priced at $15,000 (even though MS-67s routinely trade for, say, $6,500) because it is supposed to be so close to MS-68 and so much more desirable than its MS-67 counterparts. The same twelve competent dealers are surveyed. Five of the dealers are emphatic that the coin is nothing more than a so-so, dipped-out MS-65 that was certified as such last week before its dipping (and that it brought $2,000 plus a 15 percent buyer's fee at auction last month); another four insist that the coin just doesn't look right and that they would be uncomfortable paying a premium for it; and the three other dealers grade it MS-66. If this coin were represented as a "premium quality, special" MS-67 and sold for $15,000, it would be a case of white-collar overgrading.

So there is room for puffery and even out-and-out misrepresentation, even with coins certified by the best services.

What an Overgraded Coin Might Look Like

Sometimes white-collar overgrading is easy to spot. For example, look at the no-question Mint State 1903-O Morgan dollar. There are no signs of wear, but the scratches on Miss Liberty's cheek are large enough to be measured with a ruler. The cheek is one of the most grade-sensitive areas of the Morgan dollar (as well as of other "portrait" coins), and on this example, the face is so marked that it appears that Miss Liberty got involved in a violent argument.

the cheek—or hidden on the obverse. Even if the coin is desirable in every other respect, if it has an obvious problem, you will be penalized when the time comes to sell. If you see the problem when you buy and get a good enough deal, that's fine. A little scratch on a grade-sensitive area when you buy is a big problem when you sell.

Mint-Made Imperfections

A Mint-made imperfection is a defect that occurred at the mint during a coin's manufacture. One cause of dealer disillusionment with the old ANACS was the service's adherence to the principle of Mint-made imperfections not subtracting from a coin's numerical grade. However, many dealers believe that although Mint-made imperfections do not subtract from the technical level of preservation, they do subtract from the price. The 1921 Peace dollar shown has been well preserved, with exquisite hues of gold and cherry upon lustrous surfaces. But look in the left obverse field, in front of Miss Liberty's nose. A flaw in the planchet has caused a most detracting depression. This coin is a technical MS-65, based on the rule that Mint-made imperfections do not subtract from a coin's numerical grade. But this problem piece would command nothing more than an MS-64 price. Some modern grading services might assign a "net grade" of MS-MS-64 to this coin.

White-Collar Overpricing

Coins in legitimate high levels of preservation also can be used to separate you from your money. For example, coins that are not rare, but are almost perfect, are sometimes sent in to ICG, ANACS, PCGS, or NGC to be certified as MS-67. Late-date Proof half dollars can be found graded from PF-67 to PF-70. These coins are sometimes offered at a premium, but should not necessarily be worth the premium.

Another good example is the 1943-S steel cent shown. The example here is certainly a notable one: There is a dazzling contrast between the highly reflective fields and snow-white devices. The piece was graded MS-67/67 by the ANA's ANACS. Coins such as this make their way into MS-68 holders of services such as NGC and PCGS and sell for hundreds, even thousands, of dollars. This coin is less rare, though, than some people, even some dealers, think it is. And the inflated price of $1,000 is reflective of a bubble, not a solid trend. Some coins are truly rare in MS-67, even when their MS-65 counterparts are relatively common. But this 1943-S steel cent, like many other modern coins, is not an example of one of those rare coins. If this steel cent were offered for $2,000, it would be a case of white-collar overpricing.

How to Distinguish Mint State from About Uncirculated

As I stated earlier, grading practices are based on common sense. If a coin has wear, that coin is no longer Mint State. But the important question to know the answer to is, "On what part of the coin should I look for wear?" The answer is based on common sense: the high points. The highest points on a coin are what show tell-tale signs of circulation (coins wear the same way crowns on teeth do). However, each coin is different (even coins of the same denomination and year). Therefore, there can be no completely accurate textbook explanation of how each coin wears. You just have to look for the high points.

It is important to know that the first step in evaluating high-point wear and its severity is to know to look for a change in color of the high points. The following chart lists the basic coinage metals and the color of the high points that each coin possesses after it circulates.

COINAGE METAL HIGH-POINT COLOR AFTER FRICTION

Copper	Dark brown
Nickel	Dark gray
Silver	Dull gray
Gold	Dull, dark gold

It is simple to identify high-point wear. Look at the delightfully lustrous 1930 Standing Liberty quarter. Pay particular attention to the knee, which is free of friction. The weakness in the shield is not wear, but rather a weakly struck area—an area on the coin which has a corresponding weak area on the die. Now look at the other Standing Liberty quarter. Wear is evident on the knee and breast. Notice the difference in color between those high points and the rest of the coin. Even though this type of identification seems simple, people continue to buy coins like this About Uncirculated (AU) quarter as Mint State and for Mint State prices.

Let's examine another quarter which has high-point friction that is less prominent. This 1815 Bust quarter is typical of the Bust material offered as MS-63. Genuine Mint State examples are exceedingly difficult to locate. But if you are buying an AU coin, know it. Don't pay an MS-63 or even an MS-60 price. This example is nicely toned with wear evident on both sides. On the obverse, light wear is evident on the curl above the eye, the ear lobe, the curl above the ear, the nose, the tip of the ribbon, and sections of the hair. On the reverse, light wear is evident on the tips of the eagle's wings, the area above the eagle's eye, the eagle's claws, the eagle's feathers, and at the edges of the leaves.

Once you begin to realize that differentiating between About Uncirculated and Mint State is nothing more than training yourself to examine a coin's highest parts for wear, you will have overridden anyone's ability to sell you About Uncirculated coins as Mint State. Look at another AU coin. This specimen is an 1838 large cent. Have you spotted the wear? Many of the white high areas are what constitute the wear. Look at Miss Liberty's nose and at the highest points of the portrait (hair, ear, etc.). On the reverse, check the edges of the leaves. If you're able to see the wear in these photos, you ought to be able to identify wear on the actual coins. It's just as simple.

Spotting Wear on Unusual Parts of a Coin

One commonly overgraded coin is the Liberty Seated half dollar. About Uncirculated specimens graded Mint State range from almost impossible to detect to incredibly easy. The easiest specimens to identify display a lighter, duller color on the high points than the rest of the coin. Those high points are (obverse) the knees, breast, and hair above the eye and (reverse) on the eagle's head, beak, and area above the eye.

MS-65 Standing Liberty quarter obverse. This lightly toned jewel is problem-free. *ANA photograph*

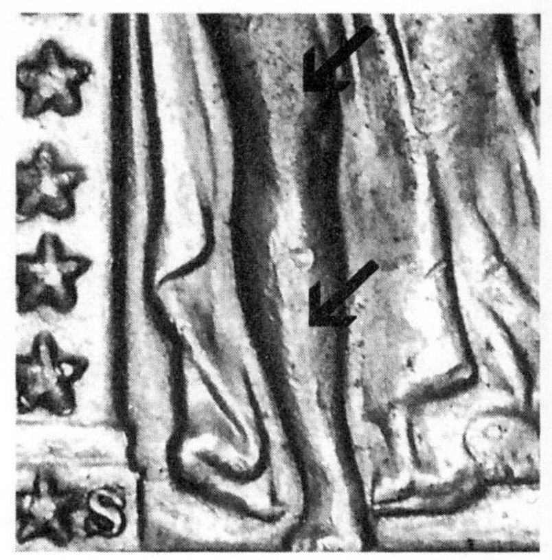

AU-55 Standing Liberty quarter obverse (detail blowup). Look at the light wear on the knee, indicated by the arrow. *ANA photograph*

Specimens that display wear on unconventional high points are more difficult to identify. I call these coins conventional high-point de-emphasis pieces. In other words, the "conventional" points of wear or parts of a coin on which you are accustomed to spotting wear do not display wear because they are not the high points; they have been de-emphasized. The high point or points exist on another area of the coin, perhaps the stars or the arm. Conventional high-point de-emphasis occurs as a result of striking. If the striking pressure is not even or if one of the dies is slightly tilted, one side of the coin may be sharply struck, while the other side may be soft in its details. Thus, the highest points of a coin shift. You could use a microscope and look at Miss Liberty's knees, breast, and hair above the eye for hours, but if the high points shifted as the result of an uneven strike, you would not find wear at those conventional points you studied. You might find the wear on the arm or even the stars. When looking for wear, look at the entire coin. Just because a grading guide or even your personal experience tells you that wear should always be on a certain place to be considered wear, don't necessarily believe it. That advice may be right 99.99 percent of the time. But that 0.01 percent error rate could mean the difference between money in your pocket or in some dealer's pocket. Wear is wear; it doesn't matter if it's on the arm or on the stars. If the coin is lightly circulated . . . well, then it isn't Mint State. Photographs of this are beyond the scope of this book.

Spotting Wear on Coins with Beautiful Toning

Presented for your examination is a very deceptive coin, an AU-55 1878 Liberty Seated half dollar. Although the wear is on the conventional high points, the coin is so beautifully toned that the wear is almost impossible to detect. The piece displays breathtaking

AU-55 Bust quarter. The slightly lighter color of the high points is wear, as indicated by the arrows. *ANA photograph*

original toning, with electric splashes of sky blue, violet, and olive green. The overall color is cherry gold, and this example is a warm, beautiful, and wholly original coin. But look closely; look very closely. First appearances may be deceiving. This half dollar displays merely a hint of wear on Miss Liberty's highest points (study where the arrows point on both obverse and reverse). This example proves that just because a coin displays original luster and has never been dipped, cleaned, or chemically enhanced, that does not guarantee that the coin is Mint State.

Gold Coins That Look Mint State

Almost all gold coins look Mint State from a distance because gold coins retain some luster indefinitely. Often, though, gold coins that are not Mint State are lacking some luster, as well as displaying wear on the high points and having a different "feel" from their Mint State counterparts. The 1926 Saint-Gaudens $20 shown was graded MS-63 by the ANA's ANACS. It is a truly stunning example, and a borderline MS-65, if not a real MS-64 that was undergraded. Look at the intense luster which emanates from the mark-free, spot-free surfaces. There are a few detractions not even worth mentioning. Of course you can see why this piece is Mint State. Now look at the 1913 Saint-Gaudens $20 featured here. That $20 gold piece is an AU-55. But it resembles many "Saints" sold as Mint State (too many). On the obverse, wear is visible on the right breast and right knee (the left breast and left knee to Miss Liberty).

An area of trouble to both dealer and nondealer is the difficulty in recognizing wear on gold pieces that have partially incuse designs. The quarter eagle shown is such a coin. This 1911 $2½ graded AU-55 appears at first glance to have no wear—or at least the

AU-55 large cent. The high points are lighter than the rest of this coin and in this picture appear white. *ANA photograph*

AU-55 Liberty Seated half dollar, obverse and reverse. This originally toned example has light, almost unnoticeable wear on its highest points. *ANA photograph*

wear isn't clearly visible. But upon close inspection, however, light signs of circulation are visible throughout the obverse portrait on the cheekbone and ever so slightly on the headdress. On the reverse, inspect the shoulder of the eagle's right wing (left wing to her), as well as the breast and head.

When buying gold coins graded Mint State, pay particular attention to the lighting details explained in chapter 3.

MS-63 Saint-Gaudens double-eagle obverse. This coin exhibits full luster and has no wear. *ANA photograph*

AU-55 Saint-Gaudens double-eagle obverse. This coin is lackluster and has been lightly circulated, as indicated by the arrows. *ANA photograph*

The Rub

When it comes to differentiating between Mint State and About Uncirculated, nothing can be more difficult to find than a "rub." Rub is the term used to identify a small area on a coin, perhaps no larger than a thumb print, which is evidence of the coin having seen circulation. Rub is an appropriate term, for it describes a coin having been rubbed. A rub is slight friction-wear which results from a coin having circulated slightly. A rub, which lowers an otherwise Mint State coin to About Uncirculated, should not be confused with a fingerprint, which, in some cases, is acceptable on an MS-65. A fingerprint is a sharp imprint; a rub is a smear, an interruption of luster, the color that circulation on each respective coinage metal assumes, and can be difficult (if not sometimes impossible) to detect unless the coin is carefully tilted and rotated, as explained in chapter 2.

The MS-65 Indian cent reverse shown displays full, fiery-red luster—undisturbed. The reverse of the Indian head cent graded AU-55 has a rub. Imagine a thumb full of perspiration touching that coin's reverse. You can see where the finger might have once touched by examining the darkened area (brown in color, while the rest of the coin is a blazing red). Examine the fields of both reverses around the words "One Cent." The Mint State field is lustrous; the About Uncirculated field displays a dullness and an interruption of the luster.

Dealers and experienced collectors occasionally buy coins as Gems, only to discover later that the Gems have rubs. These experienced numismatists have learned the hard way to take the time to examine coins closely during the buying process. You're not the only one who asks, "What rub?" Dealers and knowledgeable collectors ask it too—and sometimes discover the answer when it's too late.

AU-55 Indian head quarter eagle. The wear seems hidden but can be easily uncovered by looking for the high points that are shiny and reflect light in a uniform manner. *ANA photograph*

Strike

Strike refers to how much detail a coin exhibits the second it leaves the dies. A "poorly struck" Mint State coin was manufactured without the detail the Mint intended it to have.

Some professional numismatists might take issue with placing the subject of strike in the grading chapter. They would insist that strike is not a variable related to grade, but a separate category of study. That may be true, but so many dealers believe that strike affects the grade that including it in this chapter seemed necessary. Strike does not affect the level of preservation; however, it does affect the price. As explained earlier, Mint-made imperfections do not detract from the numerical grade. They do, however, affect the value. It's the same with strike. This is not cut-and-dried and is being heavily debated by professionals. For an explanation of how the price guides consider strike, see chapter 9.

The term "weak strike" refers to insufficient striking pressure used to manufacture the coin. "Weakly struck" specimens exhibit a softening or loss of design on the example's high relief portions. This results from the deepest areas of the die not filling adequately because of this lack of pressure. On the Morgan dollar shown, look for this loss of design on the ear and on the hair above it. Planchet luster is visible on these areas, so you can be sure the piece is Mint State.

Worn dies refer to areas of softening or loss of detail in portions of low relief on the specimen (usually at the device's edges).

On the Walking Liberty half dollar shown, you can spot the loss of design on the flag's end—the low relief part of this design. Another type of worn die strike is the "orange-

MS-65 Indian head cent reverse. Undisturbed luster. *ANA photograph*

Blowup of a weakly struck Morgan dollar obverse. The weakly struck area can be distinguished from wear because it has Mint luster. *Photograph courtesy Bill Fivaz*

peel" effect exhibited by the Roosevelt dime reverse. Notice how the orange-peel effect radiates toward the rim and the letters appear soft in execution on the illustrated example.

The terms "weak strike" and "worn dies" are often used in connection with each other. If "weak strike" is used alone, assume the simple definition for weak strike. If the description "weak strike from worn dies" is used, assume the second explanation.

AU-55 Indian head cent reverse. The slightest "rub" of circulation, as indicated by the arrows, is all that keeps this coin from the Mint State category. *ANA photograph*

Blowup of a Walking Liberty half dollar obverse, weakly struck from worn dies. Detail is missing at the flag's tip, the coin's lowest area. *Photograph courtesy Bill Fivaz*

The 1944-S Walking Liberty half dollar here is an example of a weakly struck coin. Traditionalists will tell you that although the weak strike has to be mentioned in the description, it will affect only the price, not the numerical grade. However, the weak strike greatly affects the grade at today's leading grading services. Notice the weakly struck areas, and realize that they do possess planchet luster, as this coin is Mint State.

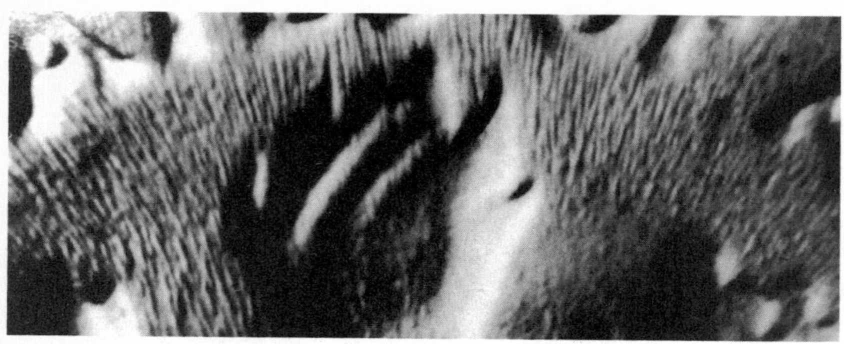

Blowup of a Roosevelt dime reverse weakly struck from worn dies. There is a distinct lack of detail. *Photograph courtesy Bill Fivaz*

Mint State, weakly struck Walking Liberty half dollar obverse. Some purists would grade this coin MS-65 weakly struck, but the marketplace would value it as an MS-63. *ANA photograph*

MS-65, weakly struck from worn dies, Buffalo nickel obverse. The luster is uninterrupted. *ANA photograph*

AU-55 Buffalo nickel observe. The luster is interrupted and thus the coin is not Mint State. *ANA photograph*

MS-65 Mercury dime reverse. The critical bands on the fasces are indicated by the arrow. *Photograph by Stephen Ritter*

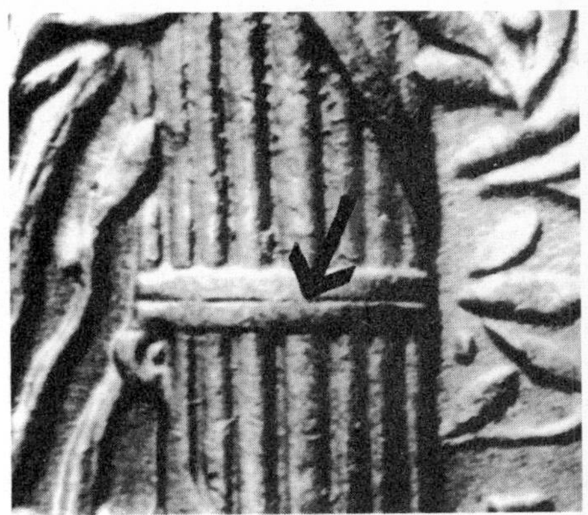

Blowup of non-split-bands Mercury dime. *Photograph courtesy Bill Fivaz*

Blowup of split-bands Mercury dime. *Photograph courtesy Bill Fivaz*

Blowup of full-split-bands Mercury dime. This is what numismatists look for when the term "full split bands" is used. *Photograph courtesy Bill Fivaz*

The 1935-D Buffalo nickel displayed is an example of a coin weakly struck from worn dies. Notice that the weak areas are the areas of low relief. Beside it is a 1913-D Variety II Buffalo nickel grading AU-55. It isn't weakly struck or weakly struck from worn dies. It has wear. Look at the lack of luster, the dullness, the high-point friction. Uncirculated coins that are weakly struck or weakly struck from worn dies have full luster. About Uncirculated coins have a diminution of that luster.

MS-65 Jefferson nickel reverse. The critical steps are indicated by the arrow. *Photograph by Stephen Ritter*

Valuable Striking Characteristics

Most coins have intricate designs, with small details in some areas. More and more people collect certain coins for the sharpness of detail in a certain small area. For this reason, a coin that exhibits some small detail may command a premium many times in excess of its counterpart that does not exhibit that small detail. The presence or absence of these details is a result of the strike. Some full-split-band Mercury dimes and full-head Standing Liberty quarters easily command six-figure prices. I can assure you of this firsthand: I have assembled some of the Number One sets of these coins on behalf of leading collectors, and I paid those prices.

Mercury Dime Bands. One of the coins most heavily collected and traded for presence of a small detail is the Mercury dime. Look at the small details on the reverse of the one shown here. Some people will pay a higher price if the two small center bands are unbroken and separated. Examine the close-up of the reverse that has bands which are not split. Now compare it to the Mercury dime reverse with "split bands." The split-bands reverse displays full separation of the two bands. Compare the split-bands reverse with the "full-split-bands" reverse illustration.

The separation is full and complete on the full-split-bands reverse. If you purchase a Mercury dime as having "full split bands," make sure it looks like the coin in the picture. The reverse bands are sometimes tampered with to create this effect (through careful manipulation of a sharp knife, such as an X-Acto). This is illustrated in the color section of this book.

Jefferson Nickel Steps. Jefferson nickels are also collected for clarity of a certain detail: the steps. You can see how small a detail it really is by examining the reverse of the Jefferson nickel illustrated. The steps are classified as Type I and Type II. Type I steps

Blowup of steps of a Type I Jefferson nickel. The Type I steps are characteristically lacking in detail. *Photograph by Steven Ritter*

Blowup of steps of a Type II five-step Jefferson nickel. *Photograph courtesy Bill Fivaz*

Blowup of full steps of a Type II six-step Jefferson nickel. This is what is required for the "full-steps" designation. *Photograph courtesy Bill Fivaz*

appear soft in detail. They are found on 1938 Jefferson nickels, some 1939 business strikes, most 1939 Proofs, and some (but not many) 1940 Proofs. There are six steps on Monticello, and coins which display these six steps are defined as "full-step nickels." Now look at the Type II steps shown. This example has five steps. Compare the five-step example with the six-step Type II example. Once you compare the two, the difference should be clearly apparent. Interestingly, some Jefferson nickels are not available with six or even five steps. In those cases, discriminating collectors have to be content with a

MS-67 Franklin half dollar reverse. The critical bell lines are indicated by the arrows. *Photograph by Steven Ritter*

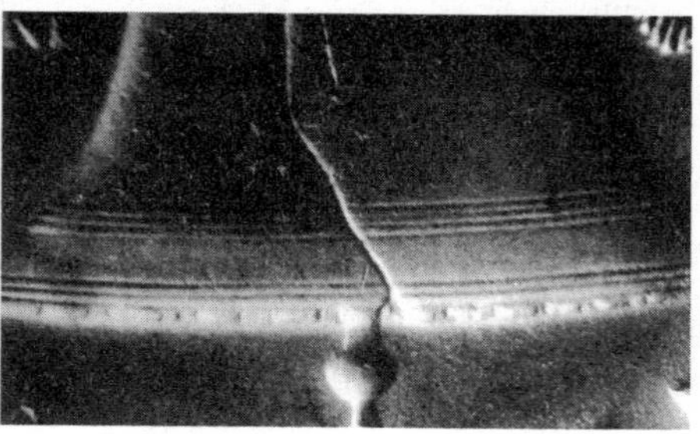

Blowup of a seven-bell-line Franklin half. This is what it takes for "full bell lines." *Photograph courtesy Bill Fivaz*

Jefferson nickel that displays four or fewer steps, as a four-step specimen might be the very best that can reasonably be found.

Franklin Half Bell Lines. The Franklin half dollar is becoming increasingly popular, and with that popularity comes attention to a small detail on its reverse: the bell lines on the bell's bottom portion; there can be seven. Take a look at a Franklin half's reverse to see what a small detail it is. Now examine the bottom half of the bell, and count the seven recessed bell lines. The lines must be complete and unbroken in order for the coin to be in the category of "full bell lines."

Standing Liberty Quarter Head. Standing Liberty quarters have attracted the attention of the "collect-by-detail" crowd. The head on Miss Liberty is what attracts attention. Type I (1916–1917) is common with full head. Type II, however, is uncommon with that detail visible. In order for a Standing Liberty quarter to be considered a "full head," it has to display a complete three leaves on the headpiece, as well as an unbroken hairline from over the forehead to the ear and ear opening. Examine the close-up of the full head shown and compare it with the 75-percent fully struck head illustration.

Roosevelt Dime Torch. Even Roosevelt dimes are collected for strike. Look at the reverse of a Roosevelt dime soft in detail on the torch. Now look at its more clearly defined counterpart. The bands display a clear separation.

Collectors pay attention to almost every small detail when it comes to buying coins. Even if a coin is not usually collected for a particular detail, chances are that some collector somewhere will pay a premium for it if it is difficult to find that coin with that detail apparent.

Toning

Toning refers to the slow and regular process by which a coin acquires color over months and years. Toning should be differentiated from tarnish, which is quick and irregular. Toning is a description of the intermediate process between a coin's period of full brilliance and full darkness. No matter how beautiful any toning may be, it does represent an intermediate stage in the coin's progression to full darkening. This is a process that can take a hundred years or more. Certain types of toning affect the grade to a major extent, and other types of toning do not affect the grade at all. This section deals with natural toning. Various aspects of toning, including artificial toning, are discussed throughout the book. Artificially toned coins are illustrated with graphic digital images in the color section.

Toning ranges from breathtakingly beautiful to unattractive; from even and consistent to odd and streaky; from exquisitely colorful and rich in hues to incredibly drab and dull; from phenomenal to despicable; and from telling to deceptive. The variety of tones is both a numismatist's best friend and most threatening enemy. Toning can downgrade a 65, upgrade a 64, and cause a lot of confusion.

What follows is a coinage metal chart, along with a brief explanation of the type of toning that each respective metal encounters and a description of how that toning may affect grade and value. Beauty of toning is so subjective that any type of toning listed as subtracting from the price might actually add to it in some transactions.

HOW TONING AFFECTS GRADE AND VALUE

Coinage Metal	Toning Description	Grade Impact	Value Impact
Copper	Cherry red	—	—
	Purple-violet	—	—
	Brown and red	—	Lowers value
	Brown	—	Lowers value
	Black spots	Lowers grade	Lowers value
Nickel	Silver-gold	—	Adds value
	Silver-gray	—	—
	Black spots	Lowers grade	Lowers value
Silver	Even iridescence	—	May add
	Uneven iridescence	May lower	May add
	Concentric circles Golden center violet periphery fading to blue and red	May add	Adds value
	Golden russet	—	May add
	Black spots	Lowers grade	Lowers value
Gold	Not applicable		

Blowup of a full-head Type I Standing Liberty quarter.
Photograph courtesy Bill Fivaz

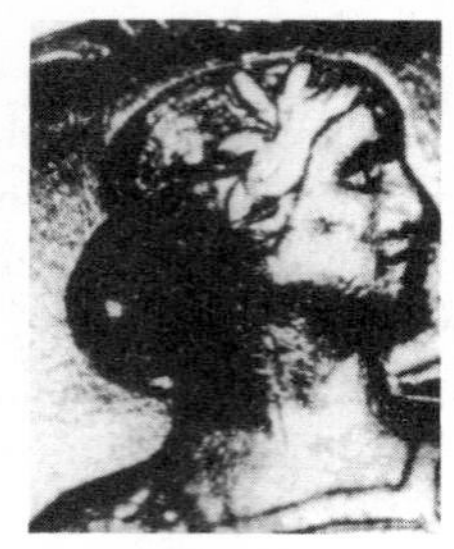

Blowup of a full-head Type II Standing Liberty quarter.
Photograph courtesy Bill Fivaz

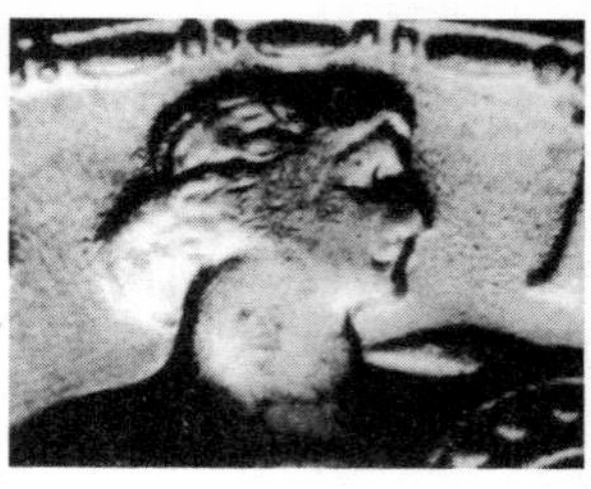

Blowup of a 75-percent full-head Type II Standing Liberty quarter.
Photograph courtesy Bill Fivaz

Beware of Heavy Toning That Covers Up Imperfections

Some dealers never purchase heavily toned coins, for fear of hidden defects or full luster not being present underneath the toning. However, the brilliant-is-best mentality is dangerous. If you take this attitude, you'll end up with nothing except cleaned coins.

At least one expert on coin chemistry has made a persuasive case for silver coins with natural toning actually being damaged goods, and this expert likens such coins to rusty cars. Other experts have made the case that far from damaging silver coins, the lovely natural toning that develops over time actually serves to protect the coins' surfaces. What's more, these experts contend, its aesthetic appeal enhances the coins' value in the eyes of knowledgeable numismatists. Mark Salzberg, chairman and CEO of NGC, has written eloquently in support of certain types of toning as a positive factor.

I am on the side of supporting certain types of toning as being an enhancement, but I respect the views of others who disagree. In time, the technology will be in place to settle this controversy once and for all. I have explored this issue at greater length in chapter 18.

Detecting Doctored Coins

Coin "doctoring" refers to a coin that has been tampered with so that its flaws are not easily visible. Coin doctors use a multiplicity of methods, but their primary approach is either to hide flaws or to add color.

In order to hide flaws, the coin doctors have been known to use epoxy, automotive body putty, and dental wax. A term associated with doctoring is thumbing, which refers to tampering with a coin's appearance by "thumbing" with nose grease. Grading services report seeing an increase in coins doctored by the addition of an

Blowup of a non-fully-struck-torch-line Roosevelt dime. *Photograph by Steven Ritter*

Blowup of a fully-struck-torch-line Roosevelt dime. The latest collecting trend dictates that the vertical bands also be fully struck in order for the coin to command a premium. The term "full split bands" is also now used to refer to fully-struck torch lines. *Photograph by Steven Ritter*

epoxy resin mixed with metallic particles and added to scratched areas of a coin. Coins' reflective properties are altered by the resin, and previously indented imperfections, from hairline scratches to major gouges, reflect light naturally and as if the flaws were not present.

One coin doctor reportedly altered a number of Indian head quarter-eagle gold pieces that originally were graded MS-61 and MS-62 by leading grading services. After hiding scratches, he resubmitted the coins for grading and apparently received grades of MS-64 and MS-65.

Coin doctoring is covered more extensively in chapter 5, and illustrations of doctored coins appear in the color section.

The Most Difficult Coins to Grade

Based on my experiences as a part-time grader at NGC in the late 1980s, I compiled a list of the coin types that I found most difficult to grade. NGC's founder John Albanese helped in preparing this list.

Line Coins

"Line coins" are coins that qualify to be graded, say, either MS-64A or MS-65C. Either grade would be fair—but with many such coins, traders have paid a price commensurate with the lower grade and are hoping to receive the higher grade from NGC.

On business strikes, it usually comes down to the quality of the surfaces; this is what determines whether a line coin gets the higher grade—although impaired luster can reduce the coin's chances for the next grade.

Blowup of the ear and adjacent areas on a doctored Proof Morgan dollar. An epoxy was used to fill in and thus conceal scratches. The epoxy is clearly visible under fluorescent black light. *Photograph courtesy Krause Publications*

Law-Breakers

If you were to assign a coin a technical grade of MS-67/64 (67 being the obverse and 64 being the reverse), any traditionalist would tell you that the overall grade would have to be MS-64, for it used to be conventional wisdom that a coin couldn't be assigned an overall grade that was higher than the lowest grade of any one side.

Wrong. The overall grade might well be MS-65, since the obverse can "carry" a coin. But if it were the other way around—an MS-64/67-the final grade probably would be MS-64.

An MS-65/65 coin with some weakness of strike might be graded MS-64—or lower—at NGC to reflect marketplace standards. NGC grades in such a way that coins can be traded sight-unseen, and a weakly struck coin graded MS-65 could restrict the fluidity of the system.

Incuse-Design Gold

Coins with incuse designs are difficult enough to grade. With gold coins, this problem is compounded. Gold retains its mint luster indefinitely, and gold coins with incuse designs—like the Indian $5 and $2½—have characteristics that make it hard to tell whether or not there is wear on the high points.

Coins with Sensational Eye Appeal

If you have a magnificent Barber quarter—one with a cameo contrast between its watery fields and snow-white devices—but the coin has a tiny hit on the obverse, can you still grade it Proof-65? Probably. Personally, I don't like seeing the 65 grade assigned to such coins, but it's the consensus that rules.

If you have a Proof Seated Liberty half dollar with light hairlines that make it a technical 63-A, can phenomenal toning make it a 64? Yes, as long as the eye appeal isn't counted for more than ½ of a point.

Rare Dates

If you come across a shimmering Proof 1936 Walking Liberty half dollar and it is identical in every respect to fifty, 1942 Walking Liberty halves which were just graded Proof-64, does the 64 grade apply to the 1936 as well? If the '36 is a technical 64-A, compensation for the date by ½ point is acceptable. Thus, the Proof-65 designation is acceptable.

Compensation for rarity is satisfactory, as long as you don't go overboard and upgrade a technical MS-62 coin to MS-65.

Small Coins

Graders spend more time examining small coins than any other kind. We have to be extremely careful about looking for imperfections, and even have to exercise more care in holding these coins. This is not to say that larger coins don't get complete consideration; it's just that smaller coins require closer scrutiny.

A tiny mark on a silver three-cent piece is weighted differently from a mark of the same size on a Morgan dollar. The three-cent silver is tiny itself, and even a tiny mark can be a considerable detraction.

Problem Coins

Coins with PVC (polyvinyl chloride) on them, or coins with imperfections, or coins that are bent or tampered with—these are problem, or "no-grade," coins.

Sometimes, however, it becomes a problem to determine whether a coin is, in fact, a no-grade—or whether it simply should have its grade lowered to reflect the imperfection.

For example, a Morgan dollar which under normal circumstances would grade MS-64 might be assigned a grade of MS-62 or MS-63 because of a rather eye-catching ding on its rim. But a Walking Liberty half dollar which normally would grade MS-67 but has a deep gouge on the obverse—a gouge so deep that it nearly travels through to the other side—would be no-graded.

Concluding Grading Tips

Knowledge is more than power; in the case of rare coins, it also can mean enormous profit. With that in mind, based on the advice given in this chapter and in earlier chapters, here is a summary of the most important grading tips:

- **Check the high points for wear.** Even if a grading service certifies a coin as Mint State-63, that doesn't mean it won't come back with a lower grade—possibly even About

Lightly circulated Liberty Seated figure. *Photograph courtesy Bill Fivaz*

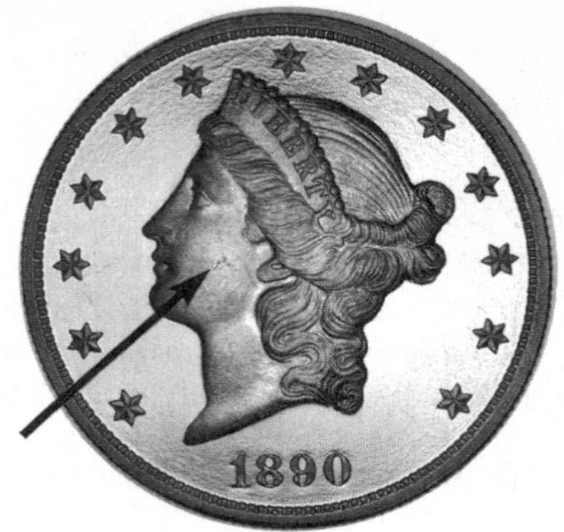

1890 Proof-64 Liberty head double eagle with a detracting mark. Dramatic cameo contrast between the golden-pond-like reflective fields and heavily frosted devices doesn't compensate for the hit on Miss Liberty's cheek. *Photograph courtesy Heritage*

Uncirculated-58—if you resubmit it. A coin should stand on its own merits; you should buy it for itself and not for the plastic. Look at the very highest points of the coin. If they're different in color from the rest of the coin, or if you see friction, the coin may not be Mint State; it may be About Uncirculated. Telltale signs of wear are indicated by the color of the high points. On coins made of copper, the high points after friction are dark brown. On coins made of nickel, the high-point color after friction is dark gray. On coins made of silver, the color is dull gray. And on coins made of gold, the high-point color after friction is dull, dark gold.

- **If it's ugly, don't buy it.** Use your common sense. Blotchy toning, obvious scratches, and spots that penetrate the surface of a coin are unattractive. And if a coin appears unattractive to you, it probably will appear that way to other people, too. Therefore, you should stay away from it. Even coins with very high grades—coins which have been certified as 67, 68, or 69 by a major certification service—are subject to personal taste, and you should always rely on yours. Rare-coin grading is subjective, and so is the beauty of coins. However, among the few characteristics which are universally attractive is concentric-circle toning. If you observe this on a coin, you should view it as a highly positive feature.

- **Examine grade-sensitive areas.** Some flaws are more obvious than others. On Morgan silver dollars, for example, a scratch on Miss Liberty's cheek is immediately apparent because that part of the coin is so smooth and open. By contrast, a scratch in her hair wouldn't be noticed as readily because it would be camouflaged by the intricate details in that portion of the design. High, exposed areas such as Miss Liberty's cheek are said to be "grade-sensitive," and you should be more hesitant to purchase any coin with an

Rare 1896-S Barber quarter with questionable toning. Suspicious gray toning, such as that shown here, can cover a multitude of imperfections. *Photograph courtesy Heritage*

Light hairline scratches as they would appear under a halogen lamp. Look carefully: This flashy 1892 Liberty head quarter eagle has hair lines that detract from its grade. *Photograph courtesy Heritage*

imperfection there, even though that coin may carry a grade of Mint State-65 or Proof-65 or above from one of the major grading services. If you have a choice between one coin graded Mint State-66 with a scratch on the cheek and another coin in the same grade without that scratch on the cheek, always opt for the latter. Everything else being equal, it's always best to purchase coins whose flaws are in non-grade-sensitive areas. Grade-sensitive areas for all the major U.S. coin series are identified and illustrated, with color grading maps, in James L. Halperin's book, *How to Grade U.S. Coins*.

- **Look beneath the toning.** This is probably the most important point of all. It's also the easiest way to determine whether a coin has artificial toning. Toning can cover up a multitude of imperfections—scratches, hairlines, tooling, thumbing, and chemical alteration, to cite just a few. Many times, coins with imperfections are artificially retoned to conceal these flaws. By examining these coins closely under a magnifying glass, you can detect not only the hidden imperfections but also the artificial toning.
- **Examine every coin under a halogen lamp or a high-intensity pinpoint light source.** When looking beneath the toning of a coin or otherwise searching for imperfections, it's essential that you use the right kind of lighting. A halogen lamp is especially beneficial when looking at proof coins. It will help you spot hairline scratches, which can detract considerably from a proof coin's overall grade. As a rule, a Tensor lamp is adequate for Mint State business-strike coins. Ordinary light sources such as floodlamps or bare-filament lights—the kind commonly used in chandeliers—make coins appear more attractive than they actually are. For that reason, if you're looking at coins at an auction-lot viewing session, you should always make sure there is a halogen lamp or a Tensor light source nearby.

Proof-62 Indian three-dollar gold piece. Visible hairline scratches are responsible for this grade. *Photograph courtesy Heritage*

Proof-64 Indian $3 gold piece. This coin is worth $5,000 more than its Proof-62 counterpart because it has fewer hairline scratches in the fields. The devices are delightfully frosted and provide for an elegant cameo contrast. *Photograph courtesy Heritage*

- **Resubmit upper-end coins—coins that are high-quality for the grade—and coins graded 67 by PCGS.** You stand a reasonably good chance of getting a higher grade if you resubmit such coins, especially if you acquired them in 1986 and 1987 when the grading services were extremely tough in assigning grades. David Hall, the founder and president of PCGS, has admitted publicly that a number of PCGS coins given a grade of 67 some years ago might well come back today at a higher grade. The difference in price between a 67 and its 68 counterpart can be tens of thousands of dollars, so this could represent a $20,000 gift for you, just for taking the trouble to crack a coin out of its holder and resubmit it.
- **"Read" every coin.** Looking at a coin is similar to proofreading a letter, as I wrote in chapter 2. And individuals who possess book knowledge combined with practical experience at buying, selling, and trading coins have learned how to look at a coin and size up its flaws rather quickly, just as expert editors have learned how to scan a manuscript for errors and typographical mistakes. Often, a coin's imperfections won't be noticeable at a glance, or even after somewhat closer perusal by an unskilled observer. This may happen, for example, when a coin has one feature so overwhelmingly attractive that it causes you to lose sight of everything else. Let's say you're shown a Saint-Gaudens double eagle with blazing golden luster; the luster may be so intense that it causes you to overlook a bump or a ding on the rim, which in turn might cause the coin to be downgraded. You should learn how to read all the key information on every coin you handle and to properly identify all the imperfections. Don't be dazzled by any one feature of a coin, no matter how attractive it may be, to the point where you miss important details in the "fine print."

Author Scott Travers at NGC. The author was a part-time occasional grader at NGC for a number of years after the service was founded in 1987. *Photograph courtesy Ed Reiter*

- **Look for hairlines.** A proof coin with overwhelmingly beautiful toning can be powerfully appealing. And, to the naked eye, its surfaces may appear pristine and original. But even on gorgeous proofs such as this, and even on coins in very high grades, you may very well find hairline scratches, and the number of hairline scratches is a very important element in determining the grade of a proof coin. Spotting hairline scratches is easier on brilliant modern proofs—proof Mercury dimes, for example. It's somewhat more difficult on older coins with heavier toning—say, Liberty Seated half dollars from the 1880s with concentric-circle toning. On coins such as these, the toning may cover the scratches.
- **Beware of the rub.** Checking for wear on the high points of a coin is relatively easy—and that's a good thing, since *wear*, after all, *is the single most crucial factor in determining grade*. Detecting rub on a coin is considerably more difficult, for rub is far more subtle. It's also far more hazardous to the health of that coin. As the term suggests, a "rub" is a small area on a coin—possibly no bigger than a thumbprint (and possibly caused by a thumbprint)—which bears evidence of friction, showing that the coin has been rubbed. The effect of such a rub can be devastating. Suppose you had a gem, pristine, magnificent coin, blazing with luster, and just one time a perspiration-soaked thumb rubbed ever so slightly across its surface. Even if the coin otherwise might have been graded 65, 66, or 67, that rub could knock it all the way down to AU-58. To identify rub, you need a good, solid Tensor lamp or pinpoint light source, and you have to tilt and rotate the coin under that lamp. You then need to envision a pencil-drawn circle fully formed. If the coin reflects light in a fully circular pattern, it's probably Mint State. But if it reflects light in a generally circular pattern but the pattern is disturbed in any way, then the coin may have a rub. Using the same analogy, that pencil-drawn circle would have just a couple of segments erased.

- **Remember that grading standards have changed a number of times since the early 1980s—and may change again.** A lot of people still own coins that they purchased in the early 1980s that were graded at that time by reputable dealers or by the ANA Certification Service. But many of these people tend to forget—or never knew—that grading standards have tightened since then and have become more consistent. Even coins purchased from reputable dealers in 1981, 1982, and 1983 may not meet today's tighter standard. There have been other periods of changing standards, and this is discussed in detail in the next chapter.

– 5 –
GRADING SERVICES AND THE PLASTIC REVOLUTION

> The word is out!!!
>
> We've had a ten year honeymoon with the coin buying public, but we've betrayed their trust, and the word is out. The word is out in the financial planning community; in the hard money circuit; and to the coin investing public. Coin dealers are rip-off artists; the rare coin market is a trap.
>
> For ten years, we've sold coins to the coin buying public as MS-65, only to tell them that the grading standards had changed and their coins graded MS-63 when it was time for them to sell.
>
> For ten years, we've told them that rare coin prices have gone up and up and up and up, only to tell them that the buyers bidding those higher prices were very fussy, very selective, sight-seen buyers who bought only the coins that they liked and not the coins that the public owned.
>
> For five years, we've supplied the telemarketers who have pounded the coin-buying public with Salomon Brothers fantasies while [selling them] viciously overgraded coins.
>
> We are currently paying the consequences of the abuses of the past ten years. And frankly, we deserve it!
>
> —David Hall, *dealer and a principal in the Professional Coin Grading Service, in a 1988 letter to coin dealers about past abuses and PCGS's new standard*

"Plastic money" has become a common term for credit cards—a term that hits home for virtually all Americans in an age when MasterCard, VISA, and American Express are almost as likely to be found in a consumer's wallet as $5, $10, and $20 bills. But credit card companies are not the only ones plasticizing Americans' money these days. Since 1986, coin-grading services have used untold tons of plastic to encapsulate rare (and sometimes not-so-rare) coins submitted to them for certification. The marketplace has witnessed a "Plastic Revolution"—one that has wrought fundamental change in the way rare coins are bought, sold, collected, saved, and displayed. In some ways, this has changed the market, and the hobby, for the better. In other ways, things have gotten worse.

David Hall is a marketing genius, a trailblazing pioneer—and, in a positive sense, a brilliant revolutionary. When he brought together a core group of major coin dealers to establish the Professional Coin Grading Service in February 1986, he ushered the rare coin market out of the Dark Ages and into a Golden Age in which the grading problem—the market's most nagging albatross at the time—appeared, at least initially, to be resolved. Hall's concept of consensus grading by experts at an independent third-party certification service appeared to be the perfect cure for the seemingly intractable plague of chronic overgrading, which was rampant at the time.

People who purchased high-grade, high-priced coins prior to the advent of PCGS ran a serious risk of paying too much and getting too little in return. The uninitiated were being thrown to the wolves—sacrificial lambs at the altar of greed that was all too pervasive in the early 1980s. The problem grew so bad that it threatened to drive the coin market all the way back to the Rock Age—and not the one that started with Elvis Presley. Other grading services sprung up in the wake of PCGS; some of them are successful and still around today, others were mere temporary blips on the market's radar screen. Certification itself survived and prospered, however, and remains a crucial component of the hobby and the industry of the 2000s.

A Tale of Two Investors

One day in the spring of 1984, a chauffeur named Ted (not his real name) answered an advertisement in *The Wall Street Journal* about rare-coin investing. A salesman contacted him and became "sort of like a friend," he recalls. Ted is married and has three children, and the salesman sympathized with the expenses involved in sending kids to college.

Ted was impressed. So he invested what he says were his life savings in rare coins: $32,650. "I figured this guy could be listened to and relied upon because he seemed to express genuine concern about my well-being," the chauffeur recounts. "He seemed so objective."

Then Ted heard that truly impartial opinions exist about rare coins. He heard about the Professional Coin Grading Service (PCGS), the Numismatic Guaranty Corporation of America (NGC), and ANACS, which render opinions as to coins' numerical grades using the 1-70 scale, encapsulating coins in hard plastic holders, and have networks of dealers who buy, sell, and trade certified coins. But by then, it was too late. The company that sold Ted the coins was out of business, and the best the grading services could do for him was confirm that his investment in coins—an investment representing his life savings—was worth a small fraction of what he thought.

In return for his hard-earned money, Ted had received ten coins, among them a 1901-S $10 gold piece graded MS-65 and priced at $4,250. That coin is covered with nicks, scratches, and gouges that are visible to the naked eye. At best, it is worth a few hundred dollars. One of the other coins he received was an 1838 $5 gold piece graded MS-63 and priced at $5,500. This coin had circulated so extensively that even a non-collector could easily spot the wear on it. It, too, probably is worth a few hundred dollars at best.

"I didn't even tell my wife yet," Ted admitted meekly after learning the awful truth. "The salesman sounded just so convincing, saying, 'Ted, I'd never do anything to hurt you.'"

Ted's story isn't unique or even unusual. Many millions of dollars have been lost by investors who were given misleading information about the vast fortunes to be made in rare coins.

The Other Side of the Coin

Peter Thompson's tale isn't as bleak.

Like many freewheeling investors, Thompson (not his real name) purchased rare coins in the late 1980s to supplement his holdings of stocks, bonds, and real estate. Thompson wasn't really a collector, but he found coins attractive, intriguing, and diverting—and despite his limited knowledge of the field, he felt secure in buying them because several Wall Street firms had started offering coins through limited-partnership funds, in much the way they marketed more traditional investment vehicles. He also felt reassured by the fact that his coins were certified—authenticated, graded, and encapsulated by an independent third-party certification service. He limited his purchases to certified coins, and by the spring of 1989, he had built up a portfolio with a market value of $100,000.

Then, in May 1989, the coin boom began to sputter. Amid allegations of improprieties in some of the coin funds, Wall Street pulled out of the rare coin market—and the coin market, in turn, suffered a sudden crisis that depressed prices sharply and set the stage for a long, steep decline that would linger well into the 1990s. Peter Thompson's portfolio plunged in value by more than 50 percent within a matter of weeks, and he and fellow investors beat a hasty retreat from a marketplace they had never fully understood.

Unlike many of the others, Thompson chose to keep his coins, rather than disposing of them at fire-sale prices. The money he had invested was discretionary in nature, and he still found the coins appealing on an emotional level, even though they had cost him tens of thousands of dollars in paper losses. He reasoned that in time, he might recoup those losses—and, in the meantime, he enjoyed owning the coins, appreciating them even though they had not appreciated for him.

Ten years later, in 1999, Thompson—newly retired—decided to check on the current market value of his coins. He had heard that rare coins were enjoying a resurgence of interest and that one particular coin, an 1804 silver dollar, had changed hands at auction for an all-time record price of more than $4 million. He obtained a current copy of the *Certified Coin Dealer Newsletter* (also known as the *Bluesheet*), the price list that gives the "sight-unseen" bid prices dealers are offering to pay for coins that have been certified by one of the major services, and looked up the prices of his coins. To his chagrin, he found that in most cases the prices remained significantly lower than what he had paid for the coins during the market boom just before the crash of 1989.

Fortunately, Thompson investigated further, rather than simply selling off the coins at what appeared to be their market value. He consulted a reputable coin dealer and discovered that his cloud had a silver lining: Grading standards had softened in the intervening years, so his coins might well be a grade or two higher in 1999 than the numbers they received in 1988 and early 1989. If that were the case, their value would correspond to higher grade levels—and higher price levels—in the current *Bluesheet*. With help from the dealer, Thompson resubmitted his coins to the certification services—and sure enough, most of them came back with higher grades. Their total combined value still fell short of his original investment; after all, he had purchased these coins at the very height of a roaring bull market. But the grading readjustment narrowed the gap and cushioned the blow considerably.

The Impact of Grading Services

By fathering PCGS, David Hall created a new generation of collectibles: certified or "papered" coins. Sure, certification had been available in the past. But the only major organization to provide that service had been ANA's ANACS. Today, there are more than twenty businesses and organizations that are in the certification business. And many dealers who first built up reputations as being reputable through the sale of "raw" coins (coins not accompanied by grading and authenticity certificates of any kind) have switched to "slabs," too.

But the buying of certified coins doesn't by any means completely solve the investor's dilemma: Some grading services are strict; others are liberal; and still others grade only the coins that they are selling to the public. To further confuse things, on occasion, even the best services have apparently slightly modified their standards. Q. David Bowers, former president of the American Numismatic Association and numismatic director of American Numismatic Rarities, LLC, says that there are as many grading standards as there are coin dealers. My variation on this theme is that there are as many grading standards as there are grading services—many!

What this means is that one dealer can call a coin Mint State–65 under one standard, and under that one standard the grade could be fair. But under another standard it could be viewed as being overgraded. When you purchase coins, always be certain that the grading standard being used is disclosed, and be certain that you are paying a price commensurate with the standards for that service.

Some Important Grading Services

It would be beyond the scope of this or any other book to list and analyze every grading service in operation today. Many grading services spring up, prosper, falter, and then disappear. It is therefore essential to take the advice given here about grading services generally, for there is no track record of long-term prosperity for any grading service.

The advent of independent grading services that encapsulate or "slab" coins has transformed the rare coin industry. It has changed the way we view ourselves and our coins. But with the revolution in rare coin grading came a revolution in rare coin trading. The establishment of the grading services attracted millions of dollars from investors and speculators who were all too eager to capitalize on the apparent systematizing of grading standards. Kidder, Peabody, and Merrill Lynch set up investment partnerships in rare coins that attracted millions of dollars. Unfortunately, these partnerships later lost millions of dollars.

In May 1989, rare coins were the hottest game in the country. Business and investment periodicals everywhere were featuring articles about coins certified by PCGS and the Numismatic Guaranty Corporation of America (NGC). *The Wall Street Journal* published an article about the coin market's newly found success; it ran on the front page, and I was quoted.

But the coin market crashed. And everywhere you turned, bewildered collectors, investors, and dealers were wondering what had happened. The answer to this question is complex.

Maurice Rosen, a prize-winning numismatic newsletter editor and publisher, is quick to point out that the coin industry is "definitely better off with slabs than without them." Writing in the May 1994 issue of his *Rosen Numismatic Advisory*, he stated: "I shudder to think where the [coin] investment market would be today were it not bound in at least the semblance of confidence and assuredness offered by the grading services."

Rosen says that although he is bullish about the coin market's future and the investment potential of many coins which have decreased in value, it is an inescapable fact that for many individuals, investing in rare coins has been a disaster. In that same May 1994 issue of his newsletter, he offered the following controversial views:

> Enormous new interest for coins was created in the face of substantially declining inflation rates and falling precious metals prices from several years earlier. The panacea: the Professional Coin Grading Service (PCGS), to be followed by the Numismatic Guaranty Corporation (NGC) in 1987. The certified ("slab") grading services had presumably provided the investor market with what it sorely wanted: relief from grading concerns; standardization of the product; increased liquidity; reduced reliance on individual client-dealer relationships; and the purported ability to play the "coin game" as a dealer without first having to master the field via education, training, and trial and error experience.
>
> The Federal Trade Commission and slabs ruined many of the sleazy telemarketers. As a result, confidence returned quickly to a market begging for deliverance. With a lot riding on their new enterprises, plus the unbridled spirit of their exuberance and self-confidence, the services made very boastful claims [about] their grading expertise and the integrity of their slabs. They seemed to

operate with a brazen air of self-assurance. This soon crumbled as subsequent developments humbled their feelings of omnipotence. In short, coin grading proved to be more difficult and complex than they originally thought and planned, plus subject to refinements and changes. Grading accuracy and consistency, in some instances, went embarrassingly awry.

The failings of the grading services, until 1989/90 generally overlooked because so many people were making so much money and wanted to believe that coins had finally achieved investment nirvana, loomed large as glaring flaws that further eroded investor confidence. And from the orthodox collector sidelines, which had looked aghast at all the former fuss, came gloated I told you so's, reminding people that within each of those plastic cases lies a coin, not solely a label.

NGC Versus PCGS: Early Market Premiums Fizzle

When the second edition of this book was released in 1988, I reported that PCGS S-mint Morgan dollars, any date, were being bid sight-unseen at $325 in MS-65; and NGC dealer high bid sight-unseen for the same type and grade was $425. PCGS Saint-Gaudens double eagles in MS-65 were being bid at $2,600, and NGC high bid was $3,750. This has changed in two respects. The values have come down dramatically for these two coin types, and at press time PCGS sight-unseen examples carry the premiums over NGC sight-unseen examples. These sight-unseen bids and, thus, values listed in the *Certified Coin Dealer Newsletter* (CCDN) are reflective of the lowest possible quality of coin for the assigned grade. Most trading in today's marketplace is on a sight-seen basis. In an exclusive study for *The Coin Collector's Survival Manual—Third Edition*, Maurice Rosen reported the following:

> Hailed as the new, more conservative grading service, NGC quickly established its superiority to the slab leader PCGS where it most counted, in the marketplace. On average, NGC-graded coins sold for higher prices than did similarly graded PCGS coins of the same issue. This situation generally lasted until mid-1989, when the pricing relationship reversed and PCGS-graded coins brought higher prices compared to NGC-graded coins.
>
> This shift in consumer taste is best shown by [extensive data compiled by Rosen] from the *Coin Dealer Newsletter Certified Coin Market Indicator*. The indicator is a weekly comparison of certified coin Bid levels relative to *CDN* sight-seen Bid levels (as 100%) sampled from 10 U.S. coin series (2 grades each; avg. is for 20 ratios). Each week, the *CDN* publishes the Low, High and Average of these 20 ratios. [Extensive data prepared by Rosen] compare the Average ratios of PCGS- and NGC-graded coins at 3-month intervals.
>
> Note that at the introduction of this indicator's publication (May 6, 1988), PCGS-graded coins, on average, brought 91.67% of *CDN* sight-seen Bid levels, whereas NGC-graded coins brought an average of 105.36%. Comparing these two percentages produces a ratio of 1.15, meaning that as of May 6, 1988, on average NGC-graded coins were Bid at a 15% premium to PCGS-graded coins of the same issue and grade.

> The near-steady diminution of this premium, and the ratio's change to a discount (shown by the ratio dipping under 1.00), tracks the decline in favor of NGC coins vis-à-vis PCGS coins in the marketplace.
>
> [Two tables of extensive numbers prepared by Rosen] show a similar analysis using two of the coin market's most popular coin issues: the 1881-S Morgan dollar in MS-65 grade and the $20 Saint-Gaudens piece, also in MS-65 grade. . . . The commanding premiums enjoyed by NGC-graded examples of these two issues relative to PCGS-graded examples of the same issues lessened over the years, giving way to a clear reversal of market preference, to the point recently where NGC-graded examples show discounts, minor for the 1881-S $1, but substantial for the $20 Saint-Gaudens.
>
> What is the market saying? It is saying that, on average, NGC-graded coins are less favored relative to PCGS-graded coins. The implication may be that market perceptions about the relative grading standards of NGC relative to PCGS have changed. As the data show, this relationship is a dynamic one, changing over time, often greatly so. It is quite possible that future observations will show further fluctuations as well. Savvy coin buyers who are able to recognize and take advantage of such swings in relative pricing can enhance their portfolio and collection values.

Grading Expert Worries About Looser Standards

John Albanese was the founder of NGC, although he sold his interest in the company. He also was one of the founders of PCGS. "I am very worried about looser standards—especially on generic gold coins—at the two major services," Albanese declared in a telephone interview (February 2005). "I have seen many gold coins, notably MS-64, MS-65, and MS-66 Saints, as well as key dates, that have been overgraded by them," he insisted. "This is creating turmoil in the marketplace."

"It's very difficult to have a sustained rally in generic coins if the buyers and market-makers don't have confidence in the product," said Albanese, now a wholesale dealer and gold coin buyer for a large coin firm. "From the end of 2004 to the beginning of 2005, we saw the price of bullion gold drop 5 percent and, correspondingly, MS-65 Saint-Gaudens double eagles drop about 30 percent. This is a disproportionate drop, and the top three supporters of the market are the top submitters of the coins." Albanese says that now, more than ever, "collectors need to learn about grading and only purchase coins that have superior surfaces and eye appeal."

Salvatore Germano, a gold coin dealer in Hawthorne, New Jersey, said that it is "still hard to get one of these coins certified as MS-66, and MS-67 remains sacred."

What's the highest grade you can hope for if you are resubmitting an MS-63+? Germano said, "It's not out of the question for one of these in an MS-63 holder from a couple of years ago to be re-graded MS-66-certain coins have a look that can lead to them being graded either higher or lower by 1 or 2 points."

PCGS said in February 2005 that it did not change its grading standards for generic gold within the last couple of months. "I do not believe that we have changed our standards for generic gold in the last two months," said David Hall, president of PCGS.

When asked whether NGC had recently modified its generic gold coin standards, its chairman, Mark Salzberg, replied, "Grading is an art, and we vigilantly police our standard. . . . NGC is committed to maintaining the most consistent and accurate standard in the industry."

At the end of February 2005, a number of dealers told me that in their opinions the grading interpretations of the standards for generic gold coins had stabilized on the side of conservatism and that, at least for the time being, their concerns were fading.

"Hey, I just sent in a group of Saints, and I got brutalized," one veteran coin dealer told me at the end of February. "No way are these guys loose now."

Helpful advice to consumers from Germano in the wake of any apparent fluctuation of grading standard interpretations:

- Cherrypick the coins.
- Don't object to paying a premium for accurately graded coins or to paying an expert a fee to pick the coins for you
- If the services are grading too tight, go out and buy similarly graded coins
- If the service are grading too loose, get them upgraded and move them out at the higher price

Albanese said that NGC has never encouraged its dealers to place bids for coins on a sight-unseen basis. "Buy the coin, not the holder," the NGC founder recommends.

The coins graded during the first several years of operation of both PCGS and NGC can be identified by their lack of a hologram; for PCGS, the holder was of a different style, too. Holograms were later adopted as a security measure. One word of caution: This is not a foolproof way to determine an earlier-graded coin, since many earlier-graded coins have been reholdered.

I urge you to create your own triple protection program when buying certified coins—generic gold or otherwise. First, use your own common sense and taste. Second, rely on grading opinions from leading services. And third, do business with a trustworthy dealer.

Grading Standards Soften at NGC and PCGS

At one time, a Hilton Head, South Carolina, dealer named Michael Keith Ruben submitted about 30,000 coins per year to NGC and paid the service about half a million dollars annually in fees. "When NGC began grading in 1987, their coins traded at a premium for two reasons," he said in 1994. "NGC standards were stricter than PCGS's and more strict than what they are in 1994; and NGC had not graded enough coins to satisfy the initial great demand for its product."

By 1994, he said, the standards were "unquestionably softer" at both services than they were just a few years before that. He pointed out that in at least one case, though, the marketplace forced a tightening of standards. "Prior to 1988, a deeply toned original coin had its grade increased, but in 1994 NGC and PCGS lowered the grade for toned specimens," Ruben noted.

Why did certain NGC coins no longer carry premiums over their PCGS counterparts? According to Ruben: "For the most part, PCGS is more conservative than NGC; but NGC is more consistent than PCGS."

"I can speak both for NGC and PCGS concerning their first six months of operation," said John Albanese, the NGC founder. "The grading standards of both services were too tight."

Albanese pointed out that during its early months, there were reasons other than tight grading standards why NGC coins commanded premiums. He related, "We limited submissions, received great publicity, and had one very large New England dealer buying up every NGC coin in sight." In an exclusive interview for the 1994 edition of this book, Albanese told me, "NGC is marginally looser in grading a certain group of coins, but overall is on par with PCGS standards. . . . Any conclusion from Rosen's statistics that NGC is generally a point looser than PCGS on anything just isn't true."

David Hall, PCGS's founder, when interviewed by me on my radio show, conceded that a small percentage of coins graded 66 and above by PCGS during its first several years might grade higher today upon resubmission. He urged consumers to submit these for regrading. (Ron Guth was named PCGS president in October 2005.)

James L. Halperin is co-chairman of the board of Heritage Capital Corporation, a coin and collectibles firm which bills itself as "the world's largest dealer and auctioneer." Halperin, whose moneymaking activities are chronicled later in this book, likes today's grading standard. "On average, NGC and PCGS standards were a little too tight in the 1980s, and today they are just about right," he stated in 2005. "Overall, I have never felt better or more confident about the numismatics profession in general."

Detecting Counterfeit PCGS Holders

In the late 1980s, the integrity and acceptance of certified coins suffered a scare when overgraded coins began turning up in counterfeit PCGS holders. Heritage co-chairman Jim Halperin uncovered the scam when he discovered an overgraded Saint-Gaudens double eagle in what appeared to be a PCGS holder. When he called PCGS and gave the certification number, he was told that the number was the identifier for a nickel five-cent piece.

IDENTIFYING ILLICIT PCGS COIN HOLDERS

Step #1 From the insert

Determine if the insert is genuine.

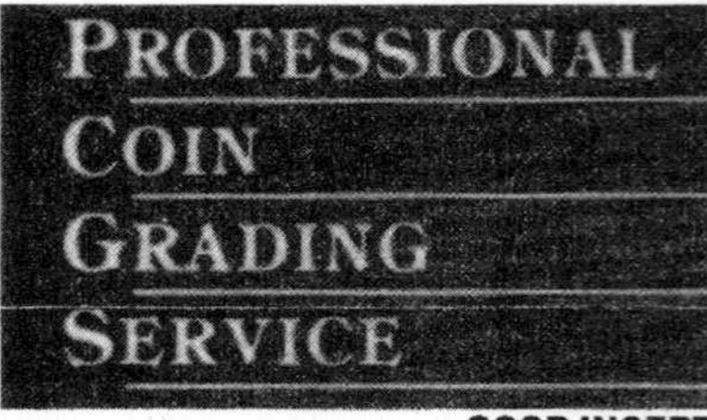

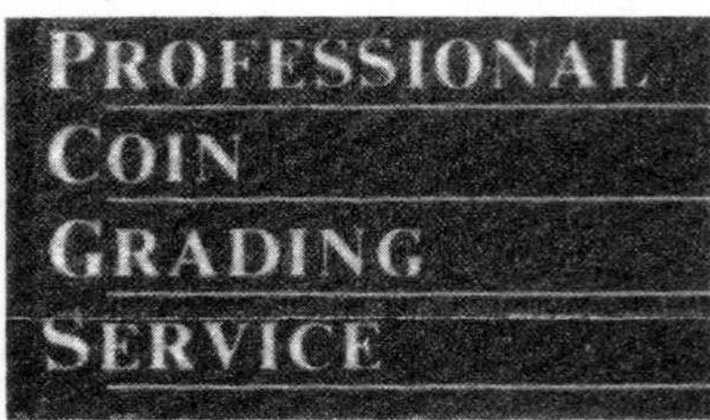

GOOD INSERT

The serifs on the good insert slant from the letters at a 45° angle. Note the S and the E in SERVICE. The serif on the G is longer.

BAD INSERT

The serifs on the bad inserts are vertical. They cut off square and do not angle out. Also there is no serif on the G.

Step #2 From The Plastic Cases

It is important to check the plastic holder even if the insert is o.k.

Area to examine on case

Bad case has a more obvious raised area which is approximately 3/16" long.

Good case has small raised area along the edge where the holder was cut from the injection molded sprue. About 1/16" long.

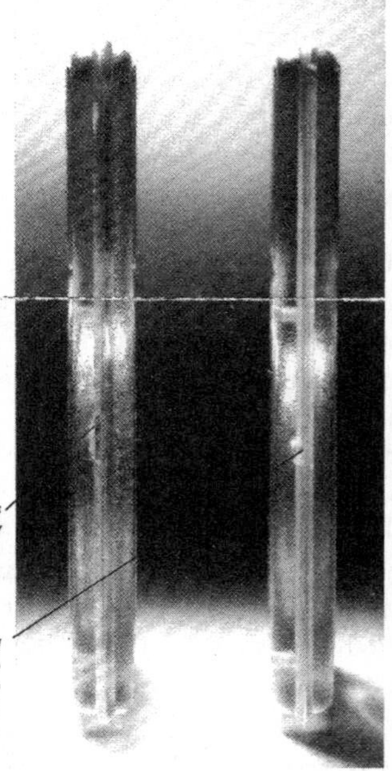

Tip sheet for identifying fake PCGS certification (old holders). PCGS has since modified and improved its holder and built in anti-tampering mechanisms such as a hologram. *Photograph courtesy Heritage*

Fortunately, the holders had fundamental flaws that permitted knowledgeable dealers and collectors—as well as the service itself—to identify them. As shown in this Heritage tipsheet for identifying fake PCGS old holders, there were small but significant differences in the lettering on the tab that is inserted in each holder. The fake holders differed, too, in having a more pronounced raised area along the side of the plastic.

Since that time, PCGS and other grading services have adopted more sophisticated techniques—including the use of holograms—to safeguard their holders and render them more difficult to counterfeit. There have been no major security problems since then, and the perpetrators of the original fraud have been brought to justice. The counterfeiter was sentenced to 46 months in prison, according to Armen R. Vartian, the PCGS lawyer who assisted the government.

Skewed Population and Census Reports

In years gone by, a coin's availability was measured by simply checking its mintage figure—the number of examples produced by the U.S. Mint of any given coin in any given year and at any given mint. There were some exceptions, to be sure; certain silver dollars and gold coins were scarcer than their mintages would suggest, for example, because many pieces had been melted over the years. But most buyers and sellers were familiar with these exceptions and, by and large, dealers and collectors accepted mintage figures as accurate reflections of available supplies.

Since the rise to prominence of independent grading services during the late 1980s, the marketplace has been given a new set of tools for measuring the supply of a given coin: the population and census reports issued by the leading grading services. These reports, pegged primarily to Mint State and Proof coins (the kinds that account for the overwhelming majority of grading-service submissions) show the certified population of every U.S. coin graded by each service—the cumulative number graded and encapsulated by PCGS, NGC, and ANACS. By checking the monthly Population Reports issued by PCGS, the corresponding Census Reports put out by NGC, and the periodic Population Reports from ANACS, buyers and sellers can see at a glance the cumulative grading activity of these companies—the total number of coins of any given type certified by each service in each of the major grade classifications.

Difficulties Interpreting Population Reports

In a sense, population and census reports are fine-tuned versions of the mintage reports issued each year by the Mint. They zoom in from the wide-angle shot of a coin's total mintage to offer a close-up look at the relative numbers available in specific grade levels—primarily in the Mint State range and in Proof. But whereas mintage figures establish an outer limit for a given coin's supply—a figure that will shrink as time goes by and coins are lost or melted—the population and census figures tend to grow in time as more and more examples are submitted to the services and certified.

Unfortunately, population and census reports are seriously flawed. Their usefulness is compromised by the fact that they fail to distinguish between coins being submitted for the first time and those being resubmitted—perhaps many, many times—in quest of an upgrade. Some submitters aren't conscientious enough to return the holder inserts from cracked-out or resubmitted coins, which would allow the respective grading service to adjust its numbers downward accordingly. Consequently, the reports' results are skewed. For example, let's say you were to resubmit the same coin fifteen different times to the same service in an attempt to get the MS-65 grade, but each time the coin was graded MS-64. The population or census report would reflect fifteen coins (not just one) being graded MS-64.

In February 2005 alone, in conjunction with a PCGS promotion, just one veteran coin dealer returned 13,535 PCGS inserts, representing hundreds of millions of dollars' worth of high-end coins he sold since 1986.

Among the old inserts returned were:

- 42 certified 1879 and 1880 $4 "Stella" pattern gold pieces with a combined estimated value of over $5 million;
- 130 round and octagonal 1915 Panama-Pacific International Exposition $50 gold commemoratives valued at over $5 million; and
- 168 High Relief 1907 Saint-Gaudens double eagles valued at over $3 million.

Before this one dealer returned these inserts, those coins were listed in PCGS's Population Report. There are, without a doubt, other dealers out there with inserts. And it is equally certain that many inserts have been destroyed and will never be returned.

For these and other reasons, the figures simply cannot be relied upon. In a sense, the close-up pictures they give us of market activity are badly out of focus—and this is too bad. Clear, sharp pictures would be worth not only a thousand words, but perhaps many thousands of dollars.

Popular and Visible Grading Services

Four grading services are viewed at press time as the marketplace's most significant services. This is a volatile situation and subject to change. Just be certain that you are not fooled by an unscrupulous telemarketer who calls you on the telephone trying to push coins graded by a service you've never heard of. One grading service in the South has reportedly certified MS-60 Morgan dollars picked from rolls as MS-65s and higher—and charged many hundreds of dollars per coin.

Grading services are not a cure-all, but we are certainly better off with them than without them. Even the very best services have not remained 100 percent consistent over years with their grading standard interpretations. They are the best we have, however, and so we need to make the best of the situation.

At press time, these are the most important grading services, in alphabetical order:

ANACS
a subsidiary of Anderson Press, Inc., parent company of Whitman Publishing, LLC, publishers since the 1930s of leading numismatic books such as *A Guide Book of United States Coins*

P.O. Box 7173
Dublin, Ohio 43017-0773
Tel.: 800-888-1861 (in Ohio: 614-791-8704)
FAX: 614-791-9103
www.anacs.com

Services offered: Accepts submissions directly from the public; guarantee linked to its own re-examination and fair market value; 6-hour Express Service; 1-, 2-, and 5-day Express Service; Economy Speed Service (turnaround time varies according to market—anywhere from 4 to 12 weeks); Pre-screen (non-binding grade opinion of coins in other services' holders); grades and authenticates error coins and varieties; attributes collector coins by die variety; verifies relevant strike details, such as 5 or 6 steps on Jefferson nickels; grades coins from more than 200 countries (will grade any coin listed in the latest edition of Krause's *Catalog of World Coins*); authenticates and encapsulates "problem" coins; conducts seminars; gives free grading opinions at selected coin shows; and publishes periodic population reports

Today's ANACS, a subsidiary of Anderson Press, Inc., has joined the mainstream of authentication and grading services by adopting as its policy the best of the past and combining that with the realities of today's marketplace. In its 15 years of operation, it has graded and encapsulated approximately 1.5 million coins. It averages 10,000-15,000 submissions per month.

This grading and encapsulation service is the successor organization to the embattled American Numismatic Association Certification Service. Although the ANA's ANACS and today's ANACS share the same acronym, they have little else in common.

The ANA's ANACS graded coins on both the obverse and reverse. Examples appear in this book of coins assigned grades of, for example, MS-65/63 by the ANA's ANACS. The old ANACS used academic grading, as was explained in the previous chapter. And the old ANACS stated its opinions in the form of authoritative-looking photo certificates.

Just imagine a Morgan dollar being struck from dies so weak that very little of Miss Liberty is visible. And upon these weakly struck surfaces is dark, ugly, black toning. Imagine further a photo certificate issued under the auspices of the ANA's ANACS offering the opinion that this weakly struck, dark, ugly Morgan dollar grades MS-65/65. Imagine no further. From 1979 through 1989, this was how the ANA's ANACS graded coins. In 1989, the ANA sold ANACS to Amos Press, Inc. for an immediate payment of $1.5 million and up to $3 million in royalties over a five-year period. Amos sold ANACS to Anderson Press, Inc. in 2005.

ANACS-certified and graded. ANACS was expected to unveil a new holder in 2006. *Photograph courtesy ANACS*

Photo certificates of authenticity and grade from the old ANACS should not be relied upon. Interestingly, many are quite accurate, but too many are not. Coins graded by the old ANACS should be submitted for grading to a contemporary respected encapsulation service.

Today's ANACS is one of those respected services. Much of the wisdom and practical knowledge of Amos Press, which also owns *Coin World*, the coin field's weekly newspaper of record, was applied over its years of ownership to enhance the structural integrity of its ANACS. Hobby leader and newest owner Anderson Press, Inc. is expected to continue to build upon this fine tradition. An overall grade is used, and this reflects the reality of the marketplace. In order to provide you with an educational tool, coins are encapsulated which have major problems or have been harshly cleaned, but always with an appropriate description attached.

Despite its lofty goals, compact and sturdy holders, accessible staff members, and decent market-sensitive grading, not all coins graded by today's ANACS are worth as much money as those with the same grades assigned by market leaders NGC and PCGS. (Consult the *Certified Coin Dealer Newsletter* for up-to-date pricing information.) That's a shame because ANACS is probably the most independent of any coin grading service out there—and its opinions are the most "arms' length distance" in the rare coin marketplace.

Independent Coin Grading Company (ICG)
7901 East Belleview Ave., Suite 50
Englewood, Colorado 80111
Toll free: 877-221-4424 (in Colorado 303-221-4424)
FAX: 303-221-5524
www.icgcoin.com

Coin certified by ICG. *Photograph courtesy Independent Coin Grading Company*

Services offered: ICG does not have a network of authorized dealers; instead, all dealers automatically receive a 20% discount on all submissions by using a Dealer Submitter Number (DSN), which they can obtain free by requesting one from ICG; dealers are sent ICG submission forms when they are assigned a DSN. Submissions are sent not to ICG but to a third-party receiving company called Corporate Security Solutions, which issues invoice numbers for incoming coins and packages and ships the coins following certification; standard service is 15 days, but coins are returned sooner if they are finished; 1-day submissions received by noon are ready the next day by 5 p.m.; there is no fee for no-grade coins, but a $5 processing fee is charged to the submitter's account; full submission fee is charged for no-grade coins deemed to be counterfeit or altered; ICG will grade, authenticate and attribute (over 75 references) any coin (including ancients), token or medal that fits into an ICG holder.

Founded in 1998, ICG is the new kid on the block among the major players in the coin certification game. It has carved out a niche for itself most clearly and successfully by pursuing and capturing the lion's share of submissions from dealers who specialize in high-grade modern U.S. coins. (This is another way of saying that ICG grades too many coins Proof-70.) This has catapulted ICG close to the top of the list among the major services in the quantity of coins currently being certified and encapsulated. However, having been in existence far longer, other services—notably PCGS and NGC—remain well ahead in terms of overall cumulative volume.

Unfortunately, ICG does not issue population or census reports, which makes it nearly impossible to know how many coins of what type it really grades.

ICG says that it is proud of its supremely qualified graders "who have, for a combined 34 years, taught coin grading and counterfeit detection for the ANA." These qualified

NGC-certified and graded.

professionals include Keith Love (CEO and senior grader), J. P. Martin (senior numismatist), and Walt Armitage (senior grader).

"Independent" is more than just a word in ICG's corporate name, claim company officials. ICG claims to take elaborate steps to ensure that its graders will not know the identity of dealers or collectors who submit coins for review. It stipulates that all coins must be sent not to ICG itself, but rather to Corporate Security Solutions, a third-party receiving company, which then removes all shipping and identification labels and assigns a computerized random tracking number to each coin before it forwards the coins to the graders. Likewise, when the coins have been certified, it is Corporate Security Solutions that processes them for return to the submitters.

ICG also offers InterceptShield coin holders that help to preserve the encapsulated item.

Consumers need to be wary of overpriced ICG modern Proof-70 coins offered in the marketplace. A number of telemarketers were recently accused of deceptive practices—much of it tied to misrepresenting the rarity and investment potential of modern Proof-70 ICG coins. The telemarketers were accused of gouging buyers by dramatically overpricing the coins.

Numismatic Guaranty Corporation of America, Inc. (NGC)
Sarasota, Florida 34230
Tel.: 800-NGC-COIN (in Florida: 941-360-3990)
FAX: 941-360-2553
www.ngccoin.com

Services offered: Consumers submit coins to NGC through a member-dealer network or by themselves if an ANA member or an NGC Collector Society member; guarantee linked to its own re-examination and the highest prevail-

Early NGC holder reverse (circa 1987) that bore an attractive molded logo. *Photograph courtesy NGC*

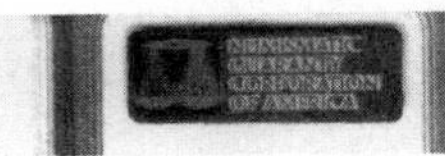

Later NGC holder reverse (left) has a hologram of NGC and the ANA. The slightly older NGC holder has just the NGC logo. A number of leading experts contend that some coins graded and encapsulated in the older holders might be graded more conservatively than their recently graded counterparts.

Latest NGC holder reverse has a hologram that features the logos of ANA and PNG.

ing bid (does not guarantee earlier-graded copper coins); same-day service (Walk Through); grading in 48 hours (Express); grading in 12 working days (Early Bird); grading in 5 working days for certain gold coins (GoldRush and Specialty Gold); grading in an estimated 21 working days for non-gold coins valued at $300 or less (Economy); resubmission evaluations; reholdering; certified pregrade (a preliminary grade assigned to a coin encapsulated by another grading service); uncertified pregrade (NGC's most economical grading service); written census reports quarterly by subscription; census reports available over the Internet updated weekly, also available by subscription; and PhotoProof digitized imaging.

Stunning white plastic holders bearing beautiful holograms showcase coins certified by the resilient NGC, one of the world's premier independent coin grading services. After 18 years of operation and surviving the longest market shakeout in numismatic history, this service still provides respectable grading, commendable efficiency, and financial stability. Through January 2005, NGC had graded more than 11 million coins since its inception, according to its chief executive officer, Steve Eichenbaum. The service was averaging about 175,000 encapsulations per month in 2004, Eichenbaum said.

NGC was founded in August 1987 by John Albanese, a former PCGS owner. Albanese temporarily gave up coin dealing to establish this service by lending his world-class, impartial skills in the grading room. Although NGC no longer has the benefit of Albanese's talented eyes, it has assembled a highly competent staff of knowledgeable experts led by the exceptionally skilled Mark Salzberg. Grades are assigned by a minimum of three grading experts. NGC's finalizer team has remained relatively constant, a factor which might help to promote consistency. The consensus approach is used.

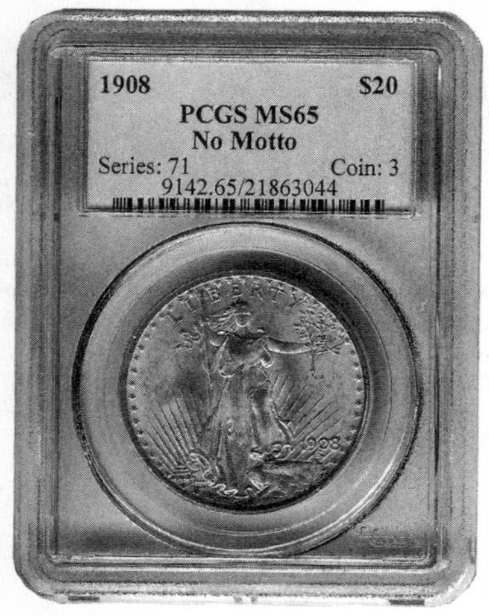

PCGS-certifed and graded.

In 1999, Albanese sold his interest in NGC. He remains active as a dealer, and is also a manufacturer of Intercept Shield.

NGC's guarantee is substantially similar to PCGS's, with two notable exceptions: NGC guarantees that each coin is graded by three graders (compared with PCGS's four graders); and NGC does not guarantee copper coins in its earlier-generation holders. The service does, however, guarantee copper coins encapsulated in current holders, on which the words NUMISMATIC GUARANTY CORPORATION appear at the bottom of the grading label.

According to NGC president Rick Montgomery, the guarantee on copper coins expires ten years from the date of grading, as copper coins occasionally deteriorate, thus lowering the grade of an already certified coin. Montgomery himself adds much to NGC: He is widely regarded as one of the world's preeminent coin authenticators.

NGC will not grade coins that have been damaged by polyvinylchloride coin holders.

Professional Coin Grading Service (PCGS)
P.O. Box 9458
Newport Beach, California 92658
Tel.: 800-447-8848 (in California: 714-833-0600)
FAX: 714-757-7699
www.pcgs.com

Services offered: Author of *The Official Guide to Coin Grading and Counterfeit Detection* (Random House, 1997, 2004). Accepts submissions directly from PCGS Collector's Club members (*www.pcgs.com/join/index.chtml*) and through a member-dealer network; guarantee linked to its own re-examination and the highest prevailing bid; turnaround guarantees; telephone grade reports; free

Newer PCGS holder reverse (left) has a hologram of PCGS and the Professional Numismatists Guild (PNG). The slightly older PCGS holder bears just the PCGS logo. A number of leading experts contend that some coins graded and encapsulated in the older holders might be graded more conservatively than their recently graded counterparts.

Latest PCGS holder reverse has a hologram that incorporates the NASDAQ symbol, CLCT, of its holding company, Collectors Universe.

grading review (restrictions apply); Show (1 day); Walkthrough (2 days); Express Special (7 days); Regular (15 days); Non-gold U.S. Coin Economy (65 days); Modern U.S. or World Coins, 1965 to present, 60 days; World Rarities, 45 days; World, 45 days; World Economy, varies; Mint Errors, 45 days; Special Issues, 30 days; Presidential Review, 10-20 days; Reholder, 10-20 days, Reholder for MS-70 and PR-70 coins, 10-20 days; pedigree certification; population reports January, April, July and October of each year, but updated weekly online (access by paid subscription); and traveling coin exhibits.

PCGS has become the most significant market force rare coin enthusiasts have ever seen. If ever there was a question of whether the rare coin industry really is an industry, certainly PCGS has confirmed that it is.

PCGS began operations in February 1986. The service grades according to a consensus: At least three expert graders look at each coin; after three graders look at the coin, a fourth grader assigns a grade. This fourth professional numismatist is called a finalizer. If the graders and finalizer agree, the grade is assigned. If there is a disagreement, the coin is passed on to more graders. This service pioneered the use of all 11 Mint State numerical grades and in the end issues one overall grade (e.g., MS-64). If a coin grades MS-63/64, PCGS would opt for the grade MS-63. Usually the lower side prevails as the overall grade, but there are a few exceptions, such as when a strong obverse "carries" the coin.

After a coin has been graded, it is sealed in a tamper-resistant holder. PCGS will not grade coins that have been damaged by polyvinylchloride coin holders.

Coins can be submitted to PCGS directly, and also through any of a number of "authorized PCGS dealers."

NUMISMATIC CERTIFICATION INSTITUTE

The Heritage Building, 311 Market Street, Dallas, Texas 75202, (214) 742-2200

1. The Numismatic Certification Institute (The Institute) guarantees this coin is genuine. If proven counterfeit, The Institute will either, at its sole option, make a suitable replacement or pay the amount of the Authenticity Insurance Coverage (AIC) shown, plus 15% of the AIC per year from issuance. 2. The Institute guarantees this coin is, in its opinion, correctly graded according to the standards of the Institute as published in the N.C.I. Grading Guide (1986). These standards represent the Institute's interpretation of prevailing commercial retail standards as interpreted in 1985, which did and do differ from the standards of others, including certain other grading services, and should not be confused with technical grading as employed by these services which is more conservative (grades lower). 3. The coin will be cataloged at the certified grade at a 20% discount off the seller's commission, subject to the standard terms and conditions through Heritage Numismatic Auctions, Inc. an affiliate of the Institute. 4. The evaluation of the original submitter for the Authenticity Insurance Coverage is: [ ] This value represents only the amount of insurance coverage extended with respect to authenticity, and is the basis on which certification fees are calculated. The Institute is not an evaluation service therefore it does NOT represent that the AIC is the current market value of the coin, nor does the Institute guarantee that if the coin were sold through public auction or other public sale, the AIC would be realized as a minimum value thereof. Therefore no implied endorsement should be taken or any reliance made on the basis of the AIC other than that of authenticity. 5. Grading is an art, not a science, and the opinion rendered by this certificate may not agree with the opinion of others (including trained experts) even while employing the N.C.I. standards, and the same experts may not grade the same coin with the same grade at two different times. Grading standards have changed in the past, and as market conditions change, may do so again in the future. Mistakes can, and do occur. Accordingly, total reliance with respect to grade should **not** be made on the basis of the certificate and any reliance which is made should be done only after understanding all relevant disclosures. 6. Because of the different standards employed by different dealers and services, there is a high degree of probability that the grade assigned may not conform to the grading standard or value expressed by publications such as Coin World Trends or the Coin Dealer Newsletter (Greysheet). However, N.C.I. coins are listed at wholesale in the Certified Coin Dealer Newsletter (C.C.D.N.). Since The Institute does not engage in the purchase or sale of coins, it cannot confirm or deny the validity of the prices listed in the CCDN. 7. The authenticity guarantee is insured by a major insurance carrier for amounts up to $1,000,000 in the aggregate. 8. A small percentage of the coins graded by The Institute may have been sold for a profit at the certified grade by an affiliate of The Institute. 9. Educational materials are available from The Institute including N.C.I. Grading Guide as well as a free booklet entitled Important Information About Buying Coins.

© 1987 Numismatic Certification Institute Incorporated

Disclosure statement appearing on photocertificates of the Numismatic Certification Institute. NCI was a grading service whose 1985 standards have become an industry benchmark. *Courtesy Heritage*

PCGS also does not grade problem coins, such as those with weak strikes or artificial toning. The grading of these coins would impair the fluidity of the sight-unseen system.

Dealers who are "market-makers" guarantee to buy certain PCGS-graded coins sight-unseen—that is, without looking at them.

Not all dealers make markets in all coins. So before you trot off to your local dealer to try to force a transaction, make certain that dealer is a market-maker who posts quotes for the coin you have for sale. Market-makers subscribe to the Certified Coin Exchange (CCE) and post both bid and ask levels.

One of the most helpful PCGS services is a population report, issued monthly, which reveals how many coins PCGS has graded, broken down by coin denomination, date, Mintmark, and grade. According to Collector's Universe senior vice president, Michael W. Sherman, PCGS grades 110,000 to 120,000 coins per month, and as of January 31, 2005, PCGS has graded a total of about 10,250,000 coins since its inception. The total declared value of coins submitted was over $12 billion.

Gradeflation and the "Other" Grading Service

Up until recently, one of the best known of the "other" grading services was the Numismatic Certification Institute (NCI), which no longer actively grades coins. NCI is a subsidiary of Dallas-based Heritage Capital Corporation, a major coin dealership. The chief grader for NCI was James L. Halperin, then and current co-chairman of the board of Heritage.

During its seven years of operation, NCI graded and encapsulated coins and issued photo certificates, too. Early in its history, only photo certificates were issued. By its own admission at the time, NCI standards were not as conservative as PCGS or NGC standards. You might well come across an NCI-graded coin, as this service was receiving about 8,000 coins per month for grading.

Some telemarketers sold NCI-graded coins to investors unfamiliar with coins and told them that NCI coins were worth the prices listed in the *Coin Dealer Newsletter*, the weekly wholesale pricing guide of the coin market. It is also referred to as the *Greysheet* because of its distinctive grey color.

Since NCI coins were generally graded according to a less conservative standard, they generally were not worth the prices listed in the *Greysheet*.

However, in February 2005, Halperin offered the opinion "that the standards currently in use at the highest volume grading services are now virtually identical, for most categories, to the standards that were in effect at NCI fifteen to twenty years ago." I agree that in many categories, the standards are now the same.

An extraordinary guide to sight-unseen values of certified coins is *The Certified Coin Dealer Newsletter*. Do not blindly buy "certified" coins unless you can identify their sight-unseen values in the *CCDN*. Stay away from certified products of grading services that do not have value listings in the *CCDN*.

Important Note: Grading standards, even at the industry's leading services, do not appear to have remained 100 percent consistent or fixed. For this reason, you should learn all you can about coins and current market conditions before you buy or sell a single coin. And, if possible, consult a trusted advisor to assist with your transaction.

Grading Fees

Grading fees are comparable at all of the major coin certification services. Typically, it costs about $30 to have a coin graded and encapsulated in the standard manner, which involves a turnaround time of about a month. Faster processing is available for a higher fee; it costs approximately $150 for "walkthrough" service, in which a coin can be certified while the submitter waits. Current fee schedules can be obtained by contacting the individual services.

Services will accept submissions from the public or through authorized dealers. Check first. Lists of dealer members can be obtained by contacting the services in question.

PCGS Versus NGC: Analyzing the Certified Coin Market Indicator

Special Analysis by Maurice Rosen

There is little argument that the two major coin grading services are PCGS and NGC. Bid quotes for many of their certified coins are published on a periodic basis. These bids are constantly referred to by dealers, collectors and investors as they contemplate and complete transactions. Little attention, however, has been given to observing the relative relationships between the published bids for coins of these two major services. In this section I will present an analysis of these long-term pricing relationships and how an understanding of them can improve your portfolio's performance.

The *Coin Dealer Newsletter* created the *Certified Coin Market Indicator(tm)* (CCMI) in July 1988. This CCMI compares the bids for sight-unseen certified coins to those of sight-seen coins, which may or may not be certified. The sight-unseen bids come from *CDN*'s weekly *Bluesheet* publication; the sight-seen bids come from the company's weekly *Greysheet* publication. To quote the *Greysheet*, "The [sight-seen] coins may be certified or 'raw' (uncertified), but the grading MUST ADHERE to the current leading standard."

These data can be used in a number of ways. One way I use them is to compare the relative values of PCGS coins vis-à-vis NGC coins. Another is to compare the sight-unseen bid levels of one service's coins to the bids for sight-seen coins. As my findings will show, the short history of certified coins has produced dynamic pricing trends and major shifts in public demand.

What Exactly Is the CCMI?

The following is taken from the *CDN Monthly Summary* for July 1988 which introduced the CCMI:

> To enhance the Indicator's value as a market index, our comparisons are made across 10 sampled series (i.e. selected Buffalo nickels) rather than specific issues (i.e. 1937-D Buffalo nickel) . . . Since we divided our 'breadbasket' into ten series, with two grades each, we have 20 different percentage levels for comparison. Of course, the Type 'series' each reflect 10 additional series, further broadening the Indicator's scope. For each of the services, we will present the lowest, the highest, and the average of the 20 percentages. Through this information we hope to make the market more aware of the varying bid levels between the grading services, leading to better informed buying and selling decisions.

On the following page is a breakdown of each of the ten series within the Indicator and the specific issues and grades represented. A total of sixty-five coin issues in each of two grades comprise the complete CCMI.

Historical Data of the CCMI

Except for the first two postings, I analyzed quarterly data (from the last issues of March, June, September, and December) as published by the weekly *CDN* to best show the long-term trend of relative pricing relationships. I must tell you up front that I have some reservations about the CCMI as presently constructed. I will discuss my opinions later, but first let's consider the data.

Remember: The percentage listings referred to here are the *Bluesheet* bids compared to the *Greysheet* bids. A reading exceeding 100 means that the *Bluesheet* bid exceeds the *Greysheet* bid, that is, the sight-unseen bid is higher than the sight-seen bid. Readings below 100 mean that the certified coin is bid at a price below that of its sight-seen counterpart.

While the actual quarterly data going back to 1988 is not presented here because of space constraints, it is available to readers of this book. Write to: Maurice Rosen, Numismatic Counseling, Inc., P.O. Box 38, Plainview, New York 11803, requesting the data. Enclosed a self-addressed stamped envelope.

Observations

1. Using the average percentages for PCGS and NGC, I determined that early on, NGC coins were generally priced higher than PCGS coins by a factor upwards of 15% (a reading of 1.15 on May 6, 1988). About a year later, the NGC premium disappeared, and PCGS coins assumed general pricing leadership, as evidenced by readings below the 1.00 level. They reached a low of .88 by the fourth quarter of 1990, then recovered to about the .94-.97 range from 1991 to 1998.

2. During 1998/99, NGC certified coin bids lost further ground relative to PCGS bids, reaching their lowest reading of .84 at first quarter 1999. That .84 reading conversely

means that PCGS coins, as presented by the CCMI data, were priced on average 19% higher than similar NGC coins. The latest reading at press time is .92, meaning that, on average, the CCMI shows that NGC coins are bid at 8% less than similar PCGS coins.

3. Comparing the *Bluesheet* bids of PCGS and NGC certified coins to the *Greysheet* bids for sight-seen coins showed a similar rollercoaster trend. On average, the amount by which *Greysheet* coins outsell coins from both services has increased over time. The latest reading shows PCGS coins to be bid at 90.05% of sight-seen *Greysheet* bids, whereas NGC bids are 83.01% of sight-seen *Greysheet* bids.

4. I made two independent analyses of individual series on my own, apart from the 65 issues within the CCMI. I created my own Type Coin indicator, consisting of ten coins each in Mint State-65 and Proof-65. On average, NGC coins were bid at 80% of PCGS bids. The other series I analyzed was MS-65 Peace Dollars. Here, NGC bids were even lower vis-à-vis PCGS bids. On average, NGC bids were 70% of PCGS bids.

Conclusions

The apparent preference that the market displays for PCGS coins vis-à-vis NGC coins may be due to the fact that PCGS entered the market a year and a half earlier than NGC (February 1986 versus August 1987). That might account for consumers developing a higher degree of comfort with and loyalty to PCGS coins. Another possibility is that, on average, consumers are slightly more pleased with the accuracy and consistency of coins in PCGS holders than they are with coins in NGC holders. To be sure, there are many exceptions, but based on the data examined here, PCGS bids, on average, and as measured and tracked by the CCMI, continue to be somewhat higher than NGC bids.

Notwithstanding the relative merits of PCGS coins versus NGC coins is the fact that even PCGS coins are largely bid at levels below the sight-seen levels in the *Greysheet*. This is because of the very nature of the listings—the *Bluesheet* uses a stricter standard to report its certified (sight-unseen) bids than the *Greysheet* observes while reporting sight-seen bids. In my Observation #2 above I mentioned that the PCGS bids were, on average, 10% below the sight-seen *Greysheet* levels and NGC's were 17% below *Greysheet* levels. This discrepancy can be termed a Certified Coin Risk Factor.

This Risk Factor will fluctuate depending upon the health and climate of the market, as well as the market's perception of the relative merits of the grading services and their coins in the marketplace. I believe that this Risk Factor would diminish if the degree of bullishness in the marketplace increased. Similarly, it is likely that the Risk Factor would increase if activity slowed and the general level of prices receded.

Limitations to the CCMI

Earlier in this chapter I told you I had certain reservations about the CCMI. While the CDN is to be commended for creating and continuing to publish data on the CCMI, it is far from a perfect tool.

1. It leans too heavily on common-date issues within each of its ten series. Better and scarcer dates are all but excluded. Each series should be greatly expanded to include many more issues.

2. It is not weighed to reflect actual market transaction volume or capitalization. The CCMI is a compilation of 20 various coinage groups (10 series in each of two grades). The various computations are averaged with equal weightings to all and the result is the CCMI. For example, this approach places equal emphasis on the 5-coin Buffalo component and the 9-coin Type component.

3. A broader picture of the market may be obtained by tracking more than two grades per coinage issue. For instance, since July 1988 the market has become very comfortable with grades higher than MS-65 and Proof-65. Such higher grades have become a much more important and sought-after part of the consumer market as evidenced by the large number of such coins certified by PCGS and NGC over the past 12 years.

The Bottom Line

It should not be inferred that coins of the same issue in the same grade certified by PCGS and by NGC are worth the same in the marketplace. Every coin is different and must be evaluated on its own merits irrespective of what grade is printed on the insert tag in any grading service's holder. Nevertheless, you should be aware of how the marketplace views the product of the major services.

It is quite possible to profit from just such a keen evaluation. As described elsewhere in this book, it is possible to crack out coins from one service's holders and resubmit them to another for the same or even a higher grade. Suppose, for example, that you are able to purchase some lovely Peace Dollars in NGC holders at significantly lower prices than if they were in equally-graded PCGS holders. I mentioned earlier that, according to my observation, NGC bids were, on average, 30% below those of PCGS. If the coins "cross" to PCGS holders you have greatly boosted your portfolio's value. Selection is critical here.

To be sure, certified coin market trading is still relatively young. Pricing and transactional data listings are bound to improve, all to the benefit of the marketplace and consumers. The *Greysheet*, *Bluesheet*, PCGS, and NGC are to be commended for providing the tools to build a better market. How you use them can determine how successful your collecting and investing endeavors will be.

Special Update for the Fifth Edition

1. The current CCMI posting for PCGS coins, on average, is 81.60%, for NGC coins 82.01%. Thus, according to this indicator, there is little price difference between the valuations for coins certified by either service. These readings compare to 90.05% for PCGS coins and 83.01% for NGC coins at the time of the last edition of this book. Thus, both weakened relative to sight-seen *Greysheet* bids, PCGS more substantially.

2. It should be noted that these CCMI readings represent discounts to current sight-seen *Greysheet* valuations of about 18% (100% less the 81.60% reading for PCGS, and the 82.01% reading for NGC). This portrays the Risk Factor for coins certified by these services, as interpreted from the CCMI data.

Special thanks to Maurice Rosen for his exclusive commentary. —S.A.T.

Changes in Grading Standards

The grading and pricing of coins have undergone a radical transformation over the past two decades. Although the actual numerical labels have remained the same, the descriptions accompanying these labels have changed.

How Grading Standard Interpretations Have Tightened

The influx of billions of investor dollars has caused industry professionals to scrutinize their acquisitions very closely. A specific coin with a tiny nick on Miss Liberty's cheek that was priced at $200 in 1980 and was accepted as MS-65 by experts of that time might no longer be considered MS-65 by experts today if the MS-65 value in a widely used guide price is $2,000. At $200, some nicks and marks might have been tolerable. But at $2,000, that coin now might have to appear flawless.

The feverish demand for coins in the highest possible levels of preservation was partially responsible for the grading and pricing revolution of the 1980s. Because of escalating values, minute distinctions in a coin's level of preservation now can play a major role in the coin's grade—and price.

The pressures placed on grading services and merchants to accept precision grading could well be a consequence of coins' needing corresponding grades to account for differences in price. Two coins valued in 1980 at $190 and $225, respectively, both could have been legitimate MS-65s during that time period. Today, if that $190 coin has a tiny nick or scratch, and that $225 coin is virtually mark-free, the $190 coin could have appreciated to $250, and the $225 coin to $2,500! Further, it is possible that the $2,500 coin would be classified as MS-65 today, while the $250 coin would be called MS-64 or lower.

Any evaluation of coins that were not purchased recently must take into consideration the grade those coins would have received at the time they were sold. The opinion of an individual or grading service (any grading service) that a certain coin purchased as MS-63 in 1980 is merely an MS-60 now cannot be relied upon unless that opinion is qualified with what that coin could have been reasonably expected to be graded at the time it was sold.

Although there are many exceptions to generalizations, these generalizations can often be of help in understanding broad trends of the marketplace. The chart presented here shows my opinion of what may have happened to grading-standard interpretations since the period predating 1981. This is anecdotal, highly unscientific, and does not detail all periods.

GRADING STANDARD INTERPRETATIONS

Pre-1981	1981–1984	1985–2003	2004 to present
MS-65	MS-63	MS-62-MS-63	MS-64 or MS-65
MS-67	MS-64	MS-63 or MS-64	MS-65
MS-67+ to MS-69	MS-65	MS-64	MS-65 or MS-66
—	MS-65+ to MS-67	MS-65	MS-66 or MS-67

ANA's Role in the Changing of Grading-Standard Interpretations

The American Numismatic Association fell prey to the pressures of the marketplace and tightened its interpretation of the grading standards. The party line—that grading standards have not changed, but that the interpretations of them have—continues to be adhered to by the ANA. The ANA's point is that the explanations set forth in its grading guide are so vague that the industry can apply them as it so desires, in response to marketplace elasticity.

The ANA was subjected to much criticism for not assuming a leadership role and for simply falling into line with what marketplace participants were doing: tightening interpretations of the standards.

A dealer who sold old ANACS-graded coins revealed the following examples, which he believes are representative of ANA's changed interpretations. In each case, the year the coin was initially graded and authenticated is followed by old ANACS's re-examination results from May 1986.

15 COINS RESUMBITTED TO ANA'S GRADING SERVICE

Coin		Old ANACS year and grade	Old ANACS 5/86 re-grade
1898	1¢	1981, PF-65/65	PF-63/63
1881	$1	1981, MS-65/65	MS-60/63
1922-S	$1	1981, MS-65/65	MS-63/63
1927	$1	1981, MS-65/65	MS-63/63
1883	1¢	1982, PF-65/65	PF-63/63
1903	1¢	1982, PF-65/65	PF-63/65
1903	5¢	1982, MS-65/65	MS-63/63
1911	5¢	1982, MS-65/65	MS-63/63
1903	$1	1982, MS-65/65	MS-63/63
1921	$1	1982, MS-65/65	MS-63/65

Coin		Old ANACS year and grade	Old ANACS 5/86 re-grade
1902	5¢	1983, PF-65/65	PF-63/63
1880	$1	1983, MS-65/65	MS-63/63
1885-O	$1	1983, MS-65/65	MS-63/65
1889	$1	1983, MS-65/65	MS-63/63
1921	$1	1983, MS-65/65	MS-63/65

Changes in Standards Through the 1980s

According to *Official ANA Grading Standards for United States Coins*, by the American Numismatic Association, "in 1985 and 1986 commercial interpretation of such grades as MS-63, MS-65, and MS-67 tightened considerably. . . ." The following chart illustrates how grading-standard interpretations changed over a short period of time at ANA's ANACS.

Michael R. Fuljenz, a former authenticator and grader for the old ANACS, submitted his personal collection of commemorative coins to old ANACS for grading in 1983. The coins were, for the most part, all graded MS-65. Fuljenz later submitted the same coins to old ANACS for grading in 1986 (see the table).

What all of this means is that your run-of-the-mill old ANACS-certified coins are worth much less than recently certified coins. Mike Fuljenz says: "[Old] ANACS certificates, unlike fine wines which age with time, turn to vinegar as time passes."

COMMEMORATIVE HALF DOLLARS GRADED BY ANA'S ANACS

Coin	Date and grade	Date and grade
1921 Alabama	10-13-83 MS-65/65	4-9-86 MS-63/63
1921 Alabama 2 x 2	10-13-83 MS-65/65	4-9-86 MS-63/65
1936 Arkansas-Robinson	10-13-83 MS-65/65	4-9-86 MS-63/65
1936-D Cincinnati	10-13-83 MS-65/65	4-9-86 MS-63/65
1925 Fort Vancouver	3-1-83 MS-65/65	4-9-86 MS-63/65
1922 Grant with star	10-13-83 MS-65/65	4-9-86 MS-63/63
1923-S Monrooe	10-13-83 MS-65/65	4-9-86 MS-63/65

Effect on Performance Charts

The changes in the interpretation of grading standards are a highly sensitive issue to professional numismatists. Many coin firms like to discuss the exceptional investment potential of rare coins. But the fact remains that if the grading-standard interpretations have undergone major shifts, then price guides and, consequently, graphs of coin performance are not nearly as accurate as some might believe.

Another way to understand this point is to realize that coins have not been registered commodities or securities over the past several years, the years that the historical price performance data specifically refers to. Let's say a collector buys a coin as Mint State-65 and later resells it as Mint State-63. There's nobody who's going to say, "Let's record this transaction as a 65 having been sold because the coin was bought as a 65." A good study on this subject is "The Fallacy of Historical Price Performance Data" (*Rosen Numismatic Advisory*, March/April 1984).

Recent Changes in Grading Standards

Consistency was a goal of the major, modern slabbing services when they began operations; all of them recognized that faithful adherence to constant grading standards would be a crucial factor in winning and keeping consumers' confidence. However, there have been perceptible deviations since the services were founded—sometimes in the direction of stricter grading, other times toward looser interpretation or enforcement of the established guidelines. For this reason, coins graded during one time period may differ by as much as a point—or even more—from virtually identical coins that passed through the same grading service at a different time. These grading differences can be disconcerting for collectors; however, they can work to the advantage of those who can identify holders from the various periods, and are thus able to determine when a particular coin was graded.

Dealer-author Q. David Bowers has monitored this situation closely over the years, showing the same keen interest he had when he headed the panel that reviewed ANA's ANACS grading in the early 1980s. "It is my opinion that grading standards, or at least interpretations of standards, are changing once again," Bowers wrote in his *Coin World* column, "The Joy of Collecting," in late 1995. "In many instances, what the grading services used to call Mint State-65 is now MS-66. In order to buy the same quality that was sold as MS-65 a few years ago, it is often necessary to buy MS-66 today."

In 1999, in his same "Joy of Collecting" column in *Coin World*, Bowers authored a series of articles under the "grade inflation" banner. In one of them, he wrote:

> . . . I spied a certified holder containing a Mint State 1839-O quarter eagle. This is quite an exciting coin to contemplate, and in more than forty-five years of professional numismatics I've seen only a handful. . . . However, upon inspection I found it, in my opinion, to be an acid-etched Extremely Fine 45 coin at best, a real "dog." . . . I would not have bought it even at a price for a Very Fine coin! It was a dog, indeed! Presumably, some bargain-seeking investor, who buys "numbers" instead of coins, owns it now.

In a later *Coin World* column he opined: "There is a peculiar aspect to certification numbers. Populations never contract. They keep getting larger!" In his column, he explained these ever-increasing population numbers as follows:

> Part of the higher numbers is due, in my opinion, to grading inflation, but the practice of resubmission is also important. I recall that one of the leading West Coast dealers once told me that he had a very nice 1916-D dime, for which there was a big jump in market price between MS-63 or MS-64 and the grade he desired, MS-65. He sent the coin in twenty-four times-yes, twenty-four times—until, finally, it was certified MS-65! The data show two dozen Mint State 1916-D dimes sent to a particular service when, in fact, only a single coin was involved.

Sight-Unseen Versus Sight-Seen

The founding of PCGS has changed the personality and appearance of the coin market. The sight-unseen medium will have a significant impact on the future accuracy of historical price-performance data. In fact, plans are being made between coin statistics guru Maurice Rosen and dealer David Hall for a definitive price-performance study.

Sight-seen transactions allow dealers to reject coins at will. In other words, if Dealer A runs a teletype buy or bid offer, and Dealer B accepts the offer and sends Dealer A the coins, Dealer A could reject them. "These coins don't meet my personal grading standards," he could argue. Dealer A could keep increasing his buy price so the price guides would reflect an increase in value, and he would be required to buy few or no coins.

With sight-unseen coin trading, Dealer A would have to buy the coins if he were a PCGS market-maker making an offer. PCGS and the sight-unseen concept will, if anything, make future price performance statistics far more reliable.

Federal Trade Commission Litigation

The Federal Trade Commission (FTC) has filed some lawsuits against coin dealers, with allegations of unfair or deceptive acts or practices in or affecting commerce.

In *Federal Trade Commission* v. *Standard Financial Management Corporation (d/b/a New England Rare Coin Galleries), Dana Willis, and Paul Taglione,* the allegations made by the FTC included, but were not limited to: "defendants have falsely represented that the value of rare coins sold by defendants at a specific grade is comparable to the prices cited for rare coins of that grade in industry pricing publications, when in fact, in numerous instances, the value of rare coins sold by defendants at a specified grade is worth substantially less than prices quoted for rare coins of that grade in industry pricing publications."

Although New England and its principals never admitted to having done anything wrong, they agreed to an out-of-court settlement (stipulated final order and judgment) which called for the closing down of the firm and liquidation of the assets.

NOTICE TO COIN BUYERS

In looking at advertisments in COINage Magazine, the reader should be aware that there is no precise or exacting science of grading coins. Opinions of two viewers of the identical coin can, and do, differ, even when they are experts, because perceptions as to the state of preservation are not always identical.

For grades that are circulated, there tend to be several well-defined and uniform criteria that are utilized, but the grades themselves may be different, because a circulated coin (and its grades) represents an impression or indication as to the amount of wear on the coin.

Uncirculated coins have no visible signs of wear, though they may have blemishes, bag marks, rim nicks, tarnish, or even be weakly struck (which often resembles wear). In uncirculated condition, there are many different grading opinions, some of which are described adjectively, others with numbers. Not all numbers have the identical meaning. This depends on the grading standard utilized.

The value of the item to the buyer should be determined by the price, not the grade. Your examination and satisfaction of the coins should be the criterion, not the grade represented by the seller, or a determination made by another.

Your best protection is your own knowledge and the trust that has developed between you and the dealer over a series of mutually satisfactory transactions.

All advertisers in COINage Magazine agree to a seven day unconditional moneyback guarantee with the exception of bullion and bullion-like coinage, whose dominant price element consists of the value of its precious metal.

If you are displeased with the purchase from an advertiser in COINage and do not receive proper satisfaction, please contact our advertising service department immediately.

Standards for grading by advertisers must specify which guideline or system is utilized. The notification may be within the context of the advertisement (if it varies from item to item), or by means of the following symbols which will appear in the bottom, right hand corner of the ad:

[A] American Numismatic Assoc. - Grading Guide
ANACS Coin is ANA Certified - Standards then in effect
[B] Brown & Dunn.
[P] Photograde.
[N] NCI
[C] Certigrade
[G] Accugrade

PCGS Professional Coin Grading Service.

Some of these names are registered trade marks, or used under license. All uses in COINage Magazine shall be strictly in accordance with such authorized use.

Any other grading standard or system utilized must be specified. A combination of any of the above standards may also be used if specified. **If there is no symbol, or other explanation, the reader must assume that the advertisers' grading standards are based upon their own personal experience.**

Uncirculated coins in Mint State (MS) may be described with numbers or adjectives. Unless the advertisement indicates otherwise, the following standards are used:

MS-67: "Superb brilliant uncirculated" or "Superb gem uncirculated"
MS-65: "Gem Brilliant Uncirculated"; "Gem Uncirculated"
MS-63: "Choice Brilliant Uncirculated"; "Choice Uncirculated"
MS-60: "Brilliant Uncirculated"; "Uncirculated"

COINage reserves the right, to which the advertisers consent, to monitor all merchandise offered in its pages and to make occasional test orders under assumed names to verify that coins are as advertised. Advertisers must agree to adhere to the minimum standards set above and understand and consent that violations may lead to suspension of advertising privileges.

Inadvertent typographical errors occur. Advertisements appearing in COINage should be considered "requests to inquire" rather than unconditional offers of sale. All prices are subject to change at any time without notice.

***COINage* magazine disclosure notice.** For years, Miller Magazines, Inc. has published this disclosure notice in each monthly issue of *COINage* magazine to inform buyers of multiple grading systems. *Courtesy Miller Magazines, Inc.*

(James L. Halperin, New England's previous owner, built that firm into one of the world's premier coin companies. In June of 1983, he sold the business, after which he says he maintained no ownership interest.)

In a telephone interview from his Andover, Massachusetts, home, former New England Rare Coin Galleries principal Dana J. Willis revealed that New England had its coins independently certified by the International Numismatic Society Authentication Bureau in Washington, D.C., a non-profit grading and authentication service which is no longer in business, but which during its years in operation had grading standards that were not as conservative as PCGS or NGC standards.

Other sources revealed that New England used INSAB only after the FTC initiated its investigation of the firm. The certificates were apparently retained by New England.

Remember, when you buy coins, be certain that the grading standard matches the price guide standard. It won't help you to buy an INSAB coin graded Proof-65 at a *Greysheet* price of $5,000, if the coin is really a Proof-64 according to *Greysheet* standards.

Another FTC case is *Federal Trade Commission* v. *Rare Coin Galleries of America, Inc., Rare Coin Galleries of Florida, Inc., Richard G. Kayne, and Edward B. Kalp.* This case was also settled out of court, with the principals surrendering just about all of their assets to the government for consumer redress.

A representative sampling of Rare Coin Galleries of America, Inc. (RCGA) coins is the purchase made by Wilbur Deck, an agent for *The Coin Dealer Newsletter*. RCGA apparently represented that its coins could be priced according to *The Coin Dealer Newsletter* and made numerous copies of the newsletter, which it distributed to clients.

The following chart shows how ANA's ANACS graded the coins and how the company apparently graded them:

COINS SOLD FOR $1,248 VALUED AT $75

Coin	RCGA grade	Old ANACS grade
1941 50¢	MS-65	AU-50/50
1942 50¢	MS-65	AU-50/50
1943 50¢	MS-65	EF-45/45

Total Price paid: $1,248.00

Approximate Value at Time of Purchase: $75.00

It doesn't matter which of the major grading services grades your coins if gross misrepresentation is involved. If you buy a coin as MS-67, and INSAB grades it EF-45, you can safely assume that you purchased an overgraded coin.

For an important historic sampling of press releases issued by the Federal Trade Commission that relate to the coin field, please see Appendix D. For those not familiar with the coin field's business history, a perusal of this list will turn up some surprises.

Premium-Quality Coins

The concept of sight-unseen coin trading has forced us to reconsider exactly what it is we're buying. If you're buying a certified product and don't mind paying a premium for a certificate, you should look for the coin certified at the lowest price. Dealer Philip Schuyler sums it up:

> There are two kinds of PCGS coins: generic quality and premium quality. Generic quality refers to coins that fall into the lower half of a grade category. They may be unsightly, darkly toned, spotty, or simply barely-made-the-grade coins. Since no grading service is perfect, a small number may even be mildly overgraded . . . Premium-quality coins are coins at the high end of the grade. Most are pieces that may have just missed the next grade up. Premium-quality pieces usually exhibit a superior strike, better luster, fewer abrasions, and better overall eye appeal than generic-quality pieces. Also, premium-quality coins cost more.

If you're a collector and don't like that S-mint dollar PCGS graded MS-65 and want to offer your dealer half of the price-guide price for it, go elsewhere. Your dealer can sell it to a market-maker sight-unseen, with no return privilege, at the market-maker's bid. These bids happen to be low, as Schuyler explains:

> Published dealer bid prices for PCGS-graded . . . coins are based on the sight-unseen bid prices of the PCGS market-makers. The market-makers . . . are committed to buy ANY sample that they have a bid for, no matter what the particular coin looks like. Black-toned, horribly spotted . . . it's immaterial. . . . Every . . . market-maker is in the same situation, so . . . all sight-unseen bids are low. Unfortunately, these bids are being published by the major price guides. And what few of the people reading those price guides realize is that they are seeing published bids for bottom-of-the-barrel coins. Since dealers must make at least 10%-15% on coins to stay in business, investors must pay at least [this same percentage range] over published bid levels FOR GENERIC-QUALITY COINS. . . . The notion that a black-toned, weakly struck coin that grades MS-64 is worth the same as a beautiful, blazing, borderline gem that also grades MS-64 is unreasonable.

If you came across a magnificent PCGS or NGC MS-65 in the 1980s, it would have cost you 20% to 40% over published bid levels. But in 1994, when the third edition of this book was being written, the premium on these coins in the $500 to $1,000 price range was nominal—in some cases $20 to $40. It appears that this premium cost factor fluctuates with market conditions. Also, a number of premium-quality coins, for which you may have paid the 20% to 40% premium, qualify today for a grading-service upgrade. NGC and PCGS graded very strictly during their early months of operation, and there is much talk about "gradeflation" at the heavy volume services in 2005.

Most important of all, don't buy a coin just because it's certified by PCGS or NGC. Buy the coin for what it is. The certified grade assists you in determining value. Many players, however, now feel that the slab services are not going to be around forever. Dealer Andrew Lustig says, "A system that values a 64 coin in a 66 slab at more than it values a 65 coin in a 65 slab is unsustainable." And Maurice Rosen bravely states, "The formerly unthinkable dissolution of a major grading service now enters the realm of possibility, with all the ugly consequences that would follow."

A number of dealers find it easier to sell PCGS premium-quality coins out of the holder and at that dealer's personal grade, rather than at the PCGS grade. Says William P. Paul of American Heritage Minting, "I know premium-quality PCGS coins exist. I break them out of the holders all the time!"

Philip Schuyler reiterates the importance of buying the coin for what it is:

> "MS-65" today does not mean what "MS-65" meant five years ago. And in five more years it could mean something else altogether. That is why wise [coin buyers] do not buy coins as certified products; they buy coins as raw coins that happen to be accompanied by certification. With a premium-quality piece, you have a rare coin investment. With a generic-quality piece, you have an investment in a certified product. . . . Grading services have yet to prove their longevity; rare coin investments have decades of strong appreciation behind them.

A Double Dividend from Premium Quality

Earlier in this chapter, I wrote about Peter Thompson, the investor whose losses were significantly reduced because the certified coins he purchased in the late 1980s were graded more conservatively than their counterparts ten years later. In some cases, Thompson actually received a double dividend: In addition to benefiting from the tighter grading standards of that earlier period, he also reaped a reward because a number of coins in his portfolio were premium-quality pieces. Those coins held their value far better than their standard-quality cousins. Indeed, some PQ coins are worth even more today than they were in the weeks leading up to the coin market crash of May 1989.

I have witnessed this phenomenon with some of my own clients. Back in the late 1980s, I strongly encouraged my clients to purchase PQ coins, even though these coins then commanded large bonus premiums. On occasion, they had to pay several times as much for these coins as the going market prices for ordinary coins of the same type and grade.

A decade later, some of those clients were thankful they had followed my advice. Under my supervision and assistance, three of them sold their coins in auctions conducted in late 1998—and because of their exceptional quality, many of the coins brought exceptional prices. This happened not just occasionally, but with dozens of coins; in fact, it was the rule, rather than the exception.

One of my favorite examples was the 1875-S Trade dollar, which had been graded Mint State-66 a decade earlier by NGC. The *Bluesheet* sight-unseen bid in the fall

GRADING SURVEY RESULTS

Coin	Date	Denomination	AU 59	MS 60	MS 61	MS 62	MS 63	MS 64	MS 65	MS 66	MS 67	Median	Mean
1	1852	cent	0	2	1	5	10	7	0	0	0	63	62.8
2	1887	cent	2	3	1	2	4	2	0	0	0	62	61.6
3	1865	3-cent Cu-Ni	3	1	8	7	5	2	0	0	0	62	61.6
4	1871	3-cent Cu-Ni	0	3	3	4	11	3	0	0	0	63	62.3
5	1858	half dime	1	1	1	6	9	6	0	0	0	63	62.6
6	1873	5-cent	1	0	3	4	14	3	0	0	0	63	62.6
7	1927	5-cent	0	2	0	2	14	7	0	0	0	63	63.0
8	1938-D	5-cent	0	0	0	2	1	18	5	0	0	64	64.0
9	1902	dime	3	5	5	8	1	0	0	0	0	61	61.0
10	1938-S	dime	0	0	0	0	6	14	5	0	0	64	64.0
11	1940-D	dime	0	0	0	1	2	11	5	3	0	64	64.3
12	1940-S	dime	0	0	0	1	3	15	6	0	0	64	64.0
13	1941	dime	0	1	0	1	11	9	0	0	0	63	63.2
14	1875-S	20-cent	0	1	2	5	16	1	0	0	0	63	62.6
15	1916-D	quarter dollar	2	5	5	0	0	0	0	0	0	60	60.3
16	1930-S	quarter dollar	0	0	0	0	15	9	1	0	0	63	63.4
17	1935-D	quarter dollar	20	1	3	1	1	0	0	0	0	59	59.5
18	1939	quarter dollar	0	0	0	0	4	18	4	0	0	64	64.0
19	1826	half dollar	1	0	0	7	13	5	0	0	0	63	62.8
20	1864	half dollar	0	3	6	9	4	0	0	0	0	62	61.6
21	1908	half dollar	0	1	2	9	8	1	0	0	0	62	62.3
22	1937	half dollar	1	0	1	8	7	2	0	0	0	62	62.4
23	1944	half dollar	0	2	1	0	10	8	4	0	0	63	63.3
24	1945-D	half dollar	7	2	2	8	7	0	0	0	0	62	61.2
25	1947-D	half dollar	0	0	0	2	6	7	1	0	0	63	63.4
26	1879-O	dollar	1	0	0	9	13	2	0	0	0	63	62.6
27	1880	dollar	0	0	0	0	16	9	0	0	0	63	63.4
28	1880-S	dollar	0	0	1	7	12	4	0	0	0	63	62.8
29	1881-S	dollar	0	0	0	6	16	4	0	0	0	63	62.9
30	1882-S	dollar	0	0	1	7	13	5	0	0	0	63	62.8
31	1883	dollar	0	0	1	0	17	8	0	0	0	63	63.2
32	1884-C	dollar	0	0	0	0	11	14	1	0	0	64	63.6
33	1889	dollar	0	0	0	4	12	5	0	0	0	63	63.0
34	1896	dollar	0	1	0	0	1	18	4	0	0	64	64.0
35	1897-S	dollar	0	0	0	0	14	11	1	0	0	63	63.5
36	1898-O	dollar	0	0	0	1	7	16	2	0	0	64	63.7
37	1921-S	dollar	0	1	0	5	16	4	0	0	0	63	62.8
38	1921	dollar	2	4	5	12	2	0	0	0	0	62	61.3
39	1922-D	dollar	1	3	2	3	14	3	0	0	0	63	62.3
40	1922-S	dollar	0	0	1	2	7	13	2	0	0	64	63.5

(Chart continued on next page.)

GRADING SURVEY RESULTS *(cont.)*

Coin	Date	Denomination	AU 59	MS 60	MS 61	MS 62	MS 63	MS 64	MS 65	MS 66	MS 67	Median	Mean
41	1924	dollar	0	0	1	3	15	4	0	0	0	63	63.0
42	1925-S	dollar	3	4	1	4	1	1	0	0	0	61	60.9
43	1893	Isabella	0	0	0	0	4	6	8	1	0	64	64.3
44	1936	Cleveland	0	0	0	4	11	11	0	0	0	63	63.3
45	1935	Connecticut	0	0	0	0	4	17	5	0	0	64	64.0
46	1938	Delaware	0	0	0	2	8	11	5	0	0	64	63.7
47	1936	Norfolk	0	0	0	0	0	3	9	12	2	66	65.5
48	1925	Vancouver	2	6	3	2	1	0	0	0	0	60	60.6
49	1905	Lewis/Clark	8	5	3	6	2	1	0	0	0	61	60.7
50	1917	McKinley	0	2	3	5	7	5	1	0	0	63	62.6
51	1926	Sesquicentennial	0	0	2	10	11	3	0	0	0	63	62.6
52	1915-S	Panama-Pacific	5	3	5	5	1	0	0	0	0	61	60.7
53	1851	gold dollar	10	9	2	3	0	0	0	0	0	60	59.9
54	1862	gold dollar	18	5	2	1	0	0	0	0	0	59	59.5
55	1879	gold dollar	0	0	0	0	3	19	4	0	0	64	64.0
56	1911	quarter eagle	1	5	8	6	5	1	0	0	0	61	61.5
57	1878	$3 gold	0	0	2	11	8	5	0	0	0	63	62.6
58	1885-S	half eagle	0	0	1	6	13	5	1	0	0	63	63.0
59	1889	half eagle	0	1	9	16	0	0	0	0	0	62	61.6
60	1903	half eagle	8	9	8	1	0	0	0	0	0	60	60.1
61	1908	half eagle	0	0	0	0	4	12	9	1	0	64	64.3
62	1904-O	eagle	6	15	5	0	0	0	0	0	0	60	60.0
63	1902-S	eagle	0	0	2	13	10	1	0	0	0	62	62.4
64	1932	eagle	3	4	6	12	1	0	0	0	0	61	61.2
65	1932	eagle	0	0	0	5	13	8	0	0	0	63	63.1
66	1895	double eagle	0	0	8	13	4	1	0	0	0	62	61.9
67	1904	double eagle	4	2	3	7	8	2	0	0	0	62	61.7
68	1907	double eagle	1	8	7	9	1	0	0	0	0	61	61.0
69	1908	double eagle	1	3	8	9	5	0	0	0	0	62	61.5
70	1915-S	double eagle	0	1	2	3	10	7	0	0	0	63	62.9
71	1924	double eagle	0	0	0	1	8	17	0	0	0	64	63.6
72	1925	double eagle	0	0	1	10	7	3	0	0	0	62	62.6
73	1926	double eagle	3	4	6	9	2	0	0	0	0	61	61.1
74	1927	double eagle	0	0	0	0	6	19	1	0	0	64	63.8
75	1928	double eagle	6	10	9	1	0	0	0	0	0	60	60.2

Results of Heritage's grading survey of 26 professional numismatists. The columns at left identify the coin. The columns at center record the number of graders assigning a specific grade. The median is the midpoint; the mean is the average. *Chart courtesy Heritage* of 1998 for an MS-66 coin of this type, year, mint, and grade with NGC certification was $10,000. If that coin were perceived to be full MS-67, its *Bluesheet* bid would have been about $30,000. But it ended up realizing even more than that: an eye-popping $46,000.

Grading by Consensus

PCGS introduced the concept of grading by consensus. Coin grading is the result of consensus of subjective opinions, which in the end makes it somewhat objective. If a coin is shown to five leading dealers, and four grade it MS-65 and the other grades it MS-64, it probably is an MS-65 (depending on the standards they're using).

But if you show the same five dealers another coin and four grade it MS-63 and the other grader calls it AU-58, who's right? Did the four dealers assigning the MS-63 grade miss some light wear that would cause a downgrading to AU-58? Grading is still subjective, and there's no real answer to that question.

A Grade Survey

Heritage Rare Coin Galleries conducted a grading consensus study. Twenty-six professional coin dealers were asked to grade 75 different coins. These results deserve your close attention and will show you just how the coin market operates. These 26 dealers make their money from their eyes: their ability to spot great coins at great prices. But some of these dealers were clearly off the mark on some of the coins. The dealer who grades the coin highest stands a good chance of buying it.

A Case for No Industry Standard

One important legal case, *Federal Trade Commission* v. *Security Rare Coin & Bullion Corp., et al.,* explored the question of whether the coin industry does, in fact, have a single recognized grading standard. David L. Ganz, a lawyer who specializes in numismatic matters, served as one of the lawyers for the defense. In a declaration filed with the court, Ganz stated the following, in his capacity as an expert consultant:

> There is no single accepted definition of grading terms or grading standards. Moreover, even within any one particular grading system, the inherent vagueness of grading standards leaves great room for subjectivity and disagreement. . . . As a result of these difficult and varied grading standards, numerous organizations have grown up whose purpose is to grade coins for a fee. . . . Given the number of organizations that perform grading, it is simply nonsensical to speak of a "market standard" or any "single standard" within the coin industry. There are numerous, often inconsistent, standards for grading coins. . . . In my experience, disagreement among experts concerning a coin's grade is in fact far more common than agreement. Such disagreements often involve many hundreds or even thousands of dollars. . . . Standards are guidelines only and there is no broad-

> based consensus about what precisely the grades represent. . . . It would be unreasonable to contend that there is a homogeneous marketplace for coins where prices are universally set. . . .

How Grading Services Determine Grade

Dealer James L. Halperin, author of *How to Grade U.S. Coins* (Ivy Press, 1986, 1990), presented in that book a series of color coin maps which illustrate coins' grade-sensitive areas. Halperin also engineered a formula designed to help you figure out the thought processes of NGC and PCGS. Halperin's formula, with accompanying text and notes, follow—updated by him for *The Coin Collector's Survival Manual, Fifth Edition*.

NGC and PCGS

In order to determine the grade of a coin using NGC or PCGS standards, use the following formula:

Note: *This formula was originally used for NCI.*

OBVERSE

Surface Preservation(1-5)	________x2	=	________
	Strike (1-5)	=	________
	Luster (1-5)	=	________
	Eye-appeal (1-5)	=	________
OBVERSE TOTAL:			________

REVERSE

Surface Preservation (1-5)	________x2	=	________
	Strike (1-5)	=	________
	Luster (1-5)	=	________
	Eye-appeal (1-5)	=	________

Now we relate these to grade:
5 to 10.49 = 60
10.5 to 12.49 = 61
12.5 to 13.99 = 62
14 to 16.99 = 63
17 to 18.99 = 64
19 to 20.99 = 65
21 to 22.49 = 66
22.5 to 25 = 67

Generally, the obverse of a coin is more important than the reverse. The consensus today is that the value of a coin is determined approximately 70/30, obverse to reverse. In other words, the obverse is about 2⅓ times more important than the reverse. Practically the only exception occurs in the case of certain commemorative coins and patterns. In these cases, it is somewhat ambiguous which side is the obverse. Both sides are of approximately equal importance in these instances.

Thus, it is considered permissible to upgrade the reverse a bit if the obverse is toward the upper end of the scale of its grade. For example, a coin with a 20 obverse and an 18.5 reverse could still be graded MS-65 in the commercial marketplace. However, a coin with an 18.5 obverse and a 20 reverse (a far more common occurrence) must still receive a technical grade of MS-64/65—or net graded MS-64.

How to Protect Yourself When You Buy Coins Certified by Leading Services

- **Be certain the holder has not been tampered with.** Check the seams and the sides. If there are any unusual cracks or openings, don't buy the coin. If you've purchased a coin you think might have been tampered with, contact the service immediately. PCGS has indicated that it will prosecute anyone it catches tampering with its holders in order to deceive the public.
- **Beware of scratches on the holder.** Someone has apparently thought of putting scratches on the indented portion of the PCGS holder where the coin is visible. This makes it more difficult to see the coin's imperfections. I've seen this technique employed on coins that grade PR-64 and PR-63 which would ordinarily have qualified for a higher grade but received lower due to some small imperfection—which the scratches on the holder may mask quite well.
- **When you pay a high price for a premium-quality coin, be certain that the coin you're buying is indeed a premium quality coin.** The demand by investors for PQ coins has caused many sellers' certified coins to have two levels: "random" or "average" quality and "PQ" quality. The difference in price can be dramatic. If the coin is a Proof, check for a cameo contrast between the fields and the devices. If the coin is a Morgan or Peace dollar graded MS-65, check the hair above the ear and confirm that the cheek is free from imperfections.
- **Remember, you're buying the coin, not just a commodity with a grade.** No matter what any certification service says, if a coin has major gouges and other imperfections, it can't be assigned a high Mint State grade. Use your common sense. Any grading service can make a mistake.
- **If your coin purchases are for trading, you should buy only coins graded by grading services listed in the *Certified Coin Dealer Newsletter.*** Even though some other coins might be graded correctly by an unknown service, use only the services listed in the *CCDN*. Otherwise, your investment's liquidity could be jeopardized.
- **Before sale, have your coins examined by a trusted expert who does a high volume in certified coins—or become an expert yourself.** In case of any recent subtle shift in standards, you will be assured of getting good value and will know if it would be wise to submit some or all of your coins for regrading.

Bands on the fasces of this Mercury dime were carefully re-engraved by a coin doctor. Exceptionally skilled, world-class grading services such as PCGS identify these alterations to help protect consumers. *Photograph courtesy Professional Coin Grading Service*

Coins with Photocertificates

- **Make sure the coin pictured on the certificate is the one you're buying.** As ridiculous as it may sound, some people have accidentally purchased coins with NCI certificates, only to find later that the coin they bought was not the one pictured. Carefully compare the photograph with the coin before you buy.
- **Be certain the coin is as well preserved as it was when examined.** Be especially cautious if the certificate is many years old—if the certificate is dated. Coins deteriorate, are mishandled, and are subjected to contaminants. Just because the certificate says "MS-65/65" does not mean the coin is still in that grade. Dealers dip coins, clean coins, and artificially retone them.

Doctored Coins and Certification

- **Don't assume that just because a coin is certified, it means that it has not been doctored.** Highly deceptive coins have slipped through the best services and into holders. Use fluorescent black light to help highlight doctored surfaces.
- **Familiarize yourself with the statistics.** PCGS founder David Hall estimates that up to 50 percent of all raw coins sold at auction have been doctored (excluding old-time collections). He believes that at least 10 percent to 20 percent of all coins submitted to grading services are doctored in some way. These numbers, if accurate, are startling.
- **Don't be critical of grading services for refusing to certify your coin because they believe it to be doctored.** Grading services have every reason to be cautious if it is true that up to 20 percent of coins submitted are doctored. Armen R. Vartian, a preeminent numismatic lawyer who represents PCGS, says: "A doctored coin in a PCGS or NGC holder is backed by those services' guarantees. If the services permit doctored coins to be certified, collectors and investors will buy such coins confidently for full market value, and handsome profits will encourage more doctoring. Moreover, the belief that

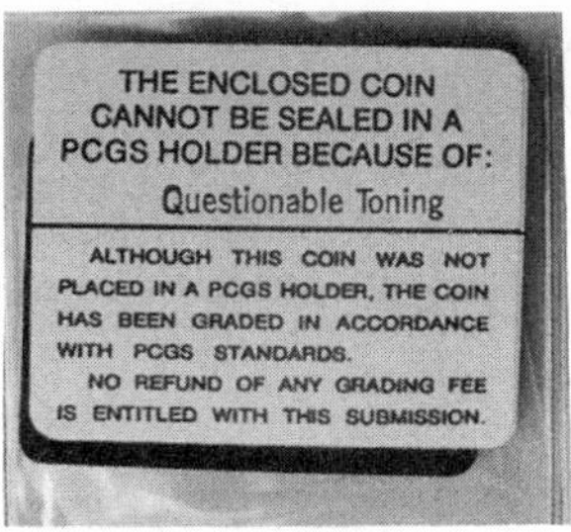
THE ENCLOSED COIN CANNOT BE SEALED IN A PCGS HOLDER BECAUSE OF:
Questionable Toning
ALTHOUGH THIS COIN WAS NOT PLACED IN A PCGS HOLDER, THE COIN HAS BEEN GRADED IN ACCORDANCE WITH PCGS STANDARDS.
NO REFUND OF ANY GRADING FEE IS ENTITLED WITH THIS SUBMISSION.

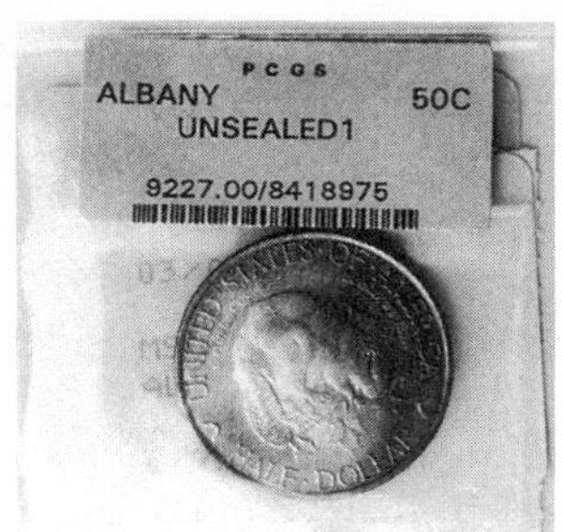

Coin returned as a "no grade" because of questionable toning. Coins returned ungraded by NGC and PCGS are sent back in a "body bag." These two services charge the same fee to "no-grade" a coin as they would to certify and encapsulate it. *Photograph courtesy Professional Coin Grading Service*

doctored coins were not scrutinized by the grading services would depress prices for all coins. . . ."

- **If you submit a coin for certification which you are certain isn't doctored, but it is returned to you by a grading service as having "altered surfaces" or "questionable toning," let the grading service know.** The grading services are fair and will listen to any facts you wish to share about why your coin is original. "What coin doctors do is make graders at grading services paranoid about doctoring," Hall observes. "Some original coins are being graded too low because there's such a worry about doctoring."
- **Use high-power magnification and a halogen lamp to carefully inspect high-priced coins.** Don't let the magnification of run-of-the-mill minor imperfections affect your grading judgment. But do let your determination of a coin having been doctored be influenced by what you see under the glass.
- **If a high-priced coin appears to have anything added to its surface, don't buy it.** Even if you like the coin and factor any potential doctoring into the price, the chemicals used for doctoring often remain active and continue to react with the coin. Carefully read the sections concerning doctoring and artificial toning.

Bombshell Interview:

A Candid Look at Coin Doctors

Far from healing the coin market's ills, as their name might suggest to some, coin doctors pose a grave and fundamental risk to the health of the hobby and also to the financial well-being of those who become unwitting victims of their "medicine." Even with all the sophisticated diagnostic equipment at their disposal, and the know-how and instincts their grading experts possess, the certification services fall prey all too often to cleverly modified coins which these "doctors" have treated in various ways. The objective of coin doctors is always the same: to make these coins appear to be more valuable than they really are by masking their deficiencies. When they succeed, they profit at the expense of unwary buyers and, when their wares elude detection, at the expense of the certification services, whose guarantees oblige them to buy back items which they overgrade or improperly authenticate.

In the interest of self-preservation, coin dealers strive to learn as much as they can about the shadowy methods employed by these malpracticing "doctors." Knowingly or otherwise, some dealers buy and sell doctored coins. At a coin show in late 1999, I interviewed a major dealer with extensive inside knowledge of coin doctors and their procedures. For obvious reasons, the dealer does not wish to be identified—and, as a precondition of the highly candid interview, I agreed not to name him in this book. Here is that interview:

TRAVERS: What are some of the successes you've had in changing the appearance of coins, even if it's just dipping a coin?

DEALER: Well, sometimes if a coin tones unevenly, you can't really tell how nice the surfaces are. Just on a hunch, many times I've looked at the surfaces and decided there was nothing really wrong with them—the toning is just unsightly or uneven. I've dipped coins that were in 64 holders and had them go 66—sometimes had them go 67. But that's the exception and not the rule.

TRAVERS: What kind of profit was involved, going from a 4 to a 7?

DEALER: Many times, I've doubled or tripled my money. But you know, on the flip side, I've also lost half my money on occasion. It's pretty much a gamble, and I just feel that I'm enough of an insider that the odds are slightly in my favor. The truth is, while your readers may want to fool with coins, it's a long, hard road. I mean, I've been fooling with coins for many years and I usually land on my feet. My pluses are greater than my [losses]. But it's not a real good deal to fool with coins—not unless you can develop some type of technology that nobody else has.

TRAVERS: What percentage of coins in holders, would you say, were doctored?

DEALER: Well, copper coins, probably 90 percent. Silver and gold coins, a much, much lower percentage. Most copper coins—when I send original copper coins to grading services, they usually no-grade because the services don't know what the [heck] they're doing there.

TRAVERS: What types of processes are used on copper coins?

DEALER: Many copper coins were cyanided many, many years ago to remove any toning or darkening. Now, when that's done to a coin, the coin does look somewhat unnatural. But if a coin is cyanided and it's left alone for 20 or 30 years, sometimes they color up just the nicest, sweetest shades of copper—because after they tone, they become just really even and gold, and actually those kinds of coins, even though they're not original, people think they're original. I know they're not original; I'm still willing to buy them because they're the most attractive copper you can get. Original copper is not the most attractive copper you can get.

TRAVERS: What modern things are done today in the doctoring of copper coinage?

DEALER: Well, I don't know exactly what people do, but I know there are certain people who remove spots . . . there are certain people who take brown coins and try to make them red-brown, and they're often successful . . . and there's other people that are taking coins that are just shaded a little bit toward red-brown and turning them full red. A lot of the red copper in holders is just so grossly unnatural that I'm surprised these guys are grading it.

TRAVERS: What kinds of upgrades have you seen in copper coins?

DEALER: I've frequently seen coins go from 65 Red Brown to 65 Red. It's really hard to doctor them into a higher grade because of the technical surface problems, but doctoring from Red Brown to Red is going on all the time. And the tragic thing is that when I send in totally original stuff, they don't understand it anymore. They're seeing so much doctored [garbage] that they forgot what original really is.

TRAVERS: The people who are doctors—what do they do? Do they charge for their services to dealers? Do they say, "I'll charge you an hourly fee and turn this from Red Brown to Red?" How does it work?

DEALER: The people that are good, they want half the profits. And the people that aren't so good, they might do it for a fee. But you know, you get what you pay for. The really smart ones, actually, just do it for themselves because there'd be no reason to spread around their technology or to have word get out. So the real shrewd ones, they just do their own stuff. But most of the people who "make" coins [get coins certified] that have big copper inventories are doctors or very close to doctors.

TRAVERS: How about silver coins?

DEALER: Silver coins—there's a lot of people who doctor them. But the smart people—I mean right now, there's a war on toned coins. So what's happening is, people are dipping nice, original coins. The owner of NGC recently came out with this article about the joys and the desirability of toned coins—which is very unusual, because he is exactly the person who's causing myself and others to dip all the coins, because they're so paranoid that the coin's going to come in for questioning, requesting a bath, that they're downgrading anything toned. So with one hand he's writing about the joys of toned coins; on the other hand, he's killing anybody who actually has to lay out their own money to buy a toned coin.

TRAVERS: What are people doing to silver coins to upgrade them? What are some of the processes used?

DEALER: Some guys are adding putty. Some guys are adding smoke. It's funny because certain guys, all their coins look alike. They're uniformly dark or they're uniformly bright. There are still a few guys dealing original coins, but trends change. Right now, white coins are more desirable than toned coins.

TRAVERS: Do people who are doctors for silver coins make the same arrangements with people as the ones who doctor copper coins? Do they split the profits?

DEALER: Yes, pretty much. And the people that have really good processes, they don't do it for other people. And there's people who work on all the different metals. I mean, the gold doctors are extremely prevalent.

TRAVERS: What processes are used on gold?

DEALER: The worst of gold is the rare-date gold market in circulated conditions, because when they first started grading this stuff—you know, if a coin had wear and had a little bit of luster, it was VF. Now, anything with luster is in an AU holder. Also, [a grading service] started liking this type of gold that's dirty—so what happened was, several coin dealers, [apparently] one [in particular], they're making this gold like smoky dark to simulate originality. But that's after it's been cleaned and brightened up. And it's working. I mean, [one service] is putting tons of this rare-date gold on the market and the price levels were established when the [material] was really rare—and at the original grade levels that the services did. And now, the typical rare-date gold coin that's been graded in the last two years has gone from 30 to 50, or 30 to 45. And in many cases, I've seen coins go from 45 into 60 holders.

TRAVERS: Is there any hope at all for the reader of my book, the consumer out there, to be able to identify the difference between a doctored coin and its original counterpart?

DEALER: It's difficult, and it's not necessarily always necessary. One should try to buy coins that are very eye-appealing. If you buy a coin you like, you're going to be able to sell it to somebody who likes coins. The readers of your book have to become knowledgeable; they have to look at a lot of coins. They have to go to coin shows, they have to interview people. It's a lot of legwork. Nobody who just wants to sit in their home and not go out and meet people and look at coins and learn should ever buy coins. On the other hand, if you're willing to do the legwork and do all the homework, you can learn a great deal and actually become more knowledgeable than the typical dealer in one particular series. The thing is, your readers should pick one series and learn it really well, because that's within the average person's grasp. If they try to learn everything, they'll never be able to outdo a dealer who does this full time. But you can learn silver dollars better than the typical dealer, you can go and learn Buffalo nickels better than the dealer—and if you're willing to just focus in on one area, you can become knowledgeable. And coins can be a really good place to put your money, as long as you buy solid value and buy eye-appealing coins that are always going to be eye-appealing.

TRAVERS: Talking about coins that aren't eye-appealing, what are a couple of the most heinously overgraded or doctored coins that actually made their way into holders—that never should have done so in a million years? You don't have to be specific as to the coin; you can just be generic and say, "A gold coin, and it was worth $2,000 as a 3 and $50,000 as a 5, and it got put in a 6 holder because it was smoked." Something like that.

DEALER: I know of many specific coins. I'd rather not mention them here. I know that things like that have happened, but that's the exception. Generally, people doctor coins to make them go up one grade—one point. The services are often mixed up and misguided, but they tend not to put $3,000 coins in $100,000 holders. The services are grading scared; they're grading liability. They might take a $40 coin and put it into a $300 holder because coins of that value, they just look at and grade and go on. They don't spend a lot of time thinking about it. They do spend quite a bit of time thinking about it before they put a $100,000 coin in a holder. You know, they tend to be risk-averse. The thing is, if a coin just barely misses like the 65 grade, somebody might do something very subtle to it just to push it over the hump. The best coin doctors are using subtlety. They're not using boiling Clorox and a flame-thrower to upgrade their coins because, you know, it's just going to [mess] them up.

TRAVERS: What are a few processes some of my readers can experiment with to see what a doctored coin looks like? You talked about Clorox and flames. What are some things people can get some interesting results from—a few recipes?

DEALER: There are some people who tone with iodine. I personally think that it makes coins ugly.

TRAVERS: Silver coins?

DEALER: Yeah. There are some people that use potash. I've never experimented with such a substance, but people are using Clorox, people are using smoke, people are using—personally, all I really do to coins is to try to clean them and brighten them, because white is selling right now. And when I dip a coin, I wash it off very, very carefully because I don't want any coin that I ever sell to change in the holder and have it come back and have somebody say something bad to me.

TRAVERS: Have you ever been stuck yourself with a doctored coin? You thought it was original, you looked at it over and over again and it was doctored.

DEALER: Many times. But I buy and sell a lot of coins. Sometimes I don't really find out unless I try to [doctor] a coin. Let's say I take a coin and think I can make it better by dipping off whatever gook is on the coin. I dip off the gook, only to reveal a comedy of horrors. And then I realize that I had been experimenting with a doctored coin. See, if I fool with a coin that's—not necessarily original, but a coin that hasn't been done by modern experts, I'll probably have good results. I'll probably be able to make the coin more attractive and more salable. If I [mess] with a coin that's been done, say, by one of the modern state-of-the-art doctors, I'm just going to make the coin worse and lose my original investment, or part of it.

TRAVERS: Based on your experience, and knowing some of the people who are doctors, what kind of people are doctors? Is there any psychological profile?

DEALER: The same kind of cross-section—the coin business is made up of the same cross-section you would find in any other part of society, in any other profession. There are coin doctors that are wearing suits and seem to have their act together. There are coin doctors that look like they just crawled out of a sewer hole. There is no profile. Coin doctors are probably a little bit more of gamblers. Some people, their interest in the coin business is to buy everything in the world and make 5 percent on it. Coin doctors are more the type that will triple up on one coin and lose half their money on the next—the same kind of people that might spend time in a casino or might be day traders.

TRAVERS: What type of alteration would you say is the easiest to detect in a holder?

DEALER: Coins that change after they're holdered. I mean, the guys that are at the grading services, while I frequently disagree with their opinions, they see plenty of coins. Anything that looks grossly artificial, they're going to body-bag it. What's dangerous is, when coins turn. Certain coin doctors do things to coins that make them keep reacting, despite the fact that there's very little air flow inside a holder. But there is some air in there, and therefore the reacting will continue in certain chemical processes. And the services have no defense against that, because if a coin changes after it's in their holder, they're [in trouble].

TRAVERS: What happens financially with the arrangements made between a coin doctor and a coin buyer if there's supposed to be a profit split and the coin doctor ruins the coin? Say you have a coin worth $20,000.

DEALER: The pre-arrangement is separate. One gets not what they deserve; one gets what they negotiate. And that's true of a retail coin buyer and his dealer; that's true of an arrangement made between a coin owner and a coin doctor; that's true of every arrangement made in life. You don't get what you deserve, you get what you negotiate.

TRAVERS: Are these arrangements in writing and contractual?

DEALER: Generally not. I mean, I've done deals for hundreds of thousands of dollars on a handshake. Most people—if they give their word, it's their word. I don't need any contract. Anybody who I would need a contract for them, they're not a person I want to do business with anyway.

TRAVERS: But what happens if a coin worth $20,000 is now worth $3,000 because the doctor ruined it? Who does what normally?

DEALER: I mean, if I give my coin to a coin doctor, I want him to at least cover half of the loss—unless I have so much faith in this guy that I'm willing to make an unsatisfactory arrangement. It happens only rarely. It could happen with copper coins, but with silver-silver and gold coins are far more resilient, and anything you can do you can usually undo.

TRAVERS: What else do you think consumers should know about doctoring?

DEALER: I think you should be doing business with somebody you trust. I think many doctors will not—I may have doctored a few coins in my life, but I'll never misrepresent the coin. If somebody asks me if a coin is doctored, I'll tell them, because I'm an honest dealer.

TRAVERS: And if they don't ask you?

DEALER: If a pure collector doesn't ask me, I'll still volunteer the information. With collectors, I'll try to guide them to what's in their best interest.

TRAVERS: How about a dealer?

DEALER: A dealer? Well, you know, they're supposed to know what . . . they're doing. With dealers, I feel, "Caveat emptor."

– 6 –

BEAUTY AND THE BEST—AUTHENTICATING PROOFS

> These days even the neophyte with only the briefest acquaintance with American coins as collectors' items will sooner or later encounter proof coins, whether as offered to the general public by the San Francisco Mint, or as offered to collectors by coin dealers. And sooner or later . . . you will come across borderline cases, claims of extreme rarity, proofs not listed in the usual reference books, coins which present frank puzzles. . . . And though there is no way to become expert overnight in even so well explored a field as United States numismatics, there is a way to raise your own level of knowledge from that of neophyte and swindlers' mark to—at least—informed amateur.
>
> —Walter Breen (1930–1993)
> *Walter Breen's Encyclopedia of U.S. and Colonial Proof Coins*

The silver quarter-dollar labeled "Proof" glistened and glimmered in the dealer's showcase. It was spectacular, as its devices appeared ivory white and its fields seemed like an antique mirror, complete with a light, even cloud of russet as testimony to its age. That coin was awesome in every respect and the epitome of originality. The cameo contrast between the fields and devices would convince almost any prospective buyer that the coin was unquestionably a Proof. But it wasn't a Proof; it was a Prooflike business strike.

Many people, including experts and leading grading services, often cannot tell whether a coin is a Proof or a business strike, a coin manufactured for everyday use. The coin just described has some characteristics of a Brilliant Proof. (Many people have just as much trouble differentiating Matte Proofs from coins which look like Matte Proofs—Proofs struck from sand-blasted dies which exhibit the same incredible detail but are granular instead of brilliant in appearance.)

A good deal of this confusion can be blamed on the Mint. During the late 1800s and early 1900s, the Mint would collect money from collectors who wanted to order Proof coins. The number of people ordering usually wouldn't exceed a couple of thousand during any given year. After the Mint made the special Proof dies and struck the few coins needed to

Proof Liberty Seated quarter, obverse and reverse. Deep chromium Proof surfaces and a spectacular contrast between the fields and devices on this Gem piece make this a no-question Brilliant Proof.

Mint State business-strike Liberty Seated quarter, obverse and reverse. This coin possesses the slightly weakly struck right-side stars characteristic of a business strike.

fill the orders, sometimes the Proof dies were saved to strike coins for circulation! A Proof coin is struck twice, a business strike once. Some coins were made for circulation with the same dies used to strike the Proofs; and the only difference between a Proof and a business strike struck from Proof dies is that the business strike is struck once by the dies, and the Proof is struck twice by the dies. It almost goes without saying that some of the earliest coins made to spend from those Proof dies look just like Proof coins.

An outstanding work, *Walter Breen's Encyclopedia of U.S. and Colonial Proof Coins* by the late Walter Breen, gives the characteristics of most early Proof dies that were made. However, useful though this book is in identifying Proof dies, if the Proof dies were used

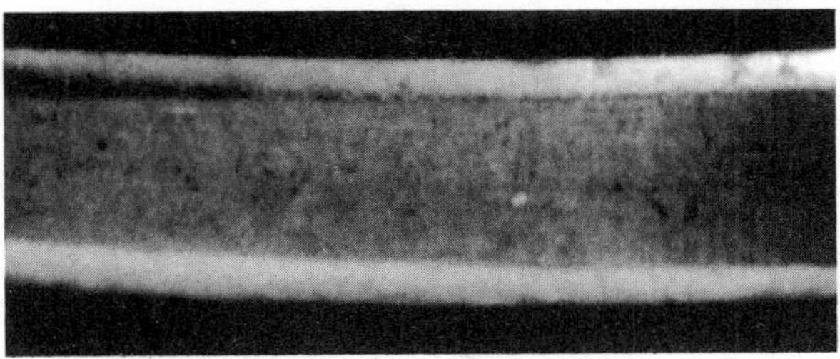

Business-strike edge. There is a prominent rounding. *Photograph courtesy Bill Fivaz*

to strike coins for circulation, you really cannot determine whether a coin is a Proof or simply Prooflike unless you know how many times that coin was struck: once or twice.

The Mint has been known on occasion to highly polish dies for coins struck for general circulation. A coin struck from these highly polished dies might look like a Proof to someone without years of experience. In this area, the Breen book is indispensable. Breen clearly identifies business-strike dies. If a coin that looks like a Proof is struck from dies used to manufacture coins for circulation, then it isn't a Proof. Period.

Knowing whether a coin is a Proof or Prooflike is an area of infinite uncertainty. Beginners have no idea what a problem this is until they are no longer beginners and find out that a coin purchased as Proof is only a Prooflike and worth a mere fraction of what a real Proof would be worth. It can happen the other way around, too: Real Proofs are sometimes sold as business-strikes when the business-strike value is higher than the Proof value.

It's so difficult to tell Proof from Prooflike for some coins that I've prepared a chart to illustrate the problems that even experts have with some issues. If you were to take Prooflike coins which look like Proofs to the country's coin dealers, these are the results you might get.

Category	Percentage of Dealers Sure	Percentage Unsure
Easy	100	0
Moderate	85	15
Difficult	25	75
Most difficult	1	99

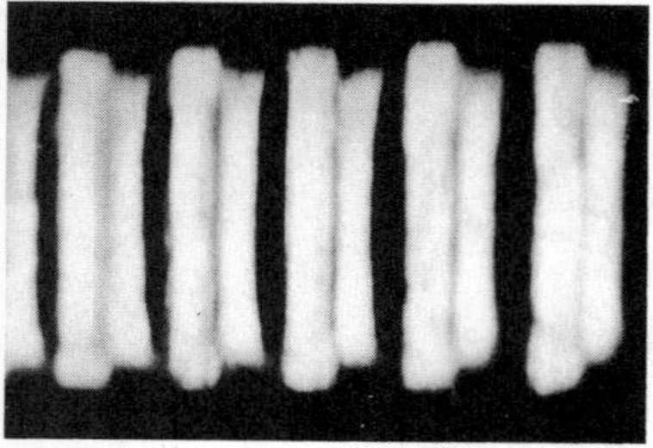

Proof coin reeding. *Photograph courtesy Bill Fivaz*

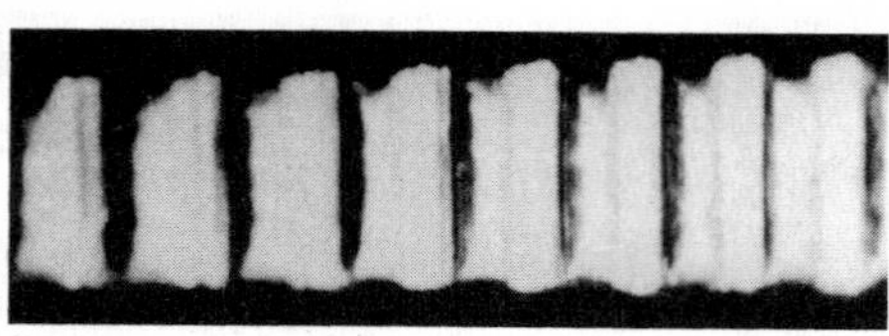

Business-strike reeding. *Photograph courtesy Bill Fivaz*

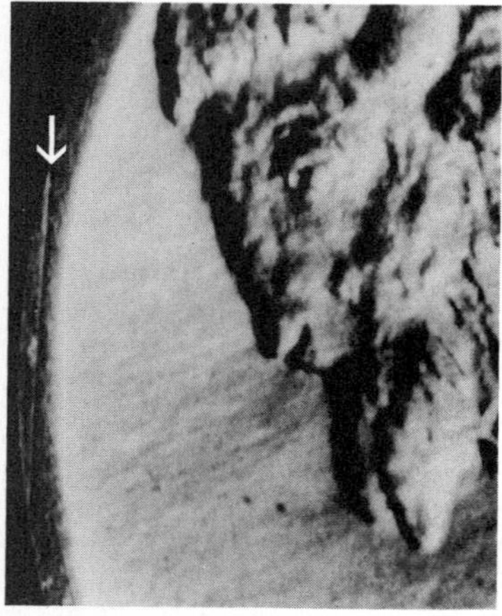

Matte Proof Buffalo nickel rim indentation. This is found on 1913 Type II, 1914, and 1915 nickels, as well as a limited number of business strikes on which the reverse die was used. *Photograph courtesy Bill Fivaz*

Matte Proof Buffalo nickel edge and rim. There is little rounding at the edge. *Photograph courtesy Bill Fivaz*

How to Tell Proof from Prooflike

Examine the overall appearance. Make sure the alleged Proof is well defined and well struck in every detail. If it isn't, it may not be a Proof. Proofs are struck twice, and they should exhibit far more detail than their non-Proof counterparts. Look at the breadth of detail on the Proof quarter shown. Compare it to the Mint State business strike displayed. The Proof is chromium-like, with spectacular definition of detail. The business strike is not as defined, not chromium-like, and exhibits no contrast between its fields and devices. The same rule applies to Matte Proofs, although they will not exhibit reflectivity, but a uniform graininess instead.

- **Check the edge.** The edge is the part your fingers touch when you hold the coin. On Proofs, the edge usually appears perfectly reflective. On non-Proofs, the edge has what look like many little parallel, vertical lines.
- **Check the rims.** The rims are the rings on both sides which encircle the coin. On Proofs, the rims usually are sharp, squared off, "knife-edge," or well defined. On business strikes, the rims are often dull, rounded-off, and poorly defined.
- **Check the reeding on reeded coins.** "Reeding" refers to vertical raised and indented lines on a coin's edge which have been manufactured there by the Mint. On Proofs, the reeding is razor sharp and extends the height of the edge. On business strikes, the reeding extends only to the areas where the rims slope.
- **Examine the depth of the reflectivity for Brilliant Proofs.** The term reflectivity refers to the depth of the mirrored surfaces. Always examine both sides to be certain a coin is a Proof. If a coin has every characteristic of being a Proof on one side and none on the other side, it isn't a Proof. If a coin has "patches" of Mint luster which interrupt highly reflective surfaces, it isn't a Proof. Is the reflectivity deep and chromium-like with breathtaking depth or does it appear fragile and not very deep? Brilliant Proofs have deep reflective surfaces. Prooflikes have surfaces that possess less depth of reflectivity.
- **Look at small details.** Make sure the surfaces are reflective inside every small unfrosted area. Check around stars and letters. Does that same mirror surface extend to inside that shield or within details of each star? If it doesn't, the coin may not be a Brilliant Proof. Also, are there striations (lines created during the manufacturing process) throughout the coin? Striations might indicate that the coin is a business strike.
- **Become suspicious if the coin possesses many detracting marks.** Proof coins were made for collectors on specially selected planchets and were handled very carefully. Non-Proofs went into circulation. Therefore, the non-Proofs are far more likely to have scratches and gouges than the Proofs are. Proofs are often mishandled, but only infrequently have the same kinds of huge marks and detractions as coins made for circulation.
- **Check for evidence of double striking.** The dies come down twice on the planchet that is to become a Proof coin. Many Proofs exhibit a slight doubling of parts of the design, especially stars, as a result of this double striking. The doubling looks like a slight shadow and is visible only under a microscope.

The Most Difficult Coins to Confirm Proof Status of

Business-strike Buffalo nickels which look like Matte Proofs are among the most difficult to tell from the real thing. One clever trick is to know about the characteristic line across the rim. This line is found on every Matte Proof of 1914 and 1915, as well as on every 1913 Type II. However, some business strikes were struck using this reverse die. A real Matte Proof, though, possesses the characteristic Matte Proof edge, with very little slope or bevel.

Proof Trade dollar, obverse and reverse.

Prooflike Trade dollar, obverse and reverse.

Look at the two attractive Trade dollars shown. The 1880 specimen is a delightfully toned Proof, complete with a spectacular chromium-like appearance and a cameo contrast between the fields and the devices. Pay attention to the incredible detail and the tiny unfrosted areas of the eagle's feathers which do not display luster but, rather, possess that chromium-like Proof reflectivity. The 1876 is a Prooflike. It's a beautiful coin, but not a

Proof. Although it's difficult to see from the photograph, areas of the reflective fields are shallow in reflectivity. This Prooflike displays patches of luster in areas, instead of the mirror-like surfaces it's supposed to be exhibiting. Also, the rim is not fully squared off. If you were to look up the 1876 Trade dollar in Walter Breen's proof encyclopedia, you would read:

> (1150 reported) Type I. Berry under claw. Exceedingly rare. (1) 1975 GENA II: 1272. (2) Anomaly from the John Zug estate; obv. perfect proof, rev. uncirculated and frosty but with the striking qualities, borders and rims of a proof. It may have been made in error using a wrong reverse-Type II. Without berry under claw. Most regular proofs seen to date of the 1876 Trade are of this type. I have not seen the copper or aluminum proofs, Judd 1476-77, AW 1480-81, but surmise that they too would be of this type. Certainly the pattern trade dollar showing motto in cartouche above date and no stars, with reverse of regular issue, Judd 1474-75, AW 1492-93, has a Type II reverse. Minor positional varieties probable.

Your ability to tell the Proof from its business strike counterpart can come only from practical experience. Even those in business for many years and who have studied Proofs for many years are not always absolutely certain whether certain coins are Proofs or Prooflikes.

The three outstanding references which provide invaluable information and illustrations of how to tell Proof from Prooflike are *Walter Breen's Complete Encyclopedia of U.S. and Colonial Coins* (Doubleday, 1988), *Walter Breen's Encyclopedia of U.S. and Colonial Proof Coins* (F.C.I. Press, 1977) and *The Encyclopedia of United States Silver & Gold Commemorative Coins 1892 to 1954*, by Anthony Swiatek and Walter Breen (Arco Publishing, 1981). The complete encyclopedia published by Doubleday is a hobby best-seller and has remained in print and widely available for years.

– 7 –
TELLING FACT FROM FICTION

Like the proverbial "bad penny," counterfeit coins have been coming back. These bad pennies are costing unwitting victims good dollars.

Fake and altered coins were a major concern for coin collectors in the early and mid 1980s. But the problem diminished greatly after the founding of third-party grading services starting in 1986. Although the certification services were intended primarily to address rampant problems with grading, they also had a major effect on cleaning up the hobby of coin collecting through authentication—addressing the genuineness of coins sent to them. Thereafter, counterfeit coins became almost a curiosity rather than a plague.

More recently, however, the old problem has reared its ugly head again because of abuses on the Internet. Online coin sellers have offered many obviously counterfeit or altered coins, taking advantage of unwary buyers with little or no knowledge.

Today, buyers are confronted not only with bad pennies, but also phony gold pieces and other fake coins offered online.

The organized coin industry's strict adherence to the Hobby Protection Act, which makes selling counterfeit coins illegal, is responsible for ridding the field of these spurious pieces. PCGS, NGC, ICG, and ANACS are to be credited with outstanding records for spotting fakes and alerting the public to their existence.

There are three basic types of inauthentic coins: altered, cast counterfeit, and die-struck counterfeit. All will be explored and illustrated with photographs taken by and reproduced here by courtesy of Pedro Collazo-Oliver.

Altered Coins

An altered coin is a real coin that has been tampered with. For example, the 1856 Flying Eagle cent is a rare, valuable, sought-after coin in all grades. Even heavily circulated ex-

Blowup of an 1858 Flying Eagle cent altered to look like an 1856. *Photograph courtesy Pedro Collazo-Oliver*

Blowup of a genuine 1856 Flying Eagle cent. *Photograph courtesy Pedro Collazo-Oliver*

Blowup of a genuine 1895 Proof Morgan dollar. *Photograph courtesy Pedro Collazo-Oliver*

Blowup of a business-strike Morgan dollar with a numeral altered to resemble a "9." *Photograph courtesy Pedro Collazo-Oliver*

Blowup of a 1922-D Lincoln cent altered by removing the Mint mark to make it resemble a 1922 Plain. *Photograph courtesy Pedro Collazo-Oliver*

amples command phenomenal premiums. But the 1858 Flying Eagle cent, although somewhat scarce, is not a major rarity. Some 1858s have been found with altered dates to resemble 1856s. Look at the altered 1856 small cent illustrated, and compare it with the real example shown. The tooling marks on the altered example are readily apparent and might even be detected without a glass. The retooling of the "8" to make it look like a "6" is obvious. Dates are altered in other ways, too. Always look closely at the date if the coin is a date rarity.

A coin sometimes found with either an altered date or removed Mint-mark is the "1895" Morgan dollar. Apparently, no examples of this coin are known to exist as business strikes, only as Proofs. But occasionally an "1895 business-strike" Morgan is offered. The 1895 Proof is worth at least $25,000 as a Proof-65. The coins offered as business strikes probably have their dates altered or their Mint-marks removed (from an 1895-O or -S). Examine the date of the genuine 1895 shown. Notice the obvious Proof rim and clear date. Now look at the altered coin. It's a business strike. The date, in this case has been altered. Possibly an 1885 was changed to an 1895. Always check for an altered date or removed Mint-mark on rare coins.

The 1922-D Lincoln head cent's Mint-mark is commonly tampered with. It sometimes can be found with a removed "D" to mislead you into thinking it's a 1922-Plain Lincoln cent. In 1922, the Philadelphia Mint didn't manufacture any Lincoln cents. The reason that 1922 cents are found without an obvious Mint-mark is that the Mint-mark on the die filled in. Real 1922-Plain cents still have a trace of the Mint-mark. So look carefully at any Lincoln cents offered as 1922-Plain. The ones with removed Mint-marks are sometimes easily spotted because the removal marks are so obvious. Also, the genuine 1922-Plain tends not to be fully struck. If you see a phenomenally well-struck 1922 Lincoln cent offered as a 1922-Plain, beware.

Blowup of a 1909 Lincoln cent with a fake "S" Mint mark added. *Photograph courtesy Pedro Collazo-Oliver*

Blowup of a 1909 Lincoln cent with an "S" Mint mark carved out of the field. *Photograph courtesy Pedro Collazo-Oliver*

Blowup of a genuine 1909-S V.D.B. cent obverse. *Photograph courtesy Pedro Collazo-Oliver*

Blowup of a genuine 1909-S V.D.B. Lincoln cent reverse. Note the slanted midsection of the "B," the most prominent distinction of the real "V.D.B." *Photograph courtesy Pedro Collazo-Oliver*

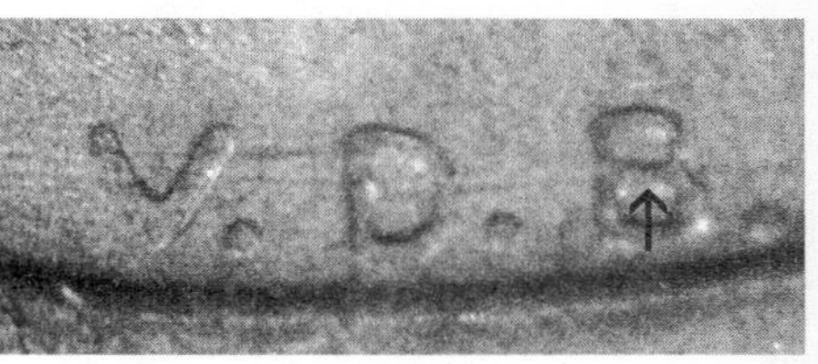

Blowup of a 1909-S Lincoln cent reverse with a fake V.D.B. added. Note the straight midsection. *Photograph courtesy Pedro Collazo-Oliver*

In general, the coins you buy that have the highest risk of being altered (and even the highest risk isn't high) are coins with rare dates and Mint-marks in great demand. The 1909-S V.D.B. Lincoln cent is another example of a rare-date coin occasionally found altered. The abbreviation V.D.B. stands for Victor David Brenner, the designer of the Lincoln cent, which was new that year. These alterations are usually in the form of an S Mint-mark added to a 1909-V.D.B. or V.D.B. added to a 1909-S. Rarely, two coins are sawed in half: a 1909-S and a 1909-V.D.B. The 1909-S obverse is then glued to the 1909-V.D.B. reverse. If you were to look at just the obverse and reverse you might be fooled. But from reading the first chapter, you know always to view the edge, which in this case would be a dead giveaway.

Blowup of an 1893 Morgan dollar with a well-positioned but fake "S" Mint mark added. *Photograph courtesy Pedro Collazo-Oliver*

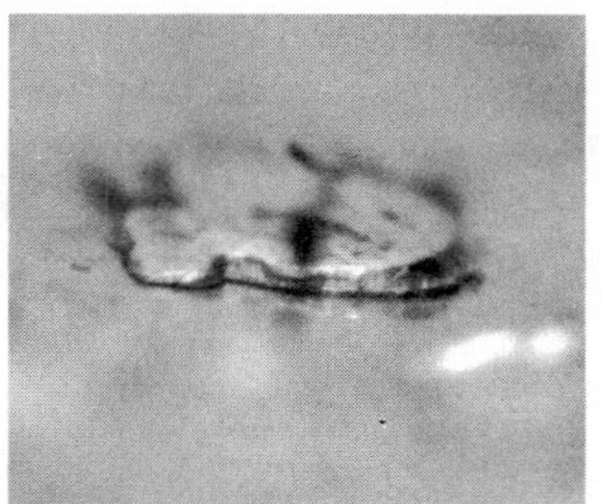

Blowup of the added Mint-mark seam. You can tell when you tilt the coin and view it under magnification that the "S" is just resting there and is not part of the coin. *Photograph courtesy Pedro Collazo-Oliver*

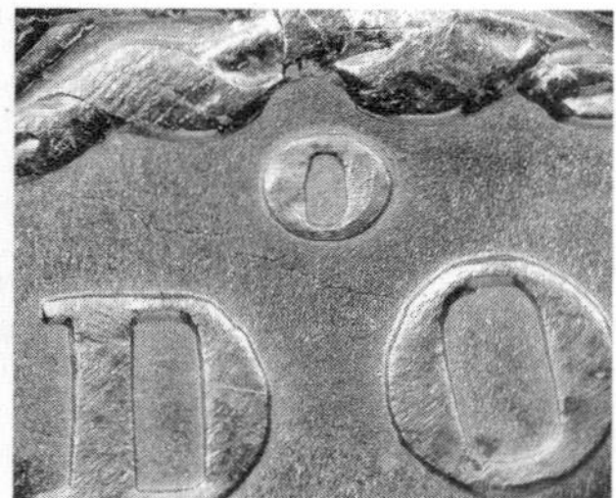

Blowup of an 1897 Morgan dollar with a fake "O" Mint mark glued to the reverse. *Photograph courtesy PCGS*

Look at the added S Mint-mark on the coin depicted. The "S" just sits there and doesn't blend in with the coin. It appears out of place—and it is. Look at another added S Mint-mark shown. In this example, the "S" has been carved out of the field. But so much concern has focused upon 1909-S V.D.B. cents turning out not to be real that collectors sometimes don't buy perfectly good ones because they are afraid the coins are altered. Collectors are often told never to buy coins that have a darkened area around the Mint-mark. This might be a good general rule of thumb, but it isn't applicable in every case. For example, the 1909-S V.D.B. Lincoln cent illustrated here with a darkened area around the Mint-mark is genuine. The darkening around the Mint-mark is die-erosion radiating outwards from the center which "is commonly encountered on this coin, mak-

Blowup of a genuine 1914-D Lincoln cent. *Photograph courtesy Pedro Collazo-Oliver*

Blowup of a 1944-D Lincoln cent altered to resemble a 1914-D. Look at the space between the 9 and the second 1. *Photograph courtesy Pedro Collazo-Oliver*

Blowup of a genuine 1916-D Mercury dime reverse. The top tail of the "D" is doubled, a characteristic of the genuine coin. *Photograph courtesy Pedro Collazo-Oliver*

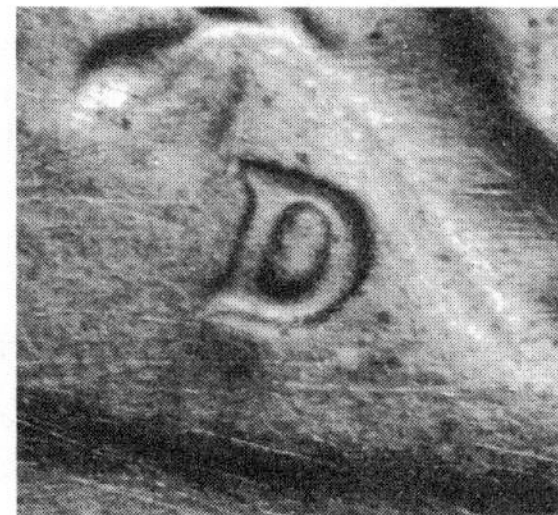

Blowup of a 1916 Mercury dime with a fake "D" added. *Photograph courtesy Pedro Collazo-Oliver*

ing the field look scratched. On the real "S," an almost unnoticeable raised marking should be visible in the top loop of the "S."

Examine the real V.D.B. reverse. Notice the slant on the midsection of the "B." Now examine an added V.D.B. Pay particular attention to the straight midsection of the "B."

Sometimes, added Mint-marks are positioned well. These, as well as many other added Mint-marks, are spotted by looking at the coin under high power magnification or under a microscope and tilting the coin to spot a seam between the added Mint-mark and the coin's surface.

Blowup of the surface of a cast counterfeit Barber half dollar. *Photograph courtesy Pedro Collazo-Oliver*

The 1914-D Lincoln is also found altered sometimes. Examine the real example shown. Now look at its altered counterpart. Observe the space between the "9" and the second "1." A 1944-D was altered to resemble a 1914-D.

Look at the Mint-mark of the 1916-D Mercury dime (a rare date). Pay attention to the doubling of the portions of the letter pointed to by the arrows. Now look at an added Mint-mark 1916 dime. The "D" might look real to someone not knowing what real should look like.

Distinguishing the real from the altered cannot be explained by listing a set of rules and examples. It's practical experience that is the only solid teacher. Get out to coin conventions and look at lots of coins. By looking at the real coins and getting an idea of what they should look like, you can avoid buying an altered coin.

Cast Counterfeits

Cast counterfeits are cast impressions of copies of genuine coins. A cast counterfeit is, therefore, a copy of a copy. As I stress throughout this book, many survival strategies in coin buying involve gaining a "feel" for the right buy and a "feel" for the wrong buy. The ability to detect cast counterfeits is based on this feel, as well as an ability to really feel and determine certain characteristics. For example, a coin that feels slimy and oily might be a cast counterfeit. If you hold it and it gets warm quickly, it might be a cast counterfeit. The less obvious "feel" is that a cast counterfeit—a copy of a copy—lacks much of the detail of its genuine, die-struck counterpart.

Detecting a cast counterfeit is easier than detecting a die-struck counterfeit, for certain tell-tale signs apply to many cast counterfeits. For example, if the coin lacks a reeded edge, a seam will be visible. This seam, though often disguised by the counterfeiter, is always there. On reeded coins, that edge has no seam. But the reeding will be less uniform

Blowup of the date of a genuine 1955 doubled-die Lincoln cent. *Photograph courtesy Pedro Collazo-Oliver*

Blowup of the date of a cast counterfeit 1955 doubled-die Lincoln cent. The cast fake is blurry. *Photograph courtesy Pedro Collazo-Oliver*

Blowup of the word "LIBERTY" on a genuine 1955 doubled-die Lincoln cent. *Photograph courtesy Pedro Collazo-Oliver*

Blowup of the word "LIBERTY" on a cast counterfeit 1955 doubled-die Lincoln cent. The doubled letters are distorted and unclear, and the surface has a low-grade texture. *Photograph courtesy Pedro Collazo-Oliver*

and even than on genuine coins. A dropped cast counterfeit won't ring true. Genuine coins have a delicate, warm ring when lightly dropped.

Because a cast counterfeit is a cast impression of a copy of a genuine coin, cast counterfeits are grainy and easily recognized for what they are. Many of the original cast counterfeits were made for circulation to fool local merchants, not astute coin collectors.

Blowup of a cast counterfeit Gobrecht dollar obverse. *Photograph courtesy Pedro Collazo-Oliver*

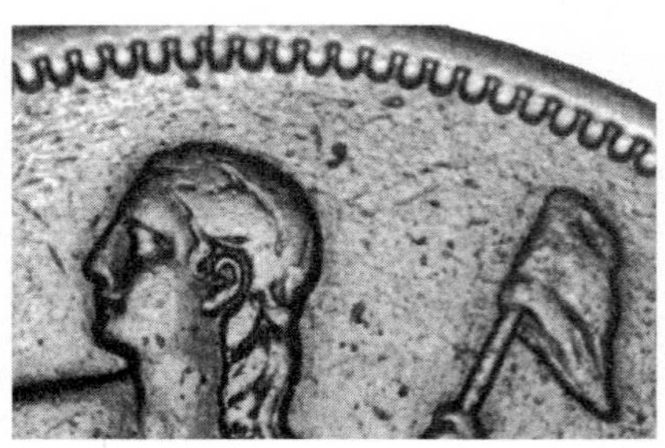

Blowup of the surface of the cast counterfeit Gobrecht dollar. The porous surface is characteristic of a cast counterfeit. *Photograph courtesy Pedro Collazo-Oliver*

Blowup of an electrotype counterfeit large cent, obverse and reverse. *Photograph courtesy Pedro Collazo-Oliver*

The closeup of the cast Barber half dollar points up the typical crude texture of a low-grade example made to pass off in circulation.

Examine the illustrations that show the sharp, genuine 1955 doubled-die Lincoln cent, a valuable Mint error caused when the dies were struck twice in misaligned positions. Compare that genuine specimen's "LIBERTY" and date with those of the cast copy

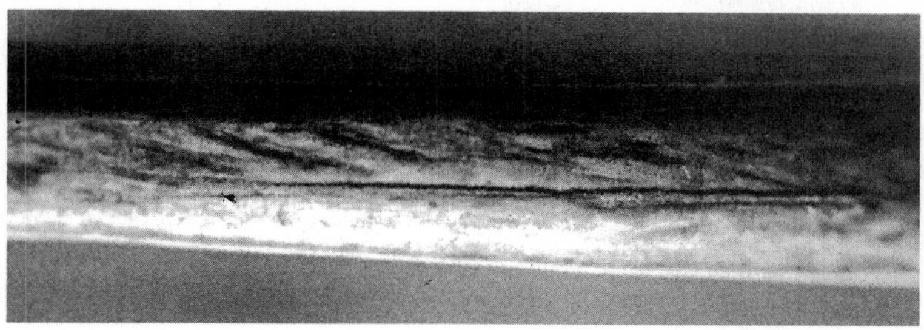

Blowup of the edge of the electrotype large cent. The telltale seam characteristic of a fake is clearly visible. *Photograph courtesy Pedro Collazo-Oliver*

illustrated. The cast copy is blurred and grainy; the genuine, sharp and clear. Cast counterfeits tend to have porous surfaces. The Gobrecht dollar shown has small holes throughout its uneven surfaces. Close examination reveals that these holes can be linked to the casting process, not circulation.

Electrotype counterfeits are similar to cast counterfeits; but whereas the cast is a copy of an impression made from a real coin, the electrotype is a direct copy of a real coin. The 1804 large cent shown might look like a genuine example at first glance. But even if you can't tell by looking at these views of the coin, if you look at the edge you can see that the seam is more prominent in electrotypes than in any other type of cast counterfeit.

Die-Struck Counterfeits

The die-struck counterfeit is the most difficult of all counterfeits to detect because it's struck with two dies—just like a genuine coin! Even some leading dealers are unable to distinguish every die-struck counterfeit that comes their way. Being able to detect a die-struck counterfeit requires many years of experience and study. Not only is it beyond the scope of this book to explain the intricacies of die-struck counterfeits, it's beyond the scope of any book to document and explain how to detect every die-struck counterfeit. If there ever were such a book, as soon as the book was released, a new type of counterfeit would be made.

Two basic methods are used to teach people how to spot die-struck counterfeits. One involves showing pictures of the characteristics of real coins. The other involves showing photos of selected counterfeits. I've chosen the latter.

Die-struck counterfeit 1799 silver dollar.
Photograph courtesy Pedro Collazo-Oliver

Blowup of the telltale sign of the fake 1799 silver dollar: The "R" is broken. *Photograph courtesy Pedro Collazo-Oliver*

The ability to spot die-struck counterfeits has a lot to do with how good a memory you have for the hundreds of die varieties of die-struck counterfeits. If you had access to an information source which enabled you to spot a good number of die-struck counterfeits, the counterfeiter would use your source to his or her advantage. For example, the 1915-S $10 gold piece displayed, a die-struck counterfeit, was featured in the American Numismatic Association's official journal, with its diagnostic characteristics listed and

Die-struck counterfeit of an Indian head $10 gold piece, obverse and reverse. *Photograph courtesy Pedro Collazo-Oliver*

Blowup of diagnostic marks on the reverse of a counterfeit Indian head $10 gold piece. *Photograph courtesy Pedro Collazo-Oliver*

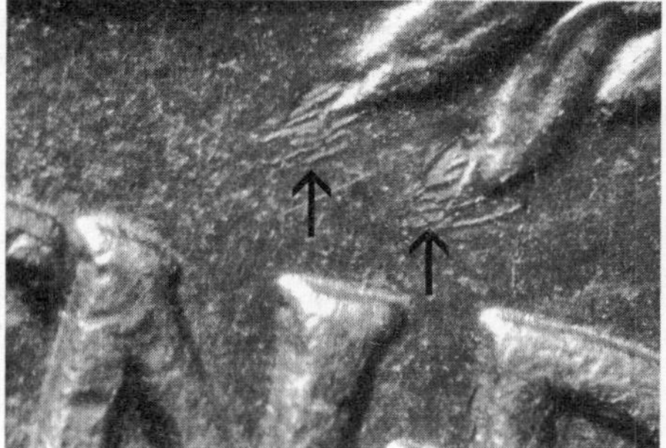

Blowup of diagnostic marks on the reverse of a counterfeit Indian head $10 gold piece, after being filled in by the counterfeiter. *Photograph courtesy Pedro Collazo-Oliver*

photographically illustrated. Two indentations are visible between the leaf and the "N" on the reverse. The counterfeiter read the article and altered his die so that those diagnostic characteristics would not be visible!

Counterfeiters do take pride in their work. One diagnostic characteristic that's evidence of this is the Omega initial. One counterfeiter placed the initial Omega on his die-struck

"Omega" counterfeit 1907 Roman-numerals high-relief Saint-Gaudens double eagle, obverse and reverse. The counterfeiter placed the Omega letter on the reverse inside the claw, where the arrow points. *Photograph courtesy Pedro Collazo-Oliver*

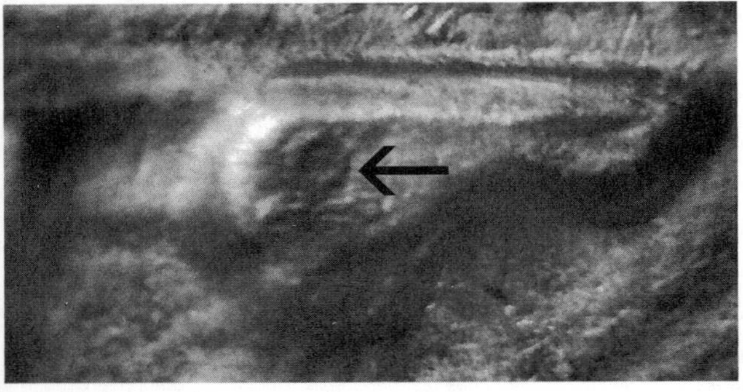

Blowup of the claw where the Omega letter is located on the double-eagle fake. *Photograph courtesy Pedro Collazo-Oliver*

"Omega" counterfeit $3 gold piece, obverse and reverse. The Omega letter is where the arrow is pointing, in the top loop of the "R." *Photograph courtesy Pedro Collazo-Oliver*

Blowup of the Omega letter on the $3 gold piece. *Photograph courtesy Pedro Collazo-Oliver*

counterfeit gold pieces. Look at the beautiful but counterfeit 1907 Roman Numerals High Relief Saint-Gaudens double eagle. Inside the eagle's claw on the reverse is the Omega initial. If you spot this initial on any coin, don't buy the coin. The 1882 $3 gold piece shown is also an Omega counterfeit. The Omega initial is located on the obverse in the top loop of the "R" in the word "LIBERTY".

Almost every die-struck counterfeit has its own separate set of diagnostic characteristics. An example of a diagnostic characteristic is the broken "R" and weak die clash of the 1799 dollar shown. A close-up is also shown.

The more familiar you become with what the real coin should look like and what the counterfeit does look like, the better you'll become at detecting counterfeits.

For Further Assistance

The following, in alphabetical order, are the most recognized authentication and grading services. For a small fee, they will authenticate coins submitted. Some also publish educational materials.

ANACS
P.O. Box 7173
Dublin, Ohio 43017-0773

Independent Coin Grading Company
7901 East Belleview Ave., Suite 50
Englewood, Colorado 80111

Numismatic Guaranty Corporation of America
P.O. Box 4776
Sarasota, Florida 34230

Professional Coin Grading Service
P.O. Box 9458
Newport Beach, California 92658

– 8 –
MAKING MONEY IN COINS RIGHT NOW

> I'm against the holders. I'm against the guys that run the business of the holders. I'm against the people who buy the stuff in the holders. I'm against the dealers who deal in the stuff in the holders. I'm against Bullet Auctions and all the other [baloney]. I'm against the morons who buy the stuff to get rich quick. I'm against everything—the whole concept. The crack-out game is a form of low-level larceny. The convention circuit boys who deal in slabs aren't interested in collectors or numismatics; these guys are parasites.
>
> Anybody who pays an extra $10,000 for a coin that grades one point higher is a nut. That one point might be smoke. You're paying ten grand extra for something that might be ephemeral.
>
> —John J. Ford, Jr., *former longtime dealer and outspoken coin collectors' advocate* (1924–2005)

The people who play the rare-coin game may be hobbyists, but the stakes can be high and the payouts can be substantial—higher and more substantial than the stakes and payouts those same people would play for if they went to a casino. On the other hand, the risks can be equally high.

At a casino, these people might put down a couple of hundred dollars and hope to double their money. In the coin market, by contrast, they might put down $60 in the slab/crack-out game and get back $500 . . . put down $150 and get back $2,500 . . . or put down $400 and get back $6,600.

It isn't pie-in-the-sky to think you might put down a couple of hundred dollars here, when you play a rare-coin game, and get back a couple of thousand dollars there. All three examples I just gave, in fact, are real-world cases you will see illustrated with actual coins in this chapter.

I want to thank James L. Halperin, co-chairman of the board of Heritage Capital Corp. of Dallas, for sharing his secrets to help make this chapter so invaluable. Jim is perhaps

Jim Halperin, one of the most financially successful coin dealers of all time, examines a coin that was cracked out of its grading-service holder.
Photograph courtesy Heritage

the most successful coin trader in the business and one of the greatest experts on coin grading standards. He understands these standards—and uses them to his advantage—better than just about anyone else. I am proud to say that Jim and I have worked together on a number of projects and have maximized the returns that were realized by coins when we sold them at public auction or in the day-to-day marketplace. With Jim's assistance, many of my clients have profited tremendously by selling their coins at the optimal time and for the most money that could reasonably have been expected, given marketplace conditions.

Jim Halperin and Steve Ivy, his fellow co-chairman of the board at Heritage, each own 12.127% of NGC, all *non-voting* stock. "It is a pure financial investment and we have no control or influence on NGC grading or other policies," Halperin stated.

The Crack-Out Game

The crack-out game, resubmitting a coin to a grading service in hopes of receiving a higher grade, is a relatively new phenomenon. It dates back to the late 1980s, when independent third-party coin grading services first appeared on the scene. Because of the strong demand for certified coins in pristine uncirculated condition, large price gaps often developed between the market values of coins in one Mint State grade level and those just a single grade higher, especially in levels of MS-65 and above. Thus, a certain type of coin might be worth $200 in MS-64 and five times that much—or more—in MS-65. Savvy traders soon began acquiring premium-quality (PQ) coins—those at the high end of their grade level—and "cracking" them out of their hard plastic holders in order to resubmit them to one of the grading services in hopes of receiving a higher grade and thereby reaping a windfall profit.

Two highly experienced expert professional numismatists examine coins in grading-service holders.

The coin crack-out game is just that—it's really a game. It's a high-stakes gamble, not unlike a poker game, where you can ante up a nominal sum of money and win a sizable pot. Jim Halperin has been playing this game for years, and winning more than his share of hefty pots. His success is apparent from the leadership position he holds as co-chairman of the board of Heritage Capital Corporation, a coin and diversified collectibles company that grosses about $350 million a year. When experts such as Jim play the crack-out game, they don't put their trust in dumb luck or random chance. They approach the game scientifically, calculating the odds and playing their hands only when they believe that those odds are in their favor. They take risks, to be sure, but only when they are justified by the potential reward. This cautious, methodical approach works for them—and it can do the same for you!

Multimillion Dollar Crack-Out Secrets

When Jim Halperin calculates the risk-reward ratio for cracking out coins and resubmitting them, he draws up three columns on a piece of paper. The center column shows a "target grade and price"—the value of each coin at its current certified grade. The left-hand column shows what it's worth in the next-lower grade; this represents the downside risk—the amount that Jim could expect to lose if the coin was downgraded the second time around. The right-hand column shows the current market value in the next-higher grade; this is the upside potential—the profit Jim would realize if the coin were upgraded instead.

Halperin follows a very simple philosophy in playing the crack-out game: "Stick with coins that have not too much risk and fantastic upside." Nobody's perfect. Everybody makes a mistake now and then in resubmitting a coin, no matter how good a grader they may be. Sometimes even premium-quality coins may be downgraded; perhaps a coin may have a hairline that you—the expert—missed. And even experts have their weaknesses. Jim Halperin, for example, has never had a lot of success getting upgrades on MS-64 Indian quarter eagles; as he admits with a laugh, "there may be certain neurons missing" in his brain when it comes to grading these coins. He admits to success, however, with MS-62 Indian quarter eagles, despite any missing neurons he might have for their MS-64 counterparts.

If you play the percentages, and develop and apply sharp grading skills, you will greatly improve the odds in your favor. Learning to play the crack-out game is a matter of practice, practice, practice; the more experience you have, the better you get. Sometimes it's also a matter of being in the right place at the right time. As Halperin remarks: "I try to get there first, but I can't get there all the time. There are an awful lot of coins out there."

The Handpicked List for Quick Cash

Jim prepared a "sample" list for me to use in my book *How to Make Money in Coins Right Now*, which served as the inspiration for this revised and comprehensive listing. All of the coins that are not specific as to NGC or PCGS ("NGC/PCGS") were added in 2005.

Let's consider one of the coins in the accompanying chart: a 1944-S Walking Liberty half dollar graded Mint State-64 by the Professional Coin Grading Service (PCGS). With a certified grade of Mint State-64, this coin is worth $56. It is worth $30 in Mint State-63 and $500 in Mint State-65. A premium-quality Mint State-64 specimen—the best candidate for an upgrade—costs $4 to $14 extra, increasing the cost to $60 to $70. Let's say you bought a PQ MS-64 example of this coin and it cost you $65. The downside risk would be negligible; even if the coin is regraded MS-63, you would only lose $35 (plus the cost of certification). But the upside potential is enormous: more than five times your cost (the purchase price of the coin plus the grading fee). If you buy a nice MS-64 coin under these circumstances, crack it out of its holder, and get it graded MS-65, it's salable for $500. If you lose out and the coin is downgraded to MS-63, it's still salable for $30. You have tremendous upside and very little downside—and that's the name of the game.

The following chart illustrates the high potential profits that exist in the crack-out game. It reflects the market values for a series of popular coins when certified and encapsulated by either PCGS or NGC in a number of Mint State grade levels. In each case, the downside risk is minimal, and the upside potential is high. The coins listed here illustrate how you can play the crack-out game and win. And as Jim Halperin notes, similar opportunities abound: "There are thousands of them around." The footnotes are Jim's.

JIM HALPERIN'S CRACK-OUT WINNERS

Coin	Service	Downgrade Grade/Price	Target Buy Grade/Price	Target Upgrade Grade/Price
1914-S 5¢	*PCGS*	MS-63 $236	MS-64 $368	MS-65 $1,670
1944-S 50¢	*PCGS*	MS-63 $30	MS-64 $56	MS-65 $500 (PQ add $4–$14)*
1888-S $1	*NGC*	MS-63 $308	MS-64 $520†	MS-65 $2,250
1921 Peace $1	*NGC/PCGS*	MS-63 $300	MS-64 $500	MS-65 $1,500
1922-S $1	*NGC/PCGS*	MS-63 $50	MS-64 $150	MS-65 $1,350
1923-S $1	*NGC/PCGS*	MS-63 $50	MS-64 $150	MS-65 $2,500
1924-S $1	*NGC/PCGS*	MS-63 $400	MS-64 $700	MS-65 $6,000
1925-S $1	*NGC/PCGS*	MS-63 $150	MS-64 $400	MS-65 $6,600
1927-D $1	*NGC/PCGS*	MS-63 $300	MS-64 $500	MS-65 $6,000
1927-S $1	*NGC/PCGS*	MS-63 $300	MS-64 $600	MS-65 $6,000
1928-S $1	*NGC/PCGS*	MS-63 $450	MS-64 $1,500	MS-65 $11,000
Common date Peace dollars	*NGC/PCGS*	MS-64 $50	MS-65 $125	MS-65 $500
Indian $1 gold T-3 (1856–89)	*PCGS*	MS-63 $655	MS-64 $940‡	MS-65 $1,580
1908 $2½ gold	*NGC/PCGS*	MS-61$275	MS-62 $550	MS-63 $1,500
1909 $2½ gold	*NGC/PCGS*	MS-61 $285	MS-62 $600	MS-63 $2,000
1910 $2½ gold	*NGC/PCGS*	MS61 $275	MS-62 $600	MS-63 $2,000
1911 $2½ gold	*NGC/PCGS*	MS61 $275	MS-62 $550	MS-63 $1,600
1911-D $2½ gold	*NGC/PCGS*	MS61 $6,450	MS-62 $11,000	MS-63 $21,250
1912 $2½ gold	*NGC/PCGS*	MS61 $265	MS-62 $625	MS-63 $2,000
1913 $2½ gold	*NGC/PCGS*	MS61 $325	MS-62 $550	MS-63 $1,400
1914 $2½ gold	*NGC/PCGS*	MS61 $400	MS-62 $1,550	MS-63 $6,000
1914-D $2½ gold	*NGC/PCGS*	MS61 $290	MS-62 $615	MS-63 $2,500
1915 $2½ gold	*NGC/PCGS*	MS61 $250	MS-62 $575	MS-63 $1,450
1925-D $2½ gold	*NGC/PCGS*	MS61 $250	MS-62 $575	MS-63 $1,250
1926 $2½ gold	*NGC/PCGS*	MS61 $250	MS-62 $575	MS-63 $1,250
1927 $2½ gold	*NGC/PCGS*	MS61 $250	MS-62 $575	MS-63 $1,250
1928 $2½ gold	*NGC/PCGS*	MS61 $250	MS-62 $575	MS-63 $1,250
1929 $2½ gold	*NGC/PCGS*	MS61 $250	MS-62 $575	MS-63 $1,250
1883-S $20	*NGC/PCGS*	MS-61 $625	MS-62 $900	MS-63 $7,000
1884-S $20	*NGC/PCGS*	MS-61 $600	MS-62 $900	MS-63 $5,000
1885-S $20	*NGC/PCGS*	MS-61 $600	MS-62 $900	MS-63 $5,000
1887-S $20	*NGC/PCGS*	MS-61 $600	MS-62 $2,000	MS-63 $10,500
1888-S $20	*NGC/PCGS*	MS-61 $600	MS-62 $700	MS-63 $4,000
1889-S $20	*NGC/PCGS*	MS-61 $600	MS-62 $800	MS-63 $5,000

Coin	Service	Downgrade Grade/Price	Target Buy Grade/Price	Target Upgrade Grade/Price
1890-S $20	*NGC/PCGS*	MS-61 $600	MS-62 $900	MS-63 $6,000
1891-S $20	*NGC/PCGS*	MS-61 $600	MS-62 $750	MS-63 $3,000
1892-S $20	*NGC/PCGS*	MS-61 $550	MS-62 $700	MS-63 $3,000
1893-S $20	*NGC/PCGS*	MS-61 $600	MS-62 $700	MS-63 $3,000
1894-S $20	*NGC/PCGS*	MS-61 $590	MS-62 $650	MS-63 $2,000
1895-S $20	*NGC/PCGS*	MS-61 $550	MS-62 $600	MS-63 $2,100
1896-S $20	*NGC/PCGS*	MS-61 $500	MS-62 $600	MS-63 $1,600
1898-S $20	*NGC/PCGS*	MS-61 $550	MS-62 $600	MS-63 $1,300
1899-S $20	*NGC/PCGS*	MS-61 $550	MS-62 $600	MS-63 $1,300
1900-S $20	*NGC/PCGS*	MS-61 $550	MS-62 $600	MS-63 $1,700
1901-S $20	*NGC/PCGS*	MS-61 $550	MS-62 $700	MS-63 $3,000
1902-S $20	*NGC/PCGS*	MS-61 $550	MS-62 $650	MS-63 $3,000
1905-S $20	*NGC/PCGS*	MS-61 $550	MS-62 $600	MS-63 $2,750
1906-S $20	*NGC/PCGS*	MS-61 $550	MS-62 $700	MS-63 $1,700
1907-S $20	*NGC/PCGS*	MS-61 $550	MS-62 $600	MS-63 $1,800
Isabella 25c	*PCGS*	MS-63 $700	MS-64 $1,050	MS-65 $2,360 (PQ add $60)
Lafayette $1	*NGC/PCGS*	MS-61 $550	MS-62 $850	MS-64 $2,200 (2-point upgrade)
1923-S 50c Monroe	*NGC/PCGS*	MS-63 $125	MS-64 $290	MS-65 $3,100
Norfolk 50c	*NGC/PCGS*	MS-66 $400	MS-67 $500	MS-68 $925
1926 50c Sesqui	*NGC/PCGS*	MS-63 $100	MS-64 $390	MS-65 $3,300
York 50c	*NGC/PCGS*	MS-66 $250	MS-67 $450	MS-68 $1,200
1905 Lewis & Clark commemorative $1 gold	*NGC*	MS-62 $720	MS-63 $1,680	MS-64 $4,000
1926 Sesqui commemorative $2½ gold	*NGC/PCGS*	MS-63 $500	MS-64 $950	MS-65 $3,800

* You have virtually no risk buying nice, premium-quality 64s, assuming you can buy them for $60 or so. You have tremendous upside—five times your cost—and they are quite liquid.

† If it goes down in grade by a point, you're risking $212. If its grade increases by a point, you stand to make $1,730.

‡ Gold type coins can be pretty wonderful because they are so liquid.

Please Note: *These prices are current as of February 2005, when Jim Halperin created this list.*

When Not to Play the Crack-Out Game

The crack-out game works best with premium-quality coins—coins that are at the high end of their grade level, such as the "A" coins described in chapter 4. If there is a question as to whether a given coin is 64A or 65C and it's certified with a grade of 64, there's a reasonable chance that it might be regraded 65 if you resubmit it. A different set of graders, a fresh perspective from the same set of graders—these and other factors could produce a higher grade the second time around, since the call is a close one anyway.

There are certain times, however, when it would be inadvisable to play the crack-out game, even with PQ coins. Coins with hairlines are unlikely to be upgraded, for example. These fine lines may be hard for the naked eye to detect, but experienced graders can spot them, and they tend to preclude an upgrade.

Jim Halperin has an interesting suggestion on how to circumvent the grading problems posed by hairlines. It isn't a quick fix, by any means, and it's certainly not a way to make money right now, but it can pay big dividends in the long run. Let's say you have a flashy white coin that looks at a glance like an MS-65, but is certified as only 63 or 64 because it has hairlines. Halperin suggests cracking out that coin, placing it in an old holder (e.g. Wayte Raymond), and storing it in your safe deposit box for several years—perhaps as long as six or seven years. Often, he says, the coin will develop beautiful, natural toning, which, in turn, will hide the hairlines completely. Then, when the coin is submitted for grading again, it may very well come back as 65. There is a degree of risk: If the toning isn't attractive, the grade of the coin might be lowered instead of raised. But if the upside potential is great and the downside risk is minimal, this might be a chance well worth taking.

You also should be wary of resubmitting coins where the downside risk is substantial. In all of the examples in Jim Halperin's chart, the price gap is modest between the target buy price and the potential downgrade value; thus, if a coin happened to lose a point during the resubmission process, the loss would not be onerous. Take the 1923-S Peace dollar, for example: The price drops from $150 to $50 between the grades of 64 and 63, so the downside risk is $100—not traumatic. On the other hand, the upside potential is handsome, for the price in 65 is a whopping $2,500. This kind of risk/reward ratio certainly would justify a crack-out. But suppose a different coin was worth $3,000 in MS-64, $5,500 in MS-65-and only $50 in MS-63. The potential reward—a $2,500 increase—would justify resubmission. The downside risk—a possible loss of $2,950—most assuredly would not. In that kind of situation, discretion would definitely be the better part of valor.

The Best Place to Buy Coins to Crack

In looking for certified coins to use in the crack-out game, your best bet is to buy them at public auction. That is Jim Halperin's view, and I agree with him. For one thing, as Jim points out, you have a safety net: The price you pay will be just one bid higher than what any dealers bidding at the sale would have paid. For another thing, the selection is

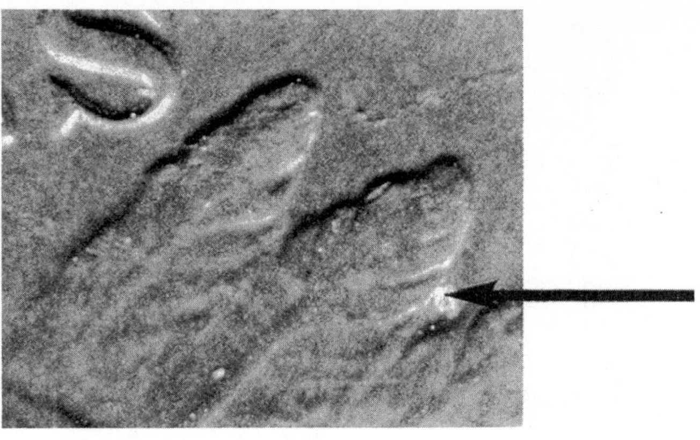

A tiny piece of plastic is a telltale sign of a cracked-out coin. Small plastic particles often adhere to a coin after it has been cracked out of a slab, unless the coin was airbrushed. *Photo courtesy Anthony Swiatek*

likely to be extensive, and some of the coins in any given sale are almost certain to be overlooked and end up selling for less than they should. When Halperin goes to an auction, he studies each coin carefully and decides "the absolute most" that he would be willing to pay. He writes that number down next to the coin's listing in his catalog and never goes higher. "Never chicken out, either," he advises. "Trust your judgment, and learn from your mistakes."

Halperin has found that premium-quality coins can often be purchased at auctions for little or no more than the going market prices for regular-quality coins of the same type. Also, if you buy them at auctions, you won't be subjected to high-pressure tactics to pay a premium; sizing up the coins and deciding what to pay will be up to you alone. By contrast, Jim observes, if you find a PQ coin in a dealer's inventory, the dealer will try to convince you that the coin will get an upgrade and charge you a higher price on that basis. Halperin reports that the "bullet sales" conducted by his own auction company include many premium-quality coins. So do the "Lightning Sales" held by my company, Scott Travers Rare Coin Galleries, LLC. Buying coins at auction is "an ideal way to practice your skills," Halperin says. "These sales are the best vehicle for learning how to grade coins . . . the best place for a person willing to do his homework to buy coins."

A word of important advice: The average consumer should not pay large premiums—say, 50 or 75 percent—for coins being sold at auction, or anywhere else for that matter, just because they look like good candidates for upgrades. Jim Halperin recommends paying no more than a 5 to 15 percent premium for a coin which appears to be PQ. He also recommends that before even bidding at an auction, would-be buyers first attend auctions at coin shows in their area and get a feel for which coins command extra pre-

Indian head quarter eagle graded MS-63 in an old PCGS holder without a hologram. This coin would regrade as an MS-64 under today's standards. Carefully examine coins in these 1986-type holders for upgrades.

miums. "The biggest danger with an auction," he says, "is getting carried away with the mood and buying coins that you ordinarily would not buy. Never get carried away with the mood."

Crack-Out Cautions

Jim Halperin estimates that 20 percent of all the coins now certified either have been cracked out or will be cracked out of their holders at least once. That is because no mere mortal can grade coins with absolute consistency, so unless a foolproof system is devised, there will always be a need to have coins re-graded based on human fallibility on the part of graders. One must also understand that a certain number of coins will always be near the borderline between one grade and the next, and thus in a position to go either way. The very same coins can be graded—and have been graded—both ways at different times. And certain coins present special problems for graders. Indian Head half eagles and quarter eagles ($5 and $2½ gold pieces) are difficult to grade, for example, because their design elements are incused, or sunken below the surface. This makes them excellent candidates for crack-outs when they're graded on the low side.

Halperin has found that if NGC grades a coin 65, then PCGS almost always will do likewise—eventually, if not immediately. He finds NGC'S grading to be "slightly more consistent" than PCGS's. "I wouldn't say that the standards are significantly different," he adds. "NGC tends to give the coin the highest grade they will give it the first time, probably because they have fewer graders."

Being active dealers, PCGS owners and their affiliates bid on PCGS coins. (Note: PCGS owners who bid on PCGS coins are not involved in the day-to-day grading.) This, Halperin says, helps explain why some PCGS-graded coins have higher sight-unseen

Jeweluster. This is a popular, mildly acidic dip.
Photo courtesy Bill Fivaz

values than their NGC counterparts. NGC coins frequently are submitted to PCGS for crossovers, he adds, because PCGS coins sometimes sell for more—and then the process becomes a self-fulfilling prophecy. "PCGS will tend to put the better NGC coins in their holders and reject the lower-grade coins—on average," Halperin says, "but that trend could reverse itself easily if there were suddenly more demand for NGC coins." It would be an interesting play, he says, to buy coins that sell for considerably less in NGC holders and wait until the NGC coins become more popular than the PCGS coins.

Dipping Coins

Silver coins often are dipped in a mildly acidic solution—thiourea—to remove toning or tarnish from their surfaces. This process, which is cumulative, can improve the appearance of a coin, making it brighter and enhancing its aesthetic appeal. Unfortunately, it also can expose underlying defects such as scratches and hairlines that were hidden by this layer before it was removed. What's more, it can leave the surfaces with a dull and washed-out look.

Coins which are original—that is to say, have never been subjected to artificial toning or other unnatural tinkering—tend to dip well. If you can't tell whether a coin is original or not, you shouldn't dip it. And if you want to test your skill, you should start with low-priced coins while you're still learning. Jim Halperin has a knack for spotting original coins, but to maximize his success rate, he has to look at coins out of their holders in order to determine if they will dip well. He can judge their potential, however, while they're still holdered. Jim has a word of advice for would-be dippers seeking to use this technique to improve their chances at upgrades: "Anyone who plays this game is going to have to pay for the education."

Superbly toned Norfolk commemorative half dollar graded MS-65 by PCGS which might qualify for an upgrade. Anthony Swiatek recommends this coin type as a prime "crackout" candidate. *Photo courtesy Heritage*

Cracking Out Commemorative Coins

Anthony J. Swiatek, a nationally known coin dealer and author from Manhasset, New York, is widely regarded as the world's preeminent authority on U.S. commemorative coins—special coins issued periodically since 1892 to honor some significant person, organization, place, or event in our nation's history. Over the years, Swiatek has followed the crack-out game closely within this important segment of the rare coin marketplace, and he has concluded that certain "commems" stand a much better chance than others of being upgraded upon resubmission.

Swiatek has identified six coins which are most likely to achieve an upgrade from MS-63 to 64, MS-64 to 65, or MS-65 to 66. All six are half dollars issued by the U.S. Mint during the "traditional" period of the nation's commemorative coinage, which extended from 1892 through 1954. (The so-called "modern" period began in 1982, after a hiatus of nearly three decades.) Here are his selections:

1. 1936 Norfolk, Virginia, bicentennial half dollar

2. 1936 Wisconsin territorial centennial half dollar

3. 1936 York County, Maine, tercentenary half dollar

4. Texas centennial half dollar, including any of the coins struck from 1934 through 1937, except for 1935-P and 1935-S (he specifically is also excluding the 1938 PDS set)

5. 1937-D Oregon Trail Memorial half dollar, a specific issue within a series that was issued sporadically from 1926 through 1939

6. 1946 Iowa centennial half dollar

In general, Swiatek says that a commemorative coin has the best chance of gaining an upgrade if its mintage is relatively high and the price spread between grades is not significant. He adds: "The coin must be eye-appealing, displaying an original white or very lightly toned lustrous surface or possessing an attractively colored toning—such as a rainbowlike play of colors—on one or both sides." What if the coin is dull, dark, or unattractive, rather than flashy? In that case, Swiatek says that the person hoping for an upgrade should practice humming or singing "The Impossible Dream."

PCGS Addresses Crack-Out Secrets

An admirably candid David Hall, founder of PCGS and its current president, originally answered my questions about crack-outs for my book *How to Make Money in Coins Right Now*. His answers are just as illuminating today as they were when he was interviewed in 1996:

TRAVERS: PCGS looks at a coin, and perhaps the coin is worth $10,000 as a 65 and $2,000 as a 64, and it's kind of splitting hairs between whether it's called 65 or 64. If you call it 65, you've created wealth—you've given possibly $8,000 to the submitter. On the other hand, if you call it a 64, in a sense you're taking wealth away. How does that make you feel?

HALL: Well, again, we didn't start PCGS to feed this arbitrage that's developed over minute differences in grade. I accept that it's part of the business. And in my mind, I think it's actually overemphasized. I think that the crack-out arbitrage artists don't do as well as they say they do. I sometimes review coins; I'm not a grader, but I sometimes review coins just to sort of see what's going on. And in my mind, the arbitrage crack-out artists take huge risk, and they lose as often as they win.

TRAVERS: Let's talk about those coins that are resubmitted—the coins that are right-at-the-edge coins, the ones where they could be the lower grade or the higher grade. How can somebody outguess the experts? What do your graders look for when they're sitting there in their rooms grading the coins?

HALL: You're asking me a couple of different questions. First is, what do the graders look for. And the graders basically look at the same thing that all coin dealers look at when they're grading coins. For Mint State coins, they're looking at strike, luster, the amount of marks, and the eye appeal of the coin. The coin that does the best at PCGS is the coin that has great eye appeal. One of the sayings in the grading room is that eye appeal adds a little and forgives a lot. So good-looking coins will do the best at PCGS.

TRAVERS: What kinds of coins are most likely to be cracked out as lower-grade coins and are most likely to get the higher grade?

HALL: The coins that are most often cracked out, at least by the professionals, are those that have the biggest spread between the grades—those with the biggest financial incentive to crack out.

TRAVERS: And the lowest downside on the lower grade?

HALL: I think that most coin dealers are huge risk-takers and don't properly assess the downside. I think a lot of them don't even think about it. It is my experience that most coin dealers aren't that sophisticated.

TRAVERS: What do you think about dipping?

HALL: I think that silver coins, in particular, can be dipped and you can't tell whether they're dipped or not. Now, they can be over-dipped, and the luster gets stripped away. Dipping is cumulative.

TRAVERS: How can someone tell if a coin will be able to take a dipping?

HALL: First of all, you have to decide what the object is. Most coins have more to lose than gain by dipping. So if a coin looks original and has a little color, that's a plus—certainly at PCGS. And there would be no reason to dip that coin. Only if perhaps there's a minor fingerprint—say, on a proof Walking Liberty half dollar—or a little bit of haze in the field. That coin could possibly—possibly—improve in appearance if it had a light dip. What you're looking for is maybe light discoloration, light haze, a light fingerprint—light, light, light, light, light. Little, little—something small. If a coin is heavily toned, in some cases it digs into the surface of the coin. That coin is going to look horrible after you dip it, so you're going to go from bad to worse. Encrusted, mottled, yucky toning—just deal with it; don't dip the coin. It's 10 to 1 that it will turn out better.

TRAVERS: What are the coins that are most likely to be on the edge, where PCGS isn't sure—where a grader like Ron Howard might actually sit there and labor over the coin and say, "I'm just not sure. Should I call this a 64 or a 65?"

HALL: As he does! I don't know what you're telling your readers, but I want to stress that in my opinion, professional crack-out artists have a difficult time. Yes, they win. Yes, some of them make a very good living at it. They are extremely talented rare-coin graders. It is, in my opinion, a total and complete waste of time for a novice to try to make a hit cracking coins out or sending them in for regrades.

TRAVERS: What coins would Ron likely labor over and say, "Should I call it 64 or call it 65?"

HALL: Coins that are on the line. A coin that's a very high-end for the grade that it's in. And how do you tell? You have to be a professional coin grader. You have to just have 20 years of experience and have looked at a hundred million dollars' worth of coins and won and lost a lot of money buying and selling coins. I do have a rare coin firm, and believe it or not, we really don't crack coins out.

TRAVERS: You never crack coins out, or you just generally don't?

HALL: Occasionally, we'll send in coins through the PCGS regrade service, maybe 5 or 10 coins a month.

TRAVERS: You own a coin firm. Do you ever grade coins at PCGS?

HALL: No.

TRAVERS: What coin types do you think people would have the greatest crack-out advantage with?

HALL: This may sound incredible, but I've never really thought of it in those terms—that a particular type is easier to make, so to speak, than the others. I know there are some coins that are really, really hard to make, and all you have to do is just look at the population report. You'll see, for instance, that a $2½ Indian in MS-67 is going to be hard to make. Therefore, if you have a $2½ Indian in MS-66, it's probably pretty foolish to try to get it to grade MS-67.

TRAVERS: Let's talk about some of the more obvious scores. How about coins in older holders, both from your service and from NGC. Coins graded maybe in 1987. Magnificent, brilliant cameo proofs in 65 holders that people might be able to crack out and get 66 or 67 on because you graded under a tighter standard in 1987. I mean, it's no secret that the standards today at both services are not what they were in 1987.

HALL: I disagree with that a little bit. I think that what was happening in '86 and '87 was, the graders were extremely reluctant to grade coins above 65. It was impossible to get a 67, 68, or 69. But in terms of coins that are 63 and 64, there are some people who will pay premiums for old-holder deals.

TRAVERS: I just had one walk in the door—all in PCGS 63 holders. Very old holders. They were graded 63. I'm reasonably certain most of those coins will grade 65. Many of them will grade 64. Some will grade 66. They were all graded in, I think, 1986 and '87.

HALL: It depends on the old-holder deal. I've seen old-holder deals that are embarrassing. In fact, through our guarantee resubmission program, we occasionally buy back coins in old holders.

TRAVERS: So are there any particular coins that you think back in 1986 were more tightly graded? Type coins, for example, that were brilliant, that are in 65 holders.

HALL: I think in general, stuff that is in 65 and 66 holders—again, I think the real difference is the total reluctance in '86 and '87 for graders to grade coins 67 and 68.

Crack-Out Coins to Buy Right Now

I'm ready to make some specific recommendations on crack-out coins that you should consider buying right now. When I first drew up this list in 1996, I sought the expertise of Jesse Lipka, one of the nation's leading crack-out coin dealers, who does business in Flemington, New Jersey, under the corporate name Numismania. In an exclusive interview in 1996, Jesse shared with me secrets he has gleaned from cracking out thousands of coins. Jesse says he no longer plays this game and now focuses almost exclusively on paper money.

Jesse's company grosses millions of dollars per year, and most of his profit used to come from successful crack-outs. Up until 1994, he said, his success rate in getting crack-out coins upgraded was phenomenal. He would go to a convention, buy coins that he considered good candidates for upgrades, and the overwhelming majority would in fact be recertified in the next-higher grade.

A Harder Game to Win

As a sign that times are changing, even the great Jesse Lipka admitted that his success rate in getting crack-out upgrades was down to about half of what it once was. The game has gotten tougher—and this should be fair warning to those of you who think you can get a coin upgraded with little or no trouble and make yourself a quick return of several thousand dollars. If Jesse Lipka, one of the very best crack-out artists in the business, used to enjoy a success rate of only 20 percent—even with his knack for picking winners and his full-time involvement in the game—then you can be pretty sure that your rate will be substantially lower.

Jesse was very selective when buying coins at conventions. His game plan, he said, was to purchase premium-quality coins for which he has to pay little or no premium. This is very similar to what Jim Halperin recommends, as I reported earlier in this chapter. With the game getting tougher, Jesse became more conservative. Today, he says, he has stopped playing it altogether.

Winning may be harder, but the game is still worthwhile, for the fruits of victory can be very sweet indeed. You can improve your chances of winning by patterning your purchases after the experts. With that said, let's examine some of the crack-out coins that you should be buying right now. The coins in this list are not necessarily presented in the order of their importance, and I have deleted some of my original recommendations because market conditions have changed.

Early Gold Type Coins Graded Mint State-62

Gold coins produced in the U.S. Mint's earliest years, from 1795 through 1839, are rare and coveted collectibles, and the price differential from one grade to the next can be many thousands of dollars. Getting an upgrade with one of these coins isn't easy; the certification services are keenly aware of the money that hangs in the balance, so they tend to be very conservative. If you are successful in getting one, however, the reward can be enormous. And the coins with the best potential for winning such an upgrade are those graded Mint State-62—although with many having increased in value, there are fewer coins that meet these conditions.

Let's consider one example of the profit you might reap. A Draped Bust $5 gold piece with a small-eagle design on the reverse—a coin type minted from 1795 through 1798—is worth $58,000 in MS-62, as graded by either PCGS or NGC. In MS-63, the price more than doubles to $125,000.

In many cases, the standards at the services in regard to gold coins are slightly looser now than they were five or so years ago. That loosening may be just a quarter of a point, but that's a significant difference for coins that are near the line from one grade level to the next—quite possibly enough to push a coin up from MS-62 to 63. If you find a really nice PQ early gold coin that was graded 62 several years ago, you might be able to get it upgraded to 63—or even 64—and make a quick profit of tens of thousands of dollars. *The odds are against you; the graders know what's at stake and err on the side of caution with such coins.* But you could make a killing with just one win.

Bust Half Dollars Graded About Uncirculated-58

Bust half dollars—large silver coins issued by the U.S. Mint from 1796 to 1839—are perennially popular with collectors and investors alike. Nice Bust halves are always in

Bust half dollar graded About Uncirculated-58 that appears to be a Mint State-64. This is just the type of coin that would upgrade to MS-64 upon resubmission: It has peerless color and surfaces, with just the slightest trace of friction on the highest points.

demand and easy to sell, even in higher circulated grades. For this reason, many have been certified in grade levels from About Uncirculated right through the Mint State range,.and that has created interesting opportunities for profitable upgrades.

Frequently, an otherwise eye-popping Bust half dollar will be graded only About Uncirculated-58 because of light rub (or friction) on the high points; the graders will reason that this is evidence of wear, however slight, and that they cannot assign a Mint State grade. At other times, however, the services will give MS grades to attractive Bust halves even if they do exhibit very slight rub. I have even heard of instances where grades as high as Mint State-66 have been given to coins with almost imperceptible—but nonetheless detectable—rub.

Jesse Lipka told me of one case where he bought a Bust half dollar graded AU-58 by NGC, cracked it out of its holder, resubmitted it to NGC, and got it regraded as Mint State-64. I wouldn't expect an upgrade from AU-58 to MS-64-or MS-66—very often, but if you succeed in getting one, you'll pocket a tidy profit. In fact, you'll do quite well even if you get that AU-58 coin upgraded to MS-62. At this writing, certified Bust halves are worth $300 in AU-58, $750 in MS-62, $1,500 in MS-63, and $3,000 in MS-64. You should look for a coin with attractive, original luster, where the surfaces are beautiful and unimpeded and which is being graded AU-58 only because it has a light rub. That kind of coin could easily be upgraded to MS-62, and might even get a higher grade than that.

Coins That Were Certified by One of the Major Grading Services During Its Formative Period

By their own admission, PCGS and NGC were much stricter in grading coins—especially in very high levels—during the time when they were first doing business. As PCGS's founder and president, David Hall, puts it, the graders were much less willing to give out grades above Mint State-65. They were frankly afraid of those higher grades during the services' very early stages. If you can locate coins that were certified during those years, you stand an excellent chance of getting upgrades. It's possible for you to distinguish coins that were graded then by checking the holders. PCGS holders have been modified since then, and NGC didn't add embedded holograms to its holders until it had been in business several years.

Your best bet is to stick with premium-quality brilliant coins. With these, you will be almost certain of upgrades much of the time. Jim Halperin confided that with brilliant coins that were certified by one of the major services from 1986 to 1988, his success rate at getting upgrades has been almost 100 percent, although he has had to resubmit some coins more than once in order to get them. Jesse Lipka helped one prominent collector get upgrades on many coins prior to the sale of a notable collection of Liberty $10 gold pieces, a sale which took place as part of a Heritage auction in Long Beach, California. After helping the collector assemble the coins in the first place, Lipka selected 110 specimens to crack out and resubmit to PCGS, largely on the basis that they had been graded originally during the early years of third-party certification. Fifty-five of these coins—fully half—received upgrades. And all 11 coins that were housed in NGC holders crossed into PCGS holders—with not a single one going down in grade.

Do not crack toned coins out of their holders—especially if the holders are early ones; toning was viewed with favor in the services' early stages, and toned coins graded then might well come back today with lower grades. By contrast, brilliant coins are very much in favor now; attractive, problem-free examples of these are universally seen as being desirable. These brilliant coins are prime candidates for crack-outs and upgrades—which could be highly lucrative for you if you handle things right.

Insights from a Crack-Out Expert

Jesse Lipka used to play the crack-out game about as well as anyone in the business, and he has made some interesting observations along the way. (He now focuses most of his attention on the paper money arena, where he has established himself as a leading authority.) According to Jesse, NGC is more likely than PCGS to become excited when it gets a group of flashy, original coins. On the other hand, he said, NGC may penalize a gem coin if it is submitted in a group that also includes inferior coins. Jesse said PCGS is much more concerned with a coin's technical qualities. For that reason, he said that it sometimes overgrades coins which comply fully with the technical requirements for a grade but which don't have much pizzazz and may even be unattractive from the standpoints of luster and eye appeal. These unappealing coins, Jesse said, are hard to sell and end up getting sold at a discount.

I asked Jesse to tell me about the crack-out that gave him the greatest satisfaction. After pondering the question, he pointed to his purchase of an 1873 doubled-die Indian Head cent, a coin which many feel is the king of Indian cents. He purchased the coin for $19,500 in a PCGS holder with a grade of Mint State-64 Red-Brown. He cracked the coin out of this holder and submitted it to NGC, which then graded it Mint State-65

Uncertified or "raw" 12-coin U.S. gold type set. These common-date generic coins appeal to investors because of the beauty of their designs and the fact that the coins are gold. *Photograph courtesy Capital Plastics*

Red-Brown. Leaving it in its new NGC holder, he then sent it to PCGS for consideration as a crossover—a process by which a coin in one service's holder is transferred to a different service's holder at the same or higher grade without having to be cracked out before submission. Lo and behold, the coin crossed over, ending up in a PCGS holder with a grade of Mint State-65 Red-Brown. Remember, this was the same coin PCGS had graded originally as Mint State-64 Red-Brown. With the coin now certified a full grade level higher, Jesse then sold it for a tremendous profit. To make this success story even sweeter, the dealer who bought it had passed on it initially when it was still in a Mint State-64 Red-Brown PCGS holder and it was offered to him then for less than what Jesse originally paid.

Profiting from Generic Gold Coins

The crack-out game—which in effect is a kind of grading arbitrage—is a wonderful way to make money in coins right now. There are other ways to turn a hefty profit, as well, and one of the best is to purchase what are known as generic gold coins and then cash them in when gold bullion rises in value. The term "generic" is applied to gold coins which are numismatic in nature but whose mintages and available populations are relatively high—common-date Saint-Gaudens double eagles, for example. A significant rise in the price of gold will trigger an even sharper rise in the value of these coins, since they possess not only precious-metal content but also the cachet of being collectibles. Yet, because they are not really rare, they often can be purchased for only a modest premium over the current value of the metal they contain.

Generic gold coins occupy a market niche midway between bullion-type gold coins and gold rarities. Bullion coins—the American Eagle, Canadian Maple Leaf, and South African Krugerrand, for example—typically are sold for just a small premium over their metal value, with metal value serving as the overriding determinant in their price at a given time. Rare-date gold pieces, such as the 1907 High-Relief Saint-Gaudens double eagle, frequently command premiums in the tens of thousands of dollars, and their value is based overwhelmingly on their low mintage, not their metal content. Generic gold coins exist in sufficient quantities to be traded as like-kind units—very much like commodities—and when the precious-metals markets are calm, their prices tend to hover not much above the value of gold bullion. But when the markets get hot, they benefit psychologically from their status as collectibles, and this drives up their value far beyond the rise in gold itself.

Precious-metal content is a key consideration in the value of generic gold coins, far more than it is for rare gold coins. This is especially true for coins in the highest circulated grades—AU-55 and AU-58—and those in the lowest Mint State grades. In these grades, generic gold coins are virtually bullion coins, very much like the American Eagle and the Maple Leaf: They rise and fall in value in lockstep with gold itself. The price differential widens, however, in grade levels of MS-63 and above. Coins in these grade levels tend to perform especially well when gold bullion gets "hot" and its price goes up dramatically within a short period of time.

Generic Gold's Price Performance

High-grade generic gold coins were flying high in May 1989, when the coin market scaled its last major peak. They plunged in value thereafter, reflecting the sharp downturn in the coin market as a whole—even though gold itself never took a similar tumble in price. As of this writing, gold is selling for about $550 an ounce—a modest advance over its average price of $372 in May 1989. Yet high-grade generic gold coins are far below the levels they enjoyed at that time; most are worth less than half of their 1989 highs. But if we were to witness meaningful upward movement in the price of gold bullion—say, $100 an ounce or more—these coins would almost certainly surge in value by hundreds of dollars apiece—far more, percentagewise, than the metal itself. Those who purchased the coins when the market was in a lull could reap a handsome dividend in the whirlwind.

Potential profits exist from trades in generic gold even during periods when the bullion market is flat. Gold itself has been remarkably steady—some would say stagnant—from 1989 through 2000, but during that time it has made modest moves on several different occasions, and high-grade generic gold coins have invariably made even stronger gains at such times. Traders who were shrewd (or fortunate) enough to ride these waves in the marketplace-buying at low ebb and selling at high tide—landed on the beach with big profits.

Consider these examples:

- On May 26, 1989, the *Bluesheet* assigned a sight-unseen bid of $3,950 to common-date Saint-Gaudens double eagles graded Mint State-65 by PCGS. As this book goes to press, those same coins are listed at $990—about 25 percent of what they were worth at that peak. But they didn't fall to this point in a straight line. For an eleven-month period during 1992–1993, they actually rose in value more than 40 percent. And similar price swings have taken place several times since 1989.

- On May 26, 1989, *Bluesheet* bid was $2,400 for Indian Head eagles ($10 gold pieces) graded Mint State-63 by PCGS. At this writing, those coins are down to $725, or a tad more than 30 percent of that amount. But again there have been significant upward spikes along the way. For instance, the price rebounded from $790 in July 1992 to $1,400 in June 1993—an increase of more than 77 percent.
- On May 26, 1989, the *Bluesheet* showed a sight-unseen bid of $3,050 for Liberty eagles with motto (dates bearing the motto IN GOD WE TRUST) graded MS-63 by PCGS. Today, those coins are bid just $675—slightly more than 22 percent of that lofty peak. But here, too, there have been some highly impressive ups along with the downs: The price bounced back, for example, from $875 in July 1992 to $1,240 in June 1993—a gain of more than 40 percent.

Not all generic gold coins have fallen as far as these—or fluctuated as greatly—since 1989. Many have experienced significant swings in value, though, creating opportunities for keen-witted traders to buy and sell advantageously, and each time they have risen, they have done so more dramatically than gold bullion.

Rolling the dice repeatedly on gold's price performance is not for the faint of heart. It's very much a gambler's game—one that can be extremely risky. In a way, it's like playing musical chairs with your money, and I don't recommend it for ordinary consumers. Even expert dealers have difficulty doing it successfully. But there's far less risk involved in rolling the dice just once, assuming you make your purchases at a time when the markets in coins and precious metals are inactive.

You should buy generic gold coins at a time when both gold itself and the coins you are acquiring are relatively low in price, compared with near-past levels. You should sell them when you see prices trending upward without much apparent economic justification. Inflation, an expanded money supply, and increased federal spending all could be viewed as true economic justification for gold and gold coins to rise in value. In their absence, a sudden rise in generic gold coins' value could simply reflect a major market promotion, and that would be a signal to sell your coins. In any case, I urge you to limit your expenditures to totally discretionary funds—money that isn't essential to your economic well-being.

Rare Gold Coins' Performance

In contrast to generic gold, rare gold coins have evidenced little price movement in recent years. Since plunging in value along with the rest of the coin market in 1989 and 1990, they were depressed almost unremittingly until the market woke up in the early 2000s. There's a simple reason for this: Rare gold coins don't exist in quantity, so they cannot be promoted by entrepreneurs. As a result, they don't enjoy the temporary price boosts created by such promotions. Rather, they lie dormant until the market regains more permanent underlying strength.

Truly rare gold coins are much better buys from the standpoint of long-term investment. They benefit more dramatically than generic gold coins when market conditions are bullish, for just as their malaise is more pronounced and persistent during slumps, their gains are more spectacular and sustained when the market is strong. They have the potential to soar far faster and higher in value when a turnaround occurs, for they are more elusive and desirable. But during bear markets, such as the one we've seen since 1989, generic gold coins offer much greater opportunities for action—and gains—in the short term.

If Gold Went Up $100 an Ounce

Gold bullion and rare coins have a symbiotic relationship. They complement each other well, and people with an interest in one of them tend to find the other appealing as well. In the 20-plus years since Americans regained the right to private gold ownership in 1974, strength in gold bullion has often gone hand-in-hand with similar strength in rare coins. The most dramatic example occurred in 1979 and 1980, when gold's amazing surge to $850 an ounce coincided with the coin market's most spectacular boom.

In recent years, the relationship between gold bullion and rare coins was a case of misery loving company. Both were in the doldrums throughout the 1990s, and both were well below the price levels they scaled in the booming 1980s. But both are participating in a turnaround as this is written in early 2005, and if that upturn continues in the bullion market, it's likely to cause a coin boom of unprecedented magnitude. And if history is any guide—as it almost always is—a surge in the price of gold will be magnified when its impact hits the coin market.

As this is written, gold is trading for about $550 an ounce. Some experts see a realistic chance that given the right combination of economic circumstances, the yellow metal's price could easily reach the $1,000 range within a short period of time. That could be an enormous boost for the coin market. I am convinced that if gold does go up even $100 an ounce, many rare coins—and even some not-so-rare coins—will jump in value. That could create tremendous opportunities for those who take advantage of the marketplace.

There is ample historical precedent for gold to go up dramatically and quickly. Just look at what happened in 1979 and 1980, when it surged within a year from $236 an ounce to $850. Even in recent years, amid the general stagnation, there have been periods when gold rose appreciably in short but significant spurts before dropping back to a dead calm. When that occurs, we see an almost immediate impact on coins that are bullion-sensitive—bullion-type coins and generic gold coins. If the increase in the price of gold bullion is sustained, the effect spreads to other gold coins with only incidental bullion value. Finally, it is felt by the marketplace as a whole, including coins with no precious metal at all.

During such periods, gold coins that possess numismatic value tend to rise in price even more sharply than the rise in gold itself.

When David Hall talks about rare coins, people listen. David was a major figure in the coin market even before he founded PCGS in 1986 and ushered in the Age of Certified Coins; for many years before that, he had been a prominent dealer. Since that time, his stature has grown even more. People who buy and sell coins hang on his every word when he comments on any aspect of the marketplace. Hall believes the coins most likely to yield big profits if the price of gold goes up are Saint-Gaudens $20s and "almost all the Liberty gold" in grades of MS-64 and 65. "The generic gold issues will be the first to feel it and they'll feel it very quickly," he told me. Hall sees it as "a relatively safe play" to buy generic gold when the market is dormant and set it aside for sale when things heat up. "You know, it's a pretty volatile world that we live in," he remarked, "but it certainly looks like a pretty safe bet."

Generic gold coins such as common-date Saint-Gaudens double eagles are looked upon as collectibles, to be sure, but their precious-metal content is also a major factor in their value. Thus, it makes sense that a rise in the price of gold would have a direct impact on the value of these coins. There's less apparent reason, though, why similar increases—or even more spectacular ones—should take place in the prices of rarer-date gold coins already selling for multiples of their precious-metal value. Yet we have seen such increases time and again, and we have even seen them, in brief but impressive bursts, when gold prices increased only temporarily.

"Every time gold bullion moves over $400 per ounce, prices seem to immediately jump up—especially for the top-quality gold coins," David Hall pointed out. "If gold makes a significant move above $400, prices could rise an additional 20 percent to 30 percent from current levels. If gold gets over $450 an ounce, prices could easily rise 30 percent to 50 percent. And if gold can get to $500 and stay there, prices could rise 50 percent to 100 percent on virtually all top-quality rare coins."

What would this mean in dollars and cents? Let's consider the no-motto Liberty $5, so named because it lacks the motto, "IN GOD WE TRUST." In Mint State-63, this genuinely rare coin type has a current market value, as this goes to press, of $5,600, or more than 20 times the value of the gold it contains. Based on David Hall's estimate, if gold were to go up $100 an ounce, we might very well see this coin rise in value to as much as $9,200. An MS-64 example, now $7,500, could shoot up in price to more than $17,000.

The impact would be felt by major rarities, too. In fact, they could enjoy an even bigger boost because they are so sensitive to even the very slightest rise in demand.

When rare collector coins react in this way to a rise in the price of gold, it's largely a matter of marketplace psychology. Bullion-market activity creates a positive climate for the coin market, too, and the newly kindled enthusiasm feeds upon itself. In a very real sense, it soon becomes a self-fulfilling prophecy. The strength in precious metals provides a kind of security blanket, reassuring buyers and making them more receptive to purchasing coins as well. We then see this strong new demand acting upon supplies that are really much scarcer than most people ever realized. This, in turn, drives prices sharply higher, attracting even more attention and bringing even more new buyers into the market.

A Spillover Effect

If a $100 rise in the price of gold bullion were sustained, the effect would soon spill over into Mint State Type coins, Proof Type coins, and other rare coins not even made of gold, and, in many instances, not even made of precious metal.

- Proof-65 Barber quarters, worth about $1,500, could very well go up more than 50 percent—to the $2,250 range—under such a scenario. Keep in mind, these coins were worth many thousands of dollars in the late 1980s.
- Proof-65 no-motto Liberty Seated quarters, now selling for $3,500, could jump almost overnight to $5,000 or more.
- Coins which are highly sensitive to changes in the population and census reports—coins graded Mint State-67 and 68 and Proof-67 and 68, for example—also are very sensitive to movements in bullion prices, and would rise in value significantly in response to a meaningful rise in the price of gold. In fact, this could prove to be the most profitable area of the marketplace if gold were to go up $100 an ounce and sustain the gain.
- Traditional U.S. commemorative coins—those issued prior to 1982—would feel the impact, too. As of this writing, beautiful white Mint State-65 examples of many of these coins are priced at $500 or less. In 1989, some of these coins carried price tags of $2,500, $3,000, or even $4,000. If gold went up $100 an ounce, the excitement could propel these coins to several times their current market value. Within a matter of weeks, they could easily become $1,500 or $2,000 coins.

Diversified Potential Winners

In 1996, David Hall and I put together a perennial list of winners. It includes both regular-issue U.S. Type coins and U.S. commemorative coins, and the price range is broad, stretching all the way from $150 to $12,000.

COIN	GRADE	WHOLESALE VALUE 2/05
Two-cent piece	MS-65 RD	$1,000
Three-cent silver	PR-65	1,200
Capped Bust 25¢	MS-65	12,000
Liberty Seated 25¢	MS-65	1,500
1854-55 Liberty Seated 25¢ with arrows beside the date	MS-65	6,300
Trade $1	MS-65	7,000
1920 Pilgrim Tercentenary 50¢	MS-65	250

COIN	GRADE	WHOLESALE VALUE 2/05
1936 Long Island Tercentenary 50¢	MS-65	250
1918 Illinois Centennial 50¢	MS-65	325
1925-S California Jubilee 50¢	MS-65	750
1936 Delaware Tercentenary 50¢	MS-65	300
1934 Texas Centennial 50¢	MS-65	150

For people on limited budgets, David Hall recommended three "ultra bargains": common-date MS-66 Mercury dimes with full bands in the fasces ("40 bucks or so—an incredible deal"); slightly better—date Buffalo nickels—any dates in the 1930s other than 1937-P and 1938-D—whose going market price is under $100; and inexpensive pre-1982 commemoratives. For big-budget people, Hall said, "The world revolves around proof gold, and proof gold is an unbelievably good long-term deal. If we were to see any move in the gold bullion market that created more activity in the coin market, proof gold prices could easily double in value," he predicted.

Hall encourages collectors to assemble coins in sets, which he regards as a good long-term strategy. However, he considers it inadvisable to pursue coins in extremely high levels of preservation. "If you want to make money right now," he said, "don't get involved in what I call the gaga grades . . . condition rarities, fairly common coins in 69, 68, even 67 condition. Whether you're buying inexpensive coins or expensive coins, don't go for the wild grades."

Coin Dealers' Role

Coin dealers play a highly pivotal role in energizing the coin market when there is a surge in the price of precious metal. They do this, in part, by alerting their clients and getting the ball rolling, so to speak. But they are active participants—and crucial ones, at that—in the whole process. Indeed, they are the ultimate consumers of many coins, and because so many coin dealers buy and sell gold in bullion forms as well, these dealers serve to cross-pollinate the interrelated coin and bullion markets. We saw graphic evidence of this during the white-hot coin market boom of 1980. Coin dealers made enormous sums of money trading in gold and silver at that time, and many of them plowed those profits right back into coins. That fueled the boom and drove up rare coins' prices even more.

Profit and Loss in a Coin Trading Fund

Rare coins received extensive—and largely unwelcome—media coverage in the spring of 2005 when an Ohio newspaper, the *Toledo Blade*, published a long series of articles detailing how the Ohio Bureau of Workers' Compensation had invested $50 million in two limited partnerships managed by Maumee, Ohio, coin dealer Thomas W. Noe, to buy and sell collectibles, particularly coins. The board, which administers monies used to pay disabled state employees, was seeking to improve the return it received from traditional investments such as stocks and bonds and set aside $500 million for an "emerging manager program." According to an editorial by Beth Deisher in *Coin World*, "Noe was one of 28 managers selected for the program and one of three whose investments would be classified as alternative as opposed to traditional."

The *Blade* raised a number of questions about Noe's handling of the bureau's millions, reporting among other things that 121 of the coins he bought for the state, worth a total of about $400,000, were apparently missing. Most of the coins were later located.

At first, Noe defended his actions and claimed that his acquisitions had realized a net profit to the fund of about $13.3 million. When the critical front-page articles continued, however, the story took a disturbing turn: With state officials demanding a full accounting of how the money had been spent, Noe's attorneys reportedly acknowledged a shortfall or gap of up to $12 million of the state funds. Ohio Gov. Bob Taft expressed outrage, and Republican office-holders up to and including President George W. Bush rushed to distance themselves from what was now being called "Coingate" by renouncing campaign contributions they had received from Noe, a major GOP fund-raiser and donor. "I am outraged, I am angered, I am saddened and I am sickened," Taft told The Associated Press. Taft later was found guilty of charges that he violated Ohio ethics law by neglecting to report golf games (some with Noe) and other gifts and was fined $4,000.

The story was still unfolding in October 2005, when an indictment was returned against Noe by a federal grand jury on three felony counts of allegedly laundering $45,400 to the Bush-Cheney reelection campaign. No others charges were filed as of that time, although a state grand jury and another federal grand jury had been convened. Noe resigned from a number of important posts, including the chairmanship of the U.S. Citizens Coinage Advisory Committee, a panel that advises the U.S. Treasury Department on coin-related matters. It also was unclear how the episode might affect the rare-coin market, since "Coingate" had been publicized well beyond Ohio by AP and other news organizations including the *New York Times*, which put the story on its front page.

Not everyone agreed with suggestions that Ohio officials acted unwisely in channeling $50 million into collectibles. "For a fund that manages $18 billion, having $50 million—less than three-tenths of 1 percent in a subset called 'rare coins'—is not imprudent," said prize-winning newsletter editor Maurice Rosen. "It is a test or pilot investment to see if this alternative area holds promise for further commitment."

D. Larry Crumbley, a tax accountant with special expertise on coin investment, agreed with Rosen's assessment. "I consider investing less than three-tenths of 1 percent into coins much safer than investing most of my retirement money into WorldCom or Enron stock," Crumbley said. "Many employees invest 50 percent to 80 percent of their retirement savings in their own company's stock." Crumbley also sought to put any coin scandal in perspective. "Fraud and abuse in the U.S. ranges from $660 billion to $1 trillion each year," he said. "I estimate state government losses to be at least $354 billion each year, local governments' loss $68 billion each year and the Federal government loses $239 billion each year to fraud and abuse."

David L. Ganz, a lawyer with an extensive background in numismatics, said Ohio officials' decision to allocate money to rare coins was "not particularly surprising, since studies by Salomon Brothers starting in the 1970s showed that rare coins consistently outperformed many other investment vehicles and offered the possibility of a high rate of return." (It is explained in chapter 17 that by the early 1990s, abuse of the Salomon surveys had caused such serious problems that the Federal Trade Commission pressured the firm to remove rare coins from its studies.) Ganz added that the Ohio bureau "lost tens of millions of dollars" on a stock-derivative investment and concluded: "Rare coins offered a more attractive alternative, and better results."

Still, many observers agreed with John Albanese, a longtime professional numismatist, when he said: "Coins or any other hard asset have no place in pension plans. These plans, by design, benefit those that invest in income-producing assets. Because of compounding, it's advantageous to leave tax-free accounts in income-producing investments."

"The Ohio Bureau of Workers' Compensation could have bought Newmont Mining common stock at $22 and sold it for $50. The way Noe's funds were run, Noe was essentially investing in businesses—coin businesses. It was like a private equity fund. After the dotcom bubble burst, a number of fund managers were looking to alternative investments. In retrospect, that was the best time to buy stocks."

Ganz said that placement of coins and other collectibles in public pension funds are legal provided that local law for the state involved follows the "prudent man" rule: Any investment is legal provided a reasonably prudent person with knowledge of all of the facts would comfortably make such an investment.

Tips on Making Coins Profitable

Making money from coins—right now or at any other time—depends to a great extent on establishing and following a set of prudent guidelines on when, what, and how to buy, on the one hand, and when, what, and how to sell on the other. The extent to which you do this will go a long way toward determining how much profit you make—or if you make any at all.

I've drawn up a list of pointers that you would do well to follow. Some may seem like simple common sense; others won't be so obvious to people outside the coin market's inner circle. All of them, however, are secrets to success for those who make money from coins—and they can help you achieve the same success.

- **Become a collector/investor.** One of the most often-heard pieces of advice in coin books and periodicals is that people who invest in coins should first become collectors. I like to turn this around, though: People should look upon coins not only as collectibles but also

This 1916-S Mercury dime in an older NGC holder (left) and graded MS-66FB was recently upgraded by PCGS to MS-67FB. Digital photographic close-ups show the coin to have possibly been dipped before submission to PCGS. The value of the upgrade is thousands of dollars, although coins in older NGC holders sometimes trade at a significant premium. *Photographs selected by Jim Halperin and courtesy Heritage*

as investments. Too often, collectors put so much emphasis on the historical, cultural, and aesthetic aspects of coins that they don't pay enough attention to the real—and important—financial implications of their purchases. Investors should indeed get a feel for the intangible aspects of coins—but by the same token, collectors should make it their business to learn all they can about the market value of coins they are considering for their sets. In years to come, the collector/investor will play an increasingly dominant role in the coin marketplace. To maximize your success, you need to possess both mentalities.

- **Know a coin's value and its current grading standards at all times.** Recently, I read an article suggesting that when a coin buyer negotiates with a seller, the buyer should always start by offering the seller a certain fixed percentage below the asking price. This is, pure and simple, one of the worst ideas I've ever heard. It totally ignores the clear and present danger that the asking price might be far above the coin's true market value. To use an extreme example, let's say a given coin is worth $1,000 and someone is offering it for sale for $10,000. It would be preposterous for you to offer to buy it for $5,000, simply because your strategy was to open negotiations at 50 percent of the asking price. Then again, if someone offered you that same $1,000 coin for just $50, there would be no point in trying to haggle the price down to $25. You would simply say, "OK, $50 is fine," buy the coin, and sell it for a very handsome profit. If you don't know the value of a coin, you shouldn't be negotiating to buy it. If you do know the value, you have a big advantage over other people who don't.
- **Crack out any slabbed coins that appear to be undergraded.** We covered this subject in great detail at the outset of this chapter. Getting a high-end coin recertified in the next-higher grade can pay you an instant dividend of hundreds—even thousands—of dollars. This is a case where knowledge is not only power but also a passkey to profit.
- **Buy low and sell high.** This is a tip that seems self-evident, but following it successfully is easier said than done. If prices have fallen sharply within a short period of time, that

might be an excellent time to buy. If prices are rising rapidly, that might be a very good time to sell. One way to avoid getting burned by fast-changing market values is to cost-average your purchases. If you plan to invest $10,000 in coins, don't spend it all at once, figuring you can outguess the marketplace—even experts have trouble doing that. Instead, spend a set amount—say, $1,000 a month—over an extended period of time. You'd make more money with a single lucky guess, but spreading out your purchases will give you far greater protection against unforeseen market changes.

- **Read books and stay informed.** Knowledge is power in the coin market, and there's really no such thing as knowing too much. The more you know about coins, the likelier it is that you'll recognize a bargain when it appears—or be able to seize an opportunity to sell a coin and pocket a hefty profit. Many excellent books are available today—more than ever before in the coin hobby's history. You also should monitor current market values by checking and analyzing the prices listed each week in the *Certified Coin Dealer Newsletter*, or *Bluesheet*, as well as its sister publication, *The Coin Dealer Newsletter*, or *Greysheet*, which covers market activity in coins that have not been certified. I also strongly recommend that you keep abreast of developments by reading all the excellent coin periodicals now being published.
- **Be decisive and take action.** Quick action pays big dividends in the coin market—more so than in almost any other field. If you order a coin through the mail and it doesn't meet your standards when you get it, don't waste time: Return it to the seller right away. The same goes for coins that you purchase at a show. The longer you wait, the less chance you will have of getting your money back and the greater the chance will be that the dealer's return privilege will expire. Conversely, if you have a coin that rises in value quickly, it would be a good idea to sell it and take your profit. Go to the cash window, celebrate—and don't even think about looking back.
- **Make sure you have the coins.** This may sound ridiculous, but I can assure you it isn't. Many people buy coins in very large quantities, much like commodities. For instance, they may order a thousand generic Morgan dollars—common-date pieces such as the 1881-S—and the coins may arrive in a box from a mail-order dealer. Months or years later, when they go to sell the coins, they may find to their chagrin that the box really contains only 600 silver dollars, not 1,000. Worse yet, the dealer from whom they bought the coins may be out of business by that time. It just stands to reason that you can't count your profits if you can't count your coins. Speaking of counting coins, always make sure that you don't get shortchanged when you purchase coins by the roll—and if you show a roll of your coins to a dealer, make sure that he doesn't palm one or two before handing it back.
- **Get rid of underperformers and junk.** Everyone accumulates losers along with winners when buying coins. You need to "weed your garden" from time to time: Pull out your off-grade modern rolls, your common coins—and yes, your junk—and sell them all, even if you have to take a loss. Better coins offer far greater opportunities for profit. Keep this in mind: Coins that are scarce today can become rare in the future, and coins which are rare today can become rarer, but coins that are common today will almost surely remain common, at least for the foreseeable future. Incidentally, I would include virtually all of the

modern commemorative coins issued by the U. S. Mint—those produced since 1982—under the heading of "common."

- **Limit yourself to coins which have been certified by leading grading services.** (Leading grading services can change, so check out the standing of services in *The Certified Coin Dealer Newsletter*.) This is among my most important pointers, but I'm putting it near the end, rather than at the beginning, because I don't want you to use the grading services as a crutch. Certification *is* crucial in the current coin marketplace. Many buyers and sellers won't even handle coins unless they have been certified by one of the major services—and it's hard to find fault with their thinking. Third-party grading removes the nettlesome guesswork that used to plague buyers and sellers, and also much of the risk that used to exist. At the same time, however, you must never lose sight of the fact that when you buy certified coins, what you're really paying for is the coin and not the holder. True, the certification gives the coin greater liquidity, but when all is said and done, the coin should stand on its own merits.
- **For the faint of heart, physically cracking a coin out of its holder to get it upgraded is not always necessary.** NGC and PCGS offer a "crossover" service that lets you send either entity an encapsulated coin graded by another grading service. (Other grading companies offer this as well.) NGC writes: "Coins will be removed from their holder[s] only if they can be graded at the same or higher than your specified minimum grade[s]. You may not request a higher minimum grade than is on the current holder." According to PCGS: "We will grade the [coin] and put [it] in a PCGS holder only if the PCGS grade meets or exceeds the other grading company's grade (unless specifically instructed differently by you). *You cannot specify a higher minimum grade.* If the PCGS grade is lower than the other grading company's grade, we will return the coin to you in the original holder. You will be charged the full grading fee even if your coin does not cross." NGC and PCGS also offer a "regrade" service for coins graded by each respective entity that you would like to have regraded at a higher grade, but not risk having downgraded: You may submit NGC coins in their holders to NGC and PCGS coins in their holders to PCGS. A number of collectors say that they are pleased with the successes they have had in getting coins upgraded using crossover services. In my professional experience, however, the most lucrative upgrades have come from cracking coins out fresh and sending them in.

Artificially toned 1853 Coronet head large cent obverse. Red was added, using a process of warm ammonia, and the coin was then retoned. *Photograph courtesy PCGS*

Artificially toned reverse. This coin's reverse is also natural-looking from a distance, but careful inspection reveals a most unnatural look. *Photograph courtesy PCGS*

Artificially frosted Lincoln head cent Proof obverse. A close inspection of the edges of the frosted devices shows seepage of the acid or auto-body putty into the fields. *Photograph courtesy PCGS*

Artificially frosted Lincoln head cent reverse. The artificially frosted devices glow unnaturally. *Photograph courtesy PCGS*

PCGS "Proof-70" Lincoln head cent that sold at auction for $39,100. PCGS later purchased the coin to take it off the market after spots appeared on the coin's surfaces following certification. *Photograph courtesy Heritage*

Reverse of the PCGS "Proof-70" Lincoln cent. The reverse is also starting to display undesirable toning. *Photograph courtesy Heritage*

Mint State Morgan dollar obverse. Color-coded for grade sensitivity. Red is the worst area for an imperfection, followed by orange, yellow, green, and blue. *Coin map courtesy James L. Halperin, copyright 1986, 1990*

Mint State Morgan dollar reverse. Coin maps by series are provided in Halperin's book *How to Grade U.S. Coins*, published by Ivy Press, Inc. *Coin map courtesy James L. Halperin, copyright 1986, 1990*

MS-68 obverse Carson City Morgan dollar. Free from flaws and possessing vibrant luster. *Photograph courtesy American Numismatic Rarities, LLC*

MS-68 reverse Carson City Morgan dollar. *Photograph courtesy American Numismatic Rarities, LLC*

BEFORE: Improper storage led to the grimy residue and uneven, unattractive toning on this Carson City Morgan dollar obverse. *Photograph courtesy NCS*

AFTER: Carson City Morgan dollar obverse. The grime and residue, as well as unattractive toning, were professionally removed, and the coin looks stunning. A tiny micron layer of metal was likely removed to rid the coin of the unattractive toning. *Photograph courtesy NCS*

MS-66 Morgan dollar obverse. Beautiful toning. The rainbow crescents are original. *Photograph courtesy American Numismatic Rarities, LLC*

MS-66 Morgan dollar reverse. Multi-colored peripheral toning enhances this specimen. *Photograph courtesy American Numismatic Rarities, LLC*

Artificial toning. 1881-O Morgan dollar obverse. Chlorine bleach and sodium sulfite were likely used to create this burnt-chestnut toning. *Photograph courtesy PCGS*

Artificial toning. 1881-O Morgan dollar reverse. The toning is more even on the reverse, but artificial nonetheless. *Photograph courtesy PCGS*

MS-63 Morgan dollar obverse. Numerous abrasions on the cheek and in the fields bring the grade down. *Photograph courtesy American Numismatic Rarities, LLC*

MS-63 Morgan dollar reverse. The reverse also has abrasions in the fields. *Photograph courtesy American Numismatic Rarities, LLC*

MS-62 Morgan dollar obverse. Huge scratches keep this coin far from Gem status, but the satin-like look gives it a boost up from MS-60. *Photograph courtesy American Numismatic Rarities, LLC*

MS-62 Morgan dollar reverse. The reverse is well matched in terms of having multiple marks obscuring the vibrant luster. *Photograph courtesy American Numismatic Rarities, LLC*

AU-58 Morgan dollar obverse. Light, almost unnoticeable wear is visible on the hair (especially the hair above the ear) and cap. An AU-58 should almost be able to pass for Mint State unless examined carefully. *Photograph courtesy American Numismatic Rarities, LLC*

AU-58 Morgan dollar reverse. Trace wear is discernible on the eagle's head and breast, as well as on the edges of the leaves. The fields are also starting to display telltale signs of the lightest rubbing. Look at the slightly darker color, most pronounced above and below the motto. *Photograph courtesy American Numismatic Rarities, LLC*

AU-50 Morgan dollar obverse. Some Mint luster still adheres, but wear is visible above the ear, at the edges of the leaves and cap, on the cheek, and in the fields. *Photograph courtesy American Numismatic Rarities, LLC*

AU-50 Morgan dollar reverse. Wear is visible on the head, breast, and tips of the wings, as well as lightly in the fields. Contact marks throughout. *Photograph courtesy American Numismatic Rarities, LLC*

EF-45 Morgan dollar obverse. Traces of Mint luster cling to the surfaces. *Photograph courtesy American Numismatic Rarities, LLC*

EF-45 Morgan dollar reverse. Hints of Mint luster are visible here, too, despite obvious wear. *Photograph courtesy American Numismatic Rarities, LLC*

EF-40 Morgan dollar obverse. Toned. Notice the obvious wear in the hair and above the ear. *Photograph courtesy American Numismatic Rarities, LLC*

EF-40 Morgan dollar reverse. The eagle's breast and feathers show wear. *Photograph courtesy American Numismatic Rarities, LLC*

VF-25 Morgan dollar obverse. Significant wear is displayed on the hair curls. *Photograph courtesy American Numismatic Rarities, LLC*

VF-25 Morgan dollar reverse. Feathers are visible but worn. *Photograph courtesy American Numismatic Rarities, LLC*

G-6 Morgan dollar obverse. Considerable wear is evident on the portrait. *Photograph courtesy American Numismatic Rarities, LLC*

G-6 Morgan dollar reverse. Some detail is still present on the lower feathers. *Photograph courtesy American Numismatic Rarities, LLC*

AG-3 Morgan dollar obverse. LIBERTY is still readable on the head. *Photograph courtesy American Numismatic Rarities, LLC*

AG-3 Morgan dollar reverse. The rim blends in with some of the lettering. *Photograph courtesy American Numismatic Rarities, LLC*

Proof-65 (circa 1985) Barber half dollar obverse. This exceptionally attractive Proof coin was graded Proof-65 in the mid-1980s. A higher grade would apply today.

Proof-65 (circa 1985) reverse. The beautiful ocean-blue and sunset-gold toning also grace the cameo reverse. Grading services assign stratospheric grades to coins like this today.

Artificially toned Barber dime obverse. The unattractive patches of silver-gray and orange splotchy toning were possibly created by sulfur dissolved in petroleum jelly. *Photograph courtesy PCGS*

Artificially toned Barber dime reverse. The unnatural character of this "second generation" toning should be obvious. *Photograph courtesy PCGS*

Artificially toned Barber quarter obverse. Chlorine bleach created the unnatural gray and brown toning. *Photograph courtesy PCGS*

Artificially toned Barber quarter reverse. *Photograph courtesy PCGS*

MS-65 PCGS Barber half dollar obverse. PCGS holds the line in grading Type coins and rare coins—and has retained a tight and consistent standard. This gray coin does not appear attractive from the photo. *Photograph handpicked by Jim Halperin, courtesy Heritage*

MS-65 PCGS reverse. *Photograph handpicked by Jim Halperin, courtesy Heritage*

Upgraded to MS-66 NGC Barber half dollar obverse. NGC maintains a conservative and consistent standard; it does not grade all PCGS Type coins higher by a point. This is simply one example of an upgraded coin. *Photograph hand-picked by Jim Halperin, courtesy Heritage*

Upgraded to MS-66 NGC reverse. PCGS also sometimes upgrades NGC coins. Grading is subjective. See Chapter 8 for an example of an NGC-graded coin that PCGS regraded at a higher grade. *Photograph hand-picked by Jim Halperin, courtesy Heritage*

Altered "1911-D" Indian head quarter eagle obverse. This was a 1914-D on which the 4 was altered to resemble a 1. Notice that in comparing both numeral ones of "1911" that they are different. Also, tooling marks are visible around the second "1." *Photograph courtesy PCGS*

Reverse shows a genuine D Mint-mark. A genuine example grading MS-65 would command $30,000 in the marketplace. *Photograph courtesy PCGS*

Altered "1927-D" Saint-Gaudens double eagle obverse. A Mint-mark was removed, most likely from a 1923-D, and added to a 1927 Philadelphia Mint example. A genuine and unaltered specimen would command $1 million or more. *Photograph courtesy PCGS*

Blow-up of the date area of the "1927-D." This is one of the most expertly executed and deceptive added Mint-mark gold coins ever seen by the Professional Coin Grading Service. Rare gold specialist Paul Nugget says the genuine specimens he has seen have marginally smaller D Mint-marks that tilt slightly to the right. *Photograph courtesy PCGS*

Reverse of the 1927 (altered to appear "1927-D") Saint-Gaudens double eagle. Nugget says that some genuine 1927-D double eagles he has examined have die lines in the rays on the reverse. *Photograph courtesy PCGS*

BEFORE: Reddish spots, frequently called copper spots, on an Indian head eagle obverse. *Photograph courtesy NCS*

BEFORE: Copper spots on an Indian head eagle reverse. *Photograph courtesy NCS*

AFTER: Indian head eagle obverse after the spots were removed by experts. Removal of these kinds of spots changed the way these coins are traded. See Chapter 18 for information on how some people remove these spots. *Photograph courtesy NCS*

AFTER: Indian head eagle reverse after the spots were professionally removed. Gold with spots like these rarely trade at a discount now between dealers, as dealers know the spots can be removed without a trace—and do not return. *Photograph courtesy NCS*

Noticeably marked MS-65 common-date Saint-Gaudens double eagle obverse graded by a major grading service. This specimen has vibrant luster and a nice "look," but displays nicks, scratches, and abrasions that in my experience are more consistent with a coin graded no better than MS-64. According to dealer John Albanese, overgraded generic gold coins made their way into the marketplace in 2004 and 2005. It is now essential that each coin be carefully inspected before acquisition. *Coin handpicked by Doug Baliko for educational purposes, photograph courtesy Heritage; coin described by Scott Travers without having seen it*

Unsightly MS-65 common-date Saint-Gaudens double eagle obverse graded by another major grading service. This coin also shows detracting marks. Its luster does not appear rich, and it has a commercial look. If the coin looks like the photograph, this is also an instance where in my experience a grade no higher than MS-64 would be warranted. Now, more than ever, it is imperative that you closely examine each coin before purchase. *Coin handpicked by Doug Baliko for educational purposes, photograph courtesy Heritage; coin described by Scott Travers without having seen it*

Environmentally damaged Indian head cent obverse. The black spot eats into the surface and, thus, cannot be successfully removed. Leading services would return this coin ungraded. *Photograph courtesy PCGS*

Environmentally damaged Indian head cent reverse. Tiny black corrosion spots eat into the coin's metal. Spots of this nature which penetrate the surface cannot be removed. *Photograph courtesy PCGS*

Environmentally damaged commemorative half dollar obverse. This Boone commemorative half dollar has environmental damage and will be returned ungraded by most grading services. The toning is more than surface-deep, as it "eats" into the surface of the coin. Notice the deep pitting throughout. *Photograph courtesy PCGS*

Environmentally damaged Proof Mercury dime reverse. Toning interspersed with a porosity which eats into the metal makes this another "no-grade." *Photograph courtesy PCGS*

BEFORE: Black toning areas detract from the aesthetic appeal of this Proof Walking Liberty half dollar reverse. The toning is superficial and can be removed. *Photograph courtesy NCS*

AFTER: Professional removal of the black toning reveals a light cameo contrast. A tiny, thin molecular layer of metal has apparently been taken off. *Photograph courtesy NCS*

Added head. 1920-S Standing Liberty quarter obverse. *Photograph courtesy PCGS*

Added head. Blow-up of the added head on the 1920-S quarter. Actual metal was probably added to the head area, and a jeweler's engraving tool was probably used to shape it. *Photograph courtesy PCGS*

Artificially toned 1918-S Standing Liberty quarter obverse. The light blushes of sky-blue toning were likely added using a small, directional gas torch and sulfur or other chemicals. *Certified as artificial by NCS; photo courtesy Heritage*

Artificially toned 1918-S Standing Liberty quarter reverse. Artificial toning is especially pronounced on the reverse. The lighter peripheral areas were likely wiped clean while the coin was still warm, or a removable mask was applied in advance. *Certified as artificial by NCS; photo courtesy Heritage*

Artificially toned 1855-O Liberty Seated half dollar with Arrows obverse. The toning was likely created by an initial application of bleach and a later enhancement with sodium sulfite. *Certified as artificial by NCS; photo courtesy Heritage*

Artificially toned reverse of the 1855-O Arrows half dollar. The artificial toning is light and multicolored—some would even say attractive. *Certified as artificial by NCS; photo courtesy Heritage*

BEFORE: 1879 Flowing Hair Stella obverse. Unattractive residue obscured the spectacular Proof surfaces. If this is just residue, the top molecular layer of metal might even remain after conservation. *Photograph courtesy NCS*

BEFORE: 1879 Flowing Hair Stella reverse. The cloudiness appears thin and removable. *Photograph courtesy NCS*

AFTER: 1879 Flowing Hair Stella obverse. The residue was removed professionally, and the coin looks lovely. *Photograph courtesy NCS*

AFTER: 1879 Flowing Hair Stella reverse after it was restored. *Photograph courtesy NCS*

– 9 –
MAKING SURE THE PRICE IS RIGHT

> *The Coin Dealer Newsletter* is an accurate reflection of values. You just have to know what the coins look like.
>
> —James L. Halperin, *co-chairman of the board, Heritage Capital Corporation*

"What's it worth?"

That's the first question most people ask when someone shows them a rare and valuable coin. Coins are correctly perceived as stores of value—and quantifying that value is one of the marketplace's most important functions. It's a function we know as pricing.

Pricing—fair, honest, accurate pricing—is the cornerstone of consumer protection for those who purchase coins as well as the key to eventually turning a profit on those coins. To get good value, you have to avoid overpaying. Those who overpay in the coin market lose their chance to reap financial gain, or at least postpone it needlessly.

Determining Value

The value of a coin is determined on the basis of three main components: grade, supply, and demand. Under certain circumstances, one of these factors might outweigh either or both of the others.

Grade: As a general statement, a coin's value tends to rise arithmetically as its level of preservation—or grade-improves within the circulated range. Thus, a given coin might be worth 10 percent more in very fine condition than in fine, the next-lower grade, and 10 percent more in extremely fine condition than in very fine. Often, however, the rate of increase becomes geometric as a coin moves up in the Mint-State range. Thus, it might be worth twice as much in Mint State-65 as in Mint State-64, and twice as much again in Mint State-66 as in Mint State-65.

Grade is a reflection of a coin's desirability. People want the best. Traditionally, the coins in the highest levels of preservation have appreciated at the fastest rates. Even for relatively common coins, fierce demand exists for coins as close to perfect as possible. The closer to MS-70, the rarer the coin and the fiercer the demand.

Supply: The term "supply" refers to the number of examples of a given coin that are available in a given level of preservation. In recent years, buyers and sellers have gained an important new tool in determining just how many coins exist for a given type, denomination, date, and mint: The major grading services have issued population and census reports stipulating the number of specimens each service has certified for every different coin in each grade level. These reports provide crucial—and often surprising—insights into the relative rarity of each coin in each different grade. A word of caution, however: Dealers sometimes resubmit the same coin over and over in hopes that it might be assigned a higher grade, and these resubmissions can seriously distort the profile of a given coin. If the same coin were submitted 10 different times, for example, the population or census report would indicate that 10 coins had been graded, masking the coin's true rarity by making it appear to be more common than it is. This is discussed in chapter 5.

The supply of a given coin is the quantity available, not the number minted. Don't look up a coin's mintage figures and assume that something is common because large numbers were minted. Mintage figures can be, and often are, very misleading. Coins can be melted or lost, and the mintage figures will not reflect this. This is especially true of silver coins, which both the government and private interests have melted for their silver content.

Demand: The term "demand" refers to the number of people who want a particular coin at a given time. A coin with a mintage of only 500 is certainly rare in an absolute sense, but its value will be greatly diminished if there are just 200 people actively seeking to acquire it. Conversely, a coin with a mintage of 500,000 can command a handsome premium—far beyond the level this figure might suggest—if 2 million people are pursuing it.

"Collector base" is another way of expressing demand. It refers to the number of collectors who specialize in a particular series and need a particular coin to complete their collections. The coins needed to complete the sets are sometimes arbitrarily determined by what spaces have been provided in coin folders and albums for coins of a given set.

How Price-Guide Listings Can Determine Values

A coin's market value can be enhanced significantly by an editor's decision—possibly quite arbitrary—to list it or change the way it is listed in a widely used price guide. This has been shown a number of times, for example, when unusual varieties and mint-error coins have been listed in *A Guide Book of United States Coins*, the price guide commonly known as the "Red Book." Consider the history of the 1866 No Motto dollar. James Halperin, then chairman of New England Rare Coin Galleries, bought one of two known examples of this coin for $48,000 from A-Mark Coin Company of California. He advertised it for resale at $97,500. The coin had been considered to be a pattern (a design for a coin struck experimentally to see what it looks like as a real coin) because the *Guide Book* had listed it as a pattern for so many years. But Halperin persuaded the *Guide Book's* editor to change the listing to that of "transition-year" (struck one year before the

Jim Halperin bought this coin for $48,000 and convinced the editor of *A Guide Book of United States Coins* to change its status from pattern to regular issue. After the change, Halperin advertised it as the world's most valuable U.S. coin. *Photograph courtesy New England Rare Coin Galleries*

official issue). The coin became a half million-dollar rarity overnight. Halperin sold it in 1982 in a private sale. Years later, the coin was sold at public auction in January 2005 by American Numismatic Rarities LLC of Wolfeboro, New Hampshire, for $1,207,500. NGC graded it Proof-63.

In February 2005, Halperin recalled for me what it took to elevate the value of his $48,000 coin to over $500,000:

> When A-Mark first offered me the 1866 No Motto dollar, it immediately seemed obvious to me that the coin was listed incorrectly in the Red Book. An 1865 No Motto dollar is a pattern, but the circumstances of the 1866 No Motto dollar were similar to the 1804 dollar and 1913 Liberty nickel, i.e., they were all the same type as earlier dates rather than subsequent dates. So after I bought the coin, I simply explained to Ken Bressett, who is a very logical and reasonable fellow, why it was a simulated series coin rather than a pattern. He agreed, and asked several other experts for their opinions just to make sure. As far as I know, not a single expert that Ken asked could come up with any compelling logic to the contrary, so he cheerfully made the change. And subsequent to the change, I'm not aware of anyone ever questioning the wisdom of his decision. The odd part is that none of the coin's previous owners seem ever to have questioned the prior, erroneous Red Book description.

One coin listed as part of a set, but which is really a pattern, is the 1856 Flying Eagle cent. Although the mintage for years was thought to be 1,000, making it a very common pattern, it's a major rarity as part of the set of United States small cents—in fact, the rarest one. Demand persists for this coin; many show up at the same place and at the same time, and each one brings top dollar. The mintage of this coin is now widely believed to be far more than 1,000.

An 1856 Proof Flying Eagle cent, obverse and reverse.

1858 Indian head cent pattern, obverse and reverse. 1859 was the first official year that the Indian head cent was made. This 1858 was struck in a small quantity to see what the design would look like as a coin.

The 1858 Indian cent is also a pattern (and scarcer than the 1856 Flying Eagle cent), but it is in less demand because it isn't listed in the *Guide Book*, and there is no hole or space for it in coin folders and albums. The first official year of the Indian cent was 1859.

Another coin with an album space for it is a mint error: the 1955 Doubled-die cent. A specimen graded MS-65 Red by PCGS recently sold at auction. There is no logical reason why this coin should be listed as part of the basic series. But it, like other coins arbitrarily chosen for inclusion in the folders and albums, continues to be popular, and to be considered part of the series. The 1858 Indian cent is valued at considerably less than its less rare counterpart pattern, the 1856 Flying Eagle. Reason: The 1856 Flying Eagle is listed; the 1858 Indian isn't.

The new generation of albums is considered to be coin grading service registry sets. Grading services, like their predecessor album designers, decide which coins to include in these online registry sets and how to weight each specimen. In today's Internet-based world, a registry listing for a coin can put intense price pressure on it. This is especially true for high-grade, low-pop coins—some of which have sold for tens of thousands of dollars. This is explored in detail in the next chapter.

Price Guides: Theory and Practice

In a coin store, a casual buyer was looking for a circulated piece to complete his collection. He had a price guide from a popular coin publication. When he came across an example of the coin he wanted in the dealer's inventory—an accurately graded "Fine-12"—he looked up the Fine-12 price for that coin in the price guide, which pegged its value at $35. But the price on the coin's holder was $50.

Popular 1955 doubled-die Lincoln cent.

"This price guide says a Fine-12 is worth $35," the buyer told the dealer.

"Write 'em a check, then," the dealer snapped back. "Our coin is $50."

"What do you mean, write 'em a check?" the buyer pressed.

"It's only a guide to what the value is, not an offering of coins," the dealer insisted.

This is typical of what goes on every day in coin stores and coin conventions throughout the country. Price guides say a coin is valued at one price, and dealers ask another price. This sort of discrepancy is a constant source of frustration to collectors, just as it is to dealers.

Price guides are imprecise listings of coin values. In most cases, the people writing the price guides don't know what the coins look like. The prices are compiled from confirmed sales between knowledgeable buyers. As explained earlier, however, grading standards change as market conditions change. Furthermore, price guides in magazines have to be compiled weeks—sometimes months—in advance. For example, just because the month is July and the magazine you hold in your hands is dated August does not mean that its price guide has August prices. The prices might have been written in May, two months before release of the magazine. If prices increased between the time the price guide was written for the magazine and the time the magazine was released, the price guide would not reflect that increase. Hence, people go to buy coins with outdated price guides.

How the Price Guides are Compiled

Price guides are generally based on figures compiled from a variety of sources, which include, but are not limited to, teletype, mail-order offerings, and auctions.

THE TELETYPE AS A REFLECTION OF COIN VALUES

The teletype is used by coin dealers to communicate and do business with one another. If a dealer wants the privilege of doing business this way, he or she has to subscribe to a coin dealer teletype network and pay a monthly fee. FACTS/CCE is the leading network. Coin-Net and Eureka are also players. The teletype works like this: Dealer A offers a certain MS-63 coin and asks $100 for it (referred to as "the ask"). Dealer B is interested in dealer A's coin—but not at "the ask." So dealer B offers $75 for the coin ("the bid"). The actual selling price is usually somewhere in between—although some transactions take place at bid, and others take place at ask (very few). Most transactions take place offline. Since there are very few asks on the system, the dealers looking to sell coins will call the highest bidders and negotiate a deal.

Transactions like this occur all day and are monitored by the people who compile the price guides. Shane Downing, publisher of *The Coin Dealer Newsletter* (*CDN*), says that he believes that his family of publications are the only price guides with formalized columns for bid and "ask." Each bid column reflects the highest visible offer that can be found from dealers nationwide; and each ask represents the lowest asking price.

For a detailed analysis of price guide manipulation, see chapter 12. *CDN* does not give as much credence anymore to uncertified coins offered for sale at lower levels.

MAIL-ORDER OFFERINGS AS A REFLECTION OF COIN VALUES

You can pick up a coin publication at any given time and find advertisements for coins described exactly alike with prices very far apart. The only way mail-order offerings can be used as a guide is if you know the grading method of the company offering the coins. Nobody can use them as the basis for listings that are both broad and accurate, price guide compilers included.

PUBLIC AUCTIONS, COIN DOCTORS, AND COIN VALUES

From shill bidding to collusion, auctions can be a minefield; and the prices realized at auctions reflect this. The prices coins bring at auction can, however, give you a rough estimate of what your own coins are worth. This method can be far more accurate than using price guides. Listings based only on auction prices are not always that helpful, though, since there can be some very tricky forces at work.

One force can be a dealer placing anticipatory bids on coins—and others who actually pay anticipatory hammer prices. If a certain coin is certified as an MS-64 (value: $500), but is very close to MS-65 (value: $5,000), some dealers might pay $4,000 for the coin in anticipation of cracking the coin out for an upgrade. Also, if bidders know of a doctoring process that will "guarantee" an upgrade, they will bid close to the next highest grade. Interestingly, sometimes the coin doesn't upgrade, or the surface alterations don't come out as well as was hoped. On the other hand, often the coin does upgrade after it has been doctored.

An extraordinary and unrivaled archive that can be used for valuation purposes and that lets you "see" coins can be accessed at no charge after free registration on the website of Heritage Galleries and Auctioneers. The site contains digital images, accompanying descriptions and information, and individual prices realized for hundreds of thousands of coins sold by Heritage Numismatic Auctions. Jim Halperin wrote the following for the benefit of my readers:

> Today, in January 2005, *HeritageCoins.com*'s 135,000 registered bidder-members have free access to 750,000 previous auction records with descriptions, enlargeable photos, and prices. Auction item pages include NGC/PCGS population data, extensive third-party pricing information, and previous-auction links to similar coins so buyers can intelligently compare quality versus price.

American Numismatic Rarities, LLC of Wolfeboro, New Hampshire, one of the nation's most highly regarded rare coin auctioneers, also has an exceptional archive available online, but the firm is relatively new, so the data doesn't go back for an extended period of time. Christine Karstedt, ANR's president, invites readers of *The Coin Collector's Survival Manual* to visit *www.anrcoins.com*. She wrote the following for readers of this book:

> Collectors can access all of our previous auctions online simply by clicking on the sale catalogue cover in order to browse lots in any area of collecting interest, small cents, Morgan dollars, half eagles, etc. Our archives also provide full-screen color photographs, scholarly descriptions, and the price realized for that particular coin.

ELECTRONIC TRADING NETWORKS

The following information has been provided by the Certified Coin Exchange, now a division of Collectors Universe:

> Since 1990, the Certified Coin Exchange (CCE) has been a key numismatic industry force. Member Firms have posted bid/ask prices on the exchange for certified coins for sight-unseen and sight-seen trades. High standards of rules enforcement and Member Firm admission have kept the exchange in the forefront of certified numismatic trading over the past decade.

CERTIFIED COIN EXCHANGE AS IT IS NOW

Currently there are over 45,000 bid and ask prices on CCE, and live trading occurs electronically between 12:00 and 5:00 Eastern Time. Bids/Asks are posted for PCGS, NGC, ANACS, and ICG certified graded coins. There are over 125 Member Firms which have the capability to place bid/ask prices and either trade based on these prices with other dealers, or propose transactions to the Member Firms who are posting these prices.

The significance of CCE prices goes beyond the potential that trades can be executed on the Certified Coin Exchange. Prices (principally bids) on CCE are frequently used as the basis for off-exchange trades between major and smaller dealers, and also the prices are a factor in formulating prices in popular printed pricing guides. As a result, market leaders who bid for coins on CCE help set a pricing benchmark for the industry.

CERTIFIED COIN EXCHANGE INTERNET

Up to the Fall of 1999, CCE executed trades over a proprietary hardware and software system that was first used in 1986. This system was designed for speed and ease of use, but was expensive to install and required a dedicated personal computer running MS-DOS.

CCE now uses an Internet-based trading system, CCE-Internet. Now, Member Firms can place bid and ask prices, execute trades and perform all other functions via an Internet browser . . . from their office, a hotel room, or a show. This is a complete numismatic trading system that enables them to:

- Post bid/ask prices on certified coins from 4 grading services (seen/unseen)
- View posted pricing on certified coins with IDs
- Execute trades against posted prices
- Send trading messages to other dealers or to all dealers
- View roster of Member Firms
- View metals prices
- Maintain a roster, including e-mail address and web URL
- Download CCE database and Program file for "Virtual Full-Time System"
- View Bullion Quotation Pages (competitive bullion listings)
- Maintain their own BQS page (if they make a market in bullion coins)
- View Teletrade auction results
- Search Open Message traffic for text strings for last 7 days
- Send messages to the CCE-list
- Use the "@atchou.com" e-mail address if desired for list traffic
- List coins free in CCE-Auction
- Mass-import from Excel or Access in CCE-Auction

Additional features and options that will be included in the future are:

- On-line Historical Pricing data
- A member's own database-driven Web site
- Automatic CCE-Auction coin listing with inventory from the member's Web site
- Automatic CCE-Auction listing from the member's CCE ask prices

- E-commerce connection from the member's Web site
- Optional descriptions on Asks posted to the CCE (importable to CCE-Auction)
- The member's own Web-driven inventory system
- Automatic import of the member's inventory to CCE-Asks/CCE-Auction
- Attractive images for most issues of U.S. rare coins for marketing purposes

MEMBERSHIP REQUIREMENTS TO BE A CCE MEMBER FIRM

While the cost to become a Member Firm on CCE has decreased thanks to the Internet, the membership requirements have not. CCE has been free of dealer defaults and other significant problems over the years, so the integrity of the system has remained intact. Membership in CCE continues to be open to dealers who meet the following requirements:

- Full-time numismatic firm
- Established place of business greater than one year
- Numismatic experience greater than three years
- 3 Member Firm dealer references, or previous satisfactory membership as a principal or executive Member Firm.

Use of the Internet by Current Full-Time CCE Member Firms

Current full-time CCE members may continue to use the satellite-based system to access and update prices as well as to execute trades. In addition, they may use the Internet to access and change their information, and also to execute trades. This can be done from anywhere on the Internet—at trade shows, while traveling, etc.

Current full-time members will be issued an Internet user ID and password on request at no additional monthly cost. Updates on the Internet are passed real-time to all full-time systems, so updates can be made simultaneously on both systems if desired. This gives full-time Member Firms the ability to keep up with the market and update and execute trades from trade shows and while traveling.

PRICING FOR CCE MEMBERSHIP

The monthly cost to be a Member Firm via CCE Internet is $295.00. Executing a trade against a bid or an ask is $0.75 per transaction. Having a trade executed against your bid or ask is $0.05 per transaction. Incentives are in place to reduce the cost of the per-transaction prices based on number of bids posted.

Contacting CCE

For sales information, call 1-800-699-3158. For trading and rules questions, call 1-713-973-1616 x22. For Customer Service, contact 1-800-733-6623 or *www.certifiedcoinexchange.com*

EUREKATRADING.COM

By far the most sophisticated coin trading system is Eureka Trading, an Internet-based system hosted by Globix. It was co-founded by former NGC grader Jeffrey Isaac and coin dealer Andrew P. Lustig.

Co-founder Isaac says that any serious trader who buys and sells coins actively would be well served to pay the $25 monthly fee and one-time $10 registration fee. "That monthly fee gives access to bulletin boards, forums, calendars, and certified coin market screens—real bids and asks, as well as sight-seen bids and the ability to post images and descriptive text." From market screens, Eureka provides access to third-party auction prices realized. Eureka now waives its fees for dealers and serious traders.

Eureka doesn't warehouse the actual coins. Instead, it serves as a sometimes commission-based coin trading facilitator. Unlike other online facilitators I have seen, this system appears to provide comprehensive information about the traders. In order to maximize use of the information, however, users will have to be meticulously attentive to detail, as the site is not straightforward to navigate.

"We are only marketing our system to the most serious traders," Isaac says. "We do not expect people who collect coins casually to be part of our system."

You can trade on Eureka via bulletin boards, market screens, or a matching engine. Eureka's matching engine appears to be its highlight; the system has both a displayed asking price and a hidden price the seller would accept. In an e-mail to me, co-founder Lustig wrote, "The matching engine simulates negotiations between traders . . . calculates the results of each potential trade, and finalizes the best of those potential trades as binding transactions."

How can a "serious" trader be certain the seller from whom he or she is buying or the buyer to whom he or she is selling will deliver the coins or the money? Here's a portion of what Eureka Trading says on its site about credit risks:

> If you think that there is a credit risk in dealing with another trader, you should set a "credit risk equalizer" for him. Eureka will then use this setting to ensure that it only matches you with the given trader when the price of the deal justifies the risk. Credit Risk equalizers are only applicable to sight-unseen trades that put you at risk, i.e., trades in which you could suffer a loss if the counterparty fails to remit payment or ship goods. The equalizers are not applicable to sight-unseen trades in which you are not at risk, nor to approval and targeted trades.
>
> If you think that there is a 2% chance that a trader will fail to remit payment or ship goods, set his credit risk equalizer at 2%. If a trade puts you at risk, Eureka will automatically compensate for that risk, as follows:
>
> When you're selling: Eureka compares all available bids to determine which is best for you. Eureka compensates for credit risks by reducing the net value (to you) of the various bids. Note that the best deal is not necessarily from the highest or most reliable bidder

Trader	Their Bid	Credit Risk	Net Value
A	$1000	2%	$980
B	975	0%	975
C	1050	8%	966

When you're buying: Credit risk equalizers effectively let you offer different prices to different sellers based on the perceived risk of non-delivery.

As for sight-unseen trades, Eureka's rules state that there is no return privilege. "The buyer assumes that the grading service's assessment of a coin is a sufficient indication of a coin's authenticity and quality."

As a visitor, you can access some of Eureka for free news, calendars, help wanted, and industry links, as well as to view the activity rankings of traders.

Where the Price Is Always Right

An accurate, readily available price guide is the single most important consumer protection tool. The certification services have removed a good deal of the risk from buying coins, somewhat obviating the need for buyers to be as knowledgeable on authentication and grading. In much the same way, a thorough, readily available annual price guide serves as a surrogate expert on the value of the coins in its listings, allowing the average consumer who has no access to trade periodicals to determine ballpark values for very rare certified coins.

Price guides come in a number of different forms, and some will appeal to a given coin buyer more than others. The important thing is not which guide a person uses, but rather that he or she uses some kind of guide before shelling out his or her hard-earned money to buy a coin. Following are some of the best-known and most popular annual price guides devoted to U.S. coins:

- *A Guide Book of United States Coins*, by R. S. Yeoman, edited by Kenneth Bressett. This book, available in both hardcover and softcover versions, has been a hobby bestseller for half a century. It is commonly referred to as the "Red Book" because of the color of its cover. Early editions are as valuable as some high-grade certified rare coins—and are as eagerly sought. (Whitman Publishing, LLC, 3101 Clairmont Road, Suite C, Atlanta, Georgia 30329)
- *Coin World Guide to U.S. Coins, Prices and Value Trends*. This softcover guide is prepared by the editors of *Coin World*, a respected weekly journal of the numismatic field. It has achieved its great success and established a market niche through its performance charts and graphs. Its value listings are conscientiously compiled and authoritative, helping to make this one of the best annual coin price guides—and a model for other collectibles fields on how to do price guides right. (Dutton Signet, division of Penguin Books USA, Inc.)

- *The Insider's Guide to U.S. Coin Values* by Scott A. Travers. This paperback guide book, which I have authored since 1993, contains pricing data on all relevant coins in both circulated and Mint State condition. Unlike some other guides, it includes prices for very high grades and very rare coins. The 2005 edition contains a value of $11,000,000 for an 1849 Coronet Portrait double eagle—the highest value listed for a coin in any annual price guide from that year. Guest chapters on popular market-related subjects of numismatic interest help this book appeal to a wide readership. (Dell Publishing, division of Random House, 1745 Broadway, New York, NY 10019)
- *The Official Blackbook Price Guide of United States Coins*, by Marc Hudgeons. This handy, pocket-size paperback provides values not only for U.S. coins but also for tokens, medals, and other related collectibles. In addition, it contains detailed tips on buying coins, a special section on grading, and other specialized articles and chapters. (House of Collectibles, imprint of Random House Information Group)
- While not an annual price guide, *United States Pattern Coins and Experimental Trial Pieces, 8th Edition*, by J. Hewitt Judd, M.D.; edited by Q. David Bowers; pricing by Robert L. Hughes (Whitman Publishing, LLC, 2004) deserves consideration as a supplement to such guides because it provides revised price valuations for coins in an important hobby specialty—one not covered in similar detail by other guides. A new edition appears every three to five years, but this latest edition appears to be a complete overhaul and an exceptionally done rewrite. This book is essential to every collector of United States coins. It lists descriptions and prices for patterns. The prices might be outdated, depending upon how recent the edition is, but Robert Hughes tells me that the popularity of the new format should assure new editions more frequently than in the past. This book uses a commonly referred to rarity rating scale:

ESTIMATE OF NUMBER STRUCK

Unique	1
R-8	2 or 3
R-7, high	4–6
R-7, low	7–12
R-6, high	13–20
R-6, low	21–30
R-5	31–75
R-4	76–200
R-3	201–500
R-2	501–1,250
R-1	1,250 +

Monthly Price Guides

For obvious reasons, yearly price guides can't be completely up-to-date; fast-changing market conditions often overtake them even before they are released. However, they do provide extremely useful facts and figures regarding relative rarity and value, and their listings serve as baseline points of reference that can be of great assistance in calculating long-term price performance. What's more, while market values may be somewhat higher or lower at any given point during the year, the listings in these books are close enough to the market to sound a clear alarm when grossly overpriced items are checked out.

Monthly price guides appear in two leading hobby magazines:

- *COINage* publishes a section called "The *COINage* Price Guide," which provides current values for selected U.S. coins in up to 14 levels of preservation. It also furnishes "*COINage* Price Averages," which track the market's overall performance in two important grade levels—Very Fine and Mint State-65. (Miller Magazines, 290 Maple Ct., Suite 232, Ventura, CA 93003-3517)
- *Coins* magazine features a "Coin Value Guide" which charts the price performance of both regular U.S. coins and commemoratives in up to nine levels of preservation. (Krause Publications, 700 E. State St., Iola, WI 54990)

Of all the printed price guides, those that appear weekly come closest to reflecting actual market values at a particular point. Instead of being prepared months before publication like listings in annual guide books, these are compiled no more than a few weeks in advance—and sometimes just a few days. Thus, while they may lack the comprehensive coverage of the yearly guides, they can offer greater immediacy and better reflect rapid movements up or down. Weekly guides to U.S. coin values can be found through the leading newspapers serving the hobby:

- *Coin World*, the largest and most widely circulated newsweekly serving coin collectors, publishes *Coin Values*, a glossy magazine, as a supplement in the first issue of each month. Weekly updates are available to *Coin World* subscribers online at no charge. *Coin Values,* in addition to comprehensive pricing for more than 45,000 U.S. coins, provides market analysis and features as well as regular columns on grading and spotting undervalued coins. A special version of *Coin Values* containing 20 percent more editorial content is available on newsstands nationwide. *Coin World* is required reading for anyone even casually interested in coins, but for the serious collector it is the bible. Subscribers to *Coin World* and *Coin Values* have access to *www.CoinValuesOnline.com* where prices for U.S. coins and market analysis are updated weekly. (Amos Press, P.O. Box 4315, Sidney, OH 45365 or *www.CoinWorld.com/CustomerService/Subscriptions*)
- *Numismatic News* contains a "Coin Market" section covering all of the popular coin series and providing accurate data on current values. In most editions, the listings contain only certain series; every four weeks, however, "Coin Market" furnishes comprehensive listings for all the coins covered by this report. *Numismatic News* is a leader in editorial content, and each issue is a numismatic treasure trove. (Krause Publications, 700 E. State St., Iola, WI 54990)

Secret Dealer Tip Sheets

Among professional numismatists, two of the most closely monitored and supremely important price guides are *The Coin Dealer Newsletter* and *The Certified Coin Dealer Newsletter*. These twin weekly publications—referred to as the *Greysheet* and the

the COIN DEALER newsletter

CDN — Our 43rd year...
Sight-Seen wholesale prices for accurately graded U.S. Coins – Certified or Raw
Single copy price $4.00 Vol. XXXXIII No. 5 February 4, 2005 *. . .a Friday morning report on the Coin Market*

GENERIC GOLD, DOLLARS LOWER
BETTER DATES REMAIN STRONG

The Market in Depth

"Overall, the market is fine." This is the opinion of many coin dealers that we have spoken to this past week as we begin February. They do acknowledge that several areas of the market, particularly some 20th century material, are beginning to suffer some weakness. They alluded to many late date Walking Liberty Half Dollars, Washington Quarters (not the key dates) and some common Buffalo Nickels. We also note that generic Morgan and Peace Dollars along with select Proof and Mint Sets are also selling freely at discounted levels. Still, dealers remain very busy and tell us that collectors are continuing to buy rare coins. At local coin shows dealers are reporting their wholesale sales to be fairly active. There was also plenty of opportunity to buy some neat material at the recently completed Houston Money Show. For example, one dealer described his purchases, including: some Draped Bust Dollars, better date Morgan Dollars, the key overdate Buffalo Nickel and a VG8 1901-S key date Barber Quarter. Superior Galleries conducted an auction of collector material in conjunction with the show that realized $140K.

While most agree that the market is doing fine, it's just "not quite as strong as it was a year ago." Gold and Silver remain saddled in their new, lower trading range but as long as Gold holds over $400 per ounce analysts believe things should be OK. The weakness in Gold Spot has continued to apply pressure to collector/investor demand for $20 Liberty and Saint-Gauden examples. Still, the demand for Gold coins is an important part of the market's health and the super demand that we are experiencing for rare date Gold shows its true strength. Naturally we are seeing more minus signs filtering in along side the plus signs. This is nothing to be alarmed about as this mix seems to be a healthy aspect of the continued bull market. Remember, some profit taking is a natural occurrence for any market that has endured the sustained increase that rare coins enjoyed. Still February is upon us and this month is usually quite active. Dealers will soon be heading west to attend the first major show and auctions of the year on the west coast. The Long Beach Coin and Collectibles Expo will be February 23-26.

This Week's Market

MERCURY DIMES: With a combination of value, rarity, beauty and realization that many potentially underrated examples exist, this could be the ultimate sleeper series. For now, challenged dealers attempt to quietly satisfy the growing legion of collectors.

WALKING LIBERTY HALVES: The key early years are exhibiting some demand with only a single gain, that belonging to the semi key 1917S (R) now Bid at $1,600 in Choice. The 1937, 1939 and 1939D are observed posting minor advances in Gem. The downward trend established for the short set continues with dealers opening up the floodgates discounting a raft of material resulting in further losses.

DOLLARS: Generic MS65s and MS66s are the main Morgan casualties in this report. However, this series has such an avid, ardent following that the demand just flows to another sector. With that said there are some impressive gains to be marveled at! The Carson City contingent remains popular with the 1879CC, 1880CC, 1884CC, 1890CC, 1891CC and 1893CC each wearing gains. The prestigious 1894 is barreling ahead wanted in multiple grades with gems commanding $28,500. DMPLs remain hot, sporting numerous increases. Peace Dollars are stable with dealers seeking slightly better dates in AU.

PROOF SETS AND MINT SETS: The 1936-1942 Proof sets remain in demand and have a ready market. All other issues are beset with more losses than gains and are attempting to stabilize.

COMMEMORATIVES: The Silver Commemorative caravan is seen steaming along taking bows in a repeat performance of last week's strong showing. With a combination of dealer support and immense collector demand this segment of the market is attracting higher Bids in virtually all areas. Not surprisingly, many issues are reflecting multiple gains. Gold Commems are quiet with the 1926 Sesquicentennial Quarter Eagle higher in MS64.

TYPE: Having just concluded an extremely active, diverse and bankroll depleting auction calendar in January, dealers appear to be content trying to acquire most common material at present levels. A review bares this out with only Trade Dollars and Twenty Cent pieces compiling modest gains in VG. Curiously, we also note that one source is attempting to acquire quantities of Cameo Liberty Nickels by offering to pay 10% over PR63-PR65 Bids.

GOLD: With Gold Spot floundering around $420 we find generic $20 Saints & Libs reporting losses across-the-board. The dealer's focus is instead positioned on the scarce and popular. Look at the $3 Type displaying several increases with MS65s now Bid $10K! $5 Indians are also chiming in with a trio of elevated Bids and the collector's favorite - $20 High Reliefs are now $38,000 in Gem.

Coin Dealer Newsletter Certified Coin Market Indicator™

SERVICE	LOW	HIGH	AVERAGE
*PCGS	58.80%	91.93%	81.62%
*NGC	56.69%	92.59%	82.06%
*ANACS	34.51%	79.98%	55.43%
ICG	59.51%	93.78%	82.24%
PCI	30.20%	68.29%	52.35%
SEGS	38.44%	81.51%	51.16%
NCI	19.00%	57.27%	31.12%
INS	17.87%	55.15%	29.20%

* These services publish population/census reports.

A weekly comparison of certified coin Bid levels relative to CDN sight-seen Bid levels (as 100%) sampled from 10 U.S. coin series (2 grades each; avg. is for the 20 ratios). All %'s relative to CDN as 100%. Data from latest issue of CDN, Monthly Supplement & Certified Coin Dealer Newsletter (sight-unseen Bids). Refer to CCDN for specific certified Bid levels. ANACS Bids & green or gold label PCI Bids are for slabbed coins only. INS bids are for blue certs. SEGS Bids are for labels without negative comments. Use this Indicator to survey the entire market, not just for a single issue; apply these ratios to CDN Bid to obtain a trading range for comparisons. For more details on the indicator and a complete listing of coins, refer to the July 1988 Monthly Supplement.

Coins certified by other services may trade at a discount; understand each services standards before using the Greysheet grades as a pricing guide.

SILVER BULLION PRICES Silver bullion items based on spot price of 6.74 per oz.

	BID	ASK	MELT
U.S. 90% Circ. Bags	4,700 /	4,650	4,876
U.S. 90% Uncirc. Bags	4,950 /	5,300	4,876
U.S. 40% Circ. Bags	1,900 /	1,980	1,994
U.S. 40% Uncirc. Bags	2,025 /	2,125	1,994
Silver Dollar Circ. Bags (AG/G)	6,500 /	6,950	5,213
Wartime 5¢ Bags	1,140 /	1,200	1,517
Canadian 80% Circ. Bags	3,540 /	3,840	4,044
Silver Eagle 1 oz.	7.39 /	8.41	6.74

BULLION, FOREIGN GOLD, & PLATINUM COINS

Bullion coins in this issue are figured on a per ounce basis of: Gold $421.80 Platinum $873.75

GOLD		BID	ASK
Amer. Eag.	1 oz.	479.80	484.10
	1/2 oz.	215.00	219.50
	1/4 oz.	108.00	111.50
	1/10 oz.	43.40	44.90
Austria	1 Du.	47.00	48.75
	4 Du.	190.40	199.90
	10 Cr.	41.00	42.50
	20 Cr.	80.10	83.60
	100 Cr.	408.70	418.95
Can. M'leaf	1 oz.	479.80	484.80
	1/2 oz.	218.90	226.20
	1/4 oz.	110.70	114.40
	1/10 oz.	46.10	46.80
China	1 oz.	429.80	434.80
	1/2 oz.	216.80	221.80
Panda	1/4 oz.	110.50	114.00
	1/10 oz.	46.00	48.50
	1/20 oz.	25.30	26.80
K'rand	1 oz.	424.80	425.30
	1/2 oz.	209.60	212.80
	1/4 oz.	105.30	108.30
	1/10 oz.	42.38	45.05
Mex.	50 Pesos	503.30	511.47
	20 Pesos	197.10	201.00
	10 Pesos	100.60	102.50
	5 Pesos	50.90	52.66
	2 1/2 Pesos	35.40	37.65
	2 Pesos	21.20	22.20
Mexico	1 oz.	417.60	428.80
	1/2 oz.	206.80	210.80
	1/4 oz.	103.30	106.30
Brit. Sovs.	(new)	99.20	103.20
Hungary	100Kr	409.60	415.10
N.E. Indies	1 Du.	45.40	48.65
Russia	10 Rubles	107.50	112.00

PLATINUM COINS

		BID	ASK
Maple	1 oz.	889.10 +	904.13
Noble	1 oz.	879.00 +	865.00
Koala	1 oz.	891.40 +	899.40

FOREIGN GOLD (Usually traded in XF/AU condition.)

	BID	ASK
Belgium 20 Fr	78.30	87.30
Colombia 5 Peso	98.70	102.70
England Sovs. (old)	100.70	105.20
France 20 Fr. (Roos)	81.40	85.90
German 20 Mark	99.40	108.40
Italy 20 Lire	78.20	82.20
Netherlands 10 Gu.	81.70	85.70
Russia 5 Rubles	58.70	62.20
Swiss 20 Fr	79.30	83.30

U.S. GOLD (Prices are for the most common date of each type.)

	VF20 BID	VF20 ASK	XF40 BID	XF40 ASK	AU50 BID	AU50 ASK	AU58 BID	AU58 ASK	MS60 BID	MS60 ASK	MS62 BID	MS62 ASK	MS63 BID	MS63 ASK	MS64 BID	MS64 ASK	MS65 BID	MS65 ASK	MS67 BID
$1.00 (I)	110	115	155	165	165	180	175	190	200	215	325	350	710	760	1,550	1,670	3,800	4,100	15,000
$1.00 (II)	230	245	340	360	430	460	1,100	1,150	2,725	3,000	4,920	5,225	11,000	11,700	17,000	18,200	30,750	32,750	78,000
$1.00 (III)	110	115	155	165	170	185	190	205	210	225	360	385	700	750	1,030	1,100	1,725	1,850	3,100
$2 1/2 Lib	135	145	160	170	180	195	190	205	220	240	450	480	660	700	900	965	1,630	1,730	4,460
$2 1/2 Indian	125	135	145	155	160	170	172	185	195	210	440	465	1,070	1,140	1,700	1,835	5,200 +	5,500	20,000
$3.00	550	600	800	865	1,075	1,175	1,525	1,650	2,000	2,150	2,820 +	3,020	4,680 +	4,950	6,000	6,450	10,000 +	11,000	44,000
$5 Lib/nm	160	170	175	185	240	260	425	455	900	975	2,350	2,525	5,100	5,600	8,000	8,750	16,000	18,000	100,250
$5 Lib/wm	120	130	125	135	132	142	140	150	160	170	325	345	620	660	1,280	1,350	3,300	3,430	11,000
$5 Indian	160	170	185	200	190	205	205	225	245	265	545 +	580	1,380 +	1,460	3,000 +	3,200	12,000	12,700	38,200
$10 Lib/nm	270	285	310	330	400	440	1,000	1,100	2,335	2,575	4,300	4,700	10,000	11,000	18,300	20,300	42,500	50,000	140,500
$10 Lib/wm	222	237	230	245	232	247	235	250	245	260	410	430	790	835	1,610 -	1,720	3,900	4,125	16,500
$10 Indian	250	265	280	295	310	325	325	340	350	370	500	535	760	810	1,530	1,615	3,700	3,975	20,500
$20 Lib (I)	480	510	490	530	650	700	1,150	1,250	1,810	1,935	4,300	4,650	5,200	5,700	6,650	7,150	9,900	10,700	90,250
$20 Lib (II)	460	490	465	500	475	520	500	550	760	835	2,650	2,875	9,330	10,000	24,400	26,500	60,000	67,000	130,500
$20 Lib (III)	440 -	460	445 -	465	450 -	470	460 -	480	500 -	520	515 -	535	660 -	690	1,230 -	1,320	4,000 -	4,300	30,000
$20 St.-Gaudens	450 -	470	455 -	475	465	485	470	490	505 -	525	515 -	535	575	690	660 -	690	1,110 -	1,180	7,300
$20 High Relief	6,200	6,650	7,000	7,550	8,400	9,100	9,800	10,700	11,200	12,200	13,200	14,200	20,300	21,500	25,000	26,500	38,000 +	40,750	115,000

The weekly COIN DEALER newsletter (the *Greysheet*) reports the national Dealer–to–Dealer wholesale coin market, monitoring all possible transactions and offers to buy and sell coins **sight–seen.** The coins may be certified or "raw" (uncertified), but the grading **MUST ADHERE** to the current leading standard. Prices reported derive from the highest legitimate Bids and lowest legitimate Asks seen nationally; they do not necessarily reflect the levels at which any particular dealer might offer to buy or sell that coin. Bids reported consider activity in the certified **sight–unseen** market, which already include consideration of certification costs. Bids for a **sight–seen** "raw" coin may be higher or lower than for a **sight–unseen** certified coin due to current market conditions. **The CDN** may not change Bid due to the bidding adjustments of the high bidder, but will be strongly influenced by Buys which are higher or Sells which are lower than current Bid/Ask levels. INVESTOR/COLLECTOR NOTE: The prices in this newsletter are from Dealer–to–Dealer transactions: you should expect to pay a premium above Ask when purchasing coins in a retail transaction; you may also commission a Dealer for your purchases.

www.greysheet.com

Sample front page of *The Coin Dealer Newsletter*, the wholesale buy-and-sell guide most widely relied upon as accurate and reliable. *Courtesy* Coin Dealer Newsletter

Bluesheet, respectively, because of their distinctive colors—are essential tools not only for those who deal in coins but also for serious collectors and investors.

The Coin Dealer Newsletter, established in 1963, provides the most accurate, up-to-date information available in printed form on current U.S. coin values. It contains detailed listings for all of the most popularly traded series, along with analysis and commentary on important market developments and trends. It uses a bid and ask format, and thus is a wholesale, rather than retail, price guide. *Greysheet* values pertain to any accurately graded coin whether certified or raw.

The Certified Coin Dealer Newsletter (*CCDN*), which began publication in 1986, parallels its sister publication, but covers coins certified by PCGS, NGC, ANACS, ICG, PCI, and SEGS. Sight-unseen bidding for these coins allows the *Bluesheet* to compile its prices. *CCDN* is "a weekly report on the *sight-unseen* certified market."

Shane Downing, publisher of *The Certified Coin Dealer Newsletter,* writes:

> *The Certified Coin Dealer Newsletter* (the *Bluesheet*) reports current wholesale market bids for coins certified by the most active grading services, determined through careful study of market activity (including the highest nationally reported sight-unseen Bids, Asks, Trades, prior levels, and auction prices.) The *CCDN* may not respond to the removal of a high Bid, but will be strongly influenced by the lowering of an unsupported high Bid or by Asks or Trades which are near or below current Bid. . . . *CCDN* does not represent that it is possible to purchase selected coins at Bid levels.

Both the *Greysheet* and the *Bluesheet* are published by The Coin Dealer Newsletter, Inc., a California company that follows the marketplace closely and understands not only the ebb and flow of price trends, but also the psychology that underlies the industry. The company also publishes *The CDN Monthly Supplement*, as well as *The CDN Quarterly*—additional supplements to its weekly price guides. The *Supplement* and *Quarterly* include bid and ask price listings for coins less frequently traded than those in the weekly newsletters. The *Summary* is distributed without charge to regular subscribers. (The Coin Dealer Newsletter, Inc., P.O. Box 11099, Torrance, CA 90510, publishes 51 issues per year)

An increasingly popular price guide is *NumisMedia*. This price guide uses fair market value rather than fair market wholesale, but even so it has developed a reputation in the dealer community for accurate pricing in areas that were previously viewed as too difficult to track. Dated gold is one such area where dealers look to *NumisMedia* for leadership.

NumisMedia uses fair market value as its valuation basis for the VF through MS-67 listings, and makes a comprehensive pricing guide of over 40 pages available monthly. (NumisMedia, 26895 Aliso Creek Road, Suite B #327, Aliso Viejo, CA 92656-5301).

Price Guide Valuation Basis

Fair-market wholesale is the price at which a coin would trade between two reasonably intelligent and knowledgeable professionals, both of whom are under no compulsion or compunction to consummate the transaction. This is generally the price a coin would bring on the dealer-to-dealer level at a coin convention or coin show.

Fair market value is the price at which a coin would change hands between two intelligent people, both of whom have no compulsion or compunction to consummate the transaction. They wouldn't necessarily be professionals. "Fair market value" would normally apply when a dealer sells a coin to a client who is knowledgeable about the marketplace.

Commercial Grading Standards

The chart below lists what coins have to look like to be worth their price-guide values. Getting top dollar for uncertified coins is difficult. PCGS- and NGC-certified coins generally meet these standards all of the time.

Price Guide Grade	Scratches	Strike
MS-67	None	Needle-sharp
MS-65	Very few	Sharp
MS-63	Some, but not in a prominent area (e.g., face)	Slight weakness allowed
MS-60	Allowed	Weak strike allowed

When the Price Is *Not* Right

Later in this chapter, I refer to a case in which an unscrupulous dealer perpetrated a scam by overpricing coins far beyond legitimate market levels. I'm pleased to report that I played a role in helping to bring the dealer in question to justice. While this is a source of great satisfaction to me, the case itself serves as an object lesson in the need for constant vigilance, for when there is a potential for enormous financial gain, abuses will inevitably occur.

The abuses were every bit as enormous as the potential benefits in that case. According to charges lodged against him by the federal government, his company defrauded more than 200 customers out of a total of $30 million by grossly overpricing coins that it represented as good investments. The coins that he sold were completely genuine; indeed, he sold nothing but certified coins whose grade had been determined independently, honestly—and, by and large, quite accurately—by either PCGS or NGC. His crime was simple and shameless: He priced the coins at levels that were astronomically higher than the going market levels at the time—and then assured clients that they were good values.

Flagrant Fraud

The United States Attorney in the district where the fraud was alleged consulted me when his office was preparing its criminal case. I then continued to furnish expertise throughout the trial. The abuses that came to light appalled and enraged me. Consider these examples:

In August 1990, he charged a client $203,150 for an 1890-CC Morgan dollar certified as Mint State-65. Its true market value at the time was just $11,000, according to NGC founder John Albanese, who served as an expert witness for the government. Four months later, in December 1990, that dealer advised the client that the coin's value had risen to $289,310. On the contrary, Albanese testified, the coin had actually lost value, and was worth only $6,000.

In July 1989, the dealer sold a different client a 1901-S Barber quarter certified as Mint State-67—a legitimately rare coin in exceptionally pristine condition. The coin was certainly worth a pretty penny: $200,000, according to Albanese. The dealer's price, however, was more than five times that amount: a staggering $1.1 million. Seventeen months later, in December 1990, the dealer told the client that the coin had soared in value to more than $2.6 million. In point of fact, Albanese said, it had lost one-fourth of its value and was worth only $150,000.

Some might say the victims of these frauds "don't deserve sympathy" because they entered into these transactions—deals involving huge amounts of money—without challenging the dealer's outlandish prices, when they could have discovered the fraud simply by purchasing a guide book costing less than $10. But this kind of attitude misses the point: Gullibility and ignorance aren't crimes; fraud is. Incredibly, The dealer might have gotten away with his scheme if overpricing the coins had been his only transgression. The prosecution's fraud case against him rested primarily not on the outrageous prices, but rather on his claims that the coins were good investments at those prices. With the help of expert witnesses such as John Albanese and prominent coin dealer Dwight Manley, the government was able to demonstrate conclusively that these claims were grossly untrue.

The dealer was convicted on eleven counts of mail fraud, four counts of interstate transportation of stolen property, and three counts of wire fraud. He was sentenced to a prison term of 76 months. The expert witnesses' testimony also was significant in establishing the point that major rarities—like all rare coins—have definable market values which can be arrived at through a process of consensus by leading authorities. Far from being isolated and arbitrary, Albanese's estimates were corroborated and reinforced by Manley and other witnesses, undercutting the argument that these were just one man's opinions.

Following the trial in 1993, the Assistant U.S. Attorney, writing for the U.S. Attorney in the jurisdiction of the case, sent me a letter expressing satisfaction with the outcome and thanking me for my efforts in helping to achieve it:

> It is a testament to your love for numismatics that you dedicated so much time and energy to our efforts without once requesting compensation. It was a pleasure working with you in common cause to punish this astonishingly successful con man . . . Someday, perhaps, there will be no need for the prosecution of coin dealers in the United States. When that day comes,

> you will be among those who can say that you helped rid the industry of unsavory characters.

After his release from prison, the dealer continues to proclaim his innocence.

Common-Sense Tips

Collectors of coins should follow the same rules in completing their collections that successful investors follow in making money with rare coins.

Don't try to outguess the market. If you plan on buying coins, don't buy them all at once. Make your coin purchases on a systematic basis. Conversely, if you plan on liquidating, don't sell all of your coins at once. Sell a few at a time.

Use your intuitive feel for people as well as your common sense when you acquire coins. If someone gives you the impression of being dishonest or less than forthright, don't deal with him or her. And if a coin looks ugly to you, don't buy it—even if it carries certification as Proof-70. There is a 1963 Lincoln cent graded Proof-70 that actually had deteriorated in the holder and was a Proof-64 at best. An explanation of what happened with that coin appears in the next chapter.

Don't follow everyone else. When everyone else is buying, sell. When everyone else is selling, buy. The coin market moves in cycles. Coins that are not increasing in value now might increase in the near future. Coins going down in value could reverse themselves sooner or later and go back up.

Diversify. No more than a small percentage (some financial professionals say 5–10 percent) of your total holdings, excluding the value of your primary residence, should be invested in your coin collection. The strongest overall financial portfolios are those that consist of different types of assets or those portfolios that are well balanced. Similarly, the financially strongest rare coin holdings are those that consist of different kinds of coins. If you are completing a set, your holdings will still be diversified, for you will be acquiring different dates and Mint-marks.

Get friendly with your dealer. You'd be surprised at the preferential treatment you'll receive if you are friendly with your dealer. You're far more likely to get a good deal and special advice if the dealer knows you than if you make a purchase in a cold, businesslike manner. If your dealer doesn't want to talk to you except to know which coins you want so he or she can write up your invoice, don't deal with that dealer.

– 10 –
REGISTRY SETS GET HIGH GRADES

Competition is ingrained in the American spirit. The drive to succeed, surmount all obstacles, and surpass all rivals can be seen in every facet of national life, from politics to athletics—and that same drive has been fueling one of the most dynamic growth areas ever witnessed in the coin market. I am speaking of registry sets, a concept so new at the time that it hardly was mentioned in the most recent previous edition of this book, but one so important today that I have given it a brand-new chapter all its own. Thousands of dedicated—even zealous—collectors are putting together registry sets as of this writing, and the effect on the market has been profound.

The Meaning of "Registry"

Registry sets were revolutionary not only in concept but also in conception. They resulted from the marriage of the coin market's Grading Revolution and the wider world's Computer Revolution. The original midwife for their birth was the Professional Coin Grading Service, which introduced its Set Registry program in booklet format in 1997 and on the Internet in 2001. Later, the Numismatic Guaranty Corporation of America launched a parallel program called the NGC Registry.

The basic idea was—and is—very simple. Most of the coins bought and sold for significant sums of money today have been certified—authenticated, graded, and encapsulated by third-party services. PCGS hit upon the idea of encouraging collectors to organize their PCGS-certified coins into sets, then "register" those sets on the company's Web site on the Internet. Collectors do this by entering the serial numbers of the coins from the holders in which they are encapsulated (or "slabbed"). Through its software, PCGS assigns ratings to these sets reflecting the rarity of the coins and the grades in which they were certified, adding or subtracting points for special characteristics or the absence of such characteristics. Certain coins, for example, may get bonus points for having deep cameo surfaces, while others may have points deducted from their score because they lack special features, such as "full heads" in the case of Standing Liberty quarters. An overall rating is determined for each set and sets are then listed sequentially

Logo for the PCGS Set Registry program.
Photograph courtesy Professional Coin Grading Service

on the Web site, from the highest rating down. Top-rated sets in various categories are singled out for special recognition.

The NGC Registry uses a similar process, but sets registered there may contain coins certified by either NGC or PCGS. "This enables our customers to include all their coins in our Registry so they do not have to make decisions based on which coin is in which holder, " said Mark Salzberg, president of NGC. "There is a marketplace reality whereby both NGC and PCGS represent a significant portion of the market."

A "Weighting" Game

Registry is really an extension of these companies' primary mission—grading coins. But in this case, they are grading *sets* of coins. According to PCGS, it "weights" these sets by taking into account three key elements: the overall rarity of each coin (whether it is rare in every grade), the rarity of each coin in the highest two or three grade levels, and the price of each coin. Price is deemed important because it reflects the degree of demand for a coin. In determining these weights, PCGS uses a spreadsheet prepared by David Hall, the company's founder, and tailored to each series. The spreadsheet is subject to modification based upon feedback from registrants. The company admits this is "not 100 percent scientific," but claims it is a reasonably accurate reflection of the relative rarity and importance of the coins. The weights assigned to individual coins are added to obtain a total weight.

There is no charge for participating in the Set Registry, and registrants even receive a number of perks, including free grading of up to five non-PCGS-certified coins once a set reaches 90 percent of completion. What motivates most collectors to take part is the program's competitive aspect—the excitement of going head-to-head with hobbyists who

Logo for the NGC Registry. *Photograph courtesy Numismatic Guaranty Corporation*

share their special passion and the keen satisfaction of being recognized publicly for their skill in pursuing that passion. They get a sense of fulfillment much like exhibitors whose coin displays win "best-of-show" awards. Although the recognition is very public, registrants often prefer to remain anonymous, using code names for their collections to avoid security problems. Nonetheless, they experience great exhilaration when their sets are singled out by PCGS. It's more than just the thrill of victory; it's the joy of validation—the pride and pleasure of being told by experts that all their time and money were well spent.

Set Registry benefits PCGS as well. On a dollars-and-cents level, it promotes submission of coins to the firm, generating substantial extra revenue. Beyond that, it creates enormous goodwill: It establishes and nurtures a bond between the company and collectors—a relationship far closer and more lasting than what would exist otherwise if registrants viewed the company as simply a supplier of useful services. By honoring collectors who assemble exceptional sets and by also fostering the formation of those sets, the company is enhancing its own image—for those blue-ribbon coin collections serve, in turn, as stunning showcases for PCGS certification.

Registry's Impact on Prices

In some marketplaces, competition leads to lower prices. Car buyers can expect to save on sticker prices, for instance, when Ford and General Motors go head-to-head for the same target audience. Likewise, Coke and Pepsi may try to outmaneuver each other by offering price incentives. The opposite has been true with registry sets: The keen competition for high-grade, high-score coins has driven prices higher—sometimes dramatically higher—for such material. As registrants vie for the finest available specimens of coins in the sets they are assembling, there is heightened upward pressure on the prices of those coins.

This coin, a "pop 1" and highest graded for the Type, has the potential to sell at auction for a sky-is-the-limit price if two bidders desperately want the best for their respective registry sets.
Photograph courtesy Scott Travers Rare Coin Galleries LLC

Having brokered the sale of thousands of coins—worth millions of dollars—bound for registry sets, I can attest to the strength of the demand for premium-quality coins that results from this spirited—sometimes even cutthroat—competition. Registry sets have had ripple effects throughout the coin market—and on the whole, their impact has been positive. They have boosted both activity and prices, and they have given rise to a whole new breed of savvy, informed collectors.

Pitfalls to Avoid

The registry set phenomenon has not been a totally unalloyed blessing. Like most things predominantly beneficial, it has spawned abuses and excesses, and these have captured sometimes jarring headlines in hobby publications, casting doubt on the merits of the program as a whole.

Before testing the water with a registry set of your own, here are potential riptides to avoid:

- **Overreliance on Population and Census Reports.** Registry sets place a premium on high quality and low quantity, as reflected in PCGS Population Reports and NGC Census Reports, which show how many examples of any given coin have been certified by that service in a particular grade. These reports are generally accurate in portraying the "condition rarity" of classic U.S. coins, most of which are genuinely scarce or even rare in the highest grades. But they're far from infallible, and may be misleading at times—for they list only coins that people have submitted for the services' review, not the entire available supply. Conversely, at other times their figures may exaggerate the number of pieces available because they may suggest that multiple resubmissions of the same coin (by submitters seeking an upgrade) are multiple coins instead. These reports should be consulted in making buying decisions for registry sets, but read through the eyes of skeptics, not true believers.

- **Pristine Examples of Coins with Relatively High Mintages, Especially Modern Coins.** Registry sets began making headlines, and raising eyebrows, when very high-grade modern coins, especially Lincoln cents, started bringing prices far beyond what their mintage figures seemed to justify. These coins were being purchased by registry-set collectors because their remarkable condition—typically Mint State-68 or 69—made them the finest examples listed in the population and census reports and qualified them for bigger registry scores. But the prices being paid (and still being paid, in some cases) clearly weren't justified. People were spending thousands of dollars for common-date coins such as the 1919-S Lincoln cent, which can be obtained for less than $50 in basic mint condition, based on the fact that few were listed in "pop reports" in exceptional mint condition. Often, however, these low numbers were due in part to the fact that relatively few examples of these coins had been submitted. Because of the common nature and modest premium value of the coins, few collectors had seen any point in paying submission fees to have them certified. Many more could be out there, just waiting for certification—and if only a few more were added to the pop reports, prices would plummet for pristine specimens.
- **Modern Proof Coins in Extremely High Condition.** Most modern proof coins, including Lincoln cents and statehood quarters, aren't really rare, even in extremely high grades, and their fair market value is considerably less than the stratospheric prices registry set owners sometimes pay for them. Modern U.S. proofs are *supposed to be* flawless, because the Mint uses the finest available equipment, material and technology in producing them. Not many have been judged to be perfect and given the designation of Proof-70 by the leading certification services, but quite a few have been graded Proof-69, a heartbeat (or maybe a hairline) from perfection. Clearly, then, it doesn't make sense to pay exorbitant premiums for such coins. As with pristine examples of common-date business-strike coins, modern proofs may not turn up in quantity in population and census reports—but again, this may be misleading: It simply may mean that few coins were submitted in the past. Today, modern coins are being submitted in far greater numbers, largely because registry sets and TV home shopping networks have created new markets at much higher price levels. Given the relatively high mintages of modern proofs, well up in the millions, additional Proof-68—or even Proof-69 or Proof-70—specimens are likely to continue turning up in pop reports, perhaps in significant quantity.

A Symbol of Excess

In January 2003, one "modern rarity"—a 1963 Lincoln cent in a PCGS Proof-70 Deep Cameo holder—changed hands for $39,100 at an auction conducted by Heritage at the FUN Show, a major event held annually by the Florida United Numismatists. It quickly became the symbol for what critics see as the dark side of registry sets. The coin was touted as the only proof Lincoln cent dated 1963 ever to receive a perfect grade from either PCGS or NGC. But the price seemed absurd to most observers—especially when the coin exhibited light toning, which some went so far as to call spotting. A year later, PCGS bought the coin for $40,250 to take it off the market. The company's founder,

David Hall, explained that the coin "had turned in the holder" and therefore was no longer Proof-70. PCGS has a buy-back guarantee for coins that deteriorate after being certified in its holders—and unlike other grading services, it extends that guarantee to copper coins.

$39,100 was not a fair market value price for a 1963 Lincoln cent—even one graded Proof-70. A fair market value price is what a willing buyer pays to a willing seller when neither is under any particular compulsion or compunction to complete the transaction—and for whatever reason, two buyers in this case appear to have been under pressure to purchase the coin with little regard for the price. In fairness, there were special circumstances involving a youngster's collection, which I cannot elaborate upon. Suffice it to say that price was no object to the buyer. He simply wanted the coin and was willing—and able—to pay whatever it took.

Time will tell whether older, more established coins in very high grades are worth the lofty prices to which registry set collectors have driven them. Unlike high-grade modern coins, these older coins have proven track records. For the most part, their mintages were considerably lower; they were set aside in far smaller numbers; and collectors can have reasonable confidence that the pop report figures accurately reflect their rarity in top condition. Over the years, these coins have performed extremely well, and I expect that to continue—with registry sets playing a major role in stimulating interest in such material.

The Future of Registry Sets

It's always hard to guess whether popular innovations will put down permanent roots. Sometimes new ideas burst upon the scene, shine brightly for a time, then fade away as quickly as they came. Hula hoops come to mind. So do 3-D movies, Nehru jackets, pet rocks, and miniskirts. All of these were fads—"for a day." It may be too soon to pass judgment on registry set programs—but far from fading away, they seem to be gaining momentum as time goes by, and I have become increasingly convinced that they will be with us for many years to come. Set registration has moved past the point where it can be dismissed as just a fad; it has taken firm root with a fast-growing segment of the hobby—including some of the most important collectors in the world.

Set registration reminds me of the role Whitman folders played in an earlier time. Introduced in 1940, the ubiquitous blue folders revolutionized the way Americans collected coins in the mid-20th century and played a major role in the hobby's rapid expansion during that era. Their role has waned in recent years, but they remain a significant tool for newer collectors, especially youngsters.

The grading services themselves are prime examples of new ideas that proved to have lasting value and therefore have endured. Certified grading and "slabs" were novel concepts in 1986, when PCGS introduced them, but today they are integral—and universally accepted—elements of our vibrant 21st-century coin market. Over the years, the services have updated and refined the services they offer to collectors, and registry sets are perhaps their most successful innovation since certification itself.

All things considered, registry sets are good for collectors, good for the grading services and good for the hobby. Collectors should be careful not to pursue them with what Alan Greenspan described as "irrational exuberance"—but with the right approach, they can be a source of healthy competition and ongoing pleasure and profit.

– 11 –
SECRETS OF CHERRYPICKING

There's something deeply satisfying about picking up a bargain—in coins as in anything else—by outsmarting somebody else, particularly when that somebody is supposed to be an expert on the subject. People who pursue hidden bargains in coins are called cherry-pickers, and their ranks have been expanding in recent years. So have their rewards, and you can grab a share of those rewards by following the guidelines provided in this chapter by leading authorities.

Success in cherrypicking is directly proportional to the effort you put in, for in almost every case, people who spot bargains are able to do so because they have done their homework and know more about a coin than the person selling that item. In years gone by, "cherrypicker" had a more general meaning; a buyer was said to have cherrypicked a dealer's inventory if he went through the dealer's coins and picked out the very best pieces—or cherries. Nowadays, the term is applied primarily to someone with specialized knowledge of die varieties. Typically, a coin will be underpriced today because it is a scarce or rare variety and the seller—not realizing this—has marked it at the price corresponding to a common or "normal" variety.

Valuable varieties can range from very obvious ones, such as the dramatic double images on the obverse of the 1955 doubled-die Lincoln cent, to subtle, almost indiscernible ones—perhaps one mint mark stamped above another, where only a magnifying glass, but nothing stronger than 10-power, will reveal that there is something out of the ordinary. Other potentially valuable varieties include coins with overdates, repunched dates, repunched mint marks—and even engraving errors. Early U.S. coinage was particularly rich in varieties because the Mint's equipment and methods were far less sophisticated. Also, it was common practice at that time, for reasons of economy, to continue using dies when a calendar year ended by punching the new year's date over the old.

Bill Fivaz, a former governor of the American Numismatic Association, is a preeminent authority on cherrypicking die varieties. He is a co-author of a best-selling

This 1971-S Proof Lincoln cent with a doubled-die obverse retails for $1,000, compared with the 75-cent value attributed to the unremarkable specimen.

Repunched dates can be subtle or very pronounced. This 1894 Indian cent will command a price over $1,000, compared with $150 for the unremarkable example.

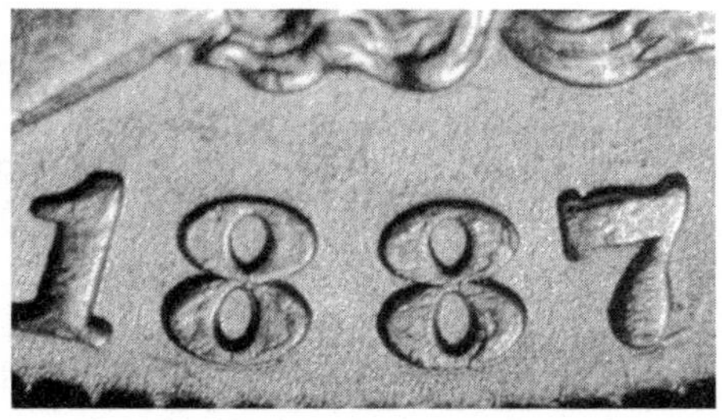

An overdate occurs when one date is punched into a die over a different date. This 1887/6-O Morgan dollar will bring as much as $7,500.

Rare variety: 1942-D Jefferson nickel with the D mint mark over a horizontal D mint mark. This repunched mint mark makes this coin worth as much as $750. The unremarkable coin is valued at $30.

hobby guidebook called *The Cherrypickers' Guide to Rare Die Varieties, Fourth Edition (Vol. 1)*, which contains descriptions and photographs of more than 400 valuable coin varieties that might very well be encountered at common-variety prices. Volume one, which covers half cents through nickels, is available from the American Numismatic Association's MoneyMarket (*www.money.org*) and Amos Advantage (*www.amosadvantage.com*).

Two other indispensable references for cherrypickers are *The Official Price Guide to Mint Errors, Sixth Edition* by Alan Herbert (House of Collectibles/Random House,

An "over mint mark," similar to an overdate, is one mint mark punched over a different mint mark. This 1950-S/D Washington quarter is a good example. Values can reach several hundred dollars for an otherwise common coin.

A "blundered die" is a variety that can cause a coin to have an unusual appearance, such as that exhibited by this 1870 Indian head cent's denticles below the date. Digits were punched in that area. Varieties are known with date punches in many different areas.

2002) and *The Error Coin Encyclopedia, Fourth Edition* by Fred Weinberg and Arnold Margolis (2004).

Fivaz recommends that anyone considering a cherrypicking expedition first stock up on knowledge by reading one of the many books available today on specific coin series and also by joining CONECA, the national club for collectors of error coins and varieties. Membership in CONECA costs $25 per year, plus a first-time application fee of $5. Inquiries should be sent to: Paul Funaiole, 35 Leavitt Lane, Glenburn, ME 04401-1013 pfunny1@adelphia.net. The CONECA web site is *www.conecaonline.org*.

Don't expect to find rare varieties right away. If they were easy to find, they wouldn't be rare or valuable. It may take months or even a year before you find your first rare variety—but once you find that first one, you'll be hooked.

With valuable coin varieties, one picture may be worth even more than a thousand words—or, for that matter, a thousand dollars. A veteran cherrypicker has generously shared some of his high-quality photographs vividly illustrating varieties you should be looking for.

When looking for these, or other valuable varieties, here are a few cherrypicking courtesies that Bill Fivaz agrees with:

- **Don't lie.** If a dealer asks you what you are looking for, tell him "varieties." But you don't have to tell everything. If the dealer persists, you can tell him about a few of the more scarce varieties, and explain that there is a market for those varieties.
- **Do not let a dealer feel cheated if you buy a coin.** You might not be invited back. It is not a good idea to brag about what you have just purchased, especially in earshot of any dealer. Be polite, courteous and friendly.

- **If you find a super variety for the price of a regular coin and don't want the dealer to focus on that one coin, buy a few other coins at the same time to draw less attention to the coin you really want.** The other coins will be saleable at or near the purchase price, and will be assured of buying that cherry at a price level that will allow you to make a tidy profit.

– 12 –
"INSIDER TRADING" OF RARE COINS

> Honest, if you buy this coin I promise I'll bid that coin to three times the level that it's listed on the sheet for now. It's the only one known. I can bid it up to any level you want. What level would you like me to bid it up to?
>
> —*Well-known market-maker with a coin listed in a certified coin population report as the only one graded for that grade.*

During my years as a coin trader, I've witnessed many examples of insider trading and observed very closely the way that information is disseminated—its ethical use, unethical use, and uneven distribution in this field.

Rare-Coin Insider Trading

Just what is rare-coin insider trading? Outsiders perceive it as the manipulation of the coin market for material gain by people who take advantage of their knowledge of inside information, knowledge not available to the general coin-buying public. In point of fact, however, a number of legal experts say that "insider trading" is a nebulous term not only in the coin market, but also in the securities industry. While there are accepted, court-sanctioned definitions for Wall Street (securities) insider trading, no one should expect a specific definition for rare coin insider trading.

Here's my definition: a number of prominent coin dealers capitalize on their knowledge of insider information to make advantageous deals. In fact, this goes on so routinely that it might even impress Kenneth Lay and Martha Stewart. The methods of market manipulation in this field are almost endless.

But be careful. Up until recently, some so-called 'insider trading' of rare coins was thought to be not only legal but essential. However, with coin dealers issuing public offerings and being subject to securities laws, the landscape has changed. So you need to use your good judgment—and maybe a good lawyer!—to stay out of trouble, or even out of jail.

People in this field don't have government agencies monitoring their day-to-day activities. For this reason, and because the coin industry is relatively small in size, savvy collectors can sometimes put themselves in the same advantageous position—the same insider position—as major dealers.

Here are two examples of "insider trading" that, depending upon the circumstances and parties involved, may or may not be legal. I am not going to give my opinion as to what is "legitimate" and what is not. Proceed at your own risk. Anyone who is unsure whether or not a transaction would be legal, or whether or not he has been treated in an unlawful manner by a party to a transaction, should consult an attorney.

- An investor purchasing a coin that he knows is the only one of its kind to which a certain grade has been assigned by a given grading service, and then offering increasingly more amounts of money for that coin—which leads to higher price guide values for the piece.
- An investor getting friendly with a dealer and learning from that contact, on a confidential basis, that five rare coins of a certain type and date were submitted by the dealer for grading and will be coming onto the market soon—and then using that knowledge to profit.

Insider Information and Rare Coins

Insider information is used routinely, of course, in many different aspects of daily life. It's used in ways that are legal and ways that are not.

Suppose your local congresswoman knows that certain property will soon be the site of a major development, and suppose she tips off her cousin, who then makes an investment in the area. That's leakage of insider information.

Suppose the chairman of the Federal Reserve Board is drafting a statement on interest rates that's likely to have a dramatic effect on the securities industry. Any number of his colleagues or associates might conceivably be aware of what he's preparing to say, and this insider information might enable them to make—or advise their friends to make—some highly lucrative deals.

Although this kind of insider information permeates the coin field, I don't believe it to be a major problem. There are mechanisms in place that will limit to a great degree, or even prevent, insider trades. And as I have noted, this industry is relatively small; insider information doesn't remain secret very long.

With that said, I must point out that there are certain types of insider information that have put some people at a tremendous advantage in the coin field and have left others at a great disadvantage.

Selling Off Right Before a Massive Downturn

We saw a good example of this phenomenon in July 1988, when coin dealers at the annual convention of the American Numismatic Association were stunned by the announcement that coins supposedly certified by the Professional Coin Grading Service had turned up in counterfeit plastic slabs. Apparently some dealers learned of the situation before the announcement was made—and based on this information, gained through insider contacts, they immediately sold many of their PCGS-graded coins. Some of the coins they sold were in counterfeit slabs and, like virtually all the coins of this type, these were overgraded and therefore overpriced. However, even the coins in genuine slabs were worth substantially less following the announcement, because the scandal shook market confidence (at least for a short time) in PCGS coins as a whole. This was a clear instance where knowledge of insider information helped certain dealers significantly.

Price Manipulation

Another common use of insider information in the coin market is price manipulation. Often this involves coins with very low populations, coins that have been graded in very small quantities in a given grade by a particular grading service.

From the insider's standpoint, the ideal population is one. The chances for price manipulation are maximized when a dealer owns the only coin of a certain kind to which a given grade has been assigned. This information can be obtained by studying the population reports issued by the major grading services. So long as the dealer is certain that no other coins of that type and that grade are available, he or she can bid up the price of that coin on the teletype system. (If another example happened to exist or got certified, the dealer would be obliged to purchase it at his or her bid price if the coin's owner belonged to the same trading network and chose to accept the bid.)

Suppose this hypothetical coin is listed initially at $2,500 in the *Certified Coin Dealer Newsletter* (or *Bluesheet*), the standard weekly price guide for coins that have been independently certified. And suppose the dealer offers progressively higher bids, upping the ante to $5,000, to $6,000, and finally to $7,000. After $7,000 has been offered for several weeks, the publishers of the *Bluesheet* may raise the coin's listed price from $2,500 to $7,000. At that point the dealer will sell it to someone who is unaware of what has been going on, perhaps to another dealer unschooled in the ways of such games or perhaps to an unsuspecting collector or investor. The dealer may even offer a "discount": With the *Bluesheet* price at $7,000, maybe the coin will be offered for "just" $6,000. Then, when the dealer stops bidding $7,000 for the coin and has sold it for $6,000, its price will go back down to where it was before and where it belongs: $2,500.

Sometimes certain types of coins are not traded because of a period of disinterest. This is referred to as a "thin" market, and one or two transactions could be responsible for the bid and ask in these popular price guides. This could invite unscrupulous individuals to attempt to manipulate the price guides. Bid and ask can be moved up or down artificially by dishonest dealers making high "bids" for low population coins. True, these dealers would have to purchase any coin offered to them at their bid—no matter how high. But if there are only three coins that were certified, and that dealer owns the three coins, then he can clearly push up the value of his own coins. His risk is if more are certified, and his bid gets hit. He would have to write a check.

Sometimes dealers will place high bids on almost-non-existent MS-65 coins, when they have a large financial interest in their relatively common MS-64 counterparts. This way, the MS-64 coin might be able to be sold for more money, and the risk of being hit to buy the MS-65 coin is minimal.

The real trick is to locate the high bidders on the coin areas in which you are interested. If you see that the only bidder on the coin graded MS-65 is the person trying to sell you that coin, you will know to exercise caution. An even more subtle technique is for you to locate the person bidding on the next higher grade.

If someone owns a large number of a certain coin, they might enter high "bids" and "asks" so that it will appear in the price guides that their coins are more valuable. If they know a certain area is about to experience a surge of interest, they might artificially depress prices in order to secure some really outstanding coins at giveaway prices.

The Coin Dealer Newsletter offers a no-charge service to subscribers in which high bidders will be identified. If you see a coin increasing in value and you want to see who the high buyer is, they will tell you. All you have to do is call and ask.

Some time ago, considerable publicity was given to an alleged manipulation of the teletype and, thus, the price guides. A few dealers were suspected of driving down prices of commemorative coins on the teletype. Anthony Swiatek, a recognized authority in the area, took such exception to this practice that in response he took out an advertisement in *Coin World*, the hobby's highest-circulation weekly, in which he wrote an "Alert":

> The drastic price decline of U.S. silver and gold commemorative coinage is a farce, a fake, a sad plot, total humbug, a fraud, a sinister deception. It was created by a few dealers who are determined to depress this beautiful area of numismatics—which in all price history has never witnessed such a drastic "unnatural" rapid drop in price. Efforts by dealers looking to buy at current levels and slightly higher previous levels have experienced the following: a) Material is not available; b) offerings are almost always overgraded. (The 63+ coin offered for the 65 coin.) Think for a moment. If many properly graded issues were not available at higher prices how can they be available now . . . Dealers can fight this negative numismatic move by using the teletype in a positive way.

Beware if you see a coin increase or decrease substantially during a short period of time with no apparent explanation. This increase or decrease could be the result of teletype manipulation. Also, the people who monitor the teletype for the price guides have to go by the descriptions as set forth by the dealers composing them. If a coin is offered on the teletype and is described as MS-67 but is only an MS-60, nobody knows except the people who look at the coin.

Today, this has become more difficult to manipulate because of the emergence of independent third-party grading services and other safeguards (e.g. dealer rejection reports). If a dealer is bidding at a certain level for a coin sight-unseen, he or she has to pay that price. The dealer can't turn sellers away by saying, "Well, this coin doesn't meet my personal standards for the grade I want." Dealers post bids on the Certified Coin Exchange.

The Inner Circle

Collectors and investors can avoid this type of manipulation by doing business with dealers who are not only honorable, but also members of the coin market's inner circle—that is, dealers who know the ins and outs of population reports and will not themselves fall victim to this kind of scam.

Keep in mind that dealers themselves can be victimized if they don't stay fully informed on all the factors involved in determining the value of a coin. If they don't pay close attention to population reports, they too can be deceived by price lists where the value reflects manipulation rather than real demand. They may think they're getting a bargain when someone comes up to their table at a show and offers them such a coin at a price well below the *Bluesheet* level. And they'll pass this "bargain" on to a customer, not because they too are trying to take advantage of someone, but because they themselves aren't very knowledgeable.

Collectors, investors, and dealers, too, should watch closely for signs of volatility in any specific area of the market. This is especially true of areas where few coins have been certified and where, for that reason, one dealer can control a complete population. Great volatility in any particular area doesn't mean that coins are being traded rapidly; it may mean that a dealer has manipulated that portion of the marketplace-manipulated it upward and then sold the specific coin or coins, causing bid levels to drop precipitously.

PCGS has the following anti-self-interest policy posted in its grading room:

> Graders!!!
>
> PCGS Anti-Self-Interest Policy
>
> PCGS graders cannot do any of the following:
>
> 1. Grade their own coins.
> 2. Grade coins they submit for clients or other dealers.
> 3. Grade coins they have a financial interest in (split-profit deals, etc.).
> 4. Verify any of the above coins.
> 5. Participate in any discussion whatsoever—inside or outside of the grading room—either before, during, or after the coins are in the grading process.

Fiduciary Responsibility

PCGS graders cannot use any information obtained inside the grading room before the information is available in the general marketplace. More specifically graders cannot do any of the following:

1. Buy coins from a dealer based on information obtained in the grading room. If a grader finds out who a coin or group of coins belongs to while the coins are in the grading process, that grader cannot contact the submitting dealer for the purpose of purchasing the coins (or obtaining first shot, etc.) until 10 days after the dealer has received his coins back from PCGS.

2. Sell or buy coins and/or coin positions based on information obtained in the grading room.

Any grader who has one substantiated violation of item No. 1 or who shows a consistent pattern of violating item No. 2 will be immediately terminated.

The Bad Old Days

In the early 1980s we witnessed market practices that were far less ethical than those we have today. Some dealers at that time occasionally drove up bid levels in *The Coin Dealer Newsletter* (or *Greysheet*), the standard weekly price guide for all U.S. coins. And they didn't have to concern themselves with rules and regulations requiring them to buy such coins if those coins were offered.

Circa-1980 dealers could take a coin listed for $400 in The Coin Dealer Newsletter, bid $600, $700, $1,000—and keep bidding higher and higher amounts on the teletype system. In those days they had no real obligation to purchase any coins that people sent; coins were not certified then, and we didn't have a sight-unseen system. The dealers would simply send the coins back, saying they didn't meet their high grading standards.

Dealer promotions and price manipulation played a big part in the marketplace confusion over grading standards. In driving up prices, dealers were looking to make bigger profits on coins they already had; they had no interest in buying such coins from anyone else. Thus, as people sent them coins, these dealers just shipped them right back. A number of people would then submit coins of the next higher grade, since the artificially inflated price levels were high enough to justify selling even these at the quoted bids. Again the dealers would send the coins back. In some cases dealers were offering to buy coins graded MS-65 at a certain price, and people were sending them coins that should have been graded as high as MS-67; even then the coins were returned.

Today's Improved Market

Although manipulation does occur today, it's more difficult to drive up price-guide levels—especially those of certified coins, since dealers must be willing to buy at least some quantity of the coin on which they are making a "sight-unseen bid." This discourages the unscrupulous from trying to manipulate prices of the more common certified coins, where hundreds or even thousands of examples may exist.

As growing numbers of coins are certified, population reports will list far fewer one-of-a-kind coins. Already the number is dwindling, even among supergrade coins bearing the very high MS and proof numbers that grading services initially assigned quite sparingly. In most cases enough coins are available to protect against price manipulation.

Clearly the coin market doesn't have a perfect trading system. But in a world where no system is completely perfect, today's system is certainly far better than yesterday's.

Promotions of Coins in Newsletters

Newsletters serve as yet another way to promote coins and influence their prices. Some mass-market coin dealers publish their own newsletters and use them on a regular basis to promote the coins they have for sale.

Often it's possible to anticipate such promotions—even without being a true market insider—simply by analyzing which coins these dealers have promoted in the past. When dealers send newsletters to thousands upon thousands of collectors and investors, obviously they can't use them to promote coins of which just three examples, or even 300, are known. They have to select coins that exist in more promotable numbers. Among the series that combine sufficient numbers with broad-based popularity are Morgan silver dollars, Saint-Gaudens double eagles, and commemoratives.

Dealers stage promotions for these and other popular coins on a regular, systematic basis. They may promote Saint-Gaudens double eagles one month, Morgan dollars the next month, and commemoratives the month after that. If you haven't seen the Morgan dollar promoted in one of these newsletters in a while, you can be quite certain that its turn will be coming very soon. That might be a good time to buy Morgan dollars—before the promotion hits, with all its attendant hype, and prices go up in response.

I recommend that you get on the mailing lists of all the large dealerships that publish and distribute such newsletters. Often they're quite informative and even entertaining, and they can help guide you in charting the direction of the market.

Insider Economics

Paul Taglione, a former principal of the now defunct New England Rare Coin Galleries, has written a number of valuable books and articles analyzing the coin market's inner workings. Taglione and the company he worked for became targets of a 1987 Federal Trade Commission lawsuit charging them with unfair or deceptive acts or practices in or affecting commerce. The company agreed to liquidate its assets and pay at least $1.5 million in refunds to consumers. Taglione, the company's former chief numismatist, signed a consent judgment and did not admit to any violation of the law, but agreed to assign to the escrow fund all of his interests in New England Rare Coins and all obligations owed to him by the company. Despite this, and to some extent because of this, his insights on the market are fascinating and illuminating. The following is an excerpt from Taglione's book, *An Investment Philosophy for the Prudent Consumer* (Numismatic Research and Service Corporation, Boston, 1986).

> Across the expanse of market actors currently active in the Numismatic Markets, technical numismatic knowledge and comprehension of the economics of the various Numismatic Markets is, in my view, extremely variable in depth and quality. An amazing number of market actors do not possess adequate technical knowledge of areas in which they trade. Incredibly enough, very few market actors seriously study the economics of the Numismatic Markets in which they participate. Any private numismatic investor can obtain an edge in a specialized area and, I am perfectly convinced, any private investor can obtain a general edge in even wider areas of the Numismatic Markets. The "investment edge," as I see it, involves a wide-ranging knowledge of the economics of the area in which one wishes to invest. A first step in obtaining this knowledge is researching and examining the supply side of an area. How many examples of this coin exist? How many come to market? Is the supply of this particular coin or class of coins inelastic to increased demand? The next step is obtaining a knowledge of the size, intensity, and quality of demand. This step must begin at the level of the individual buyer. What sort of market actor demands and desires this coin? Does the acquisition of this coin satisfy a preference or does it stimulate a preference to acquire more coins? In my opinion, the quality of demand is much more important than its size or intensity. The size or intensity of demand can be the result of dictated preference and if quality of demand is taken to include endurance and continuity (which I take it to include), then it becomes obvious that demand which derives from dictated preference is markedly lacking in these qualities. Another step in obtaining the investment edge is investigating the parameters of price at which buyers can and do acquire material. Obviously the demand for a common coin is much more sensitive to price than is the demand for a rare coin. An investor must exercise a great deal more caution in acquiring a common coin in terms of price than is required for obtaining a rarity whose market appearance in and of itself generates a value for the acquisition opportunity. Perhaps the best investment edge of all is the recognition that the edge is complicated and varies from area to area and from time to time. Part of this recognition is an awareness that choosing the elusive and storied "right dealer" might not be an edge at all; it might be a disadvantage!

Completely Legal Insider Negotiating

Once you've mastered coin grading and the mechanics of buying and selling, this is the most important section of the book. From the very first edition of this work, I have presented variations on these negotiation pointers, and have received wide praise for them. I shared this advice in my role as an instructor at the American Numismatic Association Summer Seminar, held many public forums and educational programs, and have even been videotaped delivering my most sought-after address—"How to Negotiate."

So here in a simple, condensed format is my best advice on negotiating, gleaned from nearly 30 years of hands-on experience dealing in coins worth millions of dollars—and delivered by me many times before:

- **Know the value of every coin you hope to buy or sell, or the value of the services for which you are negotiating.** Buying or selling a coin without knowing its current market value is like driving car in an area alien to you without a map or navigation system. I know of one dealer who wrote a book in which he advised readers to start out by offering half of what a dealer was asking for any given coin. Suppose the dealer was asking $10,000 but the coin was really worth only $1,000: It would be foolish to open negotiations by offering $5,000. Similarly, if you are negotiating an auction contract, you should prepare some careful projections of the auction company's costs. When I negotiate an auction contract, I'm intimately familiar with what it is costing the auction firm to conduct the sale-preparation of the catalog, labor, insurance, the staging of the sale at a hotel or convention site, and other expenses. Let the auction company make a profit; give it an incentive to obtain high prices for your coins. But don't overpay unnecessarily.
- **Let your adversary make a living.** Being a coin dealer is often a tough job. It's demanding and expensive to maintain and transport an inventory of valuable coins from city to city, show to show, sale to sale. Respect the time and effort a dealer has spent preparing for a negotiating session with you, and strive for an outcome that's fair to both of you. It isn't in your best interest to squeeze the other guy for a few extra tenths of a percent on your profit margin—not if you're planning to do business again with that dealer or others with whom he converses.
- **Master the use of your emotions.** With coins as with cards, a poker face will help you come out ahead; it keeps other people guessing about your intentions. No matter how badly you want to buy or sell a particular coin, try to appear composed and unemotional. Keep in mind, however, that every now and then, judicious use of the right emotional reaction at an appropriate time can clinch a deal for you.
- **Never bluff, and never lie.** Bluffing and lying will always get you into trouble, damaging or destroying your credibility for future dealings. They might even ruin your chances of making the deal that's at hand. Mean what you say and say what you mean. Let me assure you, if I make an offer to buy a coin and say that a certain number is my "last and final offer," I won't move up from that number by even one red cent. I would rather walk away from the deal—and I have—than go back on my word.
- **Let the other party make the first offer.** Deal-making is one situation where, quite often, it doesn't pay to go first. There's always a chance that the other person will offer to sell you a coin for substantially less than what you expect, or offer to buy a coin from you for substantially more than you would have asked. If you do have to go first, start very low in making an offer to buy. You can always come up, but you rarely can go down.
- **Simplify the issues.** "Keep it simple, stupid" is rather good advice when it comes to making deals involving rare coins. Variables tend to slow down negotiations. Boil down your discussions to a single issue or number, or at most a very few. Otherwise, you may never reach an agreement.

- **Never make an offer you're uncertain about, and never withdraw an offer once you make it.** In buying or selling rare coins, your word is your bond. You must be careful never to vacillate or dither after you make an offer.
- **Go to the top.** Pick the person with whom you want to deal, and be certain it's someone who has the needed authority—someone who can say "Yes" without getting somebody else's permission. In many cases, this eliminates the middleman. This, in turn, often eliminates unnecessary fees. It also averts the good-cop, bad-cop tactics which many used coin dealers like to use when working out a deal.
- **Find out who really owns the coin.** Many coin dealers do business routinely among themselves and handle coins on "memo" from other dealers. For this reason, it's important to negotiate with a coin's true owner. To gain this information, you need to be very active and astute at coin shows—be "in the loop," so to speak. It's worth it, though. Why pay Dealer X's bottom-line price of $25,000 when Dealer Y really owns the coin and will sell it to you for only $15,000?
- **When making an offer, count out the money or write out a check on the spot.** Being offered cash or a check on the barrelhead can be very persuasive to someone selling a coin. Say a dealer is asking $3,000 for a coin and you've offered $2,600. Chances are, he might suggest splitting the difference. But if you pull out your checkbook and write a check for $2,600, he may simply say, "OK, I'll take it," saving you $200.
- **Always assume the position of power.** Simply stated, this means giving yourself every psychological edge. When sitting down with someone to negotiate a deal, always try to get the most dominating seat. In order to look businesslike, wear professional attire. Above all, never let yourself be vulnerable; always strive to be in command. At coin shows, in an effort to level the playing field, I often go behind the other dealer's table and discuss any pending transactions back there, where we are on an equal footing. Some shows don't allow this, so if you intend to engage in this practice, check beforehand to make sure it isn't a violation—especially if you don't have a table of your own at a given show.
- **Be flexible and be ready to change the conditions of the deal on the spot.** Sometimes a deal may seem hopelessly deadlocked. Rather than lose it entirely, be prepared to improvise and modify the structure in order to save it. Suppose you're unwilling to pay more than $800 for a coin, but the dealer insists on getting $900. Look in his inventory for something else on which you can make up the difference—possibly a $600 generic gold coin you can sell elsewhere for $700. By adding that to the deal, you can still come out just the way you wanted. Similarly, if you're negotiating an auction contract and the auction company won't go any lower on its commission, you might ask the firm instead to guarantee you a photograph of that coin in the catalog. Or, if a large transaction is involved, such as the consignment of an entire collection, you might seek assurance that the auction company will do something extra to help promote it—something which might be very helpful to you in getting higher prices realized, but which would cost the company very little more, such as generating a special press release about the collection or perhaps displaying the collection at a show before the auction takes place.

- **Make the other person feel that it's in his or her best interest to make the deal.** Convince the other party that you, and only you, are the right person for this particular deal—that it's an advantage selling the coins to you, rather than any other prospective buyer.
- **Don't take things personally.** This rule is last, but certainly not least. If a dealer rejects your offer or counter-offer, don't go away mad. View negotiating as a game, even though the money involved is real. Keep a positive, enthusiastic outlook and leave the door open. He or she may even reconsider and make the deal with you after all.

Cost Averaging

Cost averaging is a technique familiar to people in financial fields. Essentially, it's a way of cushioning a loss when one investment goes down in value by purchasing a second example of the same item at the lower price.

Suppose you buy a coin for $10,000 and it plunges in value to $1,000. To cost average, you buy another coin just like it—a coin of the same denomination, date, and grade—for $1,000. What you are doing, effectively, is splitting the difference. Now you can take the attitude that you really paid $5,500 apiece for the two coins: the sum of their prices ($11,000) divided by two. It's unlikely that the market value of either coin will rebound all the way to $10,000, but chances are good that after dropping in price so sharply, the coins will regain at least part of the lost ground. They may rise to $5,000 or even $7,000 apiece. And at that point you'll break even or come out slightly ahead.

Cost averaging is a psychologically soothing way to rationalize the fact that you overpaid for a coin or bought it at the top of the cycle.

Rare Coins as Securities

David L. Ganz, a New York City lawyer who is a past president of the American Numismatic Association, writes:

> Are rare coins securities, or are they just coins? There's no easy or specific answer to that question because the courts of the nation are split on the issue—and there is no ready resolution in sight. The short answer to the question is that a coin is always a coin, but sometimes coins can be sold in such a way as to make them into a security. When they reach that status, coins become subject to a host of government regulations, and a prospective liability to purchasers.
>
> Rare coins are not generally thought of as being a security. Stocks and bonds are the most traditional types of wholly regulated investment vehicles. By contrast, the purchase and sale of rare coins is almost entirely unregulated.
>
> Coins generally lack the attributes traditionally associated with a security: fungibility (the ability to exchange one for another without noticeable difference); homogeneity (substantially identical pricing for identically described individual components); divisibility; and representation of a defined value of an otherwise regulated entity.

However, there are some coins that meet this definition—typically a generic, slabbed (or encapsulated) coin. What is always at issue is the manner in which the coins are sold to the ultimate purchaser that can transform them from a mere coin into a security.

The Securities and Exchange Commission has been curiously silent on whether or not coins are securities, except for the Brigadoon Scotch case, which determined that investment contracts for rare coins were indeed a security. Based on the sales presentation by the seller (but not the supplier), the sale of rare coins can constitute an investment contract or a security under the laws of several states.

As with every investment vehicle that is not a stock or bond, the analysis of whether or not coins sales are a security begins with the test set forth in the seminal case of *SEC* v. *W.J. Howey & Co.*, where the U.S. Supreme Court set out a three-pronged test for determining whether a transaction involves an investment contract. In Howey, the Supreme Court defined an investment contract as

1. an investment

2. in a common venture premised on the reasonable expectation of profits

3. to be derived from the entrepreneurial or managerial efforts of others.

Just as Howey was the seminal case that demonstrated that a security went beyond stocks and bonds, the principal authority that establishes that the sale of rare coins can constitute a security is *SEC* v. *Brigadoon Scotch Dist. Co. (Federal Coin Reserve)*.

The Brigadoon Scotch case involved an entity known as the Federal Coin Reserve, which marketed rare coins as an investment vehicle. The Brigadoon Scotch Court noted at the time, Federal Coin Reserve "stimulates sales by advertising in such media as airline magazines, journals used in the medical profession, and other similar outlets. It does not advertise in publications specifically addressed to amateur or professional coin collectors."

The description of what Federal Coin Reserve offered its customers is set forth in the brochure explicitly. Federal Coin Reserve promised professional selection and supervision; reinvestment of capital gains; accounting services; diversification; daily bidding; insurance; tax advice and consultation; depository vaults; and a claim that "The Federal Coin Reserve looks forward to a minimum appreciation of 100% every five (5) years. . . ." (Brochure, p. 17).

The defendants in Brigadoon Scotch (Federal Coin Reserve) denied that they were selling securities and instead asked the Court to take at face value their claims that the items offered for sale (rare coins) are just that—a mere commodity—and that there was no investment contract, which would be required as a finding under federal law.

The Brigadoon Scotch Court said, "regardless of the nature of the ultimate sales here, FCR's analysis is not in keeping with the law because an investment contract is determinable not only by the nature of what the sellers actually sell but equally by what character the investment is given . . . by the terms of offer, the plan of distribution, and the economic inducements held out to the prospect. In the enforcement of an act such as this it is not inappropriate that promoters' offerings be judged as being what they were represented to be." (citation omitted)

In Brigadoon Scotch, as indeed with almost every other investment-type case involving rare coins, "FCR customers purchase their coins as an investment for the purpose of making a profit," rather than for the purpose of collecting coins as an amateur numismatist.

The Brigadoon Scotch court put the issue succinctly: The crucial inquiry is "Whether the efforts by those other than the investor are the undeniably significant ones, those essential managerial efforts which affect the failure or success of the enterprise."

The determining factors in those schemes was that "what was being sold was an investment entrusting the promoters with both the work and the expertise to make the tangible investment pay off." *Glen-Arden Commodities, Inc.* v. *Costantino.* If a seller promises to (or does) manage the investment or uses his/her expertise to help or hinder the valuation changes in rare coins purchased, the coin sale could be a security.

Other Court cases have since been decided in which the method of selling did make the rare coin sold into securities, but for the most part, the wild, wild west attitude of the rare coin market prevails together with the classic warning of *caveat emptor*: Let the buyer beware.

– 13 –

DANGERS OF BUYING COINS ON THE INTERNET AND BY MAIL

> A while ago, we had the occasion to seriously question the values offered by an enormously successful firm. A deliberate selection of 20 or so coins were ordered from [its] hefty, profusely illustrated catalog where [it] proudly displayed [its] prestigious reputation and repeated insistence to satisfy customers. We were shocked by some of [its] coins! [Its] wonderful "BU, light rubbing" 2-cent piece was an EF; [its] BU Bust Dime was a sharp AU-50 adorned with deep scratches, too trivial to mention; [its] Unc. Trade Dollar was a polished EF; and on and on!
>
> —Maurice Rosen
> *The Rosen Numismatic Advisory*

More than 20 years have passed since Maurice Rosen, a longtime coin market analyst, wrote the above words, expressing his dismay at the quality of the coins he received by mail from a nationally known and well-regarded company. The coin market has come a long way since then, and so has the technology used in marketing coins. The more things change, however, the more they stay the same. Today, Rosen's words might easily be applied to many of the raw or uncertified coins being sold in online auctions by dealers conducting business on the Internet. His words might apply, too, to the coins sold by disreputable vendors that they "certify" themselves. These transactions are more immediate, but the perils are depressingly similar.

A good percentage of Internet transactions are just fine. Many reputable vendors are selling certified coins at fair prices. But if you don't buy a certified coin from a reputable vendor, or know the standards of the grading service whose coins you purchase, you run the risk of getting ripped off. In the Wild West world of the Internet, too many uncertified and "self-certified" coins are available from disreputable sellers.

This chapter does not focus on the 95 to 99 percent of Internet transactions that are legitimate. Instead, this chapter focuses on the small minority of transactions that are problematic.

eBay has emerged as perhaps the preeminent Internet auction facilitator.

Buying Coins on the Internet

The Computer Revolution has permeated—and permutated—virtually every area of society, and the rare-coin market is no exception. In just the last few years, computers have moved from being merely an option to becoming almost a necessity for people who buy and sell coins on a regular basis. For all but beginners and dabblers, access to the Internet is practically as important today as access to price guides and reference books. A computer has become almost as vital a tool as a magnifying glass or a high-intensity lamp for viewing coins. Knowing how to travel through cyberspace is as crucial to success as knowing how to navigate the aisles on a major coin show's bourse floor.

The vastly increased availability of almost any rare coin online has given many people access to coins and dealers that they might not have imagined a decade ago. This applies especially to people who are not in large cities.

Online Auctions

Internet auctions have become an important method of selling rare coins. Traditional auction firms have recognized the potential of the technology and established a growing presence online. In general, their Internet sales are legitimate and ethical, and these offer opportunities for buyers to obtain desirable coins more quickly and easily than through the methods of the past. High-quality digital images and detailed descriptions often accompany listings for these coins, giving prospective purchasers instant access to an online catalog without the time and expense of obtaining a printed version from the auction firm.

Some very reputable mail-order dealers are using the electronic marketplace as a way to reach new customers and expand their business—and they're even offering coins at discounted prices to help attract such buyers. But caution is always advisable.

Unfortunately, the same advantages that make Internet auctions attractive to legitimate businesses and their clients have also caught the attention of less reputable companies and individuals. They, too, conduct Internet sales, but without the safeguards and ethical considerations buyers are used to getting—and still receive online—from more established firms with names and reputations to uphold. Rip-off artists are encouraged and emboldened by the relative lack of restraint and regulation in this still untamed frontier, where swaggering sellers are free to come and go like shady traveling salespersons hawking shoddy wares to unwitting victims.

Government agencies are not striving very hard to bring order to the chaos that confronts them on the Internet. To date, their efforts have achieved only limited success. Like marshals policing the wide-open spaces in the Wild West, when they do try, they find themselves trying to track down Computer Age villains in a landscape that is vast and largely lawless. To make matters worse, some of the sophisticated Internet companies that facilitate online sales have chosen, or are forced by legal restrictions, to remain above the fray, and not only refuse to be "deputized" as crime fighters but occasionally seem to coddle and protect the guys in black hats.

Online Auction Abuses

Wherever technology leads, fast-buck artists are sure to follow. With the coming of computerized coin auctions, we have seen a proliferation of abuses carefully tailored to capitalize on the weaknesses of the system. Those weaknesses stem in no small measure from the fact that many online auction companies, including the industry's volume leader, eBay, have taken a laissez-faire approach to the business being transacted under their apparent aegis. These companies have maintained that they are merely go-betweens, providing the venue where online auctions occur but playing no role in the actual sales—and they assume little or no responsibility for anything untoward that may occur.

"The problem with eBay is one of numbers," said Michael W. Sherman, senior vice president of Collectors Universe, holding company for the Professional Coin Grading Service and other leading collectibles certification firms. "eBay has roughly 100,000 U.S. coin lots up at any time," Sherman observed. "If 20,000 or so close daily, and only 1% are bad, then there are 200 fraudulent auctions *every day*."

Sherman insists that there are many more thousands of auctions that are legitimate. "Is it fair to sound a loud warning bell about abuses that apply to fewer than 5 percent of the sales?" he asked rhetorically.

A number of abuses can and do occur. For starters, certain sellers sometimes select inferior material to offer in online sales, treating these impersonal, long-distance auctions as dumping grounds for the dregs in their store stock or the merchandise they sell at coin-show bourses. This way, they don't have to face their prospective customers up close and personal. Sometimes they assign high reserves to these coins—that is to say, prices below which the coins will not be sold. In doing so, they place themselves in a no-lose situation: If some unlucky bidder is ignorant and/or foolish enough to offer the high amount (or pay even more), the seller has made a healthy profit on a less-than-healthy coin. If the reserve isn't met, they just hold on to the coin and keep inserting it into future sales until it eventually sells.

Knowledgeable buyers possess the ability to grade coins with reasonable accuracy. If they lack this, or as a second layer of protection, they rely on the judgments of major third-party certification services. However, these are not the buyers targeted by disreputable online auctioneers. Rather, these buyers are aiming at novice collectors or people who don't collect coins at all but might be enticed to do so by slick presentations and the false sense of security imparted by the fact that a sale is taking place under the umbrella of a well-known online firm. To give themselves wiggle room to avoid potential charges of price gouging, the dealers almost always limit their online offerings to "raw" or uncertified coins—coins that have not been examined, graded, and encapsulated in hard plastic holders by one of the major services. This gives them leeway to assign whatever grade suits their purposes, and deprives their customers of a valuable safeguard.

As this is written, in mid 2005, online auctions of coins and related collectibles are taking place constantly on the Internet, attracting not only established collectors but also rank novices. Both are being lured partly by coins' traditional enticements—rarity, beauty, history, romance, and value—and partly by the convenience and immediacy of the cutting-edge technology. If anything, the profusion of such auctions is even greater today than it was in 2000, when the subject was first addressed in this book. Now, as then, this seems at first glance like a positive development, as it gives active buyers another way to acquire these tiny treasures, presumably at competitive and advantageous prices. On closer inspection, however, venomous human spiders can be seen spinning schemes on the World Wide Web, waiting to ensnare unwary victims. And while strides have been made in policing their activity, fraud still remains a concern for online buyers of coins.

To its credit, eBay finally took action in 2004 to provide recourse for those victimized in its coin auctions. In response to many complaints of such abuses, including strong criticism in my books, it joined forces with the American Numismatic Association (ANA) to establish a "Coins Community Watch Program" which offers a mechanism for filing complaints and receiving satisfaction. Still, this program is far from a total remedy and many problems persist in eBay auctions. Progress has been made, but much remains to be done.

The eBay Phenomenon

Without question, eBay is an amazing American success story. In recent years, it has facilitated the sale of an enormous number of collectibles as well as other merchandise via the Internet. It has helped to expand the field of numismatics and can be credited with bringing in thousands of new participants. Too often, however, the company has turned a blind eye and a deaf ear to serious problems involving sales of coins. Abuses in eBay auctions may or may not be worse than those in other Internet auctions, but it's clear that dubious practices do occur there, and their numbers are magnified by the sheer size and scope of the company. It's also apparent that, in the past, eBay did not respond aggressively to numerous complaints by buyers who believed they were victimized in sales.

On the contrary, eBay officials have sought consistently to disassociate their company from both the abuses and the abusers, and disavowed responsibility for both. They have likened the role of eBay to that of a hotel that rents an auction room to the actual sellers, and which thus bears no legal responsibility for the sale itself, but only for the condition of the premises. However, this is not the impression many—probably most-online bidders have when they participate in these sales. They assume, understandably, that eBay screens sellers before permitting them to use its auction "premises." More importantly, they assume that eBay will investigate apparent abuses and take action against abusers when complaints are substantiated. The reality has been decidedly very different through the years, and the jury is still out on whether the new "Coins Community Watch Program" will bring meaningful reform or just cosmetic change.

"If eBay becomes too aggressive and goes over the line in an implied warranty of safety, then it opens itself up to countless lawsuits from disgruntled buyers who can allege that it should have protected them," Sherman pointed out. "eBay either becomes the auctioneer, with all the obligations implicit in that title, or continues to simply be the parking lot where the flea market is held; I can sympathize with its position."

One of the attractions of buying coins on eBay is the simplicity of the bidding process. A consumer can browse eBay's vast database and use its search engine without even registering. One way of starting the bidding process is for a prospective buyer to first go to *www.ebay.com* and register as an eBay member. There is no charge. After the item of interest is located, the potential bidder can scroll down to the bottom of the page, enter the amount of the bid and click the review button. At this point, he or she can review the bid, enter a user ID and password, click the "place bid" button, and the bidding is complete. Simple enough, right? Yes, but behind this uncomplicated facade lurks a plethora of potholes, pitfalls, and perils. Though eBay has had no problem lending its name and prestige to the entry process, even signing up potential bidders as members of eBay, not as clients of the dealers leasing its site, it was nowhere to be found when those members tried to extricate themselves and leave with their pockets unpicked. In short, the front door has had "eBay" emblazoned upon it in large, bold letters, but the exit was unmarked and the message seemed to be: "Just go away and leave us alone."

Because of my reputation as a consumer advocate, hundreds of people have written to me with grievances about their experiences in eBay coin auctions. Many have complained about overgrading and other misrepresentation. Some said the coins they got were scratched, discolored, or otherwise defective. I've even had complaints from buyers who got nothing: Disreputable dealers simply took their money. Disturbingly, these grievances have had a common thread: Time and again, the victims sought help from eBay and got little satisfaction.

A Program to Watch

The Coins Community Watch Program offers hope that someone at eBay—and at the American Numismatic Association—will now take time to listen to such complaints. In principle, at least, it shows a sense of awareness—and, one hopes, of concern—on the part of eBay officials that there is a valid basis for these complaints and a need to address them.

Under the program, those who sell coins in eBay auctions are "encouraged" to abide by a number of conditions in a Code of Conduct. These conditions have been subject to fine-tuning and change, so you are advised not to rely on my condensed summary here. At the writing of the *Fifth Edition* some of these conditions include:

- not to knowingly sell, exhibit, trade, produce, or advertise a copy or reproduction of any numismatic item if its nature is not clearly indicated by the word "copy" or "reproduction," incused in the metal or printed on the paper thereof
- to represent a numismatic item to be genuine only when it is authentic to the best of their knowledge and belief
- not to knowingly handle or resell forgeries, unmarked copies, altered coins, or other spurious numismatic merchandise that is not clearly labeled as such
- not to knowingly participate in any way in the advertisement, sale or trade of any numismatic material using any deceptive practices including, but not limited to, false or misleading claims of sales scarcity, value, condition or investment potential
- to sell numismatic items that they own free and clear of any challenge or those that they are authorized by the owner to sell
- not to knowingly sell or buy counterfeit numismatic material
- to promptly refund the purchase price for any item that has been deemed by the ANA as other than as offered or described by the seller

Not following some of these conditions are violations of the law. The Hobby Protection Act, for example, prohibits the sale of unauthorized and unmarked reproductions.

Failure to abide by these guidelines, eBay said, "could result in disciplinary action by eBay and possible suspension or loss of selling privileges. In addition, such failure may be grounds for further disciplinary action by the ANA against its members." In describing possible actions it might take against those who violate the Code of Conduct or other rules and regulations, eBay had this to say: "eBay reserves the right, in its sole discretion, to remove any coin or paper money related item listed on its site and refund the associated listing fee, if we believe that the listing is inconsistent with the code of conduct set out by the American Numismatic Association, or inconsistent with eBay's goals of promoting the hobby and maintaining a safe trading environment. eBay reserves the right to warn, put on probation, or suspend from all eBay buying and selling activity those sellers whose coins or paper money listings have been identified as problematic. In addition, eBay cooperates fully with all law enforcement investigations into distribution of counterfeit or fraudulently mislabeled coins or paper money and will refer to law enforcement evidence of any intentional effort at distribution of counterfeit or fraudulently mislabeled coin or paper money."

My understanding of how this works behind the scenes is that a half-dozen or so volunteers check offerings and report suspicious activity to each other. If there is agreement on a suspicious listing, that listing is forwarded to the ANA, which contacts the seller. If the seller is uncooperative, or if bad listings persist, then eBay removes the lot and may remove the seller. As this book goes to press, it is my understanding that this program is focusing on counterfeits only.

This sounds highly positive, and time may demonstrate that eBay is indeed serious about cracking down on those who perpetrate fraud and other abuses through its online auctions. However, eBay officials will have to show me—through strong and meaningful actions—that it really means business about cleaning up these kinds of acts.

Nor am I the only doubting Thomas. Five months after the introduction of the Coins Community Watch Program, Ed Reiter, former Numismatics columnist for *The New York Times* and author of the award-winning book *The New York Times Guide to Coin Collecting* (St. Martin's Press, 2002), expressed skepticism about just how sincere eBay truly was. "From what I see and hear," Reiter said, "eBay is more concerned about image than improvement. To paraphrase Shakespeare, this new program seems like a lot of sound and fury signifying not much of anything. People who have reported problems and sought redress tell me they haven't gotten much satisfaction. A 'community watch' is pointless unless you go beyond just watching. Our eyes tell us there are abuses; now it's time for eBay to put some real teeth into strong corrective measures."

R.W. Julian, a renowned numismatic scholar and researcher, has filed a number of complaints about misrepresented—even apparently counterfeit—coins he saw being offered in eBay auctions. He, too, has doubts about the Community Watch program. "While this was conceived with good intentions on ANA's part," Julian told me, "the practical application has apparently resulted in no appreciable change in the nature of the marketplace. I hope and expect that the ANA will refine and improve this program to better protect the consumer." Concerning the apparent counterfeits he has seen in eBay auctions, Julian had this to say: "In those areas for which I have considerable knowledge, there appears to have been little or nothing done to protect consumers. From my personal experience, this lack of consumer protection has not changed since eBay's inception."

An Exchange of Correspondence with eBay

As an entrepreneur, I admire the spectacular success eBay has enjoyed. As a consumer advocate, though, I deplore its track record of apparent indifference in the face of repeated abuses. I am hopeful that its new joint initiative with the ANA will accomplish its stated objective "to help improve overall trading safety within the Coins category on eBay." My hopefulness is tempered, however, by the lingering memory of a disconcerting exchange of correspondence I had in 2000 with the company. At the time, I was preparing the second edition of *How to Make Money in Coins Right Now*, and I wanted to give eBay an opportunity to answer objections from critics and present its side of the story. The responses I received were curt, evasive, and even hostile. Far from discrediting the critics, these wary, legalistic responses served to validate their complaints.

In a letter to Robert Chesnut, associate general counsel of eBay, I posed a series of ten questions relating to the company's positions, policies, and activities. I asked, for example, whether eBay dealers are licensed auctioneers and what liability eBay has in the sale of counterfeit or stolen coins. The response I received came not from lawyer Robert Chesnut but from a public relations man—Kevin Pursglove, eBay's senior director of communications. And he made it clear that no answers would be forthcoming for my questions. "While Rob [Chesnut] and several other members of our legal team do occasional media interviews about specific eBay trust and safety programs, it has been our practice to decline interview requests about broader legal theories and positions," Pursglove said. "We have refused these requests due to obvious attorney-client privilege issues that could be raised by such interviews."

Seizing on the suggestion that eBay lawyers might be willing to answer questions about "specific" issues, as opposed to broader legal matters, I then distilled a single specific question:

My firm, Scott Travers Rare Coin Galleries, Inc., a New York corporation, never sold coins over eBay, but might do so soon. My firm does business from New York, NY. Do I or a representative of my firm need to have an auctioneer's license with the New York City Department of Consumer Affairs in order to sell coins over eBay?

Pursglove's reply was succinct: "With regard to your question, as with any other business venture you may consider you should consult with a New York attorney to ensure that your actions comply with the law."

To this, I replied: "I gather from your response that you believe my actions would be those of an auctioneer rather than a consignor since only an auctioneer and not a consignor must 'comply with the law.' Unless I hear from you to the contrary, I will so presume and inform my readers accordingly."

This seemed to rile Pursglove. "You may not make such a presumption," he fired back. "The reference to 'the law' below means generically all laws. eBay does not give legal advice to individual users on their particular business situations."

"Thank you for your clarification," I quickly wrote back. "I now assume from the information you have provided that persons should not consign to eBay unless and until they have consulted a lawyer. If I don't hear from you to the contrary, I will assume that this is what you mean and inform my readers of your advice."

By this time, Pursglove seemed to be growing weary from all the evasive action he was taking. This was his final response:

> Your last assumption is also incorrect. We regret that we were unable to accommodate your request for an interview on eBay legal issues. We understand and respect your deadline and desire to obtain accurate information, but we are simply not able to assist you further. We are concerned that your unconfirmed assumptions about eBay's position on these issues could lead to inaccuracies. To avoid any possible misunderstandings, please assume nothing about our position, and do not communicate any official or unofficial eBay advice or position to your readers.
>
> We will not comment further on your questions or assumptions. You may not, however, assume from our silence that we agree or disagree with your positions—only that we have no additional comment. Have a nice day!

A Coin Bidder's Guide to eBay

Barry Stuppler is a coin dealer who, as of this writing, is head of the consumer protection committee of the Professional Numismatists Guild (PNG). He previously held a similar post with the American Numismatic Association, and currently serves as a member of the ANA Board of Governors. Stuppler has drawn up a list of basic steps bidders should take "to ensure a positive and rewarding eBay coin buying experience." Here is an abbreviated version of some of them that are not covered elsewhere in this book:

- **Check the seller's feedback**

  The very first thing to do before bidding or buying is to take advantage of a remarkable evaluation tool provided by eBay—feedback. Winning bidders or outright buyers can leave positive, negative, and neutral comments about their transactions. eBay posts these comments and compiles a "feedback rating" based on them. See it by clicking the "View seller's feedback" link. A positive posting adds one point to a seller's feedback rating; a negative comment subtracts a point; a neutral statement doesn't affect the rating. eBay publishes the net number of feedbacks plus the number from unique users. To avoid being deceived by a high feedback rating created mainly by the seller's friends and relatives, be sure that a significant percentage of the positive feedbacks are from unique users. A seller who is honest, fair, and competent should have a low percentage of negative ratings. A box on the feedback page shows the number of positive, negative, and neutral ratings for the past six months. Negative ratings of more than 2% are a red flag.

- **Analyze the feedback information**

  Analyze the recent comments carefully. Remember that most eBay-ers are reluctant to post negative comments because they are afraid of retaliation. Slow delivery (which might even be attributable to the method of shipping) is less significant than bad communication, bad service, and/or bad product. Complaints from several unique users that the coins received were inferior to the coins described on eBay suggest that the seller is a predator you should avoid. Check for the "B" or "S" on the right side of feedback comments. "B" means the person receiving feedback was the buyer; "S" means he or she was the seller. Even if the feedback rating is over 100, beware if most of feedbacks show a "B." A trader can make a series of $5 and $10 purchases to build up a positive rating, then use the positive rating to scam people into buying overpriced or never-delivered big-ticket items.

- **Visit the seller's "ME" page**

  Every eBay seller can create a "ME" page. When sellers have done so, a "ME" icon appears in each of their listings, to the right of the user ID and rating. Click on it and check out the seller's self-description. See if there is a name and/or company name (not just the eBay user ID), snail mail address, and phone number (which you might want to try calling). See if there are banking and professional references.

- **Know your seller's location**

  The location of the seller is listed on each offer. eBay attracts sellers from all over the world. Many fraudulent sellers are from third-world countries. [Fraudulent sellers] can steal a photo from a legitimate offering, display it with a low reserve to attract buyers, often insist on payment by cashier's check, money order, or wire, and never deliver the product. I recommend purchasing only from sellers located in the U.S., which also avoids problems with Customs and long waits for delivery.

- **Check shipping terms, costs, and payment options**

  Scroll down below the product description to the terms of sale and read the details regarding shipping. You want to know the cost, speed, and security of the shipping process. Methods of shipping vary from seller to seller. They include parcel post, registered mail, Express Mail, and FedEx, each with or without insurance. When expensive items are involved, you want to be sure that they will be sent as quickly as possible by registered mail insured or FedEx.

- **Read the return and refund policies**

  While you are in the terms section, read the policy on returning an item. All legitimate dealers have a return policy. If you are dissatisfied with a coin, you should be able to get your money back.

- **Pay safe**

  Paying by credit card is an excellent defensive move. If you call VISA or MasterCard, for example, within 60 days of a charge on your monthly statement and say you never received the item, they will credit you for the purchase while they investigate. Unless the seller can prove you did receive the item, you will not be responsible for payment. Sellers who accept payment by credit card know that buyers are protected and are more likely to regularly deliver what they advertise, whether you pay by credit card or not. One more thing while we're on the subject of credit cards: Never, never e-mail your credit-card number—e-mail is not secure. Instead, call the seller with your number. Many eBay sellers don't accept direct payment by credit card, but do accept payment through PayPal. PayPal offers some protection for consumers, but at a lower level than most credit cards, through a more complex procedure. PayPal's Buyer Complaint Policy includes some additional protection for eBay buyers (eBay owns PayPal). Of course, you could dispute a PayPal charge through your credit-card company, but PayPal's Buyer Complaint Policy includes potential penalties for doing so. If you pay by check and want fast delivery, particularly if the seller is in a different state from you, send a money order or cashier's check. That way, the seller should be able to ship within 2-3 days, rather than waiting a week or more to be sure your personal check has cleared. To save on their PayPal or credit-card fees, many sellers offer a discount for payment by check or money order.

- **Print out the photos**

  There should be a photograph of the obverse (front) and reverse (back) of the coin (if not, e-mail the seller as suggested above). If you're the successful bidder or you use the "Buy It Now" option, print out the photo or save it to a file on your computer, then carefully compare the overall look and the details to the actual coin when it arrives. If the coin you are bidding on or buying is certified by a third-party grading service, you should see or ask the seller for a photo showing the entire capsule. The capsule should show a certification number, so that you can compare the numbers to make sure the coin you get is the coin you bought.

The Dos and Don'ts of Online Auctions

In the course of investigating complaints about online coin auctions, I have formulated my own list of tips and caveats for would-be buyers. Here are a few key do's and don'ts:

- **Do deal with reputable dealers.** As in conventional mail-order transactions, stick with dealers that have reputations to protect. Make a habit of dealing online with dealers who are members of the Professional Numismatists Guild (PNG). Check out the reputations of online auctioneers, using eBay's customer feedback section. Dealers with many "negative" comments should be avoided. And if you purchase a coin that is misrepresented or deal with an eBay dealer that is disreputable, post your opinion on eBay's feedback bulletin board and file a complaint with the Coins Community Watch Program.
- **Don't expect bargains.** Some coins sold online are offered by dealers who have resubmitted the coins multiple times to grading services. These coins are often protected by reserves that are set at or above the coins' fair market retail value. Be especially careful with coins of extreme value being offered online, as well as coins where the spread between the coin offered and the next lower grade is enormous.
- **Do assume the coin is not premium-quality.** Since you can't examine a coin from the Internet in person, some coins offered on the Net are low-end. A coin that seems like a bargain on the Internet may represent a trap because it displays poor eye appeal.
- **Don't let your emotions carry you away.** Online auctioneers count on consumers' buying coins off the Internet as impulse items and for recreational purposes. The whole on-

line auction craze is a feeding frenzy in which consumers bid each other up because of that rush of adrenaline during the bid-posting process. Use reputable price guides when you are away from the bid-posting screen, and don't exceed your reasonable estimates of fair market value.

- **Do read the fine print before bidding.** Not all online auctioneers have the same terms of sale. One online auctioneer/dealer boasted to me that he had a 15% buyer's fee hidden in his terms of sale, and that this apparently caused some bargain-hunting bidders to buy bullion coins from him at about 10% over bullion value. The bargain hunters bid 5% below the bullion value and received an invoice for that "successful" bid—plus an additional 15%.
- **Don't trust scanned images of coins.** Digitized scanners vary in quality, and even unedited scans may not be accurate depictions of a coin. Some scanners can accentuate the cameo contrast of a proof coin and hide the hairlines. Other scanners can hide otherwise obvious scratches. Image-editing software available everywhere makes it possible to sharpen, soften, and modify the color of a coin's digitized image, as well as make a host of other alterations in the image.
- **Do promptly return all overgraded material.** Don't be lazy about going to the Post Office and sending back any unacceptable coin. Do it now before you forget. When it comes to protecting your rights in mail-order/Internet transactions, time is of the essence.
- **Don't assume that all cashier's checks are genuine.** Lots of fake and stolen cashier's checks are used to pay for Internet transactions—especially from buyers in the Far East. So if you are selling a coin, be suspicious of a cashier's check coming from a buyer you have never heard of in countries such as Singapore, China, and Indonesia. In fact, be suspicious of *any* cashier's check coming from a stranger. The FDIC, through its website, *www.fdic.gov*, provides updated information on counterfeit financial instruments, including cashier's checks. You need to enter the word "counterfeit" into the search engine. The alerts can also be found in chart form at: *www.bankersonline.com/security/alertchart.html*

  Shortly after I wrote these caveats, the Federal Trade Commission (FTC) and Better Business Bureau Serving Metropolitan New York both issued advisories relating to the risks of online auctions. These organizations offered some of the same precautions that appear here.

A couple of good additional tips gleaned from these advisories are: Use a credit card when purchasing online (you have more leverage in case of non-delivery since you can reverse the credit company charge); and beware of dealers placing bogus bids on their own merchandise and "bidding" against you to get you to pay more.

Legal Aspects of Online Auctions

David L. Ganz has monitored closely the advent and growth of online coin auctions, both in his capacity as one of the nation's most prominent coin lawyers and as a major hobby leader who is a past president of the American Numismatic Association. He has prepared the following analysis of the Internet auction phenomenon especially for *The Coin Collector's Survival Manual*.

> Collectors, investors, and bidders have all been handed claims that online sales provide equality, a unified marketplace, and a "true auction" of a collectible, with each lot going to the highest bidder. What they get is something very different, with "hidden" reserves many times preventing the marketplace from setting a price, bids from the owners that cloud interest in items and boost their selling prices, and items whose descriptions are too good to be true (and whose digital images have been edited or doctored to assist in the process).
>
> To be sure, there are many legitimate auctions, descriptions, and even bidding processes, but it cannot be argued that there is no problem, for the existence of a problem is as plain as the print advertisement in a hobby periodical that offers an 1804 silver dollar for $25,000 (when that coin is worth many multiples of that sum).
>
> Auctions are not regulated by the federal government, but rather by some states and many municipalities. Rules are not uniform; they vary from state to state on both procedural and substantive bases.
>
> Are electronic auctions governed by state law? And if they are, which state law? To take it a step further, if they are governed, why haven't various electronic auctioneers given more heed to the problem?
>
> I can't, of course, answer for every auctioneer, but there is no doubt that commerce has run into local law enforcement with some regularity, and that e-auctions can be problematic in some instances.
>
> I recently took the opportunity to do an online legal database search as to the licensing requirements for an electronic auction sale, the typical e-commerce transaction for which an auction might be conducted. As was true when the prior edition of this book was published, there are currently no reported cases. That does not mean that it is not an issue; to the contrary, it means just what it says: There are no cases that have been reported to date. No case has yet been brought by a regulatory authority seeking to enforce licensing requirements in an e-commerce business, though I think that a case could easily be made as to why it should be required.
>
> The defense, that such licensing regulation would seriously impede interstate commerce, and the growth of such commerce, may be a fair one. But ultimately, the consumer needs to be protected, and cry as vendors and e-commerce participants might, it seems very likely to me that in future years, there will be such regulation, either on a piecemeal basis, or when a state attorney general decides that a particular plan or course of action is unconscionable or unreasonable.
>
> A consumer of the future may very well ask whether false claims of sale (with the intention of eventual resale) on a Web site constitute an unfair or deceptive

practice in trade or commerce. The same consumer may ask if secret reserves are legal.

I suggest that the courts of the future will litigate these and other issues, but some of the answers appear obvious. And when they finally are decided, the "Wild, Wild West" aspect of the Internet's e-commerce sales era will come to an end.

Armen R. Vartian is an attorney who serves as legal counsel to the Professional Numismatists Guild. He represents some of the leading providers of collectible goods and services on the Internet. Vartian writes:

Collectibles transactions on the Internet have increased at a tremendous rate. Most major coin dealers have the bulk of their retail offerings available online, and the traditional numismatic auction houses are encouraging Internet bidding at their sales. Huge amounts of business are done on smaller sites, by e-mail, and in non-numismatic auction venues. eBay, not a numismatic specialist by any means, is now one of the largest sellers of rare coins anywhere, with tens of thousands of coin and currency items being auctioned at any given time.

Is this a good thing for collectors from a consumer protection standpoint? The Internet should not be seen as a revolution for collectors, but rather as an easier way for them to do business with reputable people with whom they are already familiar.

Just as with mail order, in Internet transactions there is always the risk that retail buyers will send money to someone who does not then deliver the items purchased. However, the Internet allows such fraud in ways that weren't economic, or even possible, in the context of mail order. Buyers' relatively easy use of credit card numbers in Internet transactions gives fraudulent sellers better access to those numbers than ever before. It also enables dishonest sellers to cheat buyers out of $50 here and $100 there, amounts which aren't enough to keep the mail order crook in business, but which serve the new online thieves just fine given the relatively low costs of operating on the Internet. Such amounts are difficult or impractical to recover through the courts or through government agencies, most of which are far more interested in major scams focused in one area than in small crimes committed on a large scale nationwide. Even identifying the criminals can be difficult on the Internet because of the generally casual attitude toward identification.

Another risk which has been magnified by the Internet is the risk of buying overgraded or misdescribed merchandise. Looking at some non-numismatic sites such as eBay, I am amazed at the volume of uncertified coins, modern and bullion coins, and private commemorative coins which are up for auction. For the most part, these are items which traditional numismatic auction houses would advise consignors to wholesale, because the profit to be made doesn't justify the transaction costs (i.e. commissions) of selling at auction. If the sellers of these items are making much money, they must be selling at considerably above the coins' market value, which doesn't sound like a good deal for the buyers. In addition, with no central numismatic authority reviewing lot descriptions, nothing stops a crafty seller from misdescribing what he or she is selling. Yes, the buyer must beware, but the Internet brings such sellers to unwary buyers a lot more easily than was possible before.

What about the "feedback" systems and "safe harbor" protections on sites such as eBay? I'm not convinced that these address the fundamental problems satisfactorily. In 2000, a class action lawsuit, *Gentry et al.* v. *eBay, Inc.*, was filed against eBay in San Diego Superior Court by a group of collectors who purchased fake autographed sports items on eBay. The plaintiffs alleged that eBay's "safety" programs contributed to enormous damage to autographed sports memorabilia consumers because eBay allowed feedback from anyone, regardless of whether or not the person had ever conducted a successful transaction with the person whom he or she was rating. The plaintiffs alleged further that the dealers who sold them fake merchandise all had eBay "stars" and "power seller" ratings, with "Most, if not all, of these Positive Feedback ratings . . . self-generated or provided by other co-conspiring dealers." The lawsuit alleged that eBay received "an alarming number of consumer complaints" about the defendants, and "a number of warnings from government agencies that a substantial amount of forged sports memorabilia was being auctioned on eBay." Despite these complaints and warnings, the plaintiffs alleged, eBay did nothing, allowing the practices to continue "for the sole purpose of reaping millions of dollars in profits for itself." While eBay has taken some steps to prevent sellers from boosting their own feedback ratings, this was of no use to the plaintiffs in the Gentry case, where eBay successfully prevailed on the grounds that it had no legal responsibility for what others—even fraudulent dealers eBay had already received complaints about—said on eBay. The court accepted eBay's argument that eBay's advertisements that a positive feedback rating was "worth its weight in gold" were simply statements of opinion, and eBay could not be held to them.

As for the "safe harbor" concept, it looks a lot better on paper than in practice. Traditional numismatic auction houses guarantee delivery, and back those guarantees with their own money. The non-numismatic Internet venues, if they have any safe harbor at all, buy insurance policies. Claims are subject to deductibles, as well as to the length of time it takes the insurer to pay up, and other restrictions on coverage. It can take months to recover on a safe harbor claim, and chat rooms are full of complaints from disgruntled buyers who say that they filed claims and never received anything. I'm not aware of any formal statements by eBay responding to any of these allegations; in my personal opinion, eBay tends to be reticent about making such statements. But this picture seems plausible and, if true, isn't a pretty one.

The Risks of Buying Coins by Mail

It sounds so easy, so simple, so attractive. You get a coin offering in the mail. You read about a coin that sounds like the perfect addition to your collection. So you send off a check, expecting to get exactly what's advertised. If you order from a reputable dealer, you'll probably get what you pay for, since reputable dealers have integrity and strive to maintain the respect of their customers. But if you unwittingly order from a fly-by-night dealer, you could get ripped off.

The coin market is easy to enter and easy to exit. There are still few federal, state, or local laws regulating who may or may not be a coin dealer. You could get an offering in the mail from some dealer who started doing business yesterday, has no intention of really sending out the coin or coins you order, but who calls himself or herself "one of the most expert and honest dealers in the universe." However, the dealer could leave the coin business just as rapidly as he or she entered it—leaving you high and dry.

How to Identify a Disreputable Dealer

Spotting a disreputable dealer isn't easy, for there are many honest and ethical ones. However, there are a few things you should know before ordering from a dealer. Even if the answers to your questions turn out to be unfavorable, this doesn't necessarily mean that the dealer is a crook. It may mean, however, that you should inquire some more.

Membership in professional organizations in and of itself is no guarantee that a dealer is respected and honest. Nonetheless, you should make sure that your dealer belongs to the American Numismatic Association (ANA), which expels members who violate its code of ethics. Membership in this organization is not a guarantee that a dealer is honest, but non-membership might be reason enough or you to investigate further. If your dealer has been expelled from an organization (such as ANA), this may be reason to ask more questions. Keep in mind, however, that all it takes to become a member of many numismatic organizations is payment of nominal yearly dues. So don't be unduly impressed by a dealer with a long list of memberships.

Advertising in respected numismatic publications such as *Coin World*, *Numismatic News*, *COINage*, and *Coins* magazine also is not an absolute guarantee of a dealer's integrity. But these types of publications monitor the activities of their advertisers. If a fly-by-night or disreputable dealer is identified by one of the publication's consumer protection spotters, out that dealer goes. Make sure to read each publication's advertising policy before ordering. That way you'll know, for example, how long a dealer's return privilege is, even if it isn't stated in the advertisement.

Adherence to a standardized grading system is one of the most important dealer policies to check out. Some years ago, as I mentioned in the grading chapter, the absence of a "single, official standard for grading coins" caused a federal administrative law judge in Washington, D.C., to rule in favor of a San Antonio, Texas, dealer accused of selling "whizzed" and overgraded coins. According to the January 4, 1978, edition of *Coin World*:

> Judge Quentin E. Grant found the respondents, the Security National Rare Coin Corp. and Riverside Coin Co., innocent (not guilty) of allegations made by the United States Postal Service, after determining that the complainant had "failed to sustain the burden of proving the falsity of the representations alleged." . . . Among the judge's conclusions was one that "there are various, similar guides

> for the grading of United States coins, some of them widely accepted, but there is no single, official standard for grading accepted by, and binding on, all dealers and collectors. . . ." The respondent, Judge Grant found, used "its own unique system of grading, and so stated in its Riverside Coin Co. catalog"; the complainant, furthermore, "has not proved that respondent was bound, legally or morally, to use any other system." . . . The judge's opinion on "whizzing" or polishing coins was that it "is considered by some collectors to degrade a coin. For others, it enhances the desirability of a coin," he found, adding: "There is nothing illegal about 'whizzing' or polishing. There is no unanimity of opinion as to the effect of such procedures on the grading of coins, although increasing experience in collecting may tend to cause a collector to shun 'whizzed' or polished coins. . . . Therefore, I find no misrepresentation involved in respondent's practice of 'whizzing' or polishing coins."

Legally, a dealer may not be bound to conform to specific grading parameters if he or she does not state that he or she uses a specific system to grade coins, such as *Official ANA Grading Standards for United States Coins* (which was introduced shortly after the court case just mentioned in order to provide a basis for the "elimination of variations in grading on a national basis"). Although many numismatic publications may require their advertisers to conform to a specific set of grading standards, if a dealer specifically states that his coins are graded by his own system of grading, you're on your own.

There are some legal cases involving disputes concerning coin grading that establish grading to be more of a precise science than a Wild West shootout. In *U.S.* v. *Kail*, 804 F2d 441 (8th Cir. 1986), a coin dealer went to jail when it was found that coins he sold were consistently overgraded.

And in *FTC* v. *Security Rare Coin & Bullion Corp.*, 1989 US Dist. Lexis 15958, 1989 Westlaw 134002 (DCt Minn. 1989), aff'd 931 F2d 1312 (8th Cir. 1991), the Court took testimony from several expert dealers who graded many identical coins, but assigned them widely disparate grades. Expert opinions were that prices were more than double the fair market value, and a criminal conviction was sustained.

Just because a dealer refuses to use the ANA, NGC, or PCGS grading standards, that doesn't mean that he or she is dishonest. If you're buying circulated coins, for example, conformity to *Photograde* should be acceptable. Still, beware of dealers who say "all coins graded by our own unique grading system."

Bargains that seem too good to be true often are. If you see an offering from a dealer for coins at considerably below market value, no matter how respected the publication he or she is advertising in, the coins are probably below the advertised grade or else the price is probably a mistake.

A convicted felon testifying before the Senate Subcommittee on Civil Service, Post Office and General Services pointed out that greed made his coin schemes work. According to the July 7, 1982 *Coin World*, "the scheme spelled out by the convict had to do with offering counterfeit rare coins to unsuspecting buyers by mail auction." The article recapped part of the testimony:

> "I would buy a coin for $100 that looks like a 1799 silver dollar. If it were genuine, it would be worth about $5,000 . . . I played on people's greed. There were any number of people who thought they would send in a low bid 'just in case' to see if they might get a windfall." In the case of the 1799 dollar, the bids received ranged from $3,500 to $4,100, he recalled. The highest offer would be accepted and an invoice would be sent. "Those who received my invoices could not send me their money fast enough. They thought they were getting a real bargain and they wanted to push through their end of the deal before I changed my mind or something. When I received the cashier's check for $4,100, I sent the coin," recounted the convicted con man. The coin looked authentic, so the buyer was apparently satisfied with the "bargain," he indicated. Obviously, at the time, the swindler was happy with the deal, too, since he netted $4,000.

Guarantees offering the impossible often are. It's unlikely that you'll find a mail-order offering of this type in a respected numismatic publication. However, you might receive a direct-mail offering guaranteeing you, perhaps, a yearly performance percentage, such as 25 percent per year. This percentage guarantee is a gray area as far as the law is concerned, but the general consensus among hobby leaders is that the Securities and Exchange Commission (SEC) has deemed percentage guarantees to be against the law.

Deletion of a coin's major imperfection in the description is a good reason for you not to order from a particular dealer again, provided you know that he or she has seen the imperfection. If you receive a coin graded, say, VG-8, with a large, unmentioned obverse scratch, telephone the dealer and tell him or her that you spotted the imperfection. If the dealer tells you to return the coin for a prompt refund and apologizes for not having seen the scratch, you might want to give him or her another chance. If the dealer says that you're too fussy, tells you off, refuses to take back the coin, and insists that the scratch isn't important, you might think twice about buying from that dealer again.

Several years ago, some attention was given to a variation of grading which would lower a circulated coin's grade as a result of an imperfection. This system was not adopted, so don't expect a dealer to downgrade a coin as a result of an imperfection. Circulated coins are graded according to how worn they are, with any imperfections mentioned separately. This system was adopted because a lot of collectors would rather buy a worn "Fine" without imperfections than a "Very Fine" with, say, a large scratch.

Dealers offer coins that they don't have in stock far more commonly than you would think. If the filling of your order seems unreasonably slow, the dealer may be looking to buy what you ordered. This shouldn't concern you. What should concern you is a dealer who offers the same date, denomination, and Mint-mark coin cataloged five different ways and with five different prices, leading you to believe that he or she has five different coins for sale, when in actuality there is only one. If you order, say, a Very Fine Buffalo nickel and return it with more money because you've decided you want the

Extremely Fine example (a higher-grade coin) advertised, but receive the same piece back in a different holder with the higher-grade description, you have a right to return the coin and not do business with that dealer again.

Confession of a Rip-Off Coin Salesman

Reprinted here is an interview that Maurice Rosen of *The Rosen Numismatic Advisory* conducted with a former employee of a coin firm that sold coins over the telephone and sent overpriced merchandise through the mail. I think you'll find it most enlightening. ("Bob" is a pseudonym.) *Copyright © 1981 Numismatic Counseling, Inc.*

ROSEN: Bob, can you tell me something about the firm you worked for?

BOB: It was an unusual place, as all the coins that were shipped were not at all what they were supposed to be. In the beginning, I did not realize this. At first, I was so overjoyed that all my clients were getting a product that continually went up in price. However, I didn't realize that even though according to the *Greysheet* [*The Coin Dealer Newsletter*] the product went up, my clients were not participating at all.

ROSEN: Why are you now exposing the rip-off practices of this firm?

BOB: I left the firm because I realized my clients not only weren't getting the profit appreciation they thought, but, in fact, were losing tremendously, even though the market was going up. And you reach the point where it is impossible to sell to people. I had one client, a Scottish lady, who invested virtually all of her savings through me. If she had tried to liquidate her portfolio, she would lose over 75 percent.

ROSEN: What kind of numismatic experience do the account executives have?

BOB: The owners of the firm hope they have no numismatic experience at all.

ROSEN: Why?

BOB: Because they want someone to give a prepared talk and not know at all what they're saying. Then you have total confidence in what you're saying. But as soon as you learn anything about the numismatic market, you lose your confidence in that firm.

ROSEN: Was it claimed, however, that each of the account executives was an expert who would manage the account?

BOB: Of course. And in all the mailings it said: "Please call our toll-free number and speak to one of our numismatic experts." That may have meant that it would be someone who had been on the phone for two days and just found out what a coin is!

ROSEN: What is the mark-up of that firm on their average investor sale?

BOB: Recently, I sent out one coin for $15,000. We settled for $7,000, and I made 8 percent on the coin. By and large, they would add approximately 70 percent on the *Greysheet* ask price for every coin they sold. This is based on the MS-65 "ask." They bought coins as About Uncirculated (AU) and sold them as MS-65. So their mark-up is in the hundreds of percent! We also had the option of coming "all the way" down to 20 percent over "ask." And if a client was really good, we could go to 10 percent over "ask." But that had to be a super client. Still, they were doubling or tripling up at the very least.

ROSEN: Were coins cleaned to make them appear to be a higher grade?

BOB: I think that it was unusual for us to send out a coin that wasn't cleaned. It was a standard practice to be cleaning coins in a silver dip and baking soda. Then we'd send them out as Choice BU regardless of the condition of the coins.

ROSEN: Have coins ever been sent back to that firm for sale, and if so, how were the people treated when they wanted to "reap their profits"?

BOB: . . . If a customer wanted to sell coins back to us, we would say anything to change his mind. We always wanted to maintain the "cover" that the customer made a wise investment. We'd stress . . . the probability of much higher prices soon, even make false statements of appreciation in their portfolio. This would usually suffice for awhile. If that failed, we'd try to back out by telling them we didn't need their coins at the moment. Finally, we'd make an offer that was more than we paid, but still less than the customer's cost—and it would be paid over 6 to 12 months. Incidentally, those repurchased coins were sent out again at the "usual" multiple mark-up. . . . If they knew enough about our company . . . to see what we were paying for Choice BU or MS-65 coins, and they pushed, then they would get away with it if they threatened us. But situations like this were very rare.

ROSEN: How and from what sources does Firm X buy its coins?

BOB: I would say at least 90 percent of the coins are acquired through ads. . . . They receive on average 20 to 25 packages a day. They review the coins, call the sender, and make offers. If the sender knows he has good coins and wants a legitimate price, then the firm doesn't buy the coins.

ROSEN: The prices that this firm advertises to pay are related to the true market prices as you can see from the *Greysheet.* However, are you saying that they bought them for considerably less?

BOB: Definitely! Occasionally, they got really nice coins in packages. Still, the sender was told that the coins were overgraded and worth much less than the advertised buy prices. I guess the impressiveness of the ads and the smooth-talking of the buyer convinced a lot of people to sell their coins way below what they were really worth.

ROSEN: How did your firm describe the true Choice BU coins that it bought when sent out in investment packages?

BOB: If someone sent them a coin that was truly a Choice BU, every attempt would be made to buy it as a Choice AU or an AU Then it will be sold as an MS-68 or 69 at a phenomenal premium. Understand that they were routinely sending out washed up AUs as Choice BU. Can you imagine how an honest-to-goodness Choice BU would be priced?

ROSEN: How large is this company?

BOB: The average salesman was making about $1,000 a week. They were working on 8 percent commission. That would be about $12,500 a week in sales or over a half-million dollars a year per salesperson. When I left, there were 20 salespeople. They were also very big on trades, buying silver at a terribly reduced price, and trading it in for other coins at an exaggerated price.

ROSEN: How would that work?

BOB: I'm going back to early 1980 when a bag of silver was in the $30,000 range. We would buy it for $26,000 (an additional $4,000 right there because of an unwary customer) then sell him a $26,000 portfolio which in fact really cost $6,000-$10,000

ROSEN: . . . I am assuming that all the other salespeople at that firm realized that their customers were being ripped off by the unfair pricing and grading policies of the firm. Yet how could each of these salespeople, yourself included, have spoken to the people and told them about the advantages of buying rare coins and the alleged integrity of your firm, knowing that the customers were going to be ripped off? How could this have been justified?

BOB: Each of the salespeople there justified it in their own mind by the amount of money they were making. That doesn't make it right. But it happens. Here's a good example: I asked one of the best salespeople there a question about coins after I was there a short time. His answer to me was, "How the heck do I know? I don't want to know anything about coins. If I learn anything about them, I would not be as good a salesman."

ROSEN: Were you ever in contact with other dealers in the coin business to know how they operated and treated their customers?

BOB: I never had much contact with other coin dealers until I started going to local coin shows. And if I made reference to the firm that I worked for, it normally evoked a lot of laughs. Most of the people at the coin shows had a small clientele with whom they worked closely, as opposed to the situation that I had. If I showed them some of the coins that I was sending out, they would be absolutely amazed that anyone bought them.

ROSEN: Would you personally buy rare coins for investment?

BOB: Absolutely, but not from the firm I worked for!

Mail-Order Coin Guarantees

A number of dealers offer a variety of guarantees. Some are valuable, others worthless. But it all comes down to one thing: A guarantee is only as good as the company that issues it.

Don't deal with mail-order dealers whose stated policy is "All sales final." Although such a dealer may be perfectly honest, you need time to verify the value of your purchase; with uncertified coins especially, grading variations are common. Frequently, dealers have a return privilege; five or ten days is reasonable. Members of the Professional Numismatists Guild, a dealer organization, offer a thirty-day return privilege, a more than ample amount of time. Many non-member dealers also have such policies.

Many dealers are very concerned about the possibility of selling you a counterfeit and offer a virtually unlimited return period should a coin they sell you prove to be fake. Many dealers have stories to tell about coins that turned out to be counterfeit which they bought back five and ten years after they were sold. Auction houses, too, are concerned about counterfeits. If there is ever a question about the authenticity of a potential consignment, that material is often turned down. The auction company could sell a coin; give a consignor a check for the amount realized less the reasonable commission; then later have to give the successful bidder a refund if the coin turned out to be fake—when meanwhile, the consignor has the money and doesn't have to give it back.

Some firms offer not only to refund your money, but also to pay you interest on the money you spent should any coins you purchase from them prove to be counterfeit. Clearly, this is a guarantee you should request in writing.

Most grading guarantees are not binding on the dealer. The guarantee of a dealer who promises to buy back your coins at a price commensurate with the market value is a fair guarantee but not an ironclad one. Who determines what "the market" is? Who determines which price guide is used? Similarly, the guarantee of a dealer who promises to buy your coins back at the same grade at which they were purchased is also a fair guarantee but one which isn't ironclad. What if the dealer says, "Yes, these are MS-63s, but we don't need any right now and can only offer you an MS-60 price." Again, it's not the guarantee, but the dealer who offers it. Reputable dealers who offer these guarantees will bend over backward to protect their image and be sure that you are satisfied—even if it means paying the MS-63 price for coins they sold as MS-63s but don't currently need.

A few dealers offer variations of the guarantee, promising you conformity with PCGS grading standards. But even if you receive the coins graded by PCGS, this is no assurance of a good value.

Some firms guarantee that they will auction coins at the same grade at which they sold them to you via mail order. This is most helpful if you go the auction route, for you know how your coins will be cataloged, but an auction catalog grade is not a guarantee that the coin will realize a price commensurate with that grade. However, this guarantee from a top dealer is quite meaningful, for the quality of the cataloging causes bidders to become fiercely competitive and to bid liberally, using the catalog description and grade as a guide. And top dealers have loyal followings.

Professional Numismatists Guild members have the option of offering customers an organizational certificate which pledges to back the dealer's description of the coin. If the coin turns out not to be what the dealer says it is, the dealer is liable to be brought before the board of that organization. The certificate consists of a signed statement and photograph or description. Members of that organization are subject to legally binding arbitration in cases in which disgruntled customers request it.

Your Rights as a Mail-Order Coin Buyer

In a two-page flier, the Federal Trade Commission (FTC) outlines the mail-order merchandise rule as adopted by the Commission in October 1975. The FTC states:

- You must receive the merchandise when the seller says you will.
- If you are promised delivery within a certain time period, the seller must ship the merchandise no later than 30 days after your order is received.
- If you don't receive your merchandise shortly after that 30-day period, you have the right to cancel your order and get a refund.

The Commission states, in part:

> The seller must tell you if the promised delivery date (or the 30-day limit) can't be met and what the new shipping date will be. Then the seller must give you the option to either cancel the order for a full refund or agree to the new shipping date. The seller also must provide a free way to reply, such as a stamped envelope or a postage-paid postcard. If you don't answer, it means you agree to the delay. If you do not agree to the delay, the seller must return your money by the end of the first 30-day delay. If you cancel a prepaid order, the seller must mail you the refund within seven business days. Where there is a credit sale, the seller must adjust your account within one billing cycle. . . . The rule does not apply to . . . COD orders or to credit orders in which your account is not charged before the merchandise is mailed.

How to Complain and Get Results

You can pursue a number of courses of action if you think you've been ripped off by mail. You can write to the dealer or to the publication where the dealer's advertisement appeared, contact a professional organization the dealer is a member of, tell your documented story to a consumer action group, alert the United States Postal Service, complain to a government agency, or—as an absolute last resort—sue.

Write to the dealer by Certified or Registered mail, return receipt requested. Don't get mad in the letter and tell the dealer he or she is a good-for-nothing crook. Instead, be businesslike and professional. State the facts. If it's a coin you're returning within the stated return privilege, enclose the coin and request the refund politely. If it's an order you didn't receive, tell the dealer how long ago you sent your order, and, if possible, send a photocopy of the canceled check. You'd be surprised how many dealers fill their orders immediately and mail them via insured mail (up to $400), only for the package to be lost. Insured mail travels with uninsured mail and can get lost. Registered mail, however, is deemed to be extremely safe with only a small percentage lost. (In fact, the Hope diamond was mailed and insured via Registered mail.) If the package was lost in the mail, ask the dealer to file the proper insurance form with the Post Office in order for your money to be refunded. If the piece, for some reason, was not insured and didn't reach you, the dealer is responsible. If the dealer refuses to cooperate after you've handled the matter as described above, you might need to take one of the following steps:

1. Complain to the publication that carried the advertisement. In this case, too, be concise and factual. Don't make accusations which you can't back up. The most popular publications are:

 Amos Press Inc.
 (*Coin World, Coin Values*)
 P.O. Box 150
 Sidney, Ohio 45365
 Attention: Customer Service Manager

 Krause Publications
 (*Numismatic News, Coins, Coin Prices, World Coin News*)
 700 East State Street
 Iola, Wisconsin 54990
 Attention: Advertising Manager

 Miller Magazines Inc.
 (*COINage* magazine, *Coin Collector's Yearbook*)
 290 Maple Ct., Suite 232
 Ventura, California 93003-3517
 Attention: Advertising Director

 Dealers don't like being complained about to the publications in which they advertise because each legitimate complaint is held against them. At Krause Publications, for example, advertisers vie for that company's Customer Service Award, which is awarded to several advertisers every year, and a dealer receiving three or more legitimate complaints over the course of a year is ineligible for the award. Dealers given the award are allowed to display a logo in their advertisements which indicates that they received the award and the year in which they received it.

 When writing to a publication, send copies of any correspondence you had with the dealer in question. Keep copies of any correspondence you have with the publications. Send the dealer copies of any letters of complaint you send to magazines.

2. Write to numismatic organizations the dealer belongs to, following the advice stated above. Some organizations to contact are:

 American Numismatic Association
 818 N. Cascade Ave.
 Colorado Springs, Colorado 80903-3279
 (Mediation is now available to non-members, as well as members. Certain fees may apply. *www.money.org/mediationform.html*)

Professional Numismatists Guild Inc.
3950 Concordia Lane
Fallbrook CA 92028
Attention: Executive Director

The Professional Numismatists Guild offers legally binding arbitration.

3. Contact consumer action groups, such as your local chapter of the Better Business Bureau, or a television station or newspaper. Such organizations and individuals have no legal authority but can serve as useful intermediaries in disputes and can wield considerable power, especially in the case of the media. Sometimes consumer action groups will contact the appropriate government authorities so that necessary action will be taken. Send copies of pertinent documentation.

4. Complain to the Inspector in Charge of the United States Postal Service office from which your order was supposed to have been sent. The USPS usually investigates only when a pattern of allegedly suspicious dealings seem clear.

5. Contact government organizations. Sometimes, just one letter from such an organization to an errant dealer helps. Again, make absolutely certain that your gripe is warranted and well documented. Make no false statements. A few places to try are your state attorney general, your city's consumer affairs department, or the FTC's Bureau of Consumer Protection. The FTC is also responsible for enforcing the Hobby Protection Act of 1973, which makes the sale of counterfeit coins illegal, as opposed to unethical, and places restrictions on the selling of replicas (requiring the manufacturer to imprint on the replica that it isn't genuine).

6. Sue the dealer. Use this option only as a last resort. Always consult an attorney. Even if you're suing, be open to any reasonable settlement; it might be better than continuing your legal battle.

The following information is not intended to substitute for legal counsel. Allen Kamp, associate professor of law at John Marshall College of Law, Chicago, writing in the Fall-Winter 1981 edition of the no longer published *Review of Numismatics and the Law*, states:

> The sale of coins with numismatic value is governed by the provisions of Article II of the Uniform Commercial Code (UCC) . . . a statute that has been enacted into law in every state except Louisiana. . . . When a buyer receives a coin that has been stated to be of a certain grade and it appears not to meet that standard, he has several rights and remedies under the UCC. Basically, he can either send the goods back to the seller and sue for damages, or keep the goods and sue for damages. Both alternatives assume that he has been unable to achieve satisfaction without suing. [author's emphasis] He has these rights because the seller has breached his contract to the buyer. The Code provides that statements of fact about the goods such as "this is a 1979 car," and "this is of 'mint' quality"

> are express warranties. The goods must conform to these warranties or there is breach of contract. . . . What a certain grade means and whether or not the coins are of that grade are questions of fact that, if disputed, will have to be established in court. . . . Upon receiving the coins, the buyer should inspect them to determine if they conform to the grading warranties. The inspection must be done promptly or the buyer may lose his rights. . . . The Code allows one to accept or reject any commercial unit. . . . Upon rejection, the coins should be kept for the seller to pick up, or sent back if the seller so requests. (Of course, if returned they should be sent, Registered Mail and properly insured, with all receipts retained.) . . . It should be noted that the seller may contend that the coins did meet the grading standards and that, therefore, the rejection is wrongful. . . . Upon rejection, the buyer still can sue the seller for damages. The buyer can "cover," that is buy the coins elsewhere and recover the difference between the cover price and the contract price. He may also sue for the difference between the market price of the coins at the time he learned of the breach and the contract price. This is especially important if the coin in the grade ordered has appreciated significantly. If the buyer were to resell the coins, he could recover his expected lost profits, unless he were able to obtain the coins elsewhere. He may also collect his incidental damages, for such expenses as inspection, certification and storage of the rejected goods, and any commission in connection with his "cover." . . . No one should return coins claiming a breach of grading warranty just because the market has fallen. . . . These legal rights may well depend on retaining a lawyer and filing lawsuits, which are costly and risky propositions.

These basic legal rights as outlined by Kamp may appear straightforward, but they are really far more theoretical than their presentation suggests. Kamp himself admits that there is no precedent for the rights he discusses. The explanation for that might be that there are so many loopholes for the seller that no buyer could press a case. What proof is there that the coins you have in your possession are indeed the coins the dealer sold you? What proof do you have that the coins are in the precise level of preservation they were when sold? What proof do you have that the coins aren't as described if the dealer claims to grade by his or her own "unique system"? It's no wonder that no precedent exists.

Let's say you buy a coin through the mail for a nominal amount of money from a seller thousands of miles away and the coin turns out to have been misrepresented. If the seller refuses to make you whole, you might be able to recover your money without having to pay costly legal fees. Coin lawyer David L. Ganz, writing in an April 4, 1994 *Coin World* column, states:

> You don't try and seek relief from the courts in the seller's jurisdiction. You go to your own small claims court, or a court of low monetary jurisdiction, file a summons and complaint (carefully drawn, as explained here) and attempt to force a confrontation on your home turf, and in your home forum. Results of this tactic vary. . . . Except under narrow circumstances, a court in New Jersey cannot tell a resident of South Dakota that [he or she] must make a refund because the court lacks the power to enforce the decision in another state. But if the South

> Dakota firm marketed a product that caused damage in New Jersey, and entered the stream of interstate commerce, the result is different.
>
> Here's how you can apply this to your Small Claims case at the time that you bring your claim. . . . You will need to state in your complaint (or statement of claim) the following, which may have to be modified to conform to the specific requirements of the laws of your state:

- Seller, a resident of (name of state), did business and actually transacted business in (my state).
- Seller, a resident of (other state), contracted to supply goods at issue in this case to a resident of (my state).
- Seller sold defective goods to me, causing damages in contract, and regularly does business, solicits business or engages in a persistent course of conduct that derives substantial income from interstate commerce, and in particular from the citizens of (my state).
- Seller knows, or should have expected, that his actions in making the sale would have had consequences in (my state).
- Besides breach of contract, seller's actions have inflicted emotional distress upon me (tortious conduct).
- Only those items which apply to your case should be utilized.

Hanging Up on Telemarketers

Diane Piret is director of industry affairs for the Industry Council for Tangible Assets (ICTA). According to Piret, ICTA is "a national trade association that provides education on laws and regulations and also lobbies in Washington, D.C. and state legislatures to protect the interests of the rare coin and precious metals business and hobby." Although her organization allows coin dealers who use telemarketing to be members, ICTA greatly benefits consumers by helping to shape laws that promote the numismatic industry—something positive for every hobbyist and investor. Telemarketers are deservedly an unpopular bunch—few people welcome a telephone call in the middle of dinner to be solicited for overpriced modern coins. However, without ICTA, overzealous lawmakers might have outlawed the use of the phone for a sole proprietor to use when he wants to call and confirm your address to send a $10,000 check for coins he just sold for you. Piret offers this advice to consumers about the FTC's "Do Not Call" list:

> The FTC maintains a "Do Not Call" (DNC) list. This is a list where you can register your phone number so that most telemarketing companies cannot call you unless you have some existing business relationship with them. To register for the DNC list, go to the FTC site *www.donotcall.gov* or call 1-888-382-1222. Your state may have DNC laws that may be stricter than the federal rules. The DNC lists may not cover all companies. If you receive an unwanted call, say to the caller: "Please put me on your Do No Call list." An indication from you that you do not want them to call is sufficient to prevent future calls, although they will usually, correctly, advise you that it may take 30 days or so for this request to be

processed. It is our experience that once you mention the Do Not Call option, the caller will stop the sales pitch immediately. If they don't, remember that you always have the ultimate recourse—simply *hanging up the phone!* Although we don't usually like to be rude, perhaps it will help to realize that by hanging up the phone you are no longer wasting the caller's time, since you will not be making a purchase. You are doing them a favor.

ICTA is supported solely by membership dues and donations that come mostly from coin dealers and numismatic organizations, but individuals can join at a more nominal fee (only $50 per year) as well. For more information about ICTA, go to *www.ictaonline.org* or call 410-626-7005.

Violators of the Do Not Call list have faced fines by the FTC of $11,000 per violation, and many consumers and state attorneys general have filed civil lawsuits. Exemptions exist for charities and telephone calls made to "request a sales meeting," as opposed to an actual attempt to consummate a sale over the phone. A firm that has made a sale to a consumer (the so-called pre-existing business relationship) has a period of a year and a half from the last sale or payment received to contact that consumer by telephone. Any such firm is still required to abide by a consumer's request and refrain from calling if requested to do so.

Some ways to slam the phone on telemarketers include:

- **Place yourself on the FTC's Do Not Call list.** Include all of your telephone numbers, including cellphone numbers and fax lines. Business numbers are not covered. Most telemarketers have 31 days after you register to stop calling you. The registration expires after 5 years.
- **Purchase a "number is disconnected" tone for each telephone and fax line.** A popular brand is TeleZapper®. The TeleZapper is particularly effective in preventing unwanted faxes. This technology can be useful for prevention of future calls when telemarketers use automatic predictive dialing equipment. Predictive dialing refers to several telemarketing calls being made simultaneously, with the unanswered consumer phone lines being stored by the telemarketer for redialing at a later time.
- **Keep a log of all telephone sales calls and any request you made to be placed on any individual firm's Do Not Call List.** Include as much detailed information as you can in the log.
- **Become familiar with the laws of your state, and promptly sue violators, in addition to filing a complaint with the FTC.** The FTC represents consumers collectively, not individually, so your best recourse in many cases is to file a lawsuit. Federal law is summarized here: www.ftc.gov/bcp/rulemaking/tsr/tsrrulemaking/index.htm

– 14 –
CASHING IN AT SHOWS

It was 9:15 A.M. The security guard rubbed his mustache, scratched his forehead, and took his typical stroll around the exhibit area of the national coin convention. "Not much to do," he muttered to himself. There were five aisles of educational exhibits, each display having been painstakingly prepared by numismatists—advanced, intermediate, and junior. The area, along with the adjoining bourse room (the convention area where dealers gather to sell rare coins), was later to be opened to the public. But before the visitors arrived, the guard was looking at the educational displays and absorbing information.

There was one exhibit at which he stopped and stared. It consisted of small, silver coins spread out upon black velvet. The guard was transported to the evening of his first date, when he stood with his girl in the backyard and they both looked at the stars. Like gleaming stars against a dark summer nighttime sky, the silver coins glowed with magic. The simplicity of the exhibit allowed its inherent beauty to hold the attention even of a non-collector.

Meanwhile, in the room next door, dealers were preparing for the influx of people by stapling holders, setting up coins in showcases, getting their checkbooks in order, and counting hundred-dollar bills. Yet it was more like a social club than a room of cutthroat competitors. Dealers confided in one another about problems at home and at work, and they bragged to each other about sales made in the days and weeks past. In fact, if an outsider had entered to buy coins at this point, he or she would have felt like an intruder.

Upstairs, lecturers were preparing for their educational forums, and organization leaders were setting up for the specialty meetings of their groups.

This was the scene of a national coin convention. But whether the convention is international, national, regional, or local, it can provide many of the same activities for you: socializing, learning, buying and selling, auctioning, and exhibiting. The basic types of coin shows include, but are not limited to, local club meetings, local

The scene at a national convention. This show was staged by the congressionally chartered American Numismatic Association.

club shows, regional, state, or seminational conventions, national conventions, and international conventions.

Local Club Meetings

Although local club meetings are the most fundamental type of numismatic gathering, they aren't always open to everyone. Many local clubs take pride in their selectivity, even though they are primarily composed of intermediate collectors. A number of local clubs require each nonmember to be accompanied by a member when attending a meeting of the club. If you have a friend who belongs to one of these clubs, you might want to attend a meeting. If you were to attend one of these meetings, you would have the opportunity to converse with other collectors and, perhaps, to look at coins they wanted to sell. You might be given the opportunity to trade your coins for other coins, as well as to participate in the club's auction. The auction might include coins consigned by members, along with coins donated to the club. The type of individual who attends local club meetings is, in general, a person who lives within a ten-mile radius of the meeting place and who is categorized as an "intermediate" collector. But there can sometimes be really expert numismatists at these meetings.

If you educate yourself in buying and selling before the meeting and view it as a social and historically educational affair, you'll enjoy yourself immensely. Interested coin collectors can go on talking for hours. Just remember that you have to go to work the next morning!

Local Club Shows

Watch out. Some dealers at local club shows are merely part-time hobbyists. Some of these nonprofessionals are not as concerned about reputation as their professional counterparts. The author is not claiming that all part-time dealers are not ethical; in fact, many are more ethical than some of their professional counterparts. However, a part-time weekend dealer might not know all the rules of the game, might be ignorant of coin-market conditions, and might be very unhappy about your trying to return a coin. Yes, there are good deals available from part-time dealers, but a good part of the time, their material is of inferior quality and overgraded.

The cost to the dealer of renting a table at a local club show can range from $50 to $100. Often the dealers at these shows have more to sell than coins: jewelry, watches, political campaign buttons, and baseball cards. (A variation of the local club show is the local show sponsored by a commercial organization, but composed of the same types of dealers.)

Seminational Conventions: Regional and State

The seminational convention is where the action is. It is the backbone of the rare-coin industry, the place where values are determined and dealer inventory replenished. It is the place where the neophyte is educated, where the advanced collector exhibits, and where the professional numismatist wheels and deals. It is also the place where great sums of money are lost by the unknowledgeable. When you attend a seminational convention, don't hesitate to have this book at your side.

The seminational convention is sponsored by either a nonprofit or a commercial organization. When the show is sponsored by the former, you have the opportunity of placing an educational exhibit. When the show is sponsored by the latter, you do not. Although the main attraction of this type of show is the dealers who form the bourse (between seventy-five and two hundred), the seminational convention offers an impressive array of invaluable educational activities—from organized youth forums to advanced educational seminars of the highest caliber. There is also usually an important auction held in conjunction with the show.

During the 1979–1980 boom, there was almost no distinction between the seminational shows and the national conventions, for dealers from across the country would attend most coin shows; there was always a lot of business. But as market activity became less hectic, the fine line between them became more identifiable. During the boom, there were numerous complaints from the professionals about there not being enough shows. Today, the number of shows seems adequate.

Conventional wisdom says that the best place for the beginning collector is the local club show. Beginning collectors should attend the educational forums of the seminational conventions, but refrain from buying during their early learning stages. You don't get

Dealers sell their coins at conventions on rented tables.

the same feel for the hobby by only reading books before you buy. Do both; read books and attend the seminational shows.

National Conventions

The national coin convention is composed of a number of different numismatic events conducted on every level. It's also a place that might overwhelm you. Many beginners actually are scared when they first look at a national coin convention, for they don't know how to begin. There are usually several hundred dealers, dozens of educational exhibits, scores of educational activities, and a huge auction.

Beginners might find the national convention unmanageable. One way to start is by obtaining a copy of the convention program and studying it in a quiet place. But beginners should refrain from buying anything until they have attended several national conventions. National conventions also offer the young (the under-eighteen crowd) a thorough education through a series of innovative programs.

The pace of national conventions is so brisk that even an experienced dealer occasionally is a victim of the intense activity. A friend and colleague of mine walked into an auction session of a major numismatic company during a national coin convention. He was so preoccupied with other convention events that he bid $9,000 (plus a 10 percent buyer's fee) on the wrong coin! Two lots later, he informed the auctioneer of the error, but the auctioneer, also the company's president, refused to honor the request to reopen bidding on the piece. When the "successful" bidder offered the coin for sale to the underbidder, the underbidder admitted to being caught up in the bidding and was no longer interested in the coin. The story had a happy ending, for the auction company later decided to put the coin into its next auction and not force a sale. But the lesson is that everyone, even an experienced professional, has to be careful at a national convention.

International Conventions

Although this book is primarily concerned with United States coins, a discussion of the role of the coin convention would not be complete without mention of international conventions. The size of these coin shows is between the seminational and national categories discussed earlier.

For the United States resident, there are two basic types of international shows: those held in the United States and those held overseas. The international convention differs from the seminational and national in that only foreign material is allowed during international shows held in the United States, whereas there are no restrictions during regular United States shows. There are many United States dealers; even the overseas dealers speak English, and U.S. money is readily accepted. But before anyone buys coins from any coin show or convention, it is necessary to become familiar with the unwritten rules of the house.

Bourse-Room Etiquette

The following are *don'ts* for the rare-coin enthusiast:

- **Don't loudmouth a dealer for overgrading, and don't select pieces from his or her inventory and remark how ugly they are.** If you don't like the way a coin is graded or looks, don't buy it.
- **Don't deter a dealer's customer who is interested in buying the same type of material you have to sell.** If a prospective buyer is engaged in conversation with a dealer, don't interrupt. This is for your own protection, for many dealers become violent when this happens. If you want to sell your coins on the bourse floor, offer them to dealers who have tables. Or rent your own.
- **Don't interrupt a potential transaction by offering a higher price to purchase a coin than the dealer it is being offered to.** In fact, don't make any offer, even if the dealer acts disinterested. Disinterest is a clever negotiation tactic. And if you interfere, the dealer might get very angry. If you want to be offered coins in this manner, rent a table.
- **Don't remove the dealer's coin from the holder without first asking permission.** If you are given permission to remove it, make sure to hold it over a velvet tray or fabric with thumb and forefinger.
- **Don't remove the dealer's coin from the holder if your hands are dirty.** Wash your hands before you enter a bourse room. Even if a dealer doesn't mind if you hold coins

Coin buyers and sellers recognize an unwritten protocol for doing business.

with dirty hands, you should mind. If you buy a coin which you've mishandled, its value could decrease markedly at a later date.

- **Don't make a purchase offer if you don't mean it.** On the dealer-to-dealer level, purchase offers are considered binding, and dealers are rarely offered a return privilege. Even for nondealers, however, offers are often considered binding. In general, dealers don't like to take back coins purchased at conventions. If pressed, most will accept returns, but they will refuse to deal with you again.

- **Don't get mad at a dealer for asking a ridiculously high price for the piece you have been desperately searching for.** If the dealer senses your desire, he or she will put pressure on you to buy it. Remember, never allow yourself to be coerced into buying something. There is nothing wrong with asking, "What is your real bottom line? " If the dealer still won't lower the price, just say "We're too far apart." If he or she persists, tell the dealer what you're willing to pay. If you get that far, be ready to visit another table, for you might no longer be a welcome visitor. But you might get lucky and have your offer accepted.

- **Don't ask for an appraisal within listening distance of the dealer whose coin you are having appraised.** In fact, if the coin is in a flip, remove the insert bearing the dealer's name when asking another dealer's opinion. If you return the coin, don't reveal whose opinions you sought.

- **Don't fidget with price guides during an auction presale viewing session.** There are limited hours and many people waiting to view. Look at the coins first, and later determine what you want to pay—after you've finished viewing. The pros don't even bother with price guides on the bourse floor, except for an occasional, "What's bid?" Similarly, if you are offering coins for sale, know what prices you want before you offer them.

Coin conventions, while still popular, now have to compete with coin sales over the Internet.

- **Don't try to force your way in to a crowded table.** If a dealer is busy, stroll the bourse floor. Not only is it best to deal on a one-to-one basis, but dealers get nervous when there are a lot of people around, for fear of losing a coin.

  Convention-goers should take adequate security measures to help ensure their protection. For your convenience, a security checklist follows.

Security Tips for the Convention-Goer

- Take off your convention badge after you leave the bourse floor.
- Don't wear the official convention medal. If you want one, buy it and put it away. Only collectors wear the medals, and collectors often carry coins with them.
- Dress casually, and don't carry a bag if possible. During the summer months, attend in shirtsleeves, and don't wear a jacket.
- Avoid feeling your pocket where you know coins are; this alerts people to where your coins are located. Walk with your arms loosely at your sides.
- Do not boast about the coins you bought. Store your coins in a bank safe-deposit box, and if you ever discuss your numismatic holdings, remark about them being there.
- If you place an educational exhibit, be accompanied by someone upon placement and removal. Have that person accompany you with the coins back to the safe-deposit box or vault. If this is not feasible, consider not exhibiting.
- Take out insurance on collections valued above $2,500.

Author Scott Travers (r) autographs copies of his books after he held an educational forum at a coin convention.

Educational Forums

The educational forum is the main reason for individuals to attend coin conventions. In order to maximize your benefits from attending one of these forums, you should do some pre-forum planning.

First, ascertain which forum is best to attend. Second, after you decide which forum to attend, read up on the topic to be discussed. Many lecturers have written books on the subject on which they lecture, and it is a good idea to obtain copies when possible. Members of the American Numismatic Association may borrow books from the ANA library at no charge except for postage. Third, prepare a list of questions before you attend the forum. If any remain unanswered after the lecture, speak up. Ask the lecturer the unanswered question(s). It is only by going through this process repeatedly that you will be able to obtain a top-notch education.

When attending any of these seminars or forums, take notes. You may find them very useful to refer to at a later date, but there are no rules. If you believe that you will gain a better education by just sitting back and listening, do that.

Youth Programs

This country's youth program saw its beginnings in 1971 when Michigan's Florence Schook set up a program for young collectors in conjunction with a coin convention. Young numismatists (YNs) from that state and others flocked to the meeting. The attraction was simple—motivational, participatory education. Young people, some of whom were not collectors but were attending the meeting with a relative or friend, were motivated to pursue numismatics by being given gifts and participating in activities of the meeting. What a success it was! By May 1974, the program was introduced at the Greater New York Coin Convention in New York City and met with more success. Dealers were willing to donate coins to be given free of charge, as well as sponsoring luncheons. The convention organizations were so ecstatic about the number of people the programs attracted that they encouraged YN programs and advertised their existence. Within a year, Florence Schook's programs were national in scope and gained a character and momentum all their own. The programs are now famous for the numismatic spelling bee (with impressive trophies given to the winners), exhibit contests (with expert judging), young persons' presentations and coin club updates (with valuable prizes given to every speaker), and play-money auctions (with play money given to every YN in attendance to buy real coins). The programs were so well received and covered in the press that numismatic luminaries from across the country jumped at the opportunity to address the YNs. These programs, designed to maximize participation, present an ideal opportunity for YNs to broaden their numismatic knowledge and sharpen their collecting skills. Hobby organizations now sponsor scholarships to the annual ANA Summer Seminar and awards programs as well. These programs have become fiercely competitive.

There are no requirements for young people who want to attend these programs in their locale, except that they be under eighteen, have an interest in, but not necessarily any knowledge of, numismatics, and be well behaved. For further information about YN programs, write to the American Numismatic Association, 818 North Cascade Avenue, Colorado Springs, CO 80903-3279.

Persons interested in making donations of coins, material, or monies to the YN program should also contact the ANA directly and request a formal receipt for IRS purposes.

How to Design a Winning Exhibit

There is romance between coin collectors and their collections, so it follows that collectors like to prepare displays of their collections. Some displays get more attention than others. But although some exhibits interest the non-collector, such as the type of exhibit described at the beginning of this chapter, they also should be designed to please the exhibit judges.

Collectors who serve on convention committees like to believe that exhibits are the main attraction of any convention. To some degree, this is true. The judging of numismatic exhibits has evolved into a fine art, much like horse- and dog-show judging. But many persons, even the most experienced exhibitors, often wonder why judges consistently select one type of exhibit over another to win first place or best of show.

One of the country's leading exhibit judges points out that in preparing the exhibit, one must adhere to the rules prepared by the exhibit committee. Most rules are modeled after those of the ANA:

COMPETITIVE EXHIBIT POINT SPREAD

Subject	Number of Points
Numismatic Information	35
Arrangement, aesthetic appeal	30
Completeness	5
Difficulty in assembling the material	10
Condition	10
Rarity (scarcity without regard to price)	10

The method used by the convention at which you display (display case, specification, etc.) is usually outlined in the exhibit rules. There are certain tips, though, aside from the stock information, that will help you win a prize. You should make sure the title is complete as it relates to the coins displayed. If you are displaying coins which do not constitute a complete set, design your title to reflect what you're displaying. Try to have the coins stand apart from the background by placing each one on a small platform or even a small pillow. Provide adequate background information, and include an example of the coin's reverse. Do not use a background color that may bother a judge, such as red. Small items can make the difference between winning and losing because neatness counts. If your exhibit is pasted on a board which is too small for the case, place a piece of matching velvet or cloth underneath.

The exhibit judge says that the first-place award is the easiest to determine because that display stands out in all respects. The second is also not a difficult choice. But the third is most difficult because most displays left after the selection of first and second place have an equal number of faults.

How to Complain

"The dealer's risk is as great in taking your check as your risk is in taking his coin," a dealer acquaintance of mine once remarked. Every collector should make a note of this comment, for it focuses attention on the fact that every sale is a two-way street. Not only does the dealer have a responsibility, but the collector does, too. The collector should closely follow bourse-room etiquette. If a time ever arises when a collector feels that he or she has bought a misrepresented coin (whether overgraded, counterfeit, or other), he or she should not go back and tell off the dealer. Instead, the collector should quietly bring the matter to the dealer's attention. If the dealer still will not satisfactorily settle the matter, the collector may take action through the channels discussed elsewhere in this book (PNG arbitration, etc.). When at a coin convention, though, it is best to take immediate action.

In few other industries do large transactions take place in so few seconds as they do in the rare-coin industry. If you are deciding whether or not to buy a coin, it might be bought by someone else while you are taking a walk around the bourse room to make up your mind. You can't tell a dealer that you might buy a certain coin from him or her next month, for that coin could be sold tomorrow. This pressure has caused many people to buy coins, only to regret it later.

If you buy a misrepresented coin at a convention or show, dealers and organization officials agree that the best way of handling it, if talking to the dealer fails, is by contacting a high official with the show and asking his or her assistance. Dealers usually cooperate when a complaint reaches this level.

Remember, the coin industry is an easy-entry one, assumed to be self-governing. Just because a dealer has a table at a show is no assurance of high ethical standards. The shows don't police their dealers. That's up to you. The best way to complain is not to have to in the first place. Prevention is the best cure. Educate yourself so that you can never be ripped off.

Despite all the attempts at education (through organizational meetings, seminars, and exhibits), coin conventions exist for one reason only—the bourse. Just don't get the reason they exist confused with the purpose they can serve for you. The bourse is the nucleus of virtually every coin gathering. Regardless of how much planning is done by the sponsoring organization, whether profit or nonprofit, to attract top-notch speakers or have other meritorious activities, it remains an inescapable fact that were it not for the bourse, there wouldn't be a coin convention. This is obvious to even the beginning collector who may wonder why so many people flock to the bourse, compared with the few who attend the educational forums and meetings. Attractions other than the bourse exist at coin shows to lure people to the bourse. There is an analogous relationship in commercial television. Television programs exist only as a lure to get people to watch the commercials. The ANA has been stepping up its educational programs, along with trying to attract more educational exhibitors to its conventions.

Dealing with Dealers

There are a number of dealers whom you are likely to encounter at conventions—and elsewhere. The *local dealer* runs a mom-and-pop organization. The *regional dealer* has a large following from several nearby states and a hefty local following, combined with some Internet business picked up casually. The *national dealer* may have a strong local following, combined with a mail-order following throughout the country, as well as a strong following from attending coin shows and a vibrant Internet presence. The national dealer may even have locations in more than one state. The *international dealer* has several departments, as well as a following around the world. This type of dealership might have one or more overseas offices, a strong mail-order and Internet following, and a heavy travel schedule.

The coin industry is one of boom and bust. During the booms, the number of dealers in all categories grows, but many dealerships themselves grow and advance to the next category. For example, during a boom, many regional dealers will become national dealers. During a bust, dealers will exit the industry, and a number of expanded dealerships will shrink. The light regulation of the field allows dealers to enter and exit practically at will.

Increasingly, more mom and pop and regional dealers are teaming up with, or even working for, national and international dealers.

Establishing a relationship with a dealer in your locale is very important, for this dealer will serve as your central source of information, despite any other online activity you might pursue. You'll buy your coin books, your newspapers, your magazines, and, perhaps, some of your coins there. You'll hear market reports, discuss your collecting needs, and learn a great deal about buying and selling coins there—if not from the wisdom of a professional numismatist, then from your own mistakes.

Dealers acquire coins through collectors, investors, estates, auctions, coin shows, teletype, and any other source with coins for sale. In many cases, they are competing with you to buy coins. Dealers sell coins through their stores and offices to other dealers, collectors, and investors. Their other outlets include the Internet, bid board, auction, mail order, and teletype.

Establishing a relationship with a dealer might also save you money when you want a coin that another dealer possesses. For example, let's say that you establish a relationship with dealer A. One day, you discover that dealer X is offering just the coin you need to complete your collection. The coin is listed in dealer X's catalog for $3,000. You don't know how much the coin is worth because you haven't seen it. Dealer X only extends approval credit to known dealers and is hundreds of miles away. If you're a good customer, dealer A might order the coin on approval, get a wholesale price of $2,500, and sell the coin to you for $2,700, $300 less than dealer X's asking price.

The dealer you establish a relationship with might even represent you at an out-of-town convention auction for a minimal fee. For a 5-percent or 10-percent fee, you don't have to pay the transportation and lodging costs. However, this percentage fee adds up to a substantial sum of money if your auction spending is considerable. Use your judgment. If you attend yourself, it might be less expensive in the end if you know values and are self-disciplined.

Always beware of bargains. Remember, if something seems too good to be true, it probably is. Even if a coin offered to you at a convention is genuine, unaltered, and accurately graded, there could be trouble. It could be stolen. If you buy a stolen coin, you might be asked to return it. (Even if you're not asked to do so, the coin is still not legally yours.) However, dealers who care about their reputations will refund your money. If you pay too low a price, you could face criminal penalties, depending upon what state you reside in or what states are involved.

If you encounter a dealer in whom you have implicit faith who treats you fairly and with respect, embrace that dealer, and don't let go.

– 15 –
SELLING HIGH, HIGHER, HIGHEST

This is a landmark chapter—probably the most important chapter in this book, and perhaps the most important chapter you'll read in any coin book. Virtually every coin book on the market tells you how, when, and why you should buy coins, but very few offer specific advice on the coins you should sell right now.

Some other authors provide extraordinary advice on how to sell coins, once you've made the decision to do so. They neither explain to the reader what coins to sell right now nor do they offer detailed advice about the timing.

Interestingly, even numismatic newsletters rarely, if ever, tell their readers which coins to sell right away. This is not surprising, though, since most of the people who write these newsletters are coin dealers themselves and derive most of their income from selling coins. Their principal objective is getting people to buy more coins, not sell the ones they already have.

Coin auction companies can certainly be counted on to advise people to sell their coins. Some auction firms will *always* tell you to sell because an auction company needs you to sell to generate commissions. Bull market? "Sell your coins now!" Bear market? "Sell your coins now!"

Changing Strategies

In years gone by, the accepted approach to investing in coins was to buy good material and hold it as long as possible, confident in the belief that over the long term, prices would inevitably go up. But nothing is inevitable anymore—not that anything ever really was. The glory days of surefire price increases returned in the 2000s, and the gravy train of "guaranteed" profit seemed headed for the moon. The coin investment climate changed dramatically, and this calls for drastic changes in coin investors' strategy as well. In fact, it calls for a number of different investment strategies regarding coins' retention or dispersal, depending upon the nature of the coins that are involved. Some coins should be sold—even at a loss. Others should be held. And others should be traded for different coins.

Public auctions are one of the best options available to help you realize the highest prices for your coins.

There's no time like the present to review your coin collection and formulate a plan for restructuring your holdings to reflect the market realities of today. One of those realities, regrettable as it may be, is the undeniable fact that despite a bull market for coins in the early 2000s, many coins, especially popular generics like MS-65 Morgan dollars and Saint-Gaudens double eagles, are worth less today than they were at the coin market's last big peak, in May 1989.

Many coins have performed phenomenally well recently. But an overwhelming number of examples of lackluster performers can be found in every issue of the *Certified Coin Dealer Newsletter* (or *Bluesheet*), a respected weekly sight-unseen bid price guide to the current market values of certified coins—those that have been graded and encapsulated by one of the major coin certification services. Let's look at just a few of these, and then see how some very different lessons can be drawn from them:

- On May 26, 1989, the *Bluesheet* assigned a bid price of $500 to an 1880-S Morgan silver dollar certified as Mint State-65 by the Numismatic Guaranty Corporation of America (NGC). In June 2005, that same coin was listed for about $120.
- On May 26, 1989, the *Bluesheet* bid for a no-motto Liberty Seated half dollar graded Mint State-65 by the Professional Coin Grading Service (PCGS) was $23,500. In June 2005, that coin was listed at only $3,300.
- On May 26, 1989, the *Bluesheet* assigned a value of $4,060 to a common-date Saint-Gaudens double eagle ($20 gold piece) graded Mint State-65 by NGC. In June 2005, that coin is on the *Bluesheet* at just $990.

All three of these coins plunged in value. But while this gives them something important in common, a person who owned all three coins would have to use very different strategies in selling each one to maximize his or her return.

The Need for Certification

No matter which path you follow in disposing of investment coins, your first move should be to get them certified—or recertified (if they haven't been already)—by one of the major coin-grading services. If you acquired your coins in the late 1980s or thereafter, the chances are good that they were already certified when you got them. If you bought them earlier, there's a strong possibility that they may be uncertified, or "raw," to use the common marketplace term for such material. If so, you need to get them graded and encapsulated in order to be sure of just what you have and to maximize your chances to sell them or trade them advantageously.

Even if your coins have already been certified, it may be desirable to resubmit them to a certification service; grading standards have changed since the late 1980s, and they might well receive a higher grade today. You need to examine each previously certified coin to determine whether it might be a candidate for an upgrade.

As an aside, if the three bulleted coins listed earlier were upgraded by a point, their values would still be considerably lower than they were on May 26, 1989.

In theory, certification doesn't affect the grade of a coin; if a coin is Mint State-65, that should be its grade regardless of whether it's raw or in a grading-service holder. In practice, however, certification does make a tremendous difference in many potential buyers' perception of the grade, for it serves to reassure them that the coin is as described. Without this safety net, they might very well seek to purchase it at a price corresponding to a somewhat lower grade—and that could easily translate into a significant reduction in what you would get. That's why it's important to get your investment coins certified, or recertified, before you even begin to formulate plans for their dispersal.

Generic Coins

The 1880-S Morgan silver dollar is an excellent example of a generic coin. Coins in this category are available in large quantities, even in high levels of preservation. As a result, they have come to be regarded very much like commodities. This gave them great appeal to Wall Street brokerage firms and Wall Street–type investors when those outsiders entered the coin market in large numbers during the late 1980s. Their age, pristine quality, and high silver content made them seem scarcer and more valuable than they really were, and their availability made them easy to promote. All this drove their prices far beyond levels that were warranted.

Since then, generic coins have suffered a double whammy. The Wall Street crowd deserted the coin market in late 1989, returning since then only in small numbers, effectively removing most of the demand that kept these coins' prices artificially high. At the same time, the grading services have certified many thousands of additional examples, thus expanding the supply exponentially. This is clearly a formula for disaster.

At first glance, generic coins appear to be real bargains at current price levels. That 1880-S Morgan dollar in Mint State-65 condition sounds like an absolute steal at its bid of $120; after all, it would have cost you $500 or more in 1989. This is one case, however, where you do have to look a "gift horse" in the mouth. Far from being a bargain, it might be overpriced even now, at its new, lower level. So are a number of the other generic coins that used to be so popular—high-grade, common-date Peace silver dollars, Walking Liberty half dollars, and "Mercury" dimes, for example.

I recommend that you divest yourself, after recertification, of generic silver and nickel coins you now possess—even if you have to take a loss in the process. (Hold on to the generic gold coins you already have, and buy more at 2005 levels.) You can sell them outright or, if you prefer, you can trade them for other coins. It's my considered judgment that despite their drastically lower price levels, these coins aren't going anywhere but down—in the short run and especially in the long term. Dwindling demand and expanding supply add up to dismal price performance. These coins will likely see short-term and spectacular price appreciation from being promoted, but should not be viewed as a stable investment.

Many of the generics available today are not nearly of the same quality as those that were sold in 1989. Today's Mint State-65 Walking Liberty half dollar might have been only a Mint State-63 or 64 in 1989. This concept is explored in detail in chapter 5.

High-Grade Rarities

Many high-condition coins of legitimate rarity also have suffered a major loss of value in recent years. The no-motto Liberty Seated half dollar is a case in point. But unlike generic coins, these high-grade rarities remain genuinely scarce, and relatively few additional examples have been certified since 1989-especially in grades of 65 and above. The population and census reports issued by the major certification services confirm that supplies are still extremely small, despite looser grading standards. The coins' loss of value stems from reduced demand, and that, in turn, reflects the departure of unknowledgeable collectors from the coin market. A solid collector base continues to exist for these true collector coins, and it wouldn't take much additional demand to push their prices higher—perhaps dramatically so—within a short period of time. In short, they have enormous potential at their current depressed price levels, and they have potential to be big winners.

If you have many generic silver and nickel coins in your collection, it would be a great idea to sell them—even at a loss—and use the proceeds to purchase high-grade rarities such as Proof gold Type coins. Or, as an alternative, you might trade them for such coins. (This approach can have beneficial tax implications, as explained in another chapter, although these benefits primarily pertain to cases where your coins have appreciated in value, not declined.) If your holdings are extensive and valuable enough, you might even consider converting them—through sale or trade—into one single spectacular high-grade rarity. Imagine the sense of pride you would feel in owning a classic rarity with a known population of just a dozen examples. This is one case where putting all your eggs in one basket could prove to be a very wise move. Besides making you proud, it also would be highly prudent.

Generic Gold Coins

During the late 1980s, many investors—and many collector/investors, as well-purchased large quantities of generic gold coins. Often, these included common-date Saint-Gaudens double eagles in grades such as Mint State-63, or even Mint State-65, as in the case I cited earlier in this chapter. You don't want your holdings to be top-heavy in such coins, but they can be good for short-term action. No more than 30 percent of your holdings should consist of generic gold coins. Some people have nothing but generic gold in their collections, and if you're one of those people, you need to diversify and bring the percentage down.

Double eagles contain close to an ounce of gold, and as gold bullion rises in value dramatically, these coins' intrinsic value will enjoy a similar gain. In fact, they would go up in price even more percentagewise than bullion, since they have extra value as collectibles, and this would be magnified in a hot market environment. Don't be misled, however, by temporary surges triggered by upward spikes in the bullion market, or, for that matter, by hoopla and hype in the coin market. Generic gold coins were clearly overpriced in the late 1980s, and the lower price levels of the mid-1990s were far more accurate gauges of their true market value. They're certainly worth a premium over the bullion price, but not the kind of premium they commanded in the overheated marketplace of 1989.

Many investment advisors recommend keeping a certain amount of gold, including gold coins, in your portfolio. My advice would be to keep generic gold coins as an integral part of your holdings. (See Appendix D for details.) If you have about a hundred common-date Saint-Gaudens double eagles in your safe deposit box, keep a few of the better-date pieces and a number of the common-date pieces and trade the rest for coins with greater potential, such as high-grade, low-mintage U.S. gold coins.

Like-kind or like-for-like exchanges are a tax slashing concept that might benefit the holder of generic gold coins that have maxed out their potential. See chapter 16 for more information.

Five Types of Coins to Sell

There are five basic categories of coins that you should consider selling right now, and each one calls for a different kind of strategy. Let's look at them one by one:

Coins That Have Increased in Value

In a rising market, it's often very difficult to judge just when to sell your coins. If you buy a coin for $100 and it jumps in value to $1,000, that might very well be a good time to sell it—but then again, it might not be the best time: The coin might continue increasing in value to $2,000 if the positive forces at work in the market are strong and sustained enough. Should you wait to squeeze that last extra price increase out of the market and risk losing the profit you've already made on paper? My advice would be to take the money—sell the coin now—and run all the way to the bank. There's nothing wrong with taking a profit, and when coins have risen dramatically within a short period of time, you should go to the cash window and celebrate.

Of course, there's more involved in selling your coins advantageously than merely walking up to a window—or a coin dealer's counter—and picking up your money. You can sell them directly to a dealer if you wish, and this might work out well if you have a good rapport and a good working relationship with the dealer in question. But don't expect an optimal return if you simply walk in cold to a shop where you're a face without a name, or approach a dealer's table at random at a show. You'll pocket a profit, yes, if your coins have gone up significantly in value, but you may end up leaving a lot of your money on the dealer's table, or, to be more precise, in his or her wallet.

One ideal venue to sell rare coins is an auction, where the coins are showcased to maximum advantage in an eye-catching catalog, the sale is widely publicized, and all of the major interested buyers are assembled in one room at the same time, or represented there by surrogates. All of this enhances the likelihood that the coins being sold in such a sale will bring top dollar. But selling your coins in a full-scale auction can be a lengthy process; months can pass between the time you consign your coins and the moment when the gavel finally falls, and if the market is volatile, your paper profits may shrivel by the time the bidding begins.

My firm, Scott Travers Rare Coin Galleries, LLC, of New York City, offers an alternative that combines some of the advantageous features of a full-scale auction with the benefits of quick—almost overnight—sale. This format, which I call the "Lightning Sale," is a modified form of competitive offers which takes place almost at once, thereby all but eliminating the waiting risk associated with traditional auctions.

We assemble some of the most knowledgeable and influential coin buyers in the industry—the very same people you'd be likely to encounter at the biggest public auction sales—and give them an opportunity to examine the coins being sold. Then, at the consignor's sole discretion, we proceed with a private sale at once. Competition is fierce, and prices tend to be strong for existing market conditions. Thus, consignors "lock in" their profits, so to speak, avoiding the risk that the market might fizzle down the line. What's more, successful buyers wire their payments the very next day, so instead of waiting months for their money, the consignors get the proceeds from the sale right away.

Another good way to sell your coins quickly while still securing exposure to a broad range of buyers is to place them in one of telephone and Internet bid sales conducted by Teletrade(r), a Greg Manning Auctions subsidiary which conducts such sales on a regular basis by means of a sophisticated computer system accessed by Touch-Tone telephones. These sales are limited to coins that have been certified and encapsulated by one

1952 Proof set. Earlier Proof sets such as this one have appreciated in value smartly over the years.
Photo courtesy Capital Plastics, Inc.

of the leading grading services. For further information, contact Teletrade, Inc., 18022 Cowan, Suite 107, Irvine, CA 92614-6805.

Among the coins you should seriously consider selling right away are those you have been successful in getting upgraded by one of the certification services. Perhaps you had a coin that was certified as Proof-64 and you cracked it out of its holder and resubmitted it to the same service—or sent it to a different service—and it came back as Proof-65. That one-point enhancement in the grade might very well be worth several thousand dollars more in value, and that's surely something to celebrate!

In this case, I would recommend placing your coin in a full-scale, elaborate catalog auction. I have seen many coins graded Proof-64, or Mint State-64, that possessed truly remarkable visual appeal but were held back from a higher grade—initially, at least—because of some technical deficiency such as minor striations (or stress lines) on the reverse that were barely visible. It's altogether possible that bidders in an auction would look upon such coins as being premium-quality—perhaps even Proof- or Mint State-66—if they viewed them without the limiting framework of the "slab" with a stated grade of 65.

Coins That Are Unlikely to Come Back in Value

Certain coins you have in your portfolio simply may have reached a dead end. Perhaps you have some high-grade generic coins whose populations have risen astronomically during recent years because of new submissions to the certification services. Given the enormous supply now available, you may see no hope that these coins will ever rebound to anything approaching their former value. Or perhaps your holdings include some random-quality coins that you perceive as having little or no chance of being upgraded if you were to resubmit them, even with grading standards seeming to get looser all the time. These coins may have lost a substantial part of the value they had when you acquired them, but, even so, you probably should give some serious thought to selling them right now.

Selling such coins at a loss would at least allow you to use that loss to reduce your federal income tax obligation. This could be a good way to offset your capital gains from more successful investments—perhaps including windfalls from stocks and bonds. Coins that have dropped in value below your tax basis should not be traded. If you trade coins on which an outright sale would have resulted in a loss, that loss will be postponed, just as a gain is postponed through like-kind exchanges involving coins whose value has increased.

Coins You Are Finished With

There may be certain coins that you simply want to get rid of. You're through with them and never want to see them again. Perhaps you had a bag of 1,000 Morgan dollars and you picked out the 10 or 20 best pieces; now you've replaced those coins with less desirable dollars and you want to get the bag out of your way. Depending upon market conditions and your cash-flow situation, you might either sell that bag directly to a dealer who handles bullion or, alternatively, place it in auction. Either way, these are coins you should sell. It's just not productive to keep them around, and you could come out of the sale with many thousands of dollars to invest in other coins with much greater upside potential.

Another kind of coin that might well come under this heading is a certified coin you've resubmitted over and over again in an unsuccessful bid for a higher grade. Perhaps you have a coin graded Mint State-65 and it's worth $500 in that grade, but you've made a dozen fruitless attempts to get it bumped up to Mint State-66 because it would be worth $5,000 in that level. You've given up on the upgrade, and now you simply want to blow this coin out. Given your state of mind, that's exactly what you should do.

Coins You Want to Sell or Have to Sell

There are times when circumstances dictate the sale of certain coins. You may find yourself almost forced to sell them, either for financial reasons or other personal reasons.

Recently, a friend of mine confronted this kind of predicament. He had a magnificent 1909-S VDB Lincoln cent which had been graded Mint State-65 Red by the Professional Coin Grading Service, and he found himself facing a serious cash crunch. The coin was an extraordinary premium-quality piece, and the market for it seemed to be getting stronger every day. Still, my friend was strapped for cash and absolutely needed immediate funds, so he sold the coin. You could find yourself in a similarly unfortunate situation.

In selling a coin when you're under duress, by all means avoid telling potential buyers you have to sell it. Don't go to a coin show and let a dealer smell blood. Don't go to some fly-by-night dealer who's holding a liquidation sale in a room he took for the day at a local hotel. And don't go to a coin or collectibles shop where the people don't know you and let them convince you to sell that scarce coin at a fire-sale price. There's no need to engage in panic selling. The marketplace today is much more sophisticated than it used to be, and many new options are available to sellers in must-sell situations.

If you're selling a whole collection and it has substantial value, you might be able to get a generous cash advance by consigning it to an auction company. Some of the largest coin auction houses in the nation offer this type of service. These companies have a public policy of giving cash advances for up to 50 percent of the estimated value of coins that are consigned to them for sale. However, this limit can often be stretched; I've known of cases where auction firms gave advances for up to 85 percent of the value of the coins in a consignment. Naturally, you would have to sign a security agreement and pay a standard interest rate on the money you received as an advance. But you would have the funds you needed right up front, and when your coins did go on the auction block, perhaps two months later, their sale would be taking place under highly advantageous conditions, thus helping to maximize your return.

Family Accumulations Acquired Secondhand

I have had firsthand experience with numerous instances where people with little or no knowledge of rare coins inherited extensive collections, or found large accumulations in an attic or some other family hoard. Often, this material consists for the most part of high-mintage, low-value sets issued by government mints, or private-mint medals that are pretty but definitely not worth a pretty penny.

The Anatomy of a Coin Transaction

When people with limited knowledge of coins—or no knowledge at all—inherit a collection or stumble upon an old accumulation in the attic, they often tend to view it as a single entity, rather than a mosaic made up of widely differing components. This can be a serious mistake, particularly if they treat it that way when they sell it. All too often, people will take such coins to a local dealer and sell them en masse, reasoning that this is the most convenient approach, and assuming that, in any case, they'll get the same price no matter what method of dispersal they use.

The fact is, different kinds of coins require different methods of sale in order to bring the seller the best return—and sometimes need to be sold to different dealers. If you were to sell a collection or accumulation in a single transaction to just one dealer, he or she would probably use all or most of these methods in reselling the coins to others, and then the return would be maximized for that dealer, and not for you.

Let's say you came into possession of a large and diverse collection of coins, with many different kinds of material—everything from rare type coins to modern government proof sets. This may be hypothetical for the purposes of this book, but it could become very real for you or someone you know—if not right now, then somewhere down the line. Let's separate this collection into its major components and consider the best way to sell each one. In fact, let me go one step further and suggest a specific dealership which you, as a seller, might contact to get top dollar for each component. In each case, I'll select a dealer currently among the most active in that area—and also among those now paying the highest prices for such material.

These recommendations apply only at the time of this writing. Anyone with large holdings is encouraged to contact the author personally to be certain that these dealers are still active in these particular areas. This is a volatile marketplace, and active market-makers and large dealers often take turns at the helm of their respective areas of interest. You need to be certain that these dealers are still interested in such material—and even still in business—before sending any coins to them. I make these recommendations in good faith and based upon the facts as they are known to me now, but you are responsible for screening prospective buyers yourself before you sell your coins.

Let's look at each area individually:

Bullion silver coins: If you were to find yourself with large quantities of pre-1965 Washington quarters or Roosevelt dimes in circulated condition—or even in Mint State condition, chances are that you would want to sell all or most of these coins. One of several renowned bullion dealers with a national reputation is Silver Towne Coin (Leon and David Hendrickson), P.O. Box 424, R.4, Union City Pike, Winchester, IN 47394, telephone (317) 584-7481. A very honest dealer in this type of material is Salvatore Germano, S. G. Rare Coins, Inc., 625 Lafayette Ave., Hawthorne, NJ 07506, telephone (973) 304-0520.

Key-date circulated coins: If you had a collection of key-date Morgan silver dollars in circulated condition, or a collection of circulated Lincoln cents that included such key coins as the 1909-S VDB cent, and you took those coins to a local dealer, that dealer might pay you 20 or 30 percent less than the bid prices in *The Coin Dealer Newsletter*. But that dealer probably wouldn't resell those coins to a consumer—a collector—for 10 percent back of the bid price and settle for a nominal commission. Chances are that dealer would turn around and sell those coins to a company actively pursuing such material and paying top dollar to get it—a company such as Littleton Coin Company, 653 Union Street, Littleton, NH 03561, buyer telephone (603) 444-1020. You should do likewise. And keep in mind that for a collection valued at more than $35,000, Littleton will send a representative to your home to appraise and acquire your coins.

Modern government proof sets and "mint sets": If you suddenly found yourself with hundreds of late-date U.S. proof sets and uncirculated coin sets (better known as "mint sets"), it would be a big mistake to cart those sets to a coin or collectibles shop near your home, plunk them down on the counter, and take the dealer's word—and check—for their value. In all likelihood, that dealer would try to buy those sets from you for 30 or 40 percent less than the prices listed in *The Coin Dealer Newsletter*—and he would then sell them for the *CDN* bid price, or even slightly more, by shipping them off to the one or two dealers that specialize in these coins. I recommend that you sell these coins to a major market-maker in modern proof and mint sets who will pay the highest prices. Such an expert won't buy your sets unless you have a lot of them: These specialists limit their purchases to material worth a total of at least $10,000. One or two of th makers have been in a state of transition recently, so I have elected not to list a name in this edition.

Major rarities: Some dealers might keep major rarities in their inventories and sell th to regular customers, if these were among the coins in a collection that you sold to them. But chances are, many would consign such coins to a major auction firm for sale at a public auction. Auctions have long been the favored method of sale for truly rare coins because they provide the maximum exposure for these valuable but often esoteric items and bring together all of the interested buyers at a single time and place. There are many well-known national numismatic auction companies which receive my highest recommendation, such as American Numismatic Rarities, LLC; Bowers and Merena Galleries; Heritage Numismatic Auctions, Inc.; Stack's; and Superior Galleries. As a practical alternative to a full-scale auction, I also highly recommend my own Lightning Sales, which compress the time required to sell rare coins while still providing many of the advantages of an auction format. Anyone interested in learning more about this process can contact me at P.O. Box 1711, FDR Station, New York, NY 10150, telephone (212) 535-9135. A Lightning Sale is a competitive private sale, similar in format to a standard auction sale, through which people can sell their coins almost immediately in return for a nominal commission.

The value of competitive bidding was underscored recently when a woman from South Carolina decided to sell four gold coins that her father had given her years ago, telling her they would always be worth something. She needed money to pay the college tuition for her only son, so she went to some local coin dealers near her home and asked what they would give her for the coins. These local dealers offered her $200 apiece, for a total of $800. After thinking it over, she decided that the best way to find a coin dealer was by going to the library, instead of going through the Yellow Pages, so she went to the local library, picked up a copy of my book *The Coin Collector's Survival Manual*, found my phone number inside, and called me up. I submitted these coins to NGC for certification; all four received grades of Mint State-65; and the woman ended up getting more than $20,000 for them at one of my Lightning sales. That's $20,000 for a group of four coins that this woman was very close to selling for just $800 a few weeks earlier.

The lesson is clear: Competition will enable you to maximize your return when you're selling coins of high value. It isn't as crucial—and may not really matter at all—in selling more common, less valuable coins; with those, the going price is fairly well established, and the key is finding an active buyer who needs and wants your material. With higher-priced coins, however, the market value at any given time may often be a gray area—or there may be a fairly broad price range—and having several dealers vie for the right to buy them will frequently result in a higher return.

Consider the case of the woman from South Carolina. The local dealers probably viewed her four gold coins as Mint State-63 specimens and offered her Mint State-60 prices, figuring they would make a tidy—but not outrageous—profit by selling them at MS-63 prices. My professional opinion at the time was that the coins would be graded no higher ause they were so original and had full, vibrant mint luster, hough they had a few scratches. The winning bidder for all Sale was Jesse Lipka of Numismania in Flemington, New was Heritage Capital Corporation of Dallas, Texas. Both pka are active buyers. But with rarer, more valuable coins, nvironment and not just selling to one particular active coin, there could be a relatively broad value range—say, anywhere from $1,500 to $4,000. In that kind of situation, buyers—even highly reputable dealers—tend to like to pay a price at the lower end of the range. But when these items are put up for competitive bidding, the dealers usually end up paying a price at the upper end of the range, whether they like it or not. So competition can be extremely healthy for you—the seller—when you are dispersing scarce or rare coins worth thousands of dollars apiece.

Generic, fungible silver coins: High-grade, common-date silver coins—and generic nickel and copper coins, as well—should not be sold at auction; the commissions are too high for such material. If you find yourself with large numbers of these coins—1881-S Morgan silver dollars graded Mint State-65, for example—a good place to sell them might be Heritage Capital Corporation, 3500 Maple Avenue, 17th Floor, Dallas, Texas 75219-3941, telephone (800) 872-6467.

Generic gold coins: Generic gold coins require a somewhat different selling strategy from generic silver coins because their high intrinsic value gives them special appeal to a different kind of buyer. One of the most active, most reputable, and best-paying buyers for large quantities of generic gold coins is National Gold Exchange (NGE), 14309 North Dale Mabry Highway, Tampa, FL 33618, telephone (813) 969-4111. The person to contact is Mark Yaffe. Heritage is an equally strong buyer in many cases when it comes to generic gold coins. And Heritage maintains overseas buying offices. If you're selling generic gold coins certified by the Numismatic Certification Institute (NCI)—and, in some cases, PCGS and NGC generic gold coins—a good buyer to contact is Sal Germano, S.G. Rare Coins, Inc., 625 Lafayette Ave., Hawthorne, NJ 07506, telephone (973) 304-0520. If you have a quantity of generic Type coins graded by NGC, in many cases the highest sight-unseen buyer will be NGC's founder himself, John Albanese. You can contact him at John Albanese Numismatics, P.O. Box 1776, Far Hills, NJ 07931-1771, telephone (908) 781-9101.

Coin Sale Methods

Many people never realize the true value of their coins until the time comes to sell. This is true of both collectors and investors. Many collectors buy coins for their aesthetic value, only to realize years later that many of their coins are of considerably lower grades than they had believed them to be.

But when the time comes to sell—and sooner or later every coin buyer considers liquidation—the question arises, "How should I sell my coins?" The conventional means of sale are public auction, private sale, public sale, and consignment to a dealer for over-the-counter sale.

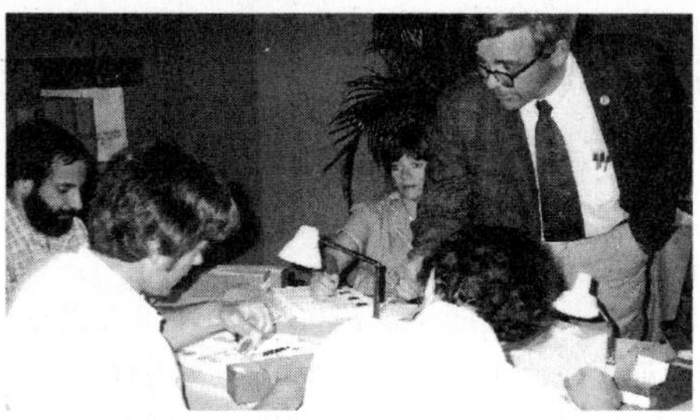

Before an auction, persons interested in buying the coins offered for sale get a chance to look at them. This is called an auction presale viewing session.

Public Auction

The price an uncertified coin realizes at public auction sometimes bears no correlation to its cataloged grade. This is because auction coins are not always cataloged with consistency. Auction sales sometimes reflect deals made between consignor and auction house. For example, if a prospective consignor approaches an auction company with a rarity valued at $250,000 and a collection of About Uncirculated-58 quarters, the auction house might want the prestige of having the valuable rarity in its sale so much that it would catalog the AU quarters as a low Mint State grade. The auction company probably would not voluntarily offer to overgrade the quarters. But if faced with losing a rarity to a competitor, it might concede to calling certain AU coins "Mint State." It might also give the benefit of the doubt to a low-end certified coin, by calling it "premium quality."

Generally, auction companies like to grade very conservatively. In fact, given a free hand, many will undergrade. Undergrading is common in estate sales. Heirs who are not numismatically knowledgeable often present their inherited coins to the auction company with complete faith that the numismatists employed by the firm are experts who will act in the best interest of the consignor. They may be experts, but they don't always act in the consignor's best interest. Undergrading is in the auction firm's best interest as it creates action on the auction floor and impresses potential consignors who don't see the coins, just the impressive prices realized. It also makes the market appear strong. Coins consigned by heirs could actually be Mint State, but be cataloged as About Uncirculated.

The auction catalog, therefore, could consist of some uncertified AU coins graded Mint State, Mint State coins graded AU, low-end certified coins described as "premium quality," and other grading inconsistencies. Of course, a respectable percentage of lots will be graded correctly. To further confuse things, mixed with the consigned coins are pieces owned by the dealer conducting the sale. But as a rule of thumb, auction houses view consignors, not bidders, as their primary clients.

I was fascinated by a very interesting deal with an auction house. There were coins that NGC had graded About Uncirculated-58, but when they were taken out of their holders they were cataloged as MS-62s and realized handsome prices of thousands of dollars apiece. As an MS-62, one of these coins sold for $5,400 plus a 10 percent buyer's fee. When it was in its slab as an AU-58, dealers did not want to buy it. One dealer refused even to make an offer on this coin; he said he wasn't interested.

In a strong market, an auction is a tremendously good method of disposal. In a weak market, it is an uneven method. An auction is often the best liquidation method for high-quality coins.

The best time to sell is in the fall, preferably November, or in the spring, preferably March. Keep away from climatic extremes—summer and winter. Avoid auctions which conclude during the early morning, such as 3:00 A.M. Also avoid small auctions, which attract too few bidders. Sometimes, big auctions can be overwhelming. If the sale contains more than 5,000 lots, consider not consigning. It's difficult for bidders to view all of the coins. And remember that an auction house's estimate of what your coins will realize may not be totally accurate.

If you're afraid that your coins will be switched for less valuable ones, photograph them before the sale, and have the auction firm initial the photos. This fear is completely unfounded with reputable auction firms, but photographs might help you prove that an auction firm damaged your coins if it did. Damage to coins is far more possible than switching. I have *never* heard of any case involving switched auction coins.

Some questions to ask the auction house include, but are not limited to, the following:

- How experienced are you at conducting numismatic auctions?
- Have you ever conducted an official ANA convention auction?
- Are my coins insured while in your possession?
- May I retain title to the coins until they are sold?
- How will you grade my coins, and what grading service, if any, will be used?
- How will you catalog my coins?
- What are the qualifications of the numismatists who will grade and catalog my coins?
- How will you determine what grading service to submit my coins to?
- If I do not like the certified grades my coins receive, may I withdraw my consignment?
- Will you resubmit coins that are assigned grades I find unsatisfactory?
- How many lots will the auction consist of?

- What time of day, and in what session, will my coins be auctioned?
- How many catalogs will be distributed?
- How are your catalogs organized: by consignment or by denomination and date?
- How many of my coins, if any, will be photographed in black-and-white or in color?
- How will you display my coins before the auction to prospective bidders?
- Will you describe my coins over the telephone to inquiring mail bidders?
- What precautions are taken to prevent collusion?
- How much of an advance on prices realized will I receive, and what will the interest charges on it be?
- What is your percentage fee?
- Are successful bidders assessed a buyer's fee?
- How soon after the auction will I be paid?
- What payment plans do you offer? (Check, cash, gold, etc.)
- What are the provisions governing "protective bids" I might want to place on some or all of my consigned coins?
- How can I get my coins to you? (Some auction firms offer bonded couriers who will pick your coins up and deliver them to the firm if a considerable holding is involved.)
- Will the auction contract specify all of the points we've discussed?

Only you can decide what answers are satisfactory.

Guidelines for Numismatic Auctioneers

The following are presented as guidelines for numismatic public auctioneers and is prepared by the Professional Numismatists Guild, Inc. as evidence of industry practices designed to protect the consumer and the consignor, with full disclosure of all items material to making an informed judgment as to an auction sale.

1. Bidders. The rights of bidders to submit bids and to return coins should be clearly and conspicuously defined in the terms of sale.

2. Opening bids. If the auctioneer may open the bidding by placing a bid on behalf of the seller, a mail bidder or any affiliate or related company, or has agreed to "cover" all lots, or not to permit a lot to be sold for less than a specified price, or if an auctioneer may bid for his or its own account, this should be conspicuously disclosed.

3. Reopening of lots. If the auctioneer reserves the right to re-open lots, or to void a hammer on account of a missed bid or misplaced bid, this should be conspicuously disclosed in the terms of the sale.

4. Tie bids. The terms of sale should provide that in the event of a tie bid, a method for determining the winning bid should be disclosed by the auctioneer.

5. Bidding increments. The terms of sale should state the general bidding increments or the auctioneer should announce the same from the floor.

6. Revealing mail bids. An auction house should never reveal a mail bid to any third party.

7. Disclosure of reserves. Consistent with such statements as are made in the terms of sale and as local law or regulation may require, bidders should be advised as to the policy with respect to reserves.

8. Estimates. When an auctioneer provides an estimate of the value of an item, it is unfair (a) if the printed estimate is lower that the known reserve price, unless the reserve price is disclosed, and (b) if the known reserve exceeds the maximum estimated price.

9. Unsold lots; buybacks; returns; prices realized. An auctioneer should not claim that a lot has been sold at an auction sale if it has not been sold. An auctioneer should not print a "selling price" in the "prices realized" of an auction sale if the item was not sold. A "buy back" or reacquisition by a consignor is not a sale. A lot that is returned is not sold. If a lot is returned after the prices realized is published, it is permissible to list such a lot as being sold in the printed prices realized. Printed prices realized should not imply that a price was received for a lot if it was not.

10. Sales to consignor. When an auctioneer knows that a lot is sold to the consignor or a known agent of the consignor, the auctioneer should not claim that the lot was sold.

11. Disclosure of reacquisitions. An auctioneer may properly provide information relative to the hammer price or the last sum cried by the auctioneer provided that if lots have been reacquired by the consignor, it is disclosed.

12. Third-party grading disclosure. When an auctioneer or auction house utilizes the grading interpretation of a third-party grading service, the auctioneer should disclose in the terms of sale whether such use means that the auctioneer agrees or disagrees or offers no opinion, with respect to the accuracy of such descriptions.

13. Grading. In the event an auctioneer does not utilize any third-party grading service, an auctioneer shall disclose the grading standards used to describe a coin. An auctioneer should make every effort to accurately describe numismatic items, including known damage or alterations to the surface or rims of a coin.

14. Pedigree or provenance. An auctioneer may offer an opinion about pedigree or provenance, but should not knowingly mislead a bidder; however, the auctioneer should not represent the pedigree or provenance of a particular item as fact unless its truth is warranted.

15. Different rights. Where the rights of a bidder by mail, fax, phone, or on the floor differ, it should be disclosed.

16. Storage of coins long term. All purchasers should be advised of the long-term effects of certain types of plastic used to temporarily store coins. Purchasers should be advised that material that is not inert may cause damage to coins.

17. Payment prior to delivery. If an auctioneer requires payment before delivering lots to a successful bidder, this should be conspicuously disclosed.

18. Imposed legal differences. Where municipal, state or other legal requirements differ materially from these industry guidelines, such facts should be conspicuously disclosed to an auctioneer's customers. These Guidelines are intended to give certain minimum rights to consignors and bidders. Nothing herein is intended to prevent an auctioneer from granting greater rights. To the extent that these Guidelines are in conflict with any law or regulation, such law or regulation shall prevail in the location where it is in effect. To the extent that these Guidelines impose greater requirements, these Guidelines shall prevail.

19. Sale of auctioneer's material. An auctioneer who includes its own material in an auction sale should disclose that it is doing so to prospective bidders.

20. Warranty of title. Each auction consignment agreement should contain a proviso that the consignor warrants good title to the property offered for sale. The terms of sale should also provide in substance that in the event it is finally determined that the purchaser has not acquired transferable title, that the auctioneer shall reimburse the purchaser for the full amount of the bid paid together with any buyer's fee upon return.

21. Limitation of damage. If an auctioneer proposed to limit the right of consequential damages, it should be disclosed to the bidder.

20. Buyer's fee disclosures. If a buyer's fee is imposed, it should be prominently disclosed in the printed catalogue, and terms of the sale should be orally announced at the start of each bidding session by the auctioneer.

22. Multiple buyer's fees. An auctioneer should not permit one bidder to pay a lower buyer's fee than another bidder without disclosing this ability to all bidders.

23. Consignor bidding. The terms of sale and consignment agreement shall state whether or not consignors are permitted to bid.

24. Assistance of pooling. An auctioneer shall not knowingly assist in the collusion between bidders.

25. Right to rescind sale. If the auctioneer claims the right to rescind the sale in the event of non-payment or breach of any warranty, this should be disclosed in the terms of sale or consignment agreement.

26. Rejection of bids. The terms of sale should state if the auctioneer has the right to reject or accept any bid.

27. Receipt for consignments. Upon receipt of a consignment, an auction house should give a proper receipt with an inventory reasonably delineating as clearly as possible the items obtained.

28. Insurance. The auctioneer should, at the time of collection of the consignment, state that the items received are insured, unless such statement is untrue. The auctioneer should provide proof of insurance upon the written or oral request of any consignor.

29. Terms of payment to consignor. Every contract issued by an auction house should clearly specify the terms of payment and remittance to the consignor. In no event, unless otherwise agreed to, should a consignor be paid later than 45 working days after a sale.

30. Service charges. Additional charges other than commissions, if any, paid by a consignor should be set forth specifically in the auction contract.

31. Consignor and bidder's right to demand arbitration. It should be disclosed to every consignor and bidder that they may elect binding arbitration against any member of the Professional Numismatists Guild, Inc., as to any dispute arising hereunder.

32. Returns to consignor. Every auction house should state in its consignment agreement when it shall return unsold goods to the consignor.

33. Applicability. These Guidelines are applicable to all member of the Professional Numismatist Guild, Inc.

34. Breach. Any breach of these Guidelines by a member of the PNG should be deemed a violation of the PNG Code of Ethics and may subject the violator to punishment in accordance with the by-laws, in addition to any legal rights or remedies that may be imposed.

35. Full disclosure. Each auctioneer–member of the PNG shall, in his dealings with the public, make full, complete, and conspicuous disclosure of all items necessary and material for a consumer to make an informed judgment concerning bidding, consigning, and conduct associated with any auction sale.

36. Regulations authorized. The PNG Board should from time to time issue or modify these regulations which should evidence industry practices and be binding upon auctioneer members.

How to Negotiate Auction Contracts

If the time comes to negotiate an auction contract and you find yourself with coins of substantial value to consign, you may want to seek legal counsel about a Uniform Commercial Code filing statement. This can be quite important in case the auction company declares bankruptcy, so that title to your coins is clear. In many states, you can file this online yourself, but I suggest you consult your attorney for further details.

Professional numismatists at a coin firm that was reputable during the many years it was in business examine some of their displayed specimens.

When you negotiate with an auction house, you also may want a cash advance. All these points are negotiable, depending on how much your coins are worth.

Many coin auction firms use a 15/10 commission structure—that is, they charge the consignor 10 percent of the "hammer price" for his or her coins and receive a 15 percent commission from each of the buyers.

If your holdings are sizable (and most auction firms won't accept a consignment worth less than a few thousand dollars), you should negotiate for a lower rate. Auction houses often reduce the seller's fee to 7 percent, 5 percent, or even less, especially if a dealer advisor is involved. In some cases I have gotten them to waive a seller's fee altogether in order to get a consignment. In cases where the auction house wanted a consignment badly enough, I have gotten them to even provide a rebate to the seller—giving him or her a share of the buyer's fees.

An Analysis of Prices Realized

Given the same coins, all the topnotch auction firms often get about the same price levels from their buyers, provided the coins don't fall into a niche area (e.g. high-grade low-pop registry set modern coins or supergrade red Lincoln cents) into which a particular firm soars above its peers. Usually the big difference is just how big a chunk of the proceeds you, the consignor, will receive and how much the firm will keep for itself. From your standpoint, how much you get—not what the coins sell for—is the real bottom line.

Let's say one firm wants to charge a 20 percent fee and won't give you any money in advance. Meanwhile, a competing firm is willing to guarantee you $800,000 on your $1 million collection, willing to give you a check for it up front without interest, and even willing to waive the seller's fee; in fact, this firm is willing to pay you a percentage or two of the buyer's fee. It seems pretty obvious which is the better deal from your standpoint. You certainly shouldn't listen to any hype you hear from the firm that wants to charge you 20 percent. These approximate numbers reflect an actual transaction I negotiated on a client's behalf.

What counts is the financial deal. It comes down to a matter of numbers, so pick the best ones. In some cases I negotiate for minimums (the minimum prices realized for certain coins) on behalf of my clients.

Private Sale

Private sale can be the most treacherous route of disposal for the non-knowledgeable or those who are not skeptical. When a dealer makes an offer on a collection, quite often it is for a fraction of the collection's true value. Dealers buy numismatic estates and count on their share of opportunities to buy collections below market value. One particular example of a large dealer buying a valuable collection for far below its market value occurred during the 1981 New Orleans ANA convention. A collection had to be liquidated, and two coin companies were invited to submit competitive bids. Each company knew of its rival's invitation. One firm, which we'll call firm A, was huge; the other, which we'll call firm B, was quite large. Both dealerships were (and are) considered highly reputable. Firm A has maintained a reputation of making offers which are not only "lowball," but laughably low. Firm B was aware of firm A making low offers and bid low also. One source in firm B told me that his firm's offer was so low that he was certain that firm A would end up buying the collection, no matter how low its offer was. But A's offer was so low that firm B was the successful bidder. Firm B was delighted to have been the winning bidder but was genuinely disturbed that any firm could have bid lower than it did.

This example points out the shortcomings of private sale. No matter how clever you may believe your sale strategy to be, dealers tend to pay very low prices for coins they are offered and can't immediately sell.

- Become knowledgeable about the marketability of your collection and each coin that it contains.
- Find out which dealers need the coins you have. If you have NGC or PCGS coins, call several market-makers.
- Approach several dealers for offers at a national coin convention. Competition is the main ingredient which will help you get the most money for your collection.
- Know the real value and grades of your coins; and don't let a dealer "talk down" your coins.
- Private sale might be required for those whose holdings fall below $2,500—the usual minimum dollar cutoff of medium-size and larger auction houses—and who don't want to consign to a small auction firm.

- Make your asking price on the high side and bargain if a dealer insists that you tell him how much you want for your coins. Try to get the dealer to make an offer instead of your telling him what your asking price is.
- To get a fair appraisal of your coins, tell the dealer that under no circumstances will you consider selling or buying coins from him or her. Offer to pay for the appraisal. This approach may only be theoretically sensible. Any dealer you show coins to, no matter what you tell him or her, knows that he or she has a chance of buying them.
- Be aware of the "percentage or sell appraisal" game. Heirs to numismatic estates sometimes fall prey to this tactic. This scheme is employed by a firm whose principals examine a collection and tell newly widowed people, orphaned children, or other bereaved people that they must pay a hefty percentage of the appraised value in appraisal fees—or sell the collection to the appraisers at their appraised value. The heirs are told this after the appraisal, and pressure is placed upon them to pay or sell.
- Beware of bad checks.

Direct Sale

Direct sale requires a great deal of work on your part, for you will be acting as the dealer. For those who have never been a dealer, it can be a devastating experience. But for those who are used to Internet, vest-pocket dealing, and having bourse tables at coin shows, it might prove profitable.

I strongly urge you not to pursue this method of disposal unless you have been or are a professional numismatist. There are too many risks, including theft, switching, and bad checks. And if you accept payment from strangers over the Internet, a bank or personal check could be more than just "bad"—it could be counterfeit. However, direct sale is one way of using competition to your advantage. If you run ads in the numismatic press or put your coins in your own Internet auction, you might be able to deal directly with the people who attend an auction or buy from the dealer you would sell your coins to.

One of the most popular direct sale methods employed by collectors is the classified section of the numismatic publications. *Coin World*, *Numismatic News*, *Coins* magazine, *Coin Prices*, and *World Coin News* offer classified advertising at very reasonable rates. You won't even have to collect sales tax if it's your personal collection, for sale of tangible, personal property is sales-tax exempt in most states. Before filling anyone's order, make sure the check more than clears—be sure the payee's bank confirms the check is genuine. Also, your asking price should be between wholesale and retail, and any description should be accurate.

Consignment to a Dealer for Over-the-Counter Sale

Dealers who have sold you coins that you want to sell back to them often suggest that you consign the coins to them. But consignment to a dealer for over-the-counter sale is a less viable means of disposal than the other methods described in this chapter. Unless you consign your coins to a scrupulously honest dealer, you can't be sure what price the coins were really sold for.

In certain cases this method may be a good strategy, for some dealers might place your coins within a few weeks. With other dealers, this might be a stall, the only way the dealer can give himself or herself more time to think about what you should do with your coins. If the dealer has grossly overgraded your coins, no auction house may accept them. And even if your holdings are considerable, when the quality is inferior (low circulated grades) and the dates aren't rare, it would be almost impossible to find any auction firm willing to accept your consignment.

Don't accept stalls. Give a deadline. When you consign to a dealer and don't get any coins sold by the deadline, insist that your coins be sold through a viable means, such as public auction. And in all cases, avoid consigning coins to a dealer for over-the-counter sale.

Sale of Slabbed Coins

The selling of slabbed coins should be approached on an individual basis. Grading is performed on a continuum. If a coin is a high-end 65, for example, you might want to break it out of the slab for the optimum price. If you believe a coin is a low-end example, you probably would get the best price by leaving the coin encapsulated.

If a coin is not certified, but has a good chance of receiving a grade beneficial to you (for example, a high-end 64 that just might get graded a 65), get it slabbed before you sell it. If you don't like the grade, you can break the coin out.

Cashing Out at the Top of a Bull Market

Buy low; sell high.

These simple, timeless words describe the lofty investment goals of everyone in virtually every investment scenario. But this is easier said than done. The psychological mindset of investors is to buy when everyone is buying: It's easy because there is strength in numbers. And the boldness required to buy when virtually everyone else is a seller seems about as easy to come by as the courage to catch a falling knife.

When the gold or silver dust settles, looking back, it is always easy to identify a market top—or a market bottom. Learning how to break away from the crowd and sell your coins at, or near, a market top is one of the most challenging concepts a coin investor must confront.

One of the first truisms to keep in mind is that being able to sell at the absolute top is extremely difficult, even for the most self-disciplined among us. In a bull market, coins will scale heights so disproportionate to reality that it is virtually impossible to pick the absolute top. Each irrational high will exceed the previous irrational high. What you *can* do with a reasonable expectation of success is to sell during the general period that coins are in favor. Sometimes you will get lucky and pick the top; other times, you will sell near the top.

Clients I have advised during previous bull markets (1980, 1986, 1989, 1992) achieved the best success rate, and risked the least, by using a "sale-average" approach. As with cost averaging, where you buy a little at a time over an extended period, you sell coins consistently over time. With sale averaging, instead of picking one moment in time to sell everything, you split up the sale over a selected period—maybe a month or two or even six months.

Skill in identifying a bull market top can be sharpened by examining the historical record of previous boom periods. The four years I mentioned earlier should each be examined in historical context, as should 1964—a watershed year for coins, when rolls reigned supreme and the curtain came down on the regular use of silver in everyday U.S. coins.

Two key bull market top indicators are extensive publicity about coins in the general press and gold bullion at a high level (try $1,000 an ounce!). Look for coins to appear as a near-mainstream investment or to be presented by financial service professionals as an "alternative to traditional modes of investment." Be very careful when you sense a prevailing attitude of "this time it's different." It's never different. The only thing different is the exact losses at the end of the bull market top when everything ends.

The key is to develop a successful action plan and try to remove your emotions from the process. Observe the signals, write down your plan—then stick to it. Try to avoid excessive trading, and don't let market players or arrogant dealers dissuade you. As values continue to escalate out of control, do not turn back. Don't feel disappointed that you missed an extra month or two of gains. After the boom is over, you can start to buy again: low. And just remember what to do during the next boom: Sell high.

– 16 –
DON'T LET UNCLE SAM PICK YOUR POCKET

Certain coin sellers stand out above the rest because of the volume of business they handle, the name recognition they enjoy, the longevity they have built up, or perhaps a combination of all these factors and others as well. American Numismatic Rarities LLC, Heritage Galleries & Auctioneers, Blanchard & Co., David Hall Rare Coins, Stack's, and Ira & Larry Goldberg Coins & Collectibles, Inc. are some of the leading sellers of coins that fall into this group.

Which of these well-known firms is the world's largest coin seller? The answer is none of the above. None of them, in fact, comes even close. That distinction belongs to a man better known to people around the planet for just about anything but: the venerable symbol of the U.S. federal government, Uncle Sam.

The United States Mint sells massive numbers of special coins and coin sets to the public every year at very substantial premiums—and though some of these products have held their value or even risen in value in the resale market, others have performed quite poorly. What's more, the Mint is conscious—and jealous—of its prerogatives as a coin seller: in January, 2005, it issued proposed federal regulations (31 CFR, part 92) to try to protect its franchise from imitation, which it clearly believes is not the highest form of flattery. Yet while Uncle Sam reaps millions of dollars a year from selling coins to collectors, he showed little concern for the hobby in 2004, when the federal government shut down the display of the National Numismatic Collection at the Smithsonian Institution in Washington, D.C. With the Mint as with any other coin seller, buyers should proceed with caution. Caveat emptor—buyer beware—remains extremely good advice.

1989 Bicentennial of the Congress half eagle. The U.S. Mint sold these gold coins for as much as much as $225 each during the year of issue. In Februrary 2005, these coins weren't worth much more than their gold bullion value: $110. *Photo courtesy U.S. Mint*

AFTERMARKET VALUE* OF SELECTED MODERN U.S. COMMEMORATIVE COINS

MODERN COMMEMORATIVE COIN	ISSUE PRICE	MARCH 2005 VALUE
DOLLAR COMMEMORATIVES		
1987-P Constitution Bicentennial, Uncirculated	$26.00	$7.00
1995-P Special Olympics World Games, Proof	35.00	18.00
HALF EAGLE ($5 GOLD) COMMEMORATIVES		
1987-W Constitution Bicentennial, Uncirculated	215.00	105.00
1987-W Constitution Bicentennial, Proof	225.00	105.00
1989-W Bicentennial of the Congress, Proof	225.00	105.00

* Prices listed were provided by Anthony J. Swiatek.

Nor is the sale of premium-priced collectibles the only way Uncle Sam sometimes picks the pockets of the nation's coin hobbyists. Federal taxes also take their toll—for while

Uncle Sam himself has no interest in collecting coins, he collects taxes avidly and has found a number of ways to turn hobbyists' profits into added internal revenue for himself. What's more, he's not alone: State and local taxmen also have their hands in collectors' pockets. It's possible to limit the damage, but those who fail to consider and insulate themselves against these tax implications run the risk of losing much of what's in their pockets—and also losing their shirts.

How the Mint Makes a Mint

As a result of the 50 State Quarters Program, the Sacagawea dollar, and the Westward Journey Nickel Series (special Jefferson nickels issued in 2004 and 2005 to commemorate the Lewis and Clark Expedition), the United States Mint has become more than ever a towering presence in the coin market—though strictly as a seller, rarely as a buyer. Each year, the Mint routinely sells hundreds of millions of dollars in premium-priced coins and coin sets to a broad cross-section of the American public, including not only established coin hobbyists but also non-collectors with little or no knowledge of rare coins. Then again, the coins being sold by the Mint are seldom truly rare; on the contrary, they are almost always struck in very significant numbers, well beyond the level that experienced collectors deem scarce, much less rare.

The supply equals the demand, at least initially; the Mint produces these items—notably Proof sets and commemorative coins—in quantities equal to the number of orders it receives. Those orders, generated by a huge mailing list and slick marketing gimmicks, used to far outstrip the core collector base for such material—until Americans by the millions started "collecting" the 50 State Quarters.

Experience has been an interesting teacher in this area, as the value of these products tended to fall for many years—often to just a very small fraction of the prices at which they were issued. However, with the release of the 50 State Quarters, Sacagawea dollars, and special Jefferson nickels—and all of the Mint products that go with them—many of these once lackluster "investments" began to appreciate in value substantially. A number of recently released Proof sets, in particular, have seen their values soar several hundred percent.

This is not to say that modern Mint products are now good investments. A phenomenon with surprising parallels to the coin boom of the early 1960s took shape in 1999 as a frenzy of collecting activity surrounded the release of the first 50 State Quarters. Once-shunned modern coins suddenly became the darlings of the coin marketplace as new collectors snapped up available Mint products that had been released over the last several years. The boom in modern Mint products taking place as of this writing is truly a craze, as much of the purchasing is being done by uninformed accumulators. Most importantly, these coins aren't rare: In some cases, millions were minted, and most have been preserved and are still available in their original high grade. Rules of thumb of coin investment that I have repeated time and again are: Coins which are common now will remain common for the foreseeable future. Coins which are scarce can become rare. Coins

This 1987 Prestige Proof Set had an issue price of $45, but can easily be purchased now for $25. A total of 435,495 sets were sold.

which are rare often become rarer. History shows that the coin boom of the early 1960s was followed by a bust and a long period of depressed prices—especially for modern Mint products.

"Collectible" coins sold by the U.S. Mint fall into four major categories: Proof sets, uncirculated coin sets (also known as "mint sets"), commemorative coins, and premium versions of the American Eagle gold and silver bullion coins. Let's take a closer look at each of these.

- Proof sets are annual coin sets containing one Proof—or specimen-quality example—of each regular U.S. coin being produced for circulation that year. The Mint produces Proofs by taking special, highly polished planchets, or coin blanks, and striking them multiple times at slower speed and with higher pressure than what it uses for standard-quality coins. The resulting coins emerge with mirror-like surfaces and very sharp detail, and often with attractive frosting on the devices, or raised portions of the design. The Mint also offers silver Proof sets, in which three coins—the dime, quarter, and half dollar—are made from a 90-percent silver alloy instead of the usual clad copper-nickel. Until being discontinued in the mid-1990s, two other options were the "Prestige set" and "Premier set," which contained the regular (non-silver) Proof coins plus a Proof example of one of the new commemorative coins being issued that year. (Prestige sets had more elaborate packaging than Premier sets.)
- Mint sets, like Proof sets, are issued each year—but they differ in two key respects. First, the coins in a mint set are a business-strike quality—that is, they are equivalent to the coins that are produced for circulation, although the Mint reportedly strives to include superior pieces in these sets. Second, a mint set contains one example of each different coin from each mint that issued that coin during the year. Thus, if cents are being struck

at both the Philadelphia and Denver mints in a certain year, the mint set for that year will include two different cents—one from each mint.

- Commemorative coins are coins produced specifically to honor some noteworthy person, place, or event, or to mark some special occasion. Typically, they are issued in just a single year and in limited quantities, and are sold to collectors and interested non-collectors for a price in excess of their face value. United States commemorative coins are divided into two categories, "traditional" and "modern," according to the time frame in which they were produced. "Traditional" commemoratives are those made by the U.S. Mint from 1892, when the program started, through 1954, when the Treasury Department suspended it because of recurrent abuses. "Modern" commemoratives are those produced by the Mint since 1982, when the program was revived following a hiatus of nearly three decades. Unfortunately, as I will show, the modern series also has been plagued by abuses.
- American Eagle bullion coins have been struck by the Mint each year since 1986. They were authorized by Congress as U.S. alternatives to existing bullion coins, such as South Africa's Krugerrand and Canada's Maple Leaf. By definition, a bullion coin is one whose price is based on the value of the metal it contains, rising or falling in direct and immediate response to rises or falls in the value of the metal itself. For example, the price of a one-ounce bullion gold coin is determined by taking the current market value of one ounce of gold and adding a small surcharge to cover the costs of producing and distributing the coin. In addition to the regular American Eagle coins, which are made in business-strike quality, the Mint has also offered special Proof versions of some or all of the coins. These are sold at premiums well above the value of the metal they contain, based upon the premise that their high quality and limited mintages give them added worth as collectibles.

Proof Sets' Price Performance

For many years, U.S. Proof sets were a marvelous buy. From 1950 through 1964, the Mint sold these sets for $2.10 apiece, and they never failed to rise—and stay-well above that level in the resale market. Many collectors ordered multiple sets from the Mint every year, keeping one or two for themselves and selling the rest at an immediate and often substantial profit. As word got around about this, even non-collectors started buying Proof sets every year and stashing them away as a "guaranteed" form of investment. They looked upon this as part of their retirement nest egg, or perhaps as a way to help put their children through college in years to come.

In truth, those Proof sets did provide good value for those who acquired them directly from the Mint, and all of them continue to be worth substantially more than their $2.10 issue price. For the most part, however, subsequent Proof sets didn't fare nearly as well until the start of the 50 States Quarter Program. The Mint suspended production of Proof sets in 1965 because it needed all of its equipment to combat a nationwide coin shortage—and when it resumed the program in 1968, the sets had a much higher price tag and much lower potential as an investment. The Mint more than doubled the issue price of the sets, from $2.10 to $5 apiece, thereby wiping out (and taking for itself) the immediate profit buyers had enjoyed in earlier years. Adding insult to this financial injury, the precious-metal content provided by previous Proof sets was now greatly reduced: The dime and quarter no longer contained any silver, and the half dollar had only 40 percent. Up to 1964, all three coins had been 90 percent silver. Thus, Proof set buyers were paying a lot more but getting much less in return. The 1968 Proof set did enjoy a speculative surge at the start, during which pent-up demand pushed its price well above $5 in the secondary market. But the bubble soon burst and for many years, the set was worth little or no premium over its issue price.

Since then, the Mint has raised the issue price of its regular Proof set seven more times. It provided something meaningful in return on only three occasions: in 1973, when it boosted the price from $5 to $7 to cover the inclusion of a new coin, the Eisenhower dollar; in 1999, when it included all five statehood quarters for that year, rather than just a single 25-cent piece as in previous years; and in 2004, when it furnished two different Jefferson nickels, rather than just one. There also was a hidden price increase in 1982, when the Mint kept the price the same despite the removal of the Susan B. Anthony dollar, whose production had been halted the previous year. In 1999, with the introduction of the 50 State Quarters Program, Proof set sales went through the roof—despite the increased issue price of $19.95 for the complete nine-coin set. (The Mint also offered a five-coin Proof set containing just the statehood quarters for an issue price of $13.95.) In 2000, the Mint added the Sacagawea dollar to its annual Proof set, increasing the number of coins per set to ten (the cent, nickel, dime, five quarter dollars, half dollar, and Sacagawea dollar); this time, the Mint actually added something (the new "golden dollar") without raising the price. By 2005, subsequent price hikes had raised the issue prices to $22.95 for the regular Proof set and $15.95 for a set of the five Proof state quarters.

Since 1999, the Mint has also offered an annual silver Proof set containing 90-percent-silver examples of the five state quarters issued during the year (along with a silver dime, a silver half dollar, and regular Proofs of all the other coins). This set carried an issue price of $31.95 in 1999, but by 2005 the Mint had raised the price to $37.95, ostensibly because of rising costs, including the higher cost of silver bullion. Actually, late-date silver Proof sets, first issued in 1992, have done quite well in the resale market. Some of the sets containing 50 State Quarters (those issued starting in 1999) have been big winners, in fact, for those who bought them directly from the Mint. The 1999 silver Proof set, for example, has a retail value of more than $250 as this is written in June 2005, while the 2001 silver Proof set is priced at more than $150.

Still, until recently, Proof sets produced since 1968 were far less successful in the secondary market than their predecessors. Every single Proof set prior to 1968 still commands a premium over its issue price, while many sets from 1968 onward were worth less than issue price until the spike brought about by the 50 State Quarters Program.

The Proof set craze since 1999 has caused a number of modern sets to experience very solid upward adjustments. The chart here illustrates just how dramatic some of those gains have been, looking at sets issued between 1995 and 1998.

This 1999 U.S. Mint 50 State Quarters Proof Set had an issue price of $13.95 and now retails for close to $100.

FIVE YEAR PRICE* COMPARISON OF SELECTED U.S. PROOF SETS, 1995–1998

PROOF SET (ISSUE PRICE)	JULY 23, 1999 VALUE	JULY 23, 2004 VALUE
1995-S ($12.50)	$38.00	$66.00
1995-S Silver (21.00)	40.00	80.00
1995-S Prem. Silver (37.50)	37.00	82.00
1996-S (12.50)	7.00	13.00
1996-S Pres. (57.00)	120.00	415.00
1996-S Silver (21.00)	24.00	41.00
1996-S Prem. Silver (37.50)	27.00	42.00
1997-S (12.50)	24.50	47.00
1997-S Silver (21.00)	23.00	75.00
1997-S Prem. Silver (37.50)	28.00	75.00
1998-S (12.50)	18.00	29.00
1998-S Silver (21.00)	24.00	32.50

**Prices listed are bid prices as recorded in* The Coin Dealer Newsletter.

Issue prices are from The Insider's Guide to U.S. Coin Values 2005, *by Scott A. Travers (Dell Publishing, 236 pages; $7.50)*

Modern Commemorative Coins

With a number of spectacular exceptions, modern U.S. commemorative coins have been losers—sometimes big losers—in the resale market. The primary reason is obvious: U.S. commemoratives issued since 1982 have been overpriced consistently by the government. Much of the blame for this lies not with the Mint but rather with Congress, which inevitably orders the Mint to tack hefty surcharges onto the prices of these coins and turn the money over to various "worthy causes." Typically, Congress mandates surcharges of $7 per coin on commemorative silver dollars and $30 per coin on half eagles (or $5 gold pieces). These charges amount to enforced contributions to the causes for which the coins are issued, such as the U.S. Olympic movement and the World Cup Soccer program. They also inflate the coins' issue prices well beyond the levels at which they otherwise could have been sold. Traditional U.S. commemoratives—those issued prior to 1955—also were sold at a premium, it's true, and also raised funds for organizations associated with their issuance. But during that era, the premiums were much smaller, often amounting to only two or three times face value.

Modern commemoratives often bring somewhat more than issue price in the resale market during the period just after their introduction. But supply soon overtakes demand as more and more of the coins are shipped to their buyers. There have been few sellouts to date, for until recently, Congress established mintage limits well above the levels it could—and should—have anticipated. At times, in fact, the limits have been ludicrously high. For instance, Congress authorized up to 10.5 million coins in three different denominations for the 1992 Olympic Games, and the Mint ended up selling fewer than 1.5 million. A similar scenario occurred the following year, when 10.75 million coins were authorized for the World Cup Soccer Games and fewer than 1.5 million were sold. In that case, the Mint even claimed to have lost money because of overproduction and other outlays tied to expectations of much higher sales.

Even with the success of the 50 State Quarters Program, many modern commemoratives still are turning in lackluster performances. There have been some notable exceptions, but these two-dozen or so "winners" are not representative of the entire series. One such exception was the 2001 American Buffalo commemorative silver dollar, which benefited from its popular design (copied from the beloved Buffalo nickel) and its relatively low mintage limit of 500,000. When the Mint declared a sellout, the coin surged in value. In June 2005, three-and-a-half years after its issuance, it was selling for more than $100—roughly three times its issue price.

The chart here illustrates how ten modern silver commemorative coins performed over a five-year period (1999–2004). Like the 2001 American Buffalo silver dollar, these are success stories.

FIVE-YEAR PRICE* COMPARISON OF SELECTED MODERN COMMEMORATIVES, 1996–1998

MODERN B.U. SILVER	JULY 23, 1999 VALUE	JULY 23, 2004 VALUE
DOLLAR COMMEMORATIVE		
1996-D Wheelchair Athlete	$55.00	$255.00
1996-D Tennis	48.00	205.00
1996-D Rowing	48.00	225.00
1996-D High Jump	48.00	255.00
1996-S Community Service	65.00	190.00
1996-D Smithsonian Anniversary	37.00	90.00
1997-P Botanic Garden	25.00	31.00
1997-S Jackie Robinson	24.00	60.00
1997-P Law Enforcement	30.00	120.00
1998-S Black Patriots	30.00	120.00

* *Prices listed are bid prices as recorded in* The Coin Dealer Newsletter.

Success stories are not the norm, however. The bottom line for buyers of modern U.S. commemoratives has been that, despite the extraordinary price performance of many of these issues, for others the resale value is far less than what the Mint charged for the coins in the first place. In 1987, for example, the Mint charged $225 for a Proof $5 gold piece celebrating the 200th anniversary of the U.S. Constitution and $215 for an Uncirculated specimen of the same coin. At this writing, eighteen years later, either coin can be purchased in the secondary market for not much more than $100—and the value has risen lately not because of heightened collector demand, but because the price of gold has been going up. In that case, the primary problem was overproduction: The Mint sold 651,659 Proofs and 214,225 Uncirculated specimens—far too many for the ultimate collector demand. That same year, the Mint sold 451,629 silver dollars commemorating the Constitution, charging an issue price of $26. At this writing, those have a fair market value of just $7 each. "The mintages of these coins were far too high, and the silver dollar's design leaves much to be desired," said Anthony J. Swiatek, a prominent dealer in commemorative coins, "For these reasons, there's little demand for these coins."

A 1990 silver dollar marking the centennial of Dwight D. Eisenhower's birth had an issue price of $25 and fifteen years later could be bought from a dealer for half that amount. A 1995 Proof silver dollar honoring the Special Olympics World Games was issued at $35 and ten years later had a retail value of $18. Nor are these isolated cases: In the long term, many modern commemoratives issued by the Mint (well over one hundred different coins so far) have plummeted below, and often well below, the issue price.

Professional numismatist Harvey G. Stack told a House of Representatives subcommittee in July of 1995 that in selling such coins to the public, the Mint should affix a warning label similar to the surgeon general's notice on cigarette packages. "These are not rare coins," Stack declared. "The only thing rarer than these modern commemoratives will be finding someone to give you a profit when you try to sell them." Then–Mint Director Phillip N. Diehl also appeared before the House subcommittee that day, and startled critics of the commemorative coin program with a frank admission. "The record is absolutely clear: These coins are not good investments," Diehl acknowledged. He said that they are authorized by Congress, and issued by the Mint, not as potential sources of profit for their purchasers, but rather as "keepsakes" and "mementos." In yet another eyebrow-raising comment, he told the gathering: "We compete with T-shirts."

Judging from the sorry track record of some of these modern commemoratives, T-shirts represent a better buy; at least their buyers have something to wear. All too often, purchasers of some of these commemoratives seem to be losing their shirts, at least in a figurative sense (and certainly in a financial sense). Beth Deisher, the savvy editor of the weekly hobby newspaper *Coin World*, told the same members of Congress that the secondary market for modern U.S. commemoratives was "weak to nonexistent." Said Deisher: "If a collector chooses to liquidate, it's difficult to find a buyer, and he or she can reasonably expect to receive from 50 to 65 percent of purchase price for an entire set of modern U.S. commemoratives."

Ten years after that testimony, the picture had brightened—largely because of the positive impact of the 50 State Quarters on modern Mint products, including some commemoratives. But whereas Proof sets seemed to be enjoying price gains virtually across the board, the advances were far less broad for commemoratives.

Traps Set by the Mint and How to Avoid Them

The U.S. Mint has been careful to avoid using the "I-word"—investment—in advertising and brochures soliciting orders for Proof sets, commemorative coins, and other "collectibles" in its growing product line. There can be little doubt, however, that these coins are represented as good values. "Keepsakes" and "mementos"—the words used by former Mint Director Diehl himself—are, after all, widely perceived as items well worth owning and passing on to future generations, at least in part because of their intrinsic worth. It's cynical for the Mint to suggest that profit motive does not play a major part in many buyers' decisions to purchase its products. On the contrary, Mint officials like to cite survey results showing that many buyers consider these products to be good investments. If buyers had purchased only the winners shown on the charts in this chapter, those purchases actually might have turned out to be good investments. Unfortunately, however, there have been many losers as well. And though the 50 State Quarters have propelled the market higher since 1999, the fact remains that for most of the last four decades, Proof sets and other Mint products have not performed well in the resale market—especially when inflation is considered.

The lesson is clear. People shouldn't buy coins—from the Mint or anyone else—until they learn enough to make an informed judgment. Uncle Sam is the nation's biggest coin seller, and his coins don't come with a price guarantee.

Tax Obligations, Record-Keeping, and Estate Planning

When they buy coins and coin sets from Uncle Sam, collectors at least have a fighting chance of coming out ahead. There's no such upside potential when it comes to paying taxes. But at least the downside risk—or exposure to financial loss—can be reduced. David L. Ganz, senior partner of the New York City law firm of Ganz & Hollinger, P.C., is a former president of the American Numismatic Association (1993–1995) and a prolific writer and author on tax and legal matters. Ganz, author of *The 90 Second Lawyer: Answers to Common Personal and Business Legal Questions* (Wiley, 1996), offers the following advice on sales and use tax:

> Consider the statements that follow generalizations. They may vary in your specific case. Always consult a competent tax professional before implementing any of the advice given here.
>
> **Sales Tax**
>
> Slightly fewer than half the states impose a sales tax on numismatic sales. The tax is usually a percentage of the gross sales price of the goods and is remitted by the dealer along with a sales tax return. In a typical over-the-counter sale of coins in those states where such tax is imposed, the dealer will add the sales tax to the invoice price.
>
> The taxable event for sales tax is an in-state retail sale. This leads to two common exemptions. First, sales tax is generally not due on wholesale (dealer-to-dealer) sales. Generally, a state will recognize this exemption only where the buyer holds a valid resale permit or certificate from that state or another state.
>
> Some states provide specific exemptions for bullion and certain numismatic items. Sales by out-of-state retailers are exempt from sales tax if (1) the customer orders goods directly from the retailer, and (2) the goods are shipped from outside the state and no in-state branch, office, outlet, or other place of business of the seller participates in the sale. The buyer may still be liable for a compensating use tax (see below).
>
> In certain states, some sales of coins are specifically exempted from sales tax for various reasons. States which do not apply sales tax to the sale of money exempt sales of "coins of the realm," defined as coins which remain legal tender of the United States or a foreign government. Others do not tax investment purchases and assume that purchases of over $500 or $1,000 are for investment. However, in many states, unless the sale falls into one of the common exemptions, sales tax will apply.
>
> **Use Tax**
>
> If you're a coin collector who lives in a state that charges sales tax on the purchase of rare coins, you'd better be prepared to pay a compensating use tax on rare coins that you purchase out of state. It's true in New York, New Jersey, and many other jurisdictions—though about half the states exempt numismatic purchases from sales tax. There's no sales tax or compensating use tax due on rare coins bought elsewhere and imported into a state that has no tax.

Sales and Use Tax Laws generally provides that an out-of-state person or entity that engages in regular and/or systematic solicitation that results in sales within the state of tangible personal property is deemed a vendor (and required to collect and remit sales tax) if the solicitation satisfies due-process and nexus requirements, i.e., regularly and systematically delivers property in the state.

A person who regularly or systematically solicits business through the distribution of catalogs (presumably including auction catalogs), advertising fliers, letters, or other means of solicitation, without regard to the location from which such solicitation originated, is presumed to regularly and systematically solicit business based on a substantiality test.

It is clear under existing law that conducting or participating in auction sales in New York one or more times each year will create a sufficient nexus. For example, a 1970 court decision involving Parke-Bernet Galleries held that bidding on an auction by phone would be sufficient contact for a New York court to have jurisdiction. Another court held that having a telephone number in a New York phone book with a foreign address was not a sufficient contact to give a New York court jurisdiction over a party.

Solicitation of business from an in-state location, with shipment from outside the state, will establish a nexus for a company. If a non-state-based company has offices in the state and solicits business in the same state where it has an office, that company will have to collect sales tax on all sales made to any state resident in any county (even if there is no office is in that county).

The constitutional test to establish a nexus with a state sufficient to require an out-of-state seller to collect and remit sales tax to that state is simply whether the facts demonstrate some definite link between that state and the person or entity from which it seeks to require to collect and remit the sales tax.

Marc D. Zand, CPA, is a partner in Shapiro Lobel LLP, a prominent New York accounting firm. Like others who discuss generic taxation issues, he advises that you always consult a competent tax professional in order to implement any tax strategies for your applicable situation. Zand writes about income tax, estate tax, and record-keeping:

Income Tax

Net income from the sale of coins is taxable. The deductibility of losses and expenses depends on whether you are classified as a collector, investor or dealer. Internal Revenue Code(IRC)§183 addresses this issue.

Under IRC§183, if an activity is not engaged in for profit, deductions will not be allowed unless the activity has gross income. However, deductions will be limited to the gross income from that activity. There is a presumption that if an activity reports a profit for three or more of the taxable years during five consecutive taxable years then the activity is considered to be an activity engaged in for profit. However, the Internal Revenue Service (IRS) can rebut this presumption. Under the IRS regulations, facts and circumstances will be taken into account to determine if an activity is engaged in for profit. The factors to be considered are the manner in which the taxpayer carries on the activity, the expertise of the taxpayer or the taxpayer's advisors, the amount of time and effort devoted by the taxpayer to the activity, an expectation that assets used will appreciate or the expectation of current or future profits, the taxpayer's experience in converting unprofitable activities into profitable enterprises, the taxpayer's history of income and losses in that activity, the amount of occasional profits, if any, that are earned, in relation to the losses, the taxpayer's financial status and elements of personal pleasure or recreation in conducting the activity (IRS Reg. §1.183-2(b)(1)–(b)(9)).

With respect to coins, upon an examination of a taxpayer's return, the IRS will apply the factors enumerated in IRC §183 to determine whether a taxpayer is functioning in a given year as a collector, as an investor, or as a dealer. If the classification for tax purposes is important to the taxpayer's overall income tax planning, they should pay careful attention to the various factors found in IRC §183 and take a forward thinking approach to the manner of handling their coins. Such attention will greatly improve the likelihood of sustaining their chosen position in an examination of their returns. The guidance of a competent tax professional will be invaluable in these instances, as the tax treatment of a given classification can vary greatly.

A collector is someone who buys and sells coins as a hobby. Collectors must report any gain on a sale of coins. A collector's loss on sale of coins is not deductible. For collectors as well as investors coins are considered capital assets. The profit on their sale is reported on Schedule D subject to a maximum federal tax rate of 28% in addition to state income tax, if applicable.

An investor is someone, determined by the factors found under IRC §183, who purchases coins as an investment; they report capital gain or loss on the sale of coins on Schedule D of their income tax returns. Expenses related to their coins are allowed as an investment deduction on Schedule A subject to the 2% adjusted gross income limitation. The investor might not receive a deduction for investment expenses if they do not exceed the 2% limitation. In addition, the benefits of these deductions might be limited due to the alternative minimum tax.

A dealer is someone who establishes that they have a trade or business. A dealer reports net gains as ordinary income, but can offset expenses and ultimately net losses from the activity against other income. Accordingly, dealers pay tax at the ordinary income tax rates when they have income.

Estate Tax

This is a complex area that involves careful planning during one's lifetime. A well- crafted estate plan can minimize the estate tax that is due. For year 2005, only estates that exceed $1,500,000 will be subject to federal estate tax. In addition, many states impose estate tax. Coin collections are subject to estate tax. Valuation of a coin collection is subjective and values can differ from expert to expert. Value can be diminished if a collection is put on sale in bulk. A professional numismatist should be consulted about valuing coins for estate tax purposes.

Record-Keeping Requirements

There are no set rules defining what constitutes the maintaining of records. However, it has been established that if there are questions from taxing authorities regarding the income reported or the expenses that were deducted, the taxpayer must furnish adequate records to substantiate all income and expenses. The burden of proof is on the taxpayer.

The dealer who operates a bona-fide business is subject to the highest record keeping standard. The dealer should maintain a general ledger, cash receipts and disbursements journal, bank statements, cancelled checks, credit card statements and receipts, sales invoices, purchase invoices, accounts payable, accounts receivable and inventory records. In addition, dealers must file a report to the IRS on Form 8300 and supply a copy to the buyer if one cash transaction or two or more related cash transactions exceed $10,000.

For the collector and investor the record-keeping requirements are not as stringent. Documentation to substantiate proof of cost basis, sales price and costs related to the coins must be maintained.

Generally, the federal statute of limitations to assess tax is three years. The statute can be extended for a variety of reasons and can vary by state, county and municipality. In the case of fraud, the statue of limitations is suspended and in theory a taxpayer can be subject to audit after a return is filed forever. Keeping records for at least ten years after the sale should cover the majority of situations.

Estate-Planning Secrets

David Ganz offers these additional shrewd pointers on estate planning gleaned from his many years of experience as a street-smart lawyer in the coin trade. Some of Ganz' opinions are controversial and open to interpretation. Accordingly, I advise you to consult with competent professionals before following any of these guidelines:

- Have a comprehensive list of your collection. The list should be complete with acquisition costs, and, if esoteric, your best estimate of the value. This is perhaps the most important thing that any collector can do. You know your own collection best of all.
- Hire appraisers who know the details of the basis of valuation. If you've come into a numismatic estate, hire a skilled appraiser—someone who is sensitive to not only the value of individual items, but also the way in which stock can be valued to lower your estate tax.
- Realize that there are multiple ways that coins and other collectibles can be valued. The liquidation value differs from the long-term disposal valuation. The IRS will allow various techniques to be used; you can pick the one that works best for your own situation.
- If your coins are held in a safety deposit box, explore having that safety deposit box not in your individual name. Individual boxes are frequently sealed at the time of the death of a holder. Corporate boxes, like corporations themselves, are "forever."

- Take the time to have a will prepared. The will should be one that is designed to minimize the total taxes that you, your spouse, and heirs will pay. Sometimes it means paying a little more now for a lot less later. If you live in a jurisdiction where probate is time-consuming or expensive, consider the option of a living trust for your collection, and perhaps other assets.
- A letter of disposition often works best. If a will states, "I give my $250,000 coin collection to my friend, Bill," it is likely to create interest from tax authorities and others. There's a better approach: a letter of disposition. A typical will clause that accomplishes this easily, without undue publicity, and in close to anonymous fashion, might read as follows: "All of my personal property, including my coin collection, should be disposed of by my executor in accordance with the instructions that I have left in a written letter that is kept in my safe deposit box." If you change your mind about the disposition, you can change the letter easily.
- Require competitive bids before a single coin is sold. How you wish to dispose of your coins is up to you, but there are some general guidelines. First, unless you have a long and established relationship with someone in the field, if an outright purchase is contemplated, you should require three separate bids to be prepared. This avoids the possibility of collusion, and, more importantly, tends to maximize the possibility of receiving the most value for the collection.
- If you decide to have the collection auctioned, it is not necessary to have all of it sold by the same auctioneer. Not all auctioneers specialize in the same areas. Some, for example, are more competent in high-quality U.S. coins than they are in ancient coins. As a collector or investor, and a purchaser of coins, you know this inherently. But your heirs won't unless you tell them. So do that in a letter to the executor or in a side letter to someone who has a power of attorney to act on your behalf. You can even negotiate estate commissions, in advance, while you are alive.

Coins and Retirement Plans

According to Dr. D. Larry Crumbley, KPMG Endowed Professor at Louisiana State University, the Federal tax laws provide substantial tax benefits for qualified retirement plans. Although rare coins and other collectibles are not allowed in many qualified retirement plans, since 1987 the American Eagle gold and silver coins have been allowed in Individual Retirement Accounts (IRAs).

In 2004, $3,000 could be placed into an IRA, and this amount jumps to $4,000 in 2005. A married couple can place a total of $8,000 into an IRA in 2005. For a traditional IRA, these amounts are deductible, and the assets grow tax-free inside the IRA, becoming taxable when you retire and withdraw the funds.

Crumbley, the author of many books and articles about collectibles and coins, says that an IRA may hold U.S.-minted gold and silver coins acquired after 1986, U.S.-minted platinum proof and bullion coins, and any coins issued under the laws of any state acquired after November 10, 1988. "American Eagle U.S. gold or silver bullion coins are allowable as IRA acquisitions, as well as any gold, silver, platinum or palladium of a fineness equal to or exceeding the minimum fineness that a contract market requires for metals which may be delivered in satisfaction of a regulated futures contract," he stated. "But this bullion must be in the physical possession of the trustee," Crumbley cautioned. He cited "IRC Section 408(m)(3)(B)."

The purchase of coins and other collectibles by an individually directed account in a tax-qualified plan is treated as a distribution (e.g., taxable). "So rare coins may *not* be used in self-directed plans," Crumbley pointed out, "but they might be used in so-called managed plans." *This is a highly subjective area that requires the advice of your tax advisor. Do not place coins into any retirement plan without competent legal and tax counsel first.*

In a paper entitled "Yes, Virginia, Rare Coins Can Be Used as Pension Plan Investments," Crumbley writes:

> Rare coins as well as American Eagles may be placed into many corporate and self-employment retirement plans. . . . A defined benefit pension plan (corporate or Keogh plan) may purchase rare coins because they do not provide for individual accounts. But a defined contribution plan (i.e., money purchase pension plan or profit-sharing plan) may be "individually directed." . . . These individually directed plans are rare, however.
>
> Sometimes, the participant may also be the trustee. Here, the person wears two hats, and he must be careful. But a self-trusteed plan is not the same as an individually directed account. The trustee-employee must direct the investments into rare coins as a trustee of the plan and not as a participant. When the "collectibles prohibition" was passed in 1981, the Joint Committee on Taxation indicated that "a participant's account in a qualified defined contribution plan is not individually directed" merely because "the participant, acting as a fiduciary with respect to the plan, directs or otherwise participates in the investment of plan assets." Be very careful here, however, and consult your tax advisor.
>
> Even for some self-directed plans there is still a dangerous escape route. The law allows a participant to borrow from the retirement plan. The borrowed monies could then be invested in collectibles outside the retirement plan. A qualified plan loan should be documented with a note signed by the participant containing a rate of interest and a repayment period within five years. A retirement plan must be created by an employer for the exclusive benefit of employees or their beneficiaries. Under a "prudent man" concept, IRS specifies four investment requirements for meeting this exclusive benefit requirement:

- The cost of the investment must not exceed the fair market value at the time of purchase.
- A fair return commensurate with prevailing rates must be provided.
- Sufficient liquidity must be maintained to permit distributions in accordance with the terms of the qualified plan.
- The safeguards and diversity that a prudent investor would adhere to must be present.

Some tax experts offer caveats on the concept of borrowing money from your retirement plan. "Not all types of plans allow loans," said widely known tax attorney Frederick W. Daily, author of *Tax Savvy for Small Business* (Nolo Press, 2004). "Even if a loan is allowed by law, there is the issue of whether it is ever prudent to borrow from your retirement for purposes other than to provide for your family's health and shelter needs," Daily stated.

Daily says that if the IRS ever rules against the legitimacy of your loan, the taxes and penalties can be brutal. "So, in any case, do not attempt to borrow money from your retirement plan without getting the advice of a good tax professional," Daily suggests.

Contributing Coins to Charity

If you donate coins to charity, there are guidelines for maximizing tax benefits. Highly respected Harvard-educated coin lawyer Armen R. Vartian of Manhattan Beach, California, presents a few of these guidelines:

- Don't donate coins which have decreased in value since you purchased them. The IRS will not allow you to deduct your loss. It is better to sell the coins and donate the proceeds so that you may deduct the investment loss and still make the contribution.
- Don't donate coins which you have held for one year or less. The IRS considers such coins "ordinary income property," and your deduction will be limited to your basis in the property (i.e., you're not allowed to deduct the full fair market value if the coins have appreciated since you purchased them).
- Keep proper records. The IRS's requirements depend upon the amount of the deduction you are claiming. Get a receipt from the charity (preferably one that has an exempt function related to coins) showing its name and address, contribution date, and a reasonably detailed description of the coins. If you are deducting between $500 and $5,000, also file IRS Form 8283 with your tax return. If deducting over $5,000, file Form 8283 and also get a signed written appraisal of the coins, preferably one from a qualified numismatist and less than 60 days old at the time of your donation (appraisal fees may be deductible as miscellaneous expenses on Schedule A).

Like-Kind Exchanges When Coins Have Increased

If you act as an investor in coins (as opposed to a hobbyist or coin dealer), here's a potential tax saver when your coins have gone up in value. If you prefer not to sell your coins with low potential (or those that are maxed out) outright, you might consider trading them for other coins that you believe possess greater potential. Tax laws permit like-kind exchanges involving rare coins. These are particularly useful in cases where your coins have gone up in value since you purchased them and you would face the prospect of being taxed on your gains if you were to sell them. By trading them for coins of similar value, you could defer the tax obligation on such gains.

Suppose you bought a coin for $1,000 and it went up in value to $5,000. Rather than simply selling the coin and having to pay taxes on your $4,000 profit, you could trade it for other coins whose current market value totals $5,000—coins that might be at the bottom of their price cycle now. Later, if those coins went up in value to $10,000, you could repeat the process. In fact, you could keep repeating it over and over for many years, all the while postponing your day of reckoning with Uncle Sam.

Eventually, of course, taxes must be paid on any gains that are realized. But if you played your cards right, you could postpone the actual sale of the coins—and payment of the taxes—until you were retired and in a lower income tax bracket, thereby greatly minimizing your obligation. Or you could escape taxes by leaving the coins to your heirs—meaning the coins would be included in the value of your estate. Eventually, of course, taxes may be due on any gains that are realized by the heirs when the coins are sold.

In recent years, losses have been more common than gains for people investing in coins, so the tax-deferral advantage of like-kind exchanges hasn't been as useful as it was in the past. In fact, there are often circumstances in this kind of hostile market climate where it might be preferable from a tax standpoint to sell coins and claim a loss, rather than trade them. You should check with your tax advisor, preferably a competent certified public accountant or tax attorney, to see which approach is better for you.

Many tax professionals advise caution in using the like-kind exchange approach described here, as some believe that only coins of the same metal may be legally exchanged (e.g., gold for gold, not gold for nickel). Further, there have been court precedents that establish that bullion for coins, or vice versa, is not allowed as a like-kind exchange, even if the bullion and the rare coins are of the same metal. Again, don't try any of this without first obtaining personalized tax advice.

A Tax-Slashing Strategy When Selling at a Loss

If you treat your coin holdings as an investment, instead of acting as a hobbyist or a coin dealer, here's another potential tax saver when selling coins at a loss. Many people have a psychological aversion to selling their coins at a loss. They may say to themselves, "Hey, I paid $10,000 for these coins. I still want to own them, and I'm not going to sell them for $1,500." Coin dealer Michael R. Fuljenz has come up with an interesting strategy that enables such people to enjoy the tax benefits of their loss without giving up the coins—at least not for very long. Fuljenz has advised clients in this kind of situation to sell such coins to their favorite dealer at the fair market wholesale value, then wait 30 days and buy comparable coins at the fair market retail value then in effect.

Let's say you paid $10,000 for a coin portfolio in 1989 and its fair market wholesale value today is just $1,500. Using the strategy formulated by Fuljenz, you could sell that portfolio to your favorite dealer for $1,500, enabling you to claim an $8,500 loss on your current or future tax returns. The tax code allows you to take capital losses on investments to the extent of any capital gains you have in that year, and up to an additional $3,000 against your ordinary income. So if you did not have any gains for the year of the sale, you would get a $3,000 tax deduction that year—and $5,500 of loss to carry over and claim in future years' tax returns.

What if you still wanted to own these coins? Fuljenz says you could buy back similar coins 31 days later for perhaps $2,000. It's essential, Fuljenz says, to avoid what tax rules call a "wash sale"—that is, the sale and repurchase of the same investment within 30 days. The IRS regulation governing this kind of transaction is Internal Revenue Code Section 1091.

I strongly recommend that you check with your accountant or financial advisor before engaging in Fuljenz's strategy. It's an interesting concept, though, and one that Michael Fuljenz has recommended to many of his customers.

– 17 –
MYTHS THAT CAN COST MILLIONS

It isn't always wise to accept conventional wisdom. All too often, people place blind faith in sage-sounding dictums that seem like solid truths but which are, in fact, merely myths and fallacies beneath a false veneer.

This is true with coins, just as with everything else. Frequently, the myths that masquerade as wisdom in the field of numismatics are teachings that have been heard for many years. Long repetition has given them an aura of inevitability—even infallibility. But no matter how many times it is repeated, a myth remains an illusion, and that's another way of saying it's a lie.

Recognizing fallacies isn't always easy. Some enjoy wide currency and thus convey a sense of false security. Even common sense may not be a perfect guide in helping you distinguish fact from myth. Still, it is essential to exercise good judgment—basic common sense—in making important decisions regarding coins. And above all, it is vital to keep an open mind: Question, analyze, and evaluate everything—even so-called axioms that seem at first like gospel truth.

Here are 6 myths that mislead the unwary in today's coin marketplace:

Myth No. 1: *Certified coins assigned the same grade are worth the same amount of money.*

This is simply not true. As I explained in chapters 4 and 5, coin grading is performed on a spectrum or continuum. Some coins rank at the high end of a grading bracket, very nearly qualifying for the next-higher level; others fall at the low end and just miss dropping to the next-lower level; and still others land right in the middle. It would be naïve to assume that buyers and sellers would view—and value—these coins precisely the same. Logic dictates that a high-end Mint State-65 coin, being almost a full grade better than a low-end 65 coin, should bring a higher price, and in practice it does: The difference in market value between two such pieces frequently amounts to many hundreds of dollars. It takes sophistication and a keen knowledge of grading to spot the difference at times, but at other times the contrast may be quite obvious.

The people who write price guides and create the pricing structure have given serious thought to listing coin values—for certain grades, at least—by showing a range of prices, rather than using a one-price-fits-all structure. Let's say a certain coin is listed at $900 in the grade of 64 and $2,000 in 65. It would probably be more accurate to list a price range of $700 to $1,400 for the 64 grade, and $1,600 to $3,000 for the 65. The point is, a coin's desirability—and value—can jump dramatically not only from one grade to the next, but also within a given grade. Coin grading is not an exact science, it's an informed opinion. People who grade coins are craftsmen, not scientists. So in analyzing a grade to determine what something is worth, we need to proceed with flexibility, not precision, and give weight not only to the big picture but also to the small but meaningful nuance.

Myth No. 2: *Price-performance data confirm that rare coins are a marvelous investment.*

In 1978, Salomon Brothers, Inc., the respected Wall Street brokerage house, began including rare coins in its annual surveys of popular investment vehicles. To the delight of the nation's coin dealers, these surveys found coins to be among the very best performers being tracked; in fact, they showed that over the long haul, rare coins had outperformed stocks, bonds, real estate, and other more traditional forms of investment. Soon, these reports were being trumpeted loudly not only by legitimate coin dealers but also by less reputable sellers drawn to the field by the lure of quick profits. This, in turn, set the stage for some serious reversals of fortune, both individually and collectively; as new investors made ill-advised purchases from seemingly omnipresent telemarketers, they helped sow the seeds for the downfall of the coin market as a whole. Initially, however, the wide dissemination of the Salomon surveys' findings created the impression among the general public that rare coins were indeed a great investment, and many continued to cling to that belief even when coin prices plunged and remained low for years thereafter.

The fact is, many coins were good investments at the outset of the Salomon Brothers' studies; in the coin and bullion boom of 1979 and 1980, high-grade coins enjoyed an astronomical rise in market value. Many had experienced healthy gains already during the 10-year period preceding coins' inclusion in the surveys (a period Salomon covered, retroactively, by using historical data). Unfortunately, though, the Salomon survey of coins was flawed from the very outset because its conclusions were based on a "market basket" of coins too small and too narrowly drawn to accurately reflect marketplace conditions as a whole. The 20 coins in this basket consisted overwhelmingly of collector-type coins in Mint-State but less than gem condition—hardly representative of a market where the action, throughout the 1980s, was in very high-grade investor-type coins. What's more, there was not a single gold coin among the 20, despite the significant role played by gold coins in the marketplace.

By the early 1990s, abuse of the Salomon surveys had caused such serious problems that the Federal Trade Commission pressured the firm to remove rare coins from its studies.

It was probably just as well: By then, it was amply clear that far from being great investment vehicles, many rare coins had been doing dismally.

Beyond the inadequacies of the Salomon Brothers studies, price-performance data tracking rare coins inevitably reflect another major deficiency that renders them highly misleading, if not downright meaningless: They fail to give proper weight—and often give no weight at all—to the changes in grading standards that occurred during the period they are covering. Well-known market analyst Maurice H. Rosen, widely cited in this book, has documented this problem in great detail. Rosen has amassed compelling evidence that grading standards industry-wide tightened dramatically in the mid-1980s, effectively reducing the grades of many coins several levels—or even more—below the ones assigned in earlier years.

We're seeing the opposite phenomenon today: Grading standards have actually loosened somewhat at some of the certification services, so coins that were processed prior to the change may now be undergraded in relation to the companies' current standards. This can have the effect of making a given coin—or even the overall marketplace—seem to be doing worse than it actually is. Let's say that in 1989 you bought a coin that PCGS had certified as Proof-64 and you paid the going price of $3,000. Today, the price in Proof-64 may be only $1,000, so on paper you seem to have lost $2,000. But that coin might very well be Proof-65 by current grading standards at PCGS, and if it had been a premium-quality 64 coin in 1989, it might even merit a Proof-66 grade today. In that event, it might be worth close to what you paid for it—say, $2,500 or so—if it were removed from its 1989 holder, resubmitted to PCGS, and graded by today's looser standards.

The lesson from all of this is clear: Price-performance data can easily be manipulated to support whatever point the company or person disseminating the data is trying to make. Rare coins can indeed be an excellent investment—even in adverse marketplace conditions—if their purchase is approached with imagination, prudence, and a well-conceived strategy. But price-performance data, in all too many instances, don't confirm a thing except the devious nature of their compilers.

Myth No. 3: *The coin market moves in regular, predictable cycles.*

It's a long-established article of numismatic faith that what goes up in the coin market will come down—and vice versa—in patterns very nearly as immutable as night following day. The fact is, however, that everything you've been taught about coin-market cycles is probably wrong today. The market has broken free from the patterns of the past, and the only thing really predictable now is that from here on, its ups and downs will be unpredictable.

The conventional wisdom relating to market cycles is rooted primarily in what took place during the 1960s and 1970s. Throughout those two decades, and right into the early 1980s, boom and bust cycles followed each other with dependable regularity at intervals of three to six years, varying only in the intensity of their highs and lows. We had a market top in 1964, when the roll-buying binge hit its peak. A down-cycle then set in, and we had a market bottom in 1967. The market recovered in the early 1970s, building to a top in 1974, then slipped back and hit another bottom around the start of 1977. Fueled by inflation and the red-hot market in gold and silver bullion, the coin market hit a spectacular top at the start of 1980 before falling back to a bottom in 1982.

The market hit a top again in 1986, and under normal conditions it would have begun sliding thereafter, possibly bottoming out in 1988 or '89. But artificial stimuli kept the boom going and made it even stronger. First came the advent of certified coins in 1986 with the establishment of PCGS, which was followed closely by the founding of its rival, NGC. Then came the influx of Wall Street money, lured by the prospect that certified coins would make it easy to buy and sell coins much like stocks. Up to that point, the coin market's booms and busts had always come in response to what Maurice Rosen calls "economic justification"—inflation pushing coin prices higher, for example, and disinflation pushing them down. But this time, the boom was artificial, and just as it's not nice to fool with Mother Nature, it also can be risky to tamper with natural rhythms in marketplace economics. When the overlong market boom finally hit its top in May 1989, it gave way to a bust that proved to be longer and deeper than anyone imagined at the outset.

As this is written, the market is doing well, thanks in no small measure to higher precious metals prices and widespread interest generated by the statehood Washington quarters. But beyond the short term, its future is by no means crystal-clear. What does seem clear is that regular market cycles are unlikely to return in their previous form. Too much has changed, not only within the coin market itself, but also in the wider investment marketplace. Investors today are much better informed and much more discriminating than their counterparts of the past, and they have a much broader selection of money-making vehicles to choose from—an immense supermarket shelf of financial products. They're unlikely to follow blindly when promoters tout coins as incredible investments; they'll demand to see tangible evidence—and that may not be easy to provide, since coins' price-performance record has now been tarnished. Unless and until the coin market gets on track again, the emphasis is likely to be on short-term trends and short-term gains, not on the long-range picture that gave coin buyers such comfort and security in the past.

Myth No. 4: *A rare coin's value varies in direct proportion to its population.*

Low mintages and high prices often go hand in hand. Thus, it's not surprising that people see big dollar signs when they come across coins with small numbers next to them in the population and census reports issued by the certification services. These reports, published periodically, list the number of pieces graded by the companies for each different date of each different coin in every grade.

Often, low figures in population reports do indeed point to coins of great rarity and value. But rarity is not the only significant factor in determining how much a coin is worth. Demand is important, too: Coins may have extremely low populations and yet command surprisingly modest premiums if the number of people pursuing them is similarly small. Then, too, numbers can and do lie. Far from suggesting great rarity, a low population actually might reflect extreme commonness: A high-mintage modern coin, for example, might have a low population in one of these reports because so few people found it worthwhile to send any in for certification. Because their premium value is so small, coins such as this aren't worth the bother and expense of being certified.

Myth No. 5: *Certified coins always represent the best deal.*

This is just not so. In the first place, grading and pricing are two separate issues, and although certification may give you reassurance regarding the grade of a coin, it doesn't guarantee that you're getting a good deal. No matter how accurately a coin may be graded, you'll get a lousy deal if it isn't fairly priced. I discussed this point in detail in chapter 9.

Beyond this, nobody's perfect—including the grading experts at the certification services—and more than a few of the coins housed in these companies' "slabs" are overgraded or otherwise problem-plagued. Some, for example, were artificially toned before being submitted to the services in order to enhance their apparent level of preservation, and these somehow eluded detection by the experts. Getting stuck with one of these coins certainly wouldn't be a good deal. The companies have been diligent about buying back their mistakes, and their graders are getting better all the time, so the number of new mistakes has declined dramatically. Still, the marketplace has to deal with all the mistakes of the past—and there are many.

Myth No. 6: *The "slabs" used to house certified coins are vacuum-sealed and contain no air.*

This is a common misconception. For the most part, the coins encapsulated in plastic by the certification services aren't vacuum-sealed but sonically sealed. NGC's founder, John Albanese, explains that sonic sealing is accomplished by using high-pitched sounds to convert energy into heat, and then using that heat to fuse together the hard plastic holder's two halves. Vacuum-sealing wouldn't be practical, Albanese says, because it would require pressing the plastic right up against the coin, much as plastic wrapping is pressed against frozen turkeys in a supermarket, and that would damage the coin. Thus, while they are airtight, coin slabs are not air-free.

– 18 –
ENDANGERED COINS—AND HOW TO RESCUE THEM

> Several years after the introduction of polyvinylchloride (PVC) to the coin storage market, some collectors began to notice greenish or bluish flecks and stains on their coins stored in PVC holders. When viewed with magnification, these flecks appeared to be thick, sticky, colored liquid which rested on the coin surface, or else appeared as patches of colored stains. Often, when the coin was removed from the holder, a green or blue "ring" remained on the plastic where the coin rim pressed against it . . . In extreme cases, coins "stuck" against the plastic so firmly that they had to be pried off, with severe damage resulting to the coin . . . Recently, due to the increase in knowledge about all plastics, it has been determined that the blue/green colored flecks and stains . . . [are] due to chemicals in the PVC bleeding out of the film onto the coin.
>
> —George Klabin
> *"Understanding PVC Damage"*

The world is a dangerous place for valuable coins. Hazards lurk in the air, in storage containers, and even on collectors' fingertips. Exposure to these hazards can subject a rare coin to irreparable damage that can greatly diminish its value. Fortunately, there are ways to guard against such risks and maintain these coins in their original, pristine condition—preserving their considerable value. Even if damage has begun from the floods of a hurricane, it is often possible to minimize its extent or even reverse the harm. There also are ways of protecting coin investments by storing them properly. All these prudent steps can make the world a much safer place for rare coins.

"Cleaning" is a term with positive connotations, but in some cases it can be extremely negative when applied to coins. Unknowledgeable individuals, in an effort to improve their coins' appearance, often end up causing devastating damage to their collectibility and resale value. When performed by someone skilled, however, certain types of cleaning can actually retard some destructive processes and enhance a coin's appearance.

Some mild types of coin cleaning under some circumstances might improve a coin's appearance. Other types of coin cleaning could destroy a Mint State coin's premium value.

Residue and unattractive toning make this 1897 Proof Barber quarter particularly undesirable and an "endangered coin." Coins caught in flood waters often look like this. *Photograph courtesy Numismatic Conservation Services LLC*

Using professional conservation techniques, the residue and unattractive toning were removed, and the final result is a rescued coin—an attractive specimen with an exceptional cameo contrast between its fields and devices. *Photograph courtesy Numismatic Conservation Services LLC*

All coin cleaning has to be done with care; coins are delicate and susceptible to damage if mishandled in the least. My advice is to leave coin cleaning of any kind to the experts, unless you have or can become competent at cleaning by practicing on non-premium-value coins.

There are two types of coin cleaning: abrasive and nonabrasive.

Abrasive Cleaning

This is the most harmful type of coin cleaning. A coin's grade is based primarily on how much wear it has if it's a circulated coin and how well it has been preserved and looks if it is a Mint State coin. Abrasive cleaning removes part of the coin and thus lowers the grade. Furthermore, abrasive cleaning activates the metal's oxidation process. Even if a coin is shining brightly one day, the next day it could turn black from having had its metal activated.

The very definition of abrasive indicates it is something to which you would not want to subject your valuable coins. Abrasive cleaning removes the top layer of metal of a coin. Using abrasive cleaning is like subjecting a coin to circulation! From the friction or rubbing on the coin's surface from cleaning, part of the coin's design is worn away

Any process is abrasive which requires that you use a wire brush to clean your coins. Also, any process that involves treating coins with acid is abrasive. The same effect can be achieved chemically that a wire brush achieves. You should never clean any coin abrasively. Coins discovered at sea as part of an underwater treasure are sometimes cleaned abrasively so that they can be identified. *This is the only acceptable numismatic use for abrasive coin cleaning.*

"But the products designed for abrasive cleaning seem so tempting . . ."

Don't listen to what the label says. If you have to use a wire brush and/or a harsh chemical, the method is abrasive.

I strongly urge you to put together your own small laboratory of coin-cleaning chemicals for experimenting on coins from circulation. You'll then become familiar with the effects of certain coin cleaners. If you do experiment, follow the warnings on the label, and always wash your hands well after each use. Wear gloves if possible during your experimentation. Remember, always experiment with coins which are not valuable.

Cleaning That Is Abrasive Only Some of the Time

Acidic 'Dips'

Some coin cleaners—for example, those designed to remove light tarnish—are mildly abrasive. Acid-type solutions used for "dipping" are often abrasive. These "dips" are controversial because they are used so often. Acids tend to leave the surface of a metal looking pitted, not scratched, as physical abrading does. A split-second dipping might not be very harmful, but immersing a coin for more than a couple of seconds could be. Do not dip any valuable coins until you have mastered the technique of dipping. Years ago, the ANA Certification Service made it a practice not to state that a coin was dipped, even if it knew the coin had been, because, authenticators claimed, dipping cannot be proven in a court of law.

Many century-old coins have been dipped. It just isn't possible for 100-year-old silver coins to be as brilliant as when they were minted. Toning is a natural part of a coin's aging process.

Each coin has many little flow lines which can be seen most clearly under a scanning electron microscope. These flow lines result from the minting process and are responsible for a Mint State coin's reflective properties. The depth and quality of these tiny little lines produce a coin's gleam. If these little lines are flattened or eliminated, a Mint State coin loses luster. It's like flattening the waves on an ocean; the ocean wouldn't reflect light at every angle from which you viewed it.

Abrasive cleaning removes these flow lines; mildly abrasive cleaning reduces their intensity. Anthony Swiatek studied this subject in his *Swiatek Numismatic Report*. Swiatek had photographs taken of a 1964 Kennedy half dollar—half of which had been dipped for fifteen seconds—under a half-million-dollar scanning electron microscope. The results caused a furor in the numismatic industry.

Look at the surface of an undipped area of that Kennedy half shown here. It is magnified 3,500 times. Notice the hundreds upon hundreds of little lines. These are Mint-

Scanning-electron microscopic view of the undipped portion, magnified 3,500 times. Many lines which the coin was made with are visible and cause the coin to reflect light. *Photograph courtesy* The Swiatek Numismatic Report

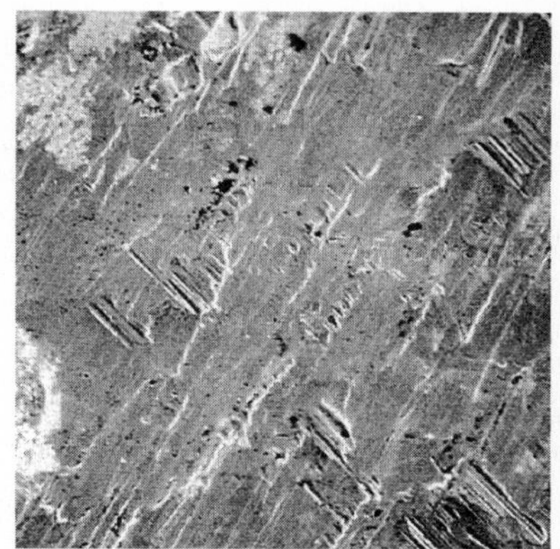

Scanning-electron microscopic view of the dipped portion (dipped for 15 seconds), magnified 3,500 times. The lighter color accounts for the toning having been removed. The acidity of the dip caused the lines to be removed, thus lowering the quality of the coin's luster. *Photograph courtesy* The Swiatek Numismatic Report

made flow lines, and they are responsible for luster. Now look at a dipped area of the half dollar shown. The color appears lighter because the cleaning removed the toning. Most important is the reduction of intensity and quality of those little lines, which have been smoothed out as a result of the dipping.

Some people may feel these results are inconclusive because coins are typically dipped for only a few seconds. However, coins re-tone and are dipped repeatedly.

Dipping is cumulative; coins lose another tiny layer from each dipping. Further, some coins have no high-quality flow lines to begin with (such as from a poor minting process, or a weak strike). If these coins are dipped, their grade will be lowered substantially. Over-dipped coins are lackluster and very unattractive. The appearance of some coins can be improved by dipping, but you have to know coin surfaces very well to know which coins can be dipped and which will lose luster.

Do not dip coins unless you are very experienced at doing so. Some coins have a surface not conducive to dipping and will be downgraded if dipped. At least 90 percent of all brilliant, untoned Mint State silver dollars have been dipped.

Hairlines

Hairlines are patches of parallel striations that interrupt a coin's reflective properties. Hairlines do not appear on Proof coins exclusively, but their presence is most detracting on Proof coins, because these are supposed to have fully reflective surfaces. Hairlines are often caused by light cleaning, such as might be done with a facial tissue to remove a fingerprint.

Blowup of hair lines on a Proof 1861 Liberty Seated quarter. *ANA photograph*

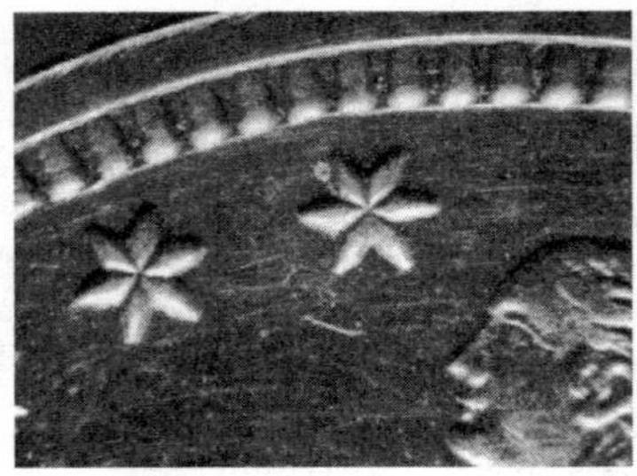

Blowup of hair lines on another section of that Proof quarter. *ANA photograph*

Hairlines usually end up as a primary grading criterion for Proof coins, because Proofs were made for collectors and usually didn't circulate. However, many Proofs were mishandled by collectors, and the Proof surface is so fragile that the least contact causes hairlines. Take a look at the closeup of the 1861 Liberty Seated quarter Proof shown. Those annoying lines on the surface are hairlines. Take another look at those hairlines from the other image shown, and you will see that these can detract considerably from the grade. A Proof-65 does not have to be completely free of hairlines. A moderately hairlined Proof, though, often grades Proof-63; and a severely hairlined Proof often deserves to be given only the Proof-60 designation.

Do not confuse hairlines with die-polishing marks, which are also patches of parallel striations. The difference is that these resulted from the polishing of the die, not of the coins. Die-polishing marks are raised, whereas hairlines are indented. Take a look at the 1938 "Mercury" dime. It has die-polishing marks, not hairlines. Since die-polishing marks are Mint-made, they don't detract from the grade, just the price.

Nonabrasive Cleaning

Nonabrasive coin cleaning does not adversely affect a coin's top layer of metal and, in a sense, does not "eat into" the coin to achieve its effect. Submersing a coin in water, for example, is a non-abrasive cleaning method. Nonabrasive cleaning methods are used to help preserve coins, for they remove particles and other chemicals from the surface which might later negatively affect the coin. For example, if you accidentally sneeze on a coin, you should use a nonabrasive method of removing the saliva. Saliva later tones the surface a dense, dark color.

Nonabrasive cleaning methods are being recommended increasingly before long-term storage. One chemical in particular, trichlorotrifluoroethane, was used for years as a de-

Whizzed 1795 13-Leaves Capped Bust eagle. The harsh, abrasive cleaning is evident from the parallel striations which crisscross the coin. *Photograph courtesy Heritage*

Die-polishing marks on a Mercury dime obverse. Die-polishing marks are Mint-made and raised. *Photograph by Steven Ritter*

greasing solvent and prized for not leaving a residue on the coin's surface. Trichlorotrifluoroethane is no longer available because the federal government identifies it as an ozone-destructive solvent and, consequently, has banned it. Preservation experts recommend the use of denatured alcohol in its place.

The loss of Dissolve (trichlorotrifluorethane) is a serious blow to collectors intent on preserving their coins from environmental damage. The same company that produced Dissolve—E&T Kointainer Company of Sidney, Ohio—has introduced a substitute solvent as a cleaning and preservation tool. The new product, called Koinsolv, is a neutral solvent which can be used to remove contaminants safely from coins, medals, tokens, and other numismatic items without disturbing any existing natural toning or natural luster. According to Bern Nagengast, the company's president, Koinsolv will remove dust, oil, tape, and PVC residue and will not leave a residue of its own. Nagengast says it will not remove oxidation, corrosion, toning, or spots.

In materials made available to me for review by the company, the contents of Koinsolv are listed as: n-Propyl bromide, 2-Propanol, Dimethoxymethane, 2-Methyl-2-Propanol, and 1,2 Epoxybutane. I would be sure to use this potent chemical combination only outside, although many will feel safe using it in a well-ventilated indoor area. I had the opportunity to test Koinsolv and found it to have an extremely strong solvent odor. The user should follow the instructions provided by the manufacturer and exercise reasonable caution and common sense.

Nagengast warns that Koinsolv should not be used with plastics unless the combination of the plastic and the Koinsolv are tested in advance. Some plastics, he cautions, will be

Koinsolv neutral coin solvent. *Photograph courtesy E&T Kointainer Co.*

attacked by the solvent and may melt or dissolve. He told me that his firm makes new proprietary tongs, called KoinTongs, that will not melt when used with Koinsolv, and he provided me with a sample for testing purposes. The first time I tried Koinsolv with the new KoinTongs, the plastic did not melt, and a coin with a thick green PVC residue came out sparkling clean. I was impressed.

Coins are essentially dirty. During their manufacture, their metal is rolled, punched, annealed, die-struck, and handled by various mechanical devices. Even the most well-preserved coins are beset by a multiplicity of contaminants: oil and grease, rag dust, bag dust, metallic particles, and others.

After coins leave the Mint, they are further contaminated by counting machines and handling. When you hold a coin, you contaminate it, too. A dandruff fleck, a drop of saliva, and the oil from your fingers all have the potential to significantly lower a coin's level of preservation.

The rate of a coin's deterioration depends a great deal on the metal of which it's made, the atmosphere, the contaminants on the coin's surface, and the handling of the coin.

Normal pollutants found in the air can cause problems by combining with oxygen to damage a coin's surface. Gases produced while a coin is housed in a plastic holder, coming from the plastic itself, also can be a cause of damage. Caustic chemicals, such as compounds containing sulfur, can harm coins, too.

When you own a coin, you can control some of these factors and thereby slow down the coins' deterioration. Unfortunately, you can't be certain that a coin is free from airborne particulate matter when it's encapsulated by a grading service. Furthermore, you're not able to clean a coin nonabrasively or "neutralize" its surfaces by dipping the coin in denatured alcohol just before it's slabbed.

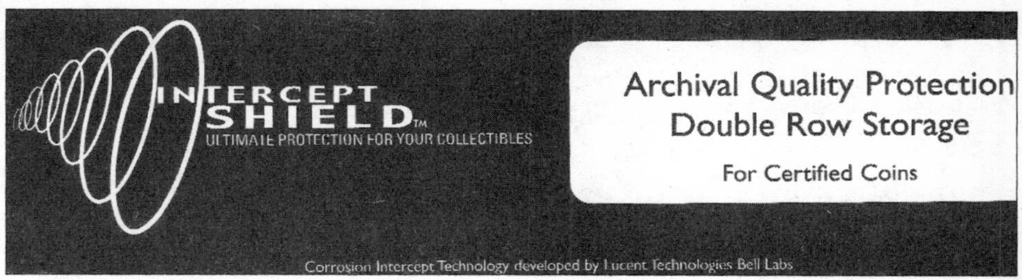

InterceptShield™, one of the very best coin storage products available, is manufactured in a number of products and formats.

It should be pointed out that my illustrations of "nonabrasive cleaning" really refer to solvent cleaning. And if you do decide to neutralize or solvent-clean a coin, you should be certain that the coin's surfaces are pristine and haven't been tampered with. The surfaces must be free from any kind of coating for your solvent cleaning to be successful and not damage the coin. Remember, also, never to use anything sharp or harsh (even cotton swabs) during solvent cleaning. The following firm specializes in coin preservation products, sells solvents which don't leave a residue, and offers a free catalog: E&T Kointainer Company, P.O. Box 103, Sidney, Ohio 45365.

There are other products available which are designed to assist in nonabrasive cleaning. However, some of them leave a residue on the coin which might attract dust or other airborne pollutants.

State-of-the-Art Protection Against Deterioration

In the late 1980s, John Albanese was one of the leaders in the Grading Revolution, which brought into being the system of independent third-party grading that permeates the coin market today. He was part of the group of inner-circle dealers that formed the Professional Coin Grading Service (PCGS) in 1986 and then, a year later, he set up a company of his own, the Numismatic Guaranty Corporation of America (NGC), which remains a major force along with PCGS. Albanese is no longer associated with NGC, but he is still as innovative as ever. Having played a key role in safeguarding the process of grading coins, he has turned his attention now to protecting their level of preservation.

Recognizing the need to keep coins safe from environmental damage, Albanese sought and found an extraordinary—and apparently revolutionary—new product which,

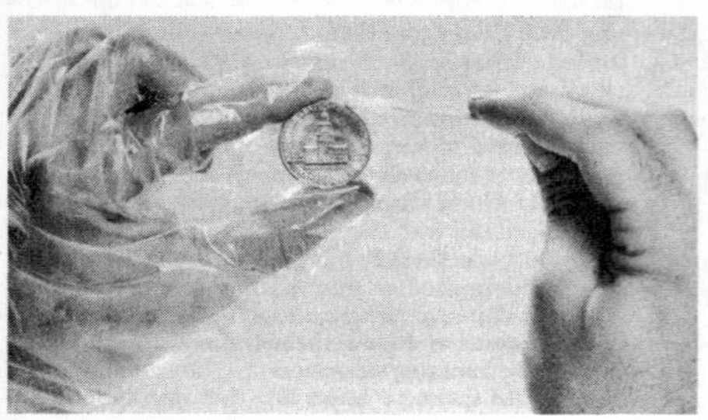

The proper way to test a coin's reaction before non-abrasively cleaning it. *Photograph courtesy Equi-Safe Corporation*

when stored with coins, will prevent them deteriorating due to contact with chemical agents in the surrounding atmosphere. The product appears to be much more effective than the vapor-phase inhibitors widely used for years to accomplish a similar objective. Whereas vapor-phase inhibitors change the molecular composition of the air, the new product reacts with, and neutralizes, potentially damaging substances.

The product, called Intercept Technology, was developed by Lucent Bell Labs—not to protect coins, but to help combat the corrosion of telephone wires and equipment. The company was searching for a method of preventing corrosive reactions involving reactive solid-state elements of its equipment. According to Lucent, the product reacts with and neutralizes all corrosive gases and keeps the environment stable for 10 years. The company says it protects both ferrous and non-ferrous metals and also prevents galvanic corrosion within its coverage area.

Intercept leaves no detectable deposit on the surfaces of the coins it protects. This is a major advantage over volatile corrosion inhibitors, which sometimes leave a residue on the coins. By cleaning trapped air of all corrosive gases, Intercept also provides a cost savings by eliminating the need for secondary packaging and cleaning. It acts as a passive bactericide and mildewcide (it kills bacteria and mildew) and eliminates the need for storing coins in an inert atmosphere. In addition, it is attractive to environmentalists, because it breaks down into polymer dust that is totally recyclable.

John Albanese formed a company to market the new product which he calls "InterceptShield." He introduced it commercially in the coin market in a number of different sizes and forms. One of these, he says, is a core that can be placed inside "slabs" (or sonically sealed plastic holders) by the various grading services as an added protection for the coins they grade and encapsulate. It also is now available to individual dealers and collectors as InterceptShield albums, boxes, and individual holders. The sizes are convenient, Albanese says, and the cost is nominal.

This is an important and exciting development and it promises to bring about fundamental changes in the way people buy, sell, and store their rare coins.

Interested readers are invited to visit the Web site for the new product: *www.interceptshield.com*

How to Clean Coins Nonabrasively

Even the most harmless products can be misused, and even good products used correctly might have a negative impact on some coins. The best way to test the impact of a coin-bathing solution is by applying a small amount to the coin's edge and observing the result. Since the rim is made from the same material and dies as the rest of the coin, you will know not to use a certain bathing solution if it reacts negatively with the edge. However, this still is not a complete assurance that the coin product tested will not harm your coin.

Artificial Toning and Doctored Coins

Often coins which have been cleaned to appear Mint State, but aren't, are artificially toned to hide the cleaning. Artificial toning can be nonabrasive, but it is usually corrosive. This toning is caused by a chemical reaction that resembles the slow, regular, natural process by which a coin tones or acquires patina. Anthony Swiatek, writing in *The Swiatek Numismatic Report*, conducted a study of artificial toning and how it is created. Here are his findings, slightly abridged:

- Directing cigar or cigarette smoke at silver coins will produce a very light brown tone. Repeated blasts will cause color to "darken to taste."
- A coin placed in a coin envelope and in an oven at 300F for a half-hour will result most often in a dull appearance. Colors of dull purple, yellowish green, and bluish purple can result.
- A weak concentration of a sulfur solution (dissolved in alcohol or water) can cause creation of a gold to golden-brown tone. A stronger solution produces purple and peacock blue colors.
- A coin baked inside an Idaho potato covered with corn oil and wrapped in foil can result in the creation of a purple-blue to an orange color.
- A mixture of motor oil and corn oil will create a bluish-purple color when placed on a coin and baked for a period of time (275°F to 300°F for one hour or less).
- Gun bluing can be painted on a coin, or an ammonia-base chemical solution used, to see a sunrise color blend behind, perhaps, the Seated Liberty on that coin type.
- A sulfur shampoo can create green, yellow, and brown colors if left on the coin for a day or longer.

Artificially toned coins are often identified by imperfect toning. Look for telltale areas of unnatural color and texture. Another telltale sign is the coin's smell. Many toning and cleaning products (such as sulfur dissolved in petroleum jelly to induce toning on copper coins) contain sulfur bases which leave an unpleasant smell on the coin. If you are in doubt about toning, smell the coin.

Another popular artificial toning method that sometimes gives the coin a beautiful, natural look involves dipping the coin in Jeweluster (a popular coin dip discussed in chapter 8). After dipping, the coin is placed in a kraft envelope within an empty Jeweluster jar so the coin is exposed to the vapors overnight. As long as the jar has a strong Jeweluster odor, the artificial toning will occur.

The primary use of artificial toning, as I have stated before, is to hide imperfections. Once you've viewed a number of coins with real toning and also have sharpened your ability to spot imperfections, you will not be easily fooled by an artificially toned coin.

An extraordinary group of digital images is used in the color section of this book to illustrate artificial toning.

PCGS's David Hall Addresses Coin Doctoring

One of the most enlightening interviews I conducted for *How to Make Money in Coins Right Now* was with David Hall, founder of PCGS—and its current president.

Hall candidly shared his views on a number of areas of the industry, but perhaps the most enlightening segment of the interview addressed doctored and altered coins:

TRAVERS: Let's give a little primer on how to identify a doctored coin. Let's talk about the most common doctoring or alteration techniques.

HALL: For a puttied coin, it won't have the typical luster, the typical shine to it. It will look subdued—but not subdued like a coin that is subdued over time. It'll look almost kind of gunky. You can smell bleaching, if that's done to a coin, but that's not so widespread anymore. Epoxy is usually used on Proofs, and it's so overly bright—especially where it shouldn't be, like over planchet flaws and hairlines and stuff—that I don't think epoxy is a big problem. The two major issues are artificial toning and then adding stuff to the surfaces. As for thumbing, this is a variation of the puttying. It's where you add a little body oil to a coin to maybe dull the luster over an area that has marks. Artificial toning is a very subjective look that's hard to describe. But if you look at original toned coins for 20 years, they have a certain way the colors look. If you look at an artificially toned coin, it's the wrong color, the wrong combination of colors, the colors aren't smooth as they run into each other.

TRAVERS: How about advising people to look beneath the surface to see whether a coin is artificially toned?

HALL: I don't think that's a way to tell whether a coin is artificially toned or not, because a nicely toned coin can have scratches, nicks, marks, planchet flaws underneath the toning.

TRAVERS: How big a problem do you think doctoring is, and artificial toning is, for coins that are sold at public auctions?

HALL: Well, if they're third-party-certified, most of the more recognized third-party services do a fairly good job of catching the doctoring. And certainly, PCGS has a grading guarantee that takes care of mistakes when they don't catch it. It's a huge problem for the grading services in that we're constantly bombarded with it. For the consumer, we're the buffer in between. For non-third-party-graded coins—coins that you would buy raw at public auction—unless you're buying them from an old-time collection . . . say, the Eliasberg Collection . . . I think that at least 50 percent of all coins sold raw have been doctored. Basically, it's a way for the dealers to dump their no-grades.

TRAVERS: What percentage of coins that have been doctored do you think have made their way into your holders?

HALL: That's hard to say, and it really depends on what you define as doctoring, and what is acceptable and what isn't acceptable. Blatantly doctored coins, I think the percentage would be very, very low. If a person were to just thumb lightly the surface of a silver dollar, often the best experts in the world can't even tell it's been done. You almost wonder why the doctors do it.

TRAVERS: And if they can tell, you might still put it in a holder anyway because it's generally accepted in the marketplace?

HALL: Right. If it was real light. And a thumbed coin can sometimes look exactly like a coin that you would pull out of an original mint-sewn bag, with a little bit of moisture haze or whatever. So it depends on the severity of the doctoring. Blatantly doctored coins, I think a very, very, very low percentage get through.

TRAVERS: How about coins with very light puttying? Would PCGS knowingly put some of those in holders once in a while if it were extremely light and not likely to interfere with the appearance that much?

HALL: If we think that it's actually been puttied, we won't do it. If we think that, well, there's a little haze on the coin—is it real or not?—and you can't tell, then haze is a negative in terms of eye appeal and it would be given an appropriately lower grade. But knowingly? If we knew that a bunch of coins had been lightly hazed, we wouldn't put them into holders.

TRAVERS: On a coin which has been thumbed, is it possible for the coin to deteriorate after it's in the holder because what's used for thumbing—the body moisture—can react with the coin and later lower its level of preservation?

HALL: It could. But if a person very lightly thumbs it, you couldn't even tell it's been thumbed. I don't think it's a big issue, because we're basically talking about silver coins. A copper coin would, of course, be much, much different. In terms of the deterioration in the holders, it is true that some coins change—some naturally, some unnaturally—and that's why PCGS has a grading guarantee and we stand behind our product. We want the consumer to be able to buy PCGS coins with confidence and know that if there is a mistake—and we certainly admit that we're not perfect—that we'll take care of it.

Toning and Corrosion

The controversy surrounding detection of artificially toned coins has caused some experts to question whether any type of toning is desirable—or if toning is merely a form of corrosion which can be likened to rust on a car. The process that causes silver coins to tone or tarnish is self-limiting, but the rusting process on a car can continue indefinitely.

My father, Harvey C. Travers, is a chemical engineer with a Master of Science degree from the Massachusetts Institute of Technology, and he has carried out extensive studies on this subject. Some of his opinions are:

- When moisture reacts with iron, there is an all-out destructive attack—corrosion—on the metal. Iron spalls or loses metal when it rusts.
- Silver is relatively inactive and does not react with oxygen in the air, even at high temperatures. It reacts with certain chemical compounds, notably those containing sulfur, if a catalyst is present-moisture, for example. The reaction, however, stops short of being an all-out destructive attack. In the case of silver coins, the sulfur causes a "protective" coating to form on the surface. If it develops quickly and tends to be unsightly, we call it tarnish; if it happens more slowly and attractively, we call it toning.
- Unlike iron, which loses metal when it rusts, silver is not eaten away—that is to say, corroded—by this limited chemical reaction. When iron rusts, it spalls and loses metal; when silver tones or tarnishes, there is no loss of metal.

The toning/corrosion controversy is an emotionally charged debate—one that is complicated by the absence of standardized numismatic definitions. Some experts argue that toning and tarnish are forms of corrosion because a small amount of metal on the surface of the coin has been irreversibly converted to a corrosion product.

All experts agree that improper storage can irreparably damage coins. So whether you call it toning or corrosion, if you don't properly store your coins, their appearance could change and lower their values.

Storing your coins—it seems simple. You buy a coin from a dealer, and it's protected—or so you think. You reason that the dealer wouldn't sell you a coin in a holder which might ruin the coin. So you take your valuable MS-67 rare coin in its pliable plastic holder and put it away in a safe-deposit box. What will happen? The coin could lose much of its premium value if the holder is made from polyvinylchloride (PVC), a plastic film which can deposit sticky chemical plasticizers on a coin and release hydrogen chloride gas at high temperatures. The hydrogen chloride gas can react with humidity in the air and form hydrochloric acid, which can eat into the surface of your coin.

Improper coin preservation is a silent killer. Every year, improper storage methods cost collectors a fortune. But most improper storage methods can be corrected, and if detected early enough, even coins affected by PVC holders can be saved. Dealers don't care how your coins are preserved. If a coin isn't in the same level of preservation as it was when you purchased it, the dealer has no obligation to buy it back or be held to a guarantee, if one was issued. (Don't think that if you store your coins properly, though, a dealer will say that they are in the same level of preservation that they were when purchased. The "not in the same level of preservation" argument is a classic reason for not honoring a grading certificate.)

Holders Can Damage Coins

PVC is in more coin holders than you think. Many of the most widely used holders contain PVC, including all of the pliable-flip types, except one brand: "Saflips," a holder made of pure polyethylene terepthalate, known as Mylar. This is the only safe coin flip available. Dealers don't have to worry about the negative effects because they move their inventory so quickly. In fact, I recommend the PVC flip-type holders if you're taking a lot of coins to a coin show for a couple of hours. These pliable pouches allow ease of handling, as well as an unobstructed view of the rim and edge. Just don't leave the coins in these holders for more than an hour or two, and don't expose the holders to heat.

Some roll holders also are made from PVC. In the illustration shown, you can see a closeup of the edge of a 1960 Small-Date Lincoln cent contaminated by PVC damage. The coin was stored in a PVC tube. If you need to use roll tubes, buy the squared-off milky polyethylene ones, which are inert.

The effects of PVC holders have been explored and documented in a study conducted by Dr. Thomas W. Sharpless, a professor of chemistry at the University of Hartford. He details his conclusions in a "Report on the Relationship Between Polyvinylchloride and Coin Corrosion." Dr. Sharpless's study was conducted some years ago, at the height of the preservation craze. That was a time when numismatic publications were paying a great deal of attention to the problems of preservation. Sharpless concluded that the PVC holders left a ring of stain when the coin was removed. Thus, just because the manufacturers of pliable flip-type holders advertise their products as "oil-free" or "safe" doesn't mean they are, if they contain PVC.

The modern attention to preservation, however, began in 1977 with the introduction of the late Walter Breen's "talking-book record," "The Care and Preservation of Rare Coins." On it, Breen says, in part:

> The problem of preservation of coins is essentially two-fold: preventing abrasion by dusts and other contaminants or by cleaning agents; and preventing access to the coins of chemical or electrochemical processes attacking the surfaces. The vast majority of these chemical agents are smog components. Others include biological residue such as cough or sneeze or sweat droplets, excreta of rodents or insects, byproducts of molds, fungi, or bacteria. Most of these require the presence of moisture. All vary in speed of action, some working in seconds, others only over the years. Ancient bronze patina is said to take centuries.

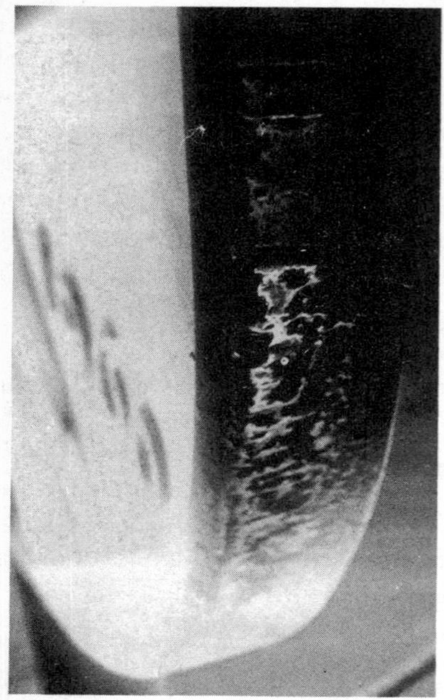

The edge of a Lincoln cent stored in a PVC tube. *Photograph courtesy Dr. Thomas W. Sharpless*

Suddenly, the numismatic community became aware of the fact that coins had to be cared for. You can't buy a coin and put it away for a few years without expecting some deterioration unless you take some necessary precautions. Dr. Sharpless, in an exclusive experiment for *The Coin Collector's Survival Manual* which he entitled "Test of Coin Containers for Their Ability to Exclude Moist Air," tested the two best "airtight" holders for their "airtightness." His conclusions for the Capital and Whitman Mylar holders surprised even me. Sharpless writes:

> The change of cobaltous chloride from its blue to its pink hydrate indicates exposure to moist air. No significant differences were found among the coin containers. Each admits moist air in a matter of hours.

Preservation Precautions

- **Store your coins in a cool, dry place.** High temperatures cause some plastics to give off harmful gases. Humidity can cause negative surface reactions even on coins which have developed a natural oxide coating. Excessive moisture causes corrosion. Copper coins are particularly vulnerable to high levels of moisture in the air, for they can suddenly break out with big black spots for apparently no reason. If you live in Florida, sell your cent collection. (Some dealers will not bring any copper coins to Florida coin shows, even for a few days.) If you do have coins in a humid environment, store silica gel with them. This will absorb the moisture. Recharge the silica gel by heating it in an oven.

Commemorative coin irreparably damaged by its high points having been abraded. Anthony Swiatek uses this photograph in his seminars to emphasize the potential for damage when using albums that have acetate slides. *Photograph courtesy Anthony Swiatek*

Kointain-brand triacetate holders, designed for safe long-term storage. *Photograph courtesy Equi-Safe Corporation*

- **Select a safe-deposit-box room that will not harm your coins.** Choose an air-conditioned safe-deposit-box room, if you store your coins there. Breen warns that the safe-deposit-box room should not contain an ozone purification system for destroying microorganisms. This type of system, according to Breen, emits a germ-killing agent as harmful to coins as chlorine gas, "and will corrode silver and copper coins very rapidly." Select a safe-deposit-box room that is not kept humid. Many are kept humid because safe deposit boxes are often used to store important documents which have to be kept moist.
- **Keep coins away from paper.** Paper contains sulfur, which can react with a coin and lower its level of preservation. Envelopes and some cardboard folders contain sulfur. Circulated coins are not as much at risk as Mint State business-strike and Proof coins.
- **Keep coins in an airtight environment.** A primary goal should be to protect the coins from airborne pollutants. A coin cannot be in an air-free environment unless it is embedded in acrylic, which is highly impractical at best. Choose an inert airtight holder. The blue plastic boxes manufactured by Whitman Coin Products, which close tightly, are good for storing your coins, which also should be in inert holders.
- **Don't store coins in albums with sliding windows.** These slides, if moved back and forth enough, could cause friction on the coins' high points.
- **Prevent deterioration by molecular change.** A product called Metal Safe Corrosion Inhibitor is available in plastic capsules through E&T. This product works by changing the molecular composition of the air. InterceptShield preservation products are also excellent.

Coin Conservation Services

As of October 2005, the only full-time professional company that preserves and conserves coins is Numismatic Conservation Services (NCS). The firm also encapsulates some coins that would otherwise be returned as ungradable by services such as NGC and

Acrylic sandwich-type holders, manufactured by Capital Plastics with safe long-term storage the aim. *Photograph courtesy Capital Plastics, Inc.*

PCGS. NCS says that it has a "mutual consulting agreement with NGC and others to provide and receive expertise when needed." Some extraordinary before-and-after photographs of NCS's work are provided in the color section of this book.

In its written promotional literature, NCS recommends that you speak with a professional at its service:

- When you notice changes in a coin, such as discoloring or spotting
- After a grading service returns a coin and issues a "no-grade" designation for reasons such as PVC, artificial toning, or residue

NCS says that it does not restore coins by making mechanical repairs such as filling holes and re-engraving detail. It also claims that it does not improve the appearance of coins through "deceptive means such as artificial toning." NCS says its most popular services are tarnish removal, gold-coin spot removal, and removal of PVC and other residue.

In a letter to dealers dated March 1, 2001, David Camire, then the company's director of operations (and now its president), wrote that NCS "enhances the credibility of the entire rare coin industry by providing a professional alternative to coin doctoring and amateur conservation."

From $460 to $4,600 in Two Easy Submissions

A typical positive experience with NCS was related to me by professional numismatist Will Rossman. He told me he had purchased an uncertified 1902 Liberty head quarter eagle for $460. The low price, he reasoned, was "because the coin had copper spots." Rossman said he submitted it to NGC, which graded the coin MS-66 and included a separate advisory that it might benefit from NCS services. As an NGC MS-66, it then had

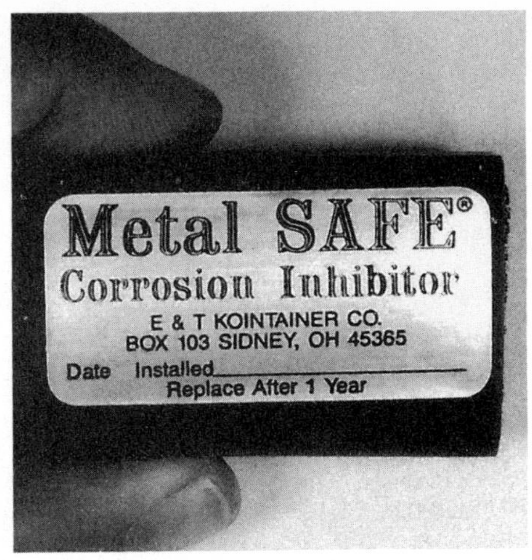

Metal Safe Corrosion inhibitor changes the molecular composition of the air to prevent deterioration.
Photograph courtesy E&T Kointainer Company

a value of $1,600. "So I sent it to NCS, which removed the copper spots, and it came back in an NGC MS-67 holder," Rossman said. The coin was elevated in value to $4,600 when it was graded MS-67 by NGC. "I was pleased with NCS's services," Rossman said. "It was professional and on time."

Fees and Contact Information

NCS says that it uses a two-part fee structure. There is an evaluation fee that covers analyzing what services, if any, would benefit the coin. NCS charges 1 percent of the pre-service value of the coin for this initial evaluation and caps this fee at $1,000. If work needs to be performed, there is a second charge of 3 percent for this service with a cap of $2,500. An expedite service is available for $50 per coin. A report on work performed is available for $75 per coin. There is a minimum evaluation fee of $5 and a minimum conservation fee of $15. NCS accepts raw and certified coins for evaluation and conservation. If you elect to have your coins graded, NCS will hand them over to NGC after conservation.

I like this service and the efficiency with which it performs the restoration function. I had a client who thought he had lost his valuable coin collection to a hurricane-spawned flood. The coins were caked with grime and appeared tarnished and heavily spotted. He *threw away* a good number of the coins because he figured there would be no way to ever salvage them.

At my suggestion, we sent the remaining coins to NCS. That was my first experience actually using NCS, so I didn't have high expectations. After just a few weeks, a box from NGC arrived in the mail. When I opened it, I found a group of magnificent—but unfamiliar—Proof and Mint State type coins in sparkling NGC holders. I went through my records to try to figure out to whom these gorgeous Gems belonged.

A problem coin which might not ordinarily qualify for encapsulation by a grading service can be slabbed by NCS and accompanied by an explanation on the insert of the coin's problem.
Photograph courtesy Numismatic Conservation Services, LLC

You guessed it.

The box contained the coins that NCS had restored. It was like a miracle. The coins looked nicer than they did when the client bought them! Ever since, I've been a believer.

For further information, contact NCS directly. NGC is also helpful in forwarding calls to NCS when requested to do so.

Numismatic Conservation Services, LLC
P.O. Box 4750
Sarasota, FL 34230
Tel: 866/NCS-COIN toll-free (in Florida: 941/360-3996)
FAX: 941/360-2559
World Wide Web: www.ncscoin.com

The $10,000 Conservation Secret

A leading dealer revealed to me that the successful removal of copper spots on business-strike and Proof gold coins is one of the most important secrets of conservation. Until now, one of those "secret" methods was so closely guarded that this leading dealer says another respected dealer paid $10,000 to someone to reveal the technique.

The copper spot removal method, he says, is to place a lighted BernzOmatic 4" torch about three inches from the coin for 3–5 seconds, until the spot in question disappears. He says he pours cold water on the coin quickly afterward to prevent himself from being burned.

Mark Yaffe, president of National Gold Exchange, perhaps the largest gold coin wholesaler in the world, cautions that it is no secret that this technique can damage a coin *and* cause injury to its owner.

"Amateurs shouldn't be playing a professional's game," Yaffe said. "If I go and read a book on general surgery, it wouldn't be advisable for me to start cutting at my appendix."

WARNING: This technique is provided for illustration purposes only as an example of how experts conserve coins. You are advised not to try this on your own.

Yaffe said he uses a chemical to remove copper spots, but that the chemical's composition is proprietary. "It doesn't hurt the coin, and the spots don't come back," Yaffe said.

Remarkable before-and-after photographs of a ten dollar Indian gold piece that had its copper spots successfully removed are provided by Numismatic Conservation Services in the color section of this book.

– 19 –
SECURITY AFTER SEPTEMBER 11 AND HURRICANE KATRINA

Security has become a constant concern of Americans since September 11, 2001. This understandable concern extends to all facets of society—including coin collecting. Safekeeping has always been a major consideration for people who possess valuable coins, but in the current climate the need for extra precautions and approaches to securing protection have taken on a new form. It is, therefore, more important than ever to store coins safely and insure them adequately against potential loss or damage—including the risks of terrorism and natural disaster.

Insurance Against Terrorism and Protection from Natural Disasters

In the immediate aftermath of the attacks of September 11, terrorism insurance premium rates skyrocketed or were in some instances unavailable. Reinsurers, entities that indemnify other insurers from taking all or part of the risk of loss, were financially unable to take on further exposure to potential terror attacks. So reinsurance became unavailable—which led insurance companies to cancel or curtail insurance coverage in all areas of American life, including numismatics.

However, in November 2002, President George W. Bush signed into law the Terrorism Risk Protection Act. The legislation was designed so that, if "spectacular events" (law enforcement's term for major catastrophes) occur, the Treasury Department will help subsidize the cost of the attacks.

With this new legislation, insurance of your numismatic items against acts of terror should now be available again at a reasonable price.

"The new problem that has emerged in this tense climate relates to simple carrying of coins," said Simon S. Codrington, international director for New York–based Hugh Wood, Inc., one of the nation's largest numismatic insurance brokers.

"With such careful inspection of carry-on bags at airports and attaché cases in office towers, it becomes public knowledge who is carrying coins," Codrington said. "And this leads to a whole host of new problems."

Reports have surfaced and insurance claims have been filed relating to dealers and collectors being targeted at airports and on airplanes. And at least one collector misplaced valuable coins after taking them out for inspection to guards at an office building.

Codrington recommends that you either have your coins transported to coin shows via armored courier—or leave your coins back home in the bank vault. However, in this new climate, he admits, "You can't even consider your neighborhood bank vault to be safe anymore."

In light of the catastrophic damage caused by Hurricane Katrina in 2005 and the potential risks from future hurricanes and other natural disasters, it would be wise to review your insurance policies and to think about how you would act if confronted by a natural disaster. Here are a few basic survival tips for you and your rare coins:

- **Escape to safety.** Know where safe shelter is in advance of any emergency, and become familiar with escape routes and alternate escape routes that would allow you to get there.
- **Protect rare coins from harm.** If you are quickly evacuating from rising floodwaters, protecting your coins can be as simple as putting them in waterproof containers and on the highest shelf possible.
- **Place your own life before the safety of your coins.** Large numbers of coins are heavy and difficult to transport, even under ideal circumstances. If you are facing an emergency evacuation, consider leaving all of the coins behind and running for your life—or quickly slipping the one or two most valuable coins in your pocket before you leave.
- **Have a pocket Emergency Alert System (EAS) radio at coin conventions and during travel, and stay informed.** The Federal Communications Commission (FCC) created EAS (*www.fcc.gov/cgb/consumerfacts/eas.html*) in cooperation with the National Weather Service (NWS) and the Federal Emergency Management Agency (FEMA). Government officials have access to EAS on all levels in order to target any selected area that requires emergency information. EAS radios can be programmed to sound an alarm in the event of an emergency. Radio Shack (*www.radioshack.com*) has an excellent selection of these handheld radios. My family and I have used EAS radios since September 11, 2001, and have found them to be most helpful.

Explosion-Resistant Safes

Insurance companies are now paying greater attention to how a safe will fare when exposed to heat and flame—or worse. The TXTL-60 rated safe, previously rarely considered because of prohibitive cost and scarcity of availability, is becoming commonplace. This designation refers to a safe that is explosion-resistant for a full hour. Standard safes are explored later in this chapter.

Educate yourself about damage temperatures. Kointains and Saflips melt at 446°F and 480°F respectively, according to the manufacturer. Floppy disks can become damaged at above approximately 125°F. If you store your coin inventory records on computer disks in a safe, look for an Underwriters Laboratory certification of 125-UL.

Safe-Deposit Box Storage

Statistically, bank safe-deposit boxes are among the safest places to store things, although they are designed for the storage of documents, not rare coins. However, mishaps do occur.

Banks rarely insure the contents of safe-deposit boxes. These boxes are provided as a service at a nominal yearly charge. Most safe-deposit box rental agreements say this in small print. Banks cannot be held responsible for negligence in guarding your valuables, and you would find it difficult to press a case if you were to sue a bank for negligence. However, you might be able to press a case for gross negligence—if you can prove it.

If you're going to store your coins in a bank safe-deposit box, take some precautions:

- **Make sure you know what's in the box.** Even people with ample insurance coverage sometimes don't bother to make an inventory of what's in their safe-deposit boxes. If you have to file an insurance claim or take a tax loss, the more detailed and itemized your listing, the better off you are. Photographs are of immense help, as I'll explain later.
- **Don't allow an attendant to hold your key.** Allowing a safe-deposit box attendant, even one that you've known for years, to hold onto your key when the attendant is out of your view is asking for trouble. Take a few seconds more to put the key in your pocket. That way, you increase your chances of your coins not going into a thief's pocket.
- **Keep your box at a consistent weight, and don't let anything jiggle around.** A considerably lighter-weight safe-deposit box after you leave your bank alerts the attendant to the fact that you removed some of the contents. The attendant would then be in a position to tip off a mugger that you have valuables on your person. If you make a major withdrawal from your safe-deposit box, replace what you have withdrawn with a "filler" of equal weight. Don't store anything in your safe-deposit box that jiggles. If the jiggle stops, the attendant will think you have removed the valuable contents.
- **Carefully read your safe-deposit box rental agreement.** This alerts you to what rights you do and don't have. If there are any unreasonable terms, change banks.
- **Store proof of purchase for coins in a separate box.** It wouldn't make any sense for you to store your receipts with your coins, for the receipts could be stolen with the coins. Make copies of all receipts and photos that you store in the separate safe-deposit box, and keep the copies in a safe place at home.
- **Carefully read your insurance policies.** Some people are covered for safe-deposit box storage of coins, but most are not. If your insurance coverage isn't adequate, buy more. Remember that just because your coins are being stored in a bank, that doesn't mean

that they are insured. If you want your coins to be stored by your bank, check out bank custodial plans. For a fee, the bank will hold your coins for you and be responsible for each one.

Home Security

Protecting Your Home or Apartment

Some common-sense precautions can be taken to protect your place of residence from a break-in:

- **Don't have coin publications delivered to your home.** These are a tip-off that you collect and might have some valuable coins at home. Rent a Post Office Box. Some people have no coins at home, but receive these numismatic publications at a P.O. Box anyway, just to make sure they have no confrontations with an intruder who gets upset that no coins are available. Don't read coin publications in public places. There's no need to give the wrong person any ideas. Similarly, if you order by mail, make sure the package gives no hints of what it contains. Tell the dealer to leave off words such as "coin" and "numismatic."
- **Don't leave a message on your telephone answering machine which states that you're not at home.** I have a friend who recorded a message which says that he is "not available to answer your call and available by appointment only." Anything is better than saying you're not at home. If you don't have a telephone answering machine and are out of the house, unplug your phone from the wall. Burglars sometimes call from a phone booth and then go to your house to find out if the phone's still ringing and you're not at home.
- **Use timers to fool people into thinking that you're at home.** Timers can be used to turn lights or radios on and off at different times of the day. A radio turned on for a few hours each day when you aren't at home is helpful. A car parked in the driveway, as well as children's toys scattered throughout the yard, also can be helpful.
- **Use a good burglar alarm, and test it periodically.** Check with reputable alarm companies to see which alarm is best suited to your needs. Also ask your local police department's opinion about the effectiveness of certain types of alarms and locks for your area. An impressive alarm which notifies the police that you need help at the touch of a button doesn't appear that impressive after you find out that the notification by alarm is given a low priority by police and may not be responded to for an extended period of time. Use an electrical burglar alarm with a battery backup, and test the batteries at regular intervals.
- **Most importantly, use common sense.** Use the peephole on your door to screen visitors. Don't let strangers in. Ask repair people for identification. If you go out of your house or apartment, lock all doors and windows. Some burglars make their livings by going from door to door and entering only those dwellings which have open doors. You would be amazed at all of the people with the most advanced alarms available who leave their homes and don't lock the door!

- **If all else fails, file an insurance claim.** Even people who take every possible precaution are sometimes the victims of theft. Make sure your insurance policy covers your risks. Many homeowners policies do not cover coin collections. Check the fine print. If you want insurance designed especially for your collection, the group insurance plan offered by the insurance company contracted by the American Numismatic Association might interest you. You must be an ANA member to qualify. For more information, contact: ANA Group Insurance Plans, Hugh Wood, Inc., 35 Broadway, 3rd Floor, New York, NY 10006, Internet: *www.hwint.com/usa/hughwood/ana/index.html*

Home Safes

During many home burglaries, home safes are either lifted away or wheeled away—sometimes on their own wheels! Many people make the mistake of buying fire safes, as opposed to burglar-resistant safes. Safes are available to suit both purposes, but are extremely expensive. If you buy a home safe, follow these guidelines:

- **Bolt your safe to the floor.** Securing your safe so it cannot be easily transported is one of the most important steps you can take in protecting your rare coins with a home safe. Bolting your safe to the floor helps to compensate for underweight safes, too.
- **Buy a burglar-resistant safe, not a fire-resistant one.** Make sure the lock is of high quality and that the door and structure are steel. If you absolutely insist on using a fire-resistant safe, buy a burglar resistant safe that it will fit into. Fire-resistant safes have walls that are well insulated and conducive to moisture absorption. That's why fire-resistant safes are fire-resistant: they have moist insulation that keeps the temperature inside the safe low. Moisture, as discussed in the last chapter, is potentially harmful to coins. Store silica gel inside a sealed inert plastic box with your coins, and store the box in the fire-resistant safe.
- **If you use a fire-resistant safe, weight it down.** Fire resistant safes are big and bulky, not heavy. The bulkiness is due to the thick insulation. Place boxes of cents, available at face value from some banks in boxes of $25, in your safe to weight it down if you have any space left over.
- **Pay attention to the UL rating.** The better the rating of your safe from Underwriters Laboratories, the more favorable your insurance rates will be. Some insurance companies require safes to meet a certain minimum rating before issuing a policy for coins stored in them. Check with your insurance company before buying a safe.

How to Buy a Safe

by Robert F. McLaughlin

McLaughlin has extensive experience dealing in safes and offers his expertise for you here.

Cost

High security safes vary in cost from $1,000 to $10,000, based on the level of protection you need and the size of the safe.

You should expect a wide variety of prices in the many safe categories, as well as varying delivery and installation fees.

Insurance Demands

If you need or wish to insure the contents of your safe against burglary, your insurance underwriter will advise that a certain minimum Underwriters Laboratories (UL) tested, approved, and labeled safe be utilized.

Every insurance underwriter has some formal guidelines. Their willingness to insure the contents of your safe is dictated by the degree of security your safe offers against various types of burglar attacks.

It is important to note that although the UL rating of the safe is a major part of the policy acceptance, location, alarms, etc. are also part of what they consider. They take together all the security factors.

Burglar Protection

There are several UL safe ratings, each one offering more protection than the last. Many of the lower ratings no longer exist in current manufacturing or have lost their popularity since more advanced models offer much greater protection at an only slightly higher price.

The most popular UL ratings used today are the TL-15, TL-30, TL-30X6 and TRTL-30X6:

TL-15. This safe will resist entry when attacked on the door only with common hand tools, picking tools, mechanical or portable electric tools, carbide drills, and pressure applying devices or mechanisms for a total attack time of 15 minutes.

TL-30. This safe has the same specifications as the TL-15, but will resist attack for a period of 30 minutes.

TL-30X6. This safe offers the same 30-minute protection as the TL-30 above, but it resists attacks on all six sides.

TRTL-30X6. This safe offers the same six-sided, 30-minute protection as the TL-30X6 above but in addition resists attacks from oxy-fuel gas cutting or welding torch (quantity of gas consumed in one test limited to 1,000 cubic ft. combined total oxygen and fuel gas).

It should be noted that the indicated attack time is the minimum length of time a safe must resist attack to receive a certain rating. A safe may resist for more than the indicated time.

Fire Protection

Underwriters Laboratories has established three major categories which express the degree to which the contents are protected from fire.

Class A: 4 hour protection at 2000°F

Class B: 2 hour protection at 1850°F

Class C: 1 hour protection at 1700°F

The most popular in the coin and jewelry industries are the Class B and Class C.

The "2 hour safe," Class B, keeps the safe's interior temperature below 350°F, even if the outside temperature reaches 1850°F.

The "1 hour safe," Class C, keeps the safe's interior temperature below 350°F, even if the outside temperature reaches 1700°F.

In the heat testing, a reheat test and a mechanical drop test are included.

Most materials resist heat to a point, but steel, being a conductor, offers very little resistance and can cause an oven burning effect on the contents. Today's state-of-the-art composite safes dissipate heat and offer great resistance to heat.

Construction

State-of-the-art composite safes offer the best protection against burglar attacks and fire.

Older safes were only designed to withstand attacks by burglar tools and techniques in existence at the time they were built. Today, with new high-tech compound nuggets buried deep within a high-stress concrete aggregate, and with internal drill deflector bars that are encapsulated between extra-hard steel plates, penetration by any means is extremely difficult, if not impossible.

Size

Consideration must be given to the size of the safe. Does it have the appropriate dimensions for your trays or storage containers? Is there extra room for memo items, consignments, or other unforseen additions? The best solution is to figure exactly what you need, then double it! Also, please remember that buying an additional safe at a later date can be costly; and also that once you are investing in a high security safe, the next size larger costs very little more.

Weight/Installation

When installing the safe, choose a location that offers you the most efficient access. The weight of the safe must be considered. Floor weight-bearing capacities limit the location. A ground floor is the best. Elevators can be problem, because of their capacity; doorways can also limit access. A safe can only be installed if the floor and access pathway allows. This also may determine the size of safe you can purchase.

Locks

There are a great variety of locks that are available, in terms of operation, security, and convenience.

The basic safe is usually equipped with a main combination lock. This main lock often has an additional auxiliary key lock. These locks, either main or auxiliary, can be of the mechanical combination, key, or electronic keypad design.

The electronic lock allows immediate lock programming and change, and can also be connected to a duress (silent alarm) contact in the security system.

Boltwork

Most safes are supplied with bolts on the hinged and leading-edge door. Today, most high-security safes are supplied with door bolts in all directions to defend against attacks on all four sides. The fewer moving parts in the interior boltwork design, the better the security. Multiple welding of parts and multiple gearing offer a better chance of failure for a thief.

Relockers

The best security in a safe is offered by internal relockers. These can be either active or passive. They are hidden in the door, and when the safe is attacked by jackhammer, heavy shock, high speed drills, carbide desk, torch, or explosives, they cause the system to lock the bolts closed.

Alarm Systems

Many safes are equipped with external alarm contacts, and internal (out-of-sight) alarms can also be provided. Heat sensors can be also supplied.

Warranty

Usually safe manufacturers offer a one-year warranty on parts, labor, and material. In many instances your safe supplier will extend the warranty.

Photographs and Digital Images

An unretouched 35mm photograph is like a fingerprint. Many fingerprints look similar, but, if you look closely, you will discover that each is unique. It is the same with an unretouched 35mm coin photograph. Although a coin in an unretouched photograph may at first resemble a coin other than the one photographed, if you closely compare photo to coin, you'll discover there's no way of switching. Use a magnifying glass, and look for some tiny characteristic on the coin. That same characteristic will be on the photograph. Photographs are an important identification aid, and might even assist you in recovering your coins if they are ever stolen.

For many years, collectors relied on the Polaroid Collector System, with a built-in Spectra II AF camera. The camera has a table that places the coin at the correct angle to be photographed so that it appears perfectly round.

Today, digital cameras are the norm, and the results can be astounding. For images of coins, I use an 8 megapixel digital camera, with close-up lens attachments. Outstanding digital cameras are made by Canon, Kodak, Minolta, Nikon, Sony, and others. Online reviews of the latest digital cameras can be found at *CNET.com*.

However, with the advent of these cameras, manipulation of a coin's digital image is easy. Occasionally, unscrupulous online merchants will modify digital files so that coins will appear to be of higher grades.

For insurance purposes, digital image files should be stored separately and offsite from your coins. In the event of a natural or other disaster, images of your coins stored with a relative or friend in another state would come in handy.

APPENDICES

Value Chart for United States and Canadian Silver Coins

Value Chart for Commonly Traded United States Coins and World Gold Coins

Specifications for American Eagle Silver and Gold Bullion Coins

Internet Resources

Calamity Insurance: Gold Coins as a Safe Haven

VALUE CHART FOR UNITED STATES AND CANADIAN SILVER COINS

Silver Price Per Ounce	$9.00	$9.25	$9.50	$9.75	$10.00	$10.25	$10.50	$10.75
U.S. 5¢ .350 Fine (Wartime Nickels)	.51	.52	.53	.55	.56	.58	.59	.60
U.S. 50¢ .400 Fine (1965–1970 Clad)	1.33	1.37	1.40	1.44	1.48	1.52	1.55	1.59
U.S. $1.00 .400 Fine (Collector's Coins)	2.85	2.93	3.00	3.08	3.16	3.24	3.32	3.40
U.S. 10¢ .900 Fine (Pre-1965)	.65	.67	.69	.71	.72	.74	.76	.78
U.S. 25¢ .900 Fine (Pre-1965)	1.63	1.67	1.72	1.76	1.81	1.85	1.90	1.94
U.S. 50¢ .900 Fine (Pre-1965)	3.26	3.34	3.44	3.53	3.61	3.71	3.80	3.89
U.S. $1.00 .900 Fine (Pre-1971)	6.96	7.15	7.35	7.54	7.73	7.93	8.12	8.31
Canada 10¢ .800 Fine (1920–1967)	.54	.56	.57	.59	.60	.62	.63	.65
Canada 25¢ .800 Fine (1920–1967)	1.35	1.39	1.43	1.46	1.50	1.54	1.58	1.61
Canada 50¢ .800 Fine (1920–1967)	2.70	2.78	2.85	2.93	3.00	3.08	3.15	3.23
Canada $1.00 .800 Fine (1935–1967)	5.40	5.55	5.70	5.85	6.00	6.15	6.30	6.45
Canada 10¢ .500 Fine (1967 & 1968)*	.34	.35	.36	.37	.38	.38	.39	.40
Canada 25¢ .500 Fine (1967 & 1968)*	.84	.87	.89	.91	.94	.96	.98	1.01

Source: Courtesy Krause Publications, Inc. All Rights Reserved.
*The 1967 Canadian 10¢ and 25¢ were produced in both .800 and .500 Fine.

$11.00	$11.25	$11.50	$11.75	$12.00	$12.25	$12.50	$12.75	$13.00	$13.25	$13.50	$13.75
.62	.63	.65	.66	.68	.69	.70	.72	.73	.75	.76	.77
1.63	1.66	1.70	1.74	1.78	1.81	1.85	1.89	1.92	1.96	2.00	2.03
3.48	3.56	3.64	3.72	3.80	3.87	3.95	4.03	4.11	4.19	4.27	4.35
.80	.81	.83	.85	.87	.89	.90	.92	.94	.96	.98	.99
1.99	2.03	2.08	2.12	2.17	2.22	2.26	2.31	2.35	2.40	2.44	2.49
3.98	4.07	4.16	4.25	4.34	4.43	4.52	4.61	4.70	4.79	4.88	4.97
8.51	8.70	8.89	9.09	9.28	9.47	9.67	9.86	10.05	10.25	10.44	10.63
.66	.68	.69	.71	.72	.74	.75	.77	.78	.80	.81	.83
1.65	1.69	1.73	1.76	1.80	1.84	1.88	1.91	1.95	1.99	2.03	2.06
3.30	3.38	3.45	3.53	3.60	3.68	3.75	3.83	3.90	3.98	4.05	4.13
6.60	6.75	6.90	7.05	7.20	7.35	7.50	7.65	7.80	7.95	8.10	8.25
.41	.42	.43	.44	.45	.46	.47	.48	.49	.50	.51	.52
1.03	1.05	1.08	1.10	1.13	1.15	1.17	1.20	1.22	1.24	1.27	1.29

Silver Price Per Ounce	$14.00	$14.25	$14.50	$14.75	$15.00	$15.25	$15.50	$15.75
U.S. 5¢ .350 Fine (Wartime Nickels)	.79	.80	.82	.83	.84	.86	.87	.89
U.S. 50¢ .400 Fine (1965–1970 Clad)	2.07	2.11	2.14	2.18	2.22	2.26	2.29	2.33
U.S. $1.00 .400 Fine (Collector's Coins)	4.43	4.51	4.59	4.66	4.74	4.82	4.90	4.98
U.S. 10¢ .900 Fine (Pre-1965)	1.01	1.03	1.05	1.07	1.09	1.10	1.12	1.14
U.S. 25¢ .900 Fine (Pre-1965)	2.53	2.58	2.62	2.67	2.71	2.76	2.80	2.85
U.S. 50¢ .900 Fine (Pre-1965)	5.06	5.15	5.24	5.33	5.43	5.52	5.61	5.70
U.S. $1.00 .900 Fine (Pre-1971)	10.83	11.02	11.21	11.41	11.60	11.79	11.99	12.18
Canada 10¢ .800 Fine (1920–1967)	.84	.86	.87	.89	.90	.92	.93	.95
Canada 25¢ .800 Fine (1920–1967)	2.10	2.14	2.18	2.21	2.25	2.29	2.32	2.36
Canada 50¢ .800 Fine (1920–1967)	4.20	4.28	4.35	4.43	4.50	4.58	4.65	4.73
Canada $1.00 .800 Fine (1935–1967)	8.40	8.55	8.70	8.85	9.00	9.15	9.30	9.45
Canada 10¢ .500 Fine (1967 & 1968)*	.53	.53	.54	.55	.56	.57	.58	.59
Canada 25¢ .500 Fine (1967 & 1968)*	1.31	1.34	1.36	1.38	1.41	1.43	1.45	1.48

$16.00	$16.25	$16.50	$16.75	$17.00	$17.25	$17.50	$17.75	$18.00	$18.25	$18.50	$18.75
.90	.91	.93	.94	.96	.97	.98	1.00	1.01	1.02	1.04	1.05
2.37	2.40	2.44	2.48	2.51	2.55	2.59	2.62	2.66	2.70	2.74	2.77
5.06	5.14	5.22	5.30	5.38	5.45	5.53	5.61	5.69	5.77	5.85	5.93
1.16	1.18	1.19	1.21	1.23	1.25	1.27	1.28	1.30	1.32	1.34	1.36
2.89	2.94	2.98	3.03	3.07	3.12	3.16	3.21	3.26	3.30	3.35	3.39
5.79	5.88	5.97	6.06	6.15	6.24	6.33	6.42	6.51	6.60	6.69	6.78
12.37	12.57	12.76	12.96	13.15	13.34	13.54	13.73	13.92	14.12	14.31	14.50
.96	.98	.99	1.01	1.02	1.04	1.05	1.07	1.08	1.10	1.11	1.13
2.40	2.44	2.48	2.51	2.55	2.59	2.63	2.66	2.70	2.74	2.78	2.81
4.80	4.88	4.95	5.03	5.10	5.18	5.25	5.33	5.40	5.48	5.55	5.63
9.60	9.75	9.90	10.05	10.20	10.35	10.50	10.65	10.80	10.95	11.10	11.25
.60	.61	.62	.63	.64	.65	.66	.67	.68	.68	.69	.70
1.50	1.52	1.55	1.57	1.59	1.62	1.64	1.66	1.69	1.71	1.73	1.76

VALUE CHART FOR COMMONLY TRADED UNITED STATES COINS AND WORLD GOLD COINS

Gold Price Per Ounce	**$360**	**$370**	**$380**	**$390**	**$400**	**$410**	**$420**	**$430**	**$440**	**$450**	**$460**	**$470**
USA $1.00 .900 Fine	17.42	17.90	18.38	18.87	19.35	19.84	20.32	20.80	21.29	21.77	22.25	22.74
USA $2.50 .900 Fine	43.53	44.74	45.95	47.16	48.37	49.58	50.79	52.00	53.21	54.41	55.62	56.83
USA $3.00 .900 Fine	52.29	53.75	55.20	56.65	58.10	59.56	61.01	62.46	63.91	65.37	66.82	68.27
USA $5.00 .900 Fine	87.07	89.49	91.91	94.33	96.75	99.17	101.59	104.01	106.42	108.84	111.26	113.68
USA $10.00 .900 Fine	174.15	178.99	183.82	188.66	193.50	196.34	203.17	208.01	212.85	217.69	222.52	227.36
USA $20.00 .900 Fine	348.30	357.97	367.65	377.32	387.00	396.67	406.35	416.02	425.70	435.37	445.05	454.72
Australia $200 .916 Fine	106.10	109.05	112.00	114.94	117.89	120.84	123.78	126.73	129.68	132.63	135.57	138.52
Austria 1 Ducat .986 Fine	39.84	40.95	42.05	43.16	44.27	45.37	46.48	47.59	48.69	49.80	50.91	52.01
Austria 4 Ducat .986 Fine	159.36	163.79	168.21	172.64	177.07	181.49	185.92	190.35	194.77	199.20	203.63	208.05
Austria 10 Francs .900 Fine	33.60	34.54	35.47	36.40	37.34	38.27	39.21	40.14	41.07	42.01	42.94	43.87
Austria 20 Francs .900 Fine	67.21	69.08	70.94	72.81	74.68	76.54	78.41	80.28	82.14	84.01	85.88	87.75
Austria 10 Corona .900 Fine	35.29	36.27	37.25	38.23	39.21	40.19	41.17	42.15	43.13	44.12	45.10	46.08
Austria 20 Corona .900 Fine	70.57	72.53	74.49	76.46	78.42	80.38	82.34	84.30	86.26	88.22	90.18	92.14
Austria 100 Corona .900 Fine	352.87	362.67	372.47	382.28	392.06	401.88	411.68	421.48	431.29	441.09	450.89	460.69
Belgium 20 Francs .900 Fine	67.21	69.08	70.94	72.81	74.68	76.54	78.41	80.28	82.14	84.01	85.88	87.75
Britain ½ Sovereign .916 Fine	42.38	43.55	44.73	45.91	47.09	48.26	49.44	50.62	51.79	52.97	54.15	55.33

Note: These values reflect the approximate gold value contained in standard coins of the indicated units, and do not take into consideration wear to which a coin might be subjected in circulation. Neither do they allow for numismatic value considerations. All values, except the per dollar values in the extreme right column, are rounded to the nearest cent.

Source: Courtesy Krause Publications, Inc.

$480	$490	$500	$510	$520	$530	$540	$550	$560	$570	$580	$590	$600	$610	$620	Changes in value per dollar
23.22	23.71	24.19	24.67	25.16	25.64	26.13	26.61	27.09	27.58	28.06	28.54	29.03	29.51	30.00	.0484
58.04	59.25	60.46	61.67	62.88	64.09	65.30	66.51	67.72	68.93	70.13	71.34	72.55	73.76	74.97	.1209
69.72	71.18	72.63	74.08	75.53	76.99	78.44	79.89	81.34	82.80	84.25	85.70	87.15	88.61	90.06	.1453
116.10	118.52	120.94	123.36	125.77	128.19	130.61	133.03	135.45	137.87	140.29	142.71	145.12	147.54	149.96	.2419
232.20	237.04	241.87	246.71	251.55	256.39	261.22	266.06	270.90	275.74	280.57	285.41	290.25	295.09	299.92	.4837
464.40	474.07	483.75	493.42	503.10	512.77	522.45	532.12	541.80	551.47	561.15	570.82	580.50	590.17	599.85	.9675
141.74	144.42	147.36	150.31	153.26	156.20	159.15	162.10	165.05	167.99	170.94	173.89	176.84	179.78	182.73	.2947
53.12	54.23	55.33	56.44	57.55	58.65	59.76	60.87	61.97	63.08	64.19	65.29	66.40	67.51	68.61	.1107
212.48	216.91	221.33	225.76	230.19	234.61	239.04	243.47	247.89	252.32	256.75	261.17	265.60	270.03	274.45	.4427
44.81	45.74	46.67	47.61	48.54	49.47	50.41	51.34	52.27	53.21	54.14	55.07	56.01	56.94	57.87	.0933
89.61	91.48	93.35	95.21	97.08	98.95	100.81	102.68	104.55	106.42	108.28	110.15	112.02	113.88	115.75	.1867
47.06	48.04	49.02	50.00	50.98	51.96	52.94	53.92	54.90	55.88	56.86	57.84	58.82	59.80	60.78	.0980
94.10	96.06	98.02	99.98	101.94	103.90	105.86	107.82	109.78	111.74	113.70	115.66	117.62	119.58	121.54	.1960
470.49	480.30	490.10	499.90	509.70	519.50	529.31	539.11	548.91	558.71	568.51	578.32	588.12	597.92	607.72	.9802
89.61	91.48	93.35	95.21	97.08	98.95	100.81	102.68	104.55	106.42	108.28	110.15	112.02	113.88	115.75	.1867
56.50	57.68	58.86	60.03	61.21	62.39	63.57	64.74	65.92	67.10	68.27	69.45	70.63	71.80	72.98	.1177

Gold Price Per Ounce	**$360**	**$370**	**$380**	**$390**	**$400**	**$410**	**$420**	**$430**	**$440**	**$450**	**$460**	**$470**
Britain 1 Sovereign .916 Fine	84.75	87.11	89.46	91.82	94.17	96.53	98.88	101.23	103.59	105.94	108.30	110.65
Britain 2£ .916 Fine	169.51	174.22	178.92	183.63	188.34	193.05	197.76	202.47	207.18	211.88	216.59	221.30
Britain 5£ .916 Fine	423.77	435.54	447.31	459.08	470.85	482.62	494.40	506.17	517.94	529.71	541.48	553.25
Canada $100 .583 Fine	90.00	92.50	95.00	97.49	99.99	102.49	104.99	107.49	109.99	112.49	114.99	117.49
Canada Maple Leaf .999 Fine	359.60	369.59	379.58	389.57	399.56	409.54	419.53	429.52	439.51	449.50	459.49	469.48
Chile 100 Pesos .916 Fine	215.70	221.70	227.69	233.68	239.67	245.66	251.65	257.65	263.64	269.63	275.62	281.61
Colombia 5 Pesos .916 Fine	84.75	87.11	89.46	91.82	94.17	96.53	98.88	101.23	103.59	105.94	108.30	110.65
France 10 Francs .900 Fine	33.60	34.54	35.47	36.40	37.34	38.27	39.21	40.14	41.07	42.01	42.94	43.87
France 20 Francs .900 Fine	67.21	69.08	70.94	72.81	74.68	76.54	78.41	80.28	82.14	84.01	85.88	87.75
German States 10 Mark .900 Fine	41.48	42.64	43.79	44.94	46.09	47.25	48.40	49.55	50.70	51.86	53.01	54.16
German States 20 Mark .900 Fine	82.97	85.27	87.58	89.88	92.19	94.49	96.80	99.10	101.41	103.71	106.02	108.32
Hong Kong $1000 .916 Fine	169.51	174.22	178.92	183.63	188.34	193.05	197.76	202.47	207.18	211.88	216.59	221.30
Hungary 10 Korona .900 Fine	35.29	36.27	37.25	38.23	39.21	40.19	41.17	42.15	43.13	44.12	45.10	46.08
Hungary 20 Korona .900 Fine	70.57	72.53	74.49	76.46	78.42	80.38	82.34	84.30	86.26	88.22	90.18	92.14
Hungary 100 Korona .900 Fine	352.87	362.67	372.47	382.28	392.08	401.88	411.68	421.48	431.29	441.09	450.89	460.69
Iran 1 Pahlavi .900 Fine	84.38	86.72	89.06	91.41	93.75	96.10	98.44	100.78	103.13	105.47	107.81	110.16
Jamaica $100 .900 Fine	118.13	121.41	124.69	127.97	131.25	134.53	137.81	141.10	144.38	147.66	150.94	154.22
Mexico 2 Pesos .900 Fine	17.35	17.84	18.32	18.80	19.28	19.76	20.25	20.73	21.21	21.69	22.18	22.66
Mexico 2.5 Pesos .900 Fine	21.70	22.30	22.90	23.51	24.11	24.71	25.31	25.92	26.52	27.12	27.73	28.33
Mexico 5 Pesos .900 Fine	43.40	44.60	45.81	47.01	48.22	49.42	50.63	51.83	53.04	54.25	55.45	56.66
Mexico 10 Pesos .900 Fine	86.80	89.21	91.63	94.04	96.45	98.86	101.27	103.68	106.09	108.50	110.92	113.33
Mexico 20 Pesos .900 Fine	173.61	178.43	183.25	188.07	192.90	197.72	202.54	207.36	212.19	217.01	221.83	226.65
Mexico 50 Pesos .900 Fine	434.03	446.08	458.14	470.20	482.25	494.31	506.37	518.42	530.48	542.53	554.59	566.65
Mexico Onza Oro .900 Fine	359.99	369.99	379.99	389.99	399.99	409.99	419.99	429.99	439.99	449.99	459.99	469.99

$480	$490	$500	$510	$520	$530	$540	$550	$560	$570	$580	$590	$600	$610	$620	Changes in value per dollar
113.00	155.36	117.71	120.07	122.42	124.78	127.13	129.48	131.84	134.19	136.55	138.90	141.26	143.61	145.96	.2354
226.01	230.72	235.43	240.14	244.84	249.55	254.26	258.97	263.68	268.39	273.10	277.80	282.51	287.22	291.93	.4709
565.02	576.80	588.57	600.34	612.11	623.88	635.65	647.42	659.20	670.97	682.74	694.51	706.28	718.05	729.82	1.1771
119.99	122.49	124.99	127.49	129.99	132.49	134.99	137.49	139.99	142.49	144.99	147.49	149.99	152.49	154.99	.2500
479.47	489.46	499.44	509.43	519.42	529.41	539.40	549.39	559.38	569.37	579.36	589.34	599.33	609.32	619.31	.9989
287.60	293.60	299.59	305.58	311.57	317.56	323.56	329.55	335.54	341.53	347.52	353.51	359.51	365.50	371.49	.5992
113.00	115.36	117.71	120.07	122.42	124.78	127.13	129.48	131.84	134.19	136.55	138.90	141.26	143.61	145.96	.2354
44.81	45.74	46.67	47.61	48.54	49.47	50.41	51.34	52.27	53.21	54.14	55.07	56.01	56.94	57.87	.0933
89.61	91.48	93.35	95.21	97.08	98.95	100.81	102.68	104.55	106.42	108.28	110.15	112.02	113.88	115.75	.1867
55.31	56.47	57.62	58.77	59.92	61.08	62.23	63.38	64.53	65.68	66.84	67.99	69.14	70.29	71.45	.1152
110.63	112.93	115.24	117.54	119.85	122.15	124.45	126.76	129.06	131.37	133.67	135.98	138.28	140.59	142.89	.2305
226.01	230.72	235.43	240.14	244.84	249.55	254.26	258.97	263.68	268.39	273.10	277.80	282.51	287.22	291.93	.4709
47.06	48.04	49.02	50.00	50.98	51.96	52.94	53.92	54.90	55.88	56.86	57.84	58.82	59.80	60.78	.0980
94.10	96.06	98.02	99.98	101.94	103.90	105.86	107.82	109.78	111.74	113.70	115.66	117.62	119.58	121.54	.1960
470.49	480.30	490.10	499.90	509.70	519.50	529.31	539.11	548.91	558.71	568.51	578.32	588.12	597.92	607.72	.9802
112.50	114.85	117.19	119.53	121.88	124.22	126.56	128.91	131.25	133.60	135.94	138.28	140.63	142.97	145.31	.2344
157.50	160.78	164.07	167.35	170.63	173.91	177.19	180.47	183.75	187.03	190.32	193.60	196.88	200.16	203.44	.3281
23.14	23.62	24.10	24.59	25.07	25.55	26.03	26.51	27.00	27.48	27.96	28.44	28.92	29.41	29.89	.0482
28.93	29.53	30.14	30.74	31.34	31.94	32.55	33.15	33.75	34.36	34.96	35.56	36.16	36.77	37.37	.0603
57.86	59.07	60.27	61.48	62.68	63.89	65.09	66.30	67.51	68.71	69.92	71.12	72.33	73.53	74.74	.1205
115.74	118.15	120.56	122.97	125.38	127.79	130.21	132.62	135.03	137.44	139.85	142.26	144.67	147.08	149.50	.2411
231.48	236.30	241.12	245.94	250.77	255.59	260.41	265.23	270.06	274.88	279.70	284.52	289.35	294.17	298.99	.4822
578.70	590.76	602.82	614.87	626.93	638.99	651.04	663.10	675.15	687.21	699.27	711.32	723.38	735.44	747.49	1.2056
479.99	489.99	499.99	509.99	519.99	529.99	539.99	549.99	559.98	569.98	579.98	589.98	599.98	609.98	619.98	1.0000

Gold Price Per Ounce	**$360**	**$370**	**$380**	**$390**	**$400**	**$410**	**$420**	**$430**	**$440**	**$450**	**$460**	**$470**
Netherlands 10 Gulden .900 Fine	70.09	72.04	73.99	75.94	77.88	79.83	81.78	83.72	85.67	87.62	89.57	91.51
Netherlands 1 Ducat .986 Fine	39.87	40.98	42.09	43.20	44.30	45.41	46.52	47.63	48.74	49.84	50.95	52.06
Panama 100 Balboa .900 Fine	85.00	87.36	89.72	92.08	94.45	96.81	99.17	101.53	103.89	106.25	108.61	110.97
Peru 1/5 Libra .916 Fine	16.98	17.45	17.92	18.39	18.86	19.33	19.81	20.28	20.75	21.22	21.69	22.16
Peru 1/2 Libra .916 Fine	42.38	43.55	44.73	45.91	47.09	48.26	49.44	50.62	51.79	52.97	54.15	55.33
Peru 1 Libra .916 Fine	84.75	87.11	89.46	91.82	94.17	96.53	98.88	101.23	103.59	105.94	108.30	110.65
Peru 100 Soles .900 Fine	487.61	501.16	514.70	528.25	541.79	555.34	568.88	582.43	595.97	609.52	623.06	636.60
Russia 5 Roubles .900 Fine	44.80	46.05	47.29	48.54	49.78	51.03	52.27	53.51	54.76	56.00	57.25	58.49
Russia Chervonets .900 Fine	89.61	92.09	94.58	97.07	99.56	102.05	104.54	107.03	109.52	112.01	114.50	116.98
South Africa 1 Rand .916 Fine	42.38	43.55	44.73	45.91	47.09	48.26	49.44	50.62	51.79	52.97	54.15	55.33
South Africa 2 Rands .916 Fine	84.75	87.11	89.46	91.82	94.17	96.53	98.88	101.23	103.59	105.94	108.30	110.65
South Africa Krugerrand .916 Fine	360.00	370.00	380.00	390.00	400.00	410.00	420.00	430.00	440.00	450.00	460.00	470.00
Switzerland 10 Francs .900 Fine	33.60	34.54	35.47	36.40	37.34	38.27	39.21	40.14	41.07	42.01	42.94	43.87
Switzerland 20 Francs .900 Fine	67.21	69.08	70.94	72.81	74.68	76.54	78.41	80.28	82.14	84.01	85.88	87.75
Turkey 100 Piastres .916 Fine	76.57	78.70	80.83	82.95	85.08	87.21	89.34	91.46	93.59	95.72	97.84	99.97
Turkey 500 Piastres .916 Fine	382.85	393.48	404.11	414.75	425.38	436.02	446.65	457.29	467.92	478.56	489.19	499.83

$480	$490	$500	$510	$520	$530	$540	$550	$560	$570	$580	$590	$600	$610	$620	Changes in value per dollar
93.46	95.41	97.35	99.30	101.25	103.20	105.14	107.09	109.94	110.98	112.93	114.88	116.82	118.77	120.72	.1947
53.17	54.27	55.38	56.49	57.60	58.70	59.81	60.92	62.03	63.13	64.24	65.35	66.46	67.56	68.67	.1108
113.34	115.70	118.06	120.42	122.78	125.14	127.50	129.86	132.22	134.59	136.95	139.31	141.67	144.03	146.39	.2361
22.63	23.11	23.58	24.05	24.52	24.99	25.46	25.94	26.41	26.88	27.35	27.82	28.29	28.77	29.24	.0472
56.50	57.68	58.86	60.03	61.21	62.39	63.57	64.74	65.92	67.10	68.27	69.45	70.63	71.80	72.98	.1177
113.00	115.36	117.71	120.07	122.42	124.78	127.13	129.48	131.84	134.19	136.55	138.90	141.26	143.61	145.96	.2354
650.15	663.69	677.24	690.78	704.33	717.87	731.42	744.96	758.51	772.05	785.60	799.14	812.69	826.23	839.78	1.3545
59.74	60.98	62.23	63.47	64.72	65.96	67.20	68.45	69.69	70.94	72.18	73.43	74.67	75.92	77.16	.1245
119.47	121.96	124.45	126.94	129.43	131.92	134.41	136.90	139.39	141.88	144.36	146.85	149.34	151.83	154.32	.2489
56.50	57.68	58.86	60.03	61.21	62.39	63.57	64.74	65.92	67.10	68.27	69.45	70.63	71.80	72.98	.1177
113.00	115.36	117.71	120.07	122.42	124.78	127.13	129.48	131.84	134.19	136.55	138.90	141.26	143.61	145.96	.2354
480.00	490.00	500.00	510.00	520.00	530.00	540.00	550.00	560.00	570.00	580.00	590.00	600.00	610.00	620.00	1.0000
44.81	45.74	46.67	47.61	48.54	49.47	50.41	51.34	52.27	53.21	54.14	55.07	56.01	56.94	57.87	.0933
89.61	91.48	93.35	95.21	97.08	98.95	100.81	102.68	104.55	106.42	108.28	110.15	112.02	113.88	115.75	.1867
102.10	104.22	106.35	108.48	110.61	112.73	114.86	116.99	119.11	121.24	123.37	125.50	127.62	129.75	131.88	.2127
510.46	521.09	531.73	542.36	553.00	563.63	574.27	584.90	595.54	606.17	616.81	627.44	638.08	648.71	659.34	1.0635

SPECIFICATIONS FOR AMERICAN EAGLE SILVER AND GOLD BULLION COINS

Silver
U.S. $1 .999 Fine; 1 troy ounce
Diameter: 40.60 millimeters (1.598 inches)
Thickness: 2.96 millimeters (0.117 inches)
Silver: .999 troy ounces

Gold
U.S. $50 .917 Fine; 1.0909 troy ounces
Diameter: 32.70 millimeters (1.287 inches)
Thickness: 2.83 millimeters (0.111 inches)
Gold: 1 troy ounce

U.S. $25 .917 Fine; 0.5455 troy ounces
Diameter: 27.0 Millimeters (1.063 inches)
Thickness: 2.16 millimeters (0.085 inches)
Gold: 0.5 troy ounces

U.S. $10 .917 Fine; 0.2727 troy ounces
Diameter: 22 millimeters (0.866 inches)
Thickness: 1.79 millimeters (0.07 inches)
Gold: 0.25 troy ounces

U.S. $5 .917 Fine; 0.1091 troy ounces
Diameter: 16.5 millimeters (0.65 inches)
Thickness: 1.27 millimeters (0.05 inches)
Gold: 0.1 troy ounces

Note: These coins are traded for a small premium above their gold content.

INTERNET RESOURCES

The author cannot endorse any commercial vendors except himself, and does not monitor the text or images contained on sites other than his own. Information is provided here solely as a convenience to Internet users.

Auctions (primarily Internet-based)

eBay
www.ebay.com

Teletrade
www.teletrade.com

Consumer Protection

California Consumer Affairs on Telemarketing
www.dca.ca.gov/r_r/telemark.htm

Federal Trade Commission Coin Alert
www.ftc.gov/bcp/conline/pubs/alerts/coinalrt.htm

Federal Trade Commission Press Releases (sampling)
www.ftc.gov/opa/predawn/F93/pcgs-coin8.txt

www.ftc.gov/opa/predawn/F89/hert.txt

www.ftc.gov/opa/predawn/F87/sfmc.txt

www.ftc.gov/opa/predawn/F87/rarecoins2.txt

Numismatic Consumer Alliance, Inc.
www.stopcoinfraud.org

Scott Travers Rare Coin Consumer Protection
www.pocketchangelottery.com/travers3.htm

Federal Reserve Banks

Atlanta
www.frbatlanta.org/

Minneapolis
woodrow.mpls.frb.fed.us/

New York
www.ny.frb.org/

St. Louis
www.stls.frb.org/

Grading Services

ANACS
www.anacs.com

Independent Coin Grading Company
www.icgcoin.com

Numismatic Guaranty Corporation of America, Inc.
www.ngccoin.com

Professional Coin Grading Service
www.pcgs.com

Information Resources

Certified Coin Exchange
www.certifiedcoinexchange.com

Coin Club Locator
www.coinclubs.com

Scott Travers Articles
www.pocketchangelottery.com/articles.htm

U.S. Coin On-line Encyclopedia
www.coinfacts.com

U.S. Department of the Treasury/Mint/B.E.P.
www.bep.treas.gov/

www.treas.gov/mint/

www.usmint.gov/

U.S. National Numismatic Collection/Smithsonian Institution
americanhistory.si.edu/collections/numismatics/

Worldwide Coin Show Directory
coinshows.com

Numismatic Literature

Brooklyn Gallery Coins & Stamps
www.brooklyngallery.com

Charles Davis Numismatic Literature
www.abebooks.com/home/numismat

George Frederick Kolbe Fine Numismatic Books
www.numislit.com

Krause Publications
www.krausebooks.com

Scott Travers Information Services
www.pocketchangelottery.com

Organizations

American Israel Numismatic Association
www.amerisrael.com

American Numismatic Association
www.money.org

American Numismatic Society
www.amnumsoc.org

British Art Medal Society
www.bams.org.uk

Canadian Numismatic Association
www.canadian-numismatic.org

Canadian Numismatic Research Society
www.nunetcan.net/cnrs.htm

Classical and Medieval Numismatic Society
www.nunetcan.net/cmns.htm

CoinMasters On-line Coin Club
www.coinmasters.org/mainpage.html

Combined Organizations of Numismatic Error Collectors of America
hermes.csd.net/~coneca

Early America Coppers
eacs.org

International Bank Note Society
www.public.coe.edu/~sfeller/IBNSJ

John Reich Collectors Society
www.logan.com/jrcs

Numismatic Bibliomania Society
www.coinbooks.org

Numismatic Literary Guild
www.numismaticliteraryguild.org

Professional Numismatists Guild
www.pngdealers.com

Royal Numismatic Society
www.rns.dircon.co.uk

Society of U.S. Pattern Collectors
www.uspatterns.com

Token & Medal Society
www.money.org/clubs/tams/index.html

Periodicals

The Celator
www.celator.com

The Coin Dealer Newsletter
www.greysheet.com

COINage magazine
www.coinagemag.com

Coins magazine
www.krause.com

Coin World
www.coinworld.com

Numismatic News
www.krause.com

World Coin News
www.krause.com

E-mail Addresses for Editors of Publications

Beth Deisher
Editor, *Coin World*
bdeisher@coinworld.com

Marcy Gibbel
Managing Editor, *COINage* magazine
CoinMag2@aol.com

Barbara Gregory
Editor, *Numismatist*
gregory@money.org

David C. Harper
Editor, *Numismatic News*
harperd@krause.com

Ed Reiter
Senior Editor, *COINage* magazine
EdEditor@aol.com

Robert R. VanRyzin
Editor, *Coins* magazine
vanryzinr@krause.com

CALAMITY INSURANCE: GOLD COINS AS A SAFE HAVEN

This section has been prepared exclusively for *The Coin Collector's Survival Manual* by the award-winning coin investment newsletter publisher Maurice Rosen.

Gold has been a timeless store of value through the ages. It is the basis for our monetary system and is universally recognized for its brilliant luster and resilience as a noble metal. Consequently, certain gold coins can be regarded as a safe-haven insurance policy against an uncertain world. That role can often be adequately satisfied by the premier denomination among regularly issued U.S. coins: the $20 gold piece, also known as the double eagle. This coin was minted in two broad design types: the Liberty head, from 1850 to 1907 (with three minor design variations), and the Saint-Gaudens, issued from 1907 to 1933 (with two minor design variations). Each of these coin types has characteristics than can add a fair measure of balance and reduced risk to the asset holdings of many individuals.

Let's look at the features of these coins. Each contains nearly a full ounce of pure gold—0.9675 oz., to be exact. Millions each of the Liberty and Saint-Gaudens coins exist today. They are among the most actively traded U.S. coins, are highly liquid, and offer buyers and sellers relatively low price spreads between what a dealer pays for them and what he or she charges for them. These are very attractive features, as they help minimize your transactional risk and provide you with coins possessing a high degree of visible value.

The safe-haven status of these coins relates directly to their cost and the actual value of the gold they contain. There is a term for this: Premium Over Melt (POM). Here's an example. Assume that the price of a $20 Liberty is $475. If the price of an ounce of gold is $425, the coin would contain $411.18 worth of gold ($425 x 0.9675). Based on the $475 coin price, this Liberty would be worth 16 percent more than the full value of the gold it contains. ($475 ÷ $411.18 × 100% = 116%). This means that the POM is 16 percent.

Such premiums can and do vary according to market conditions, notably the supply and demand for the coins. In fact, over the last twenty years of market price history, the POM has varied from a low of about 5 percent to a high approaching 100 percent.

The prospect of buying these coins near the lower end of this range presents a potentially attractive opportunity, and the prospect of selling them near the high end of that range is certainly enticing. These coins represent a better safe-haven alternative at lower POMs than at higher ones.

Besides the risk of the POM declining after you buy the coins, the biggest risk is the fluctuation in the price of gold. This risk is the "cost" of your safe-haven insurance. As has often been the case in the past, the gold price increases—sometimes dramatically—when traditional paper investment vehicles such as stocks and bonds are not doing well.

1907 $20 Liberty, substantially abraded, just makes the MS-61 grade, although the MS-60 designation is tempting. *ANA photograph*

1900 $20 Liberty, likely to grade MS-64 at a leading grading service, has great luster and eye appeal but is marred by some minor abrasions on the neck. Coins such as this in older holders are sometimes graded MS-63 but can be resubmitted for an upgrade. *ANA photograph*

Therefore, the better relative performance of gold might cushion the poorer performance of traditional investments. On the other hand, gold tends not to be a good performer when stocks and bonds are performing well. Thus, gold coins can serve as an "insurance" component of your holdings.

$20 Liberty Gold Pieces

Minted from 1850 to 1907, the Liberty double eagle is a proud, hefty reminder of a young, growing and vibrant country. At a time when $20 may have been one or two weeks' wages for a working man, these coins rarely ended up in the pockets of most Americans. The coins tended to see more circulation in Western states than Eastern ones, because the gold was mined in the West.

Today $20 "Libs" often trade in bulk quantities in grades from Very Fine to the lower levels of Mint State (from MS-60 to MS-63). In circulated grades, they tend to trade as raw, or uncertified, coins. This is because the cost of certification would add disproportionately to the cost of the coins. Also, the difference in value between grades in the VF–AU range is relatively modest, thus typically making certification less important. Moreover, since these coins lend themselves to bulk trading, they are more efficiently shipped and stored in rolls or tubes than in a grading service's bulky individual slabs.

In Mint State condition, the most actively traded $20 Libs are graded MS-61 and MS-62. The MS-61 coins typically sell for about a 5 percent premium over AU coins. In MS-62, there might be only a 3 to 5 percent price premium over the MS-61 coin. The grade MS-63 represents a "Choice Uncirculated" specimen, which starts to get into the range of better-quality gold coins. Consequently, while certified MS-63s also often trade in bulk quantities, their prices reflect this added relative scarcity and appeal. MS-63s are often valued at premiums of 30 percent or more above their MS-62 counterparts.

Saint-Gaudens Double Eagles

Called by many "the most beautiful U.S. coin," the Saint-Gaudens double eagle made its debut in 1907. Whereas some 100 million $20 Liberties were produced from 1850 to 1907, around 70 million Saint-Gaudens double eagles were minted through 1933. The "Saints" that exist today tend to be in better condition than the Libs. This is because the Libs had been circulating for decades before the Saints came on the scene. When huge quantities of U.S. gold coins were sent to Europe during the 1930s due to the currency turmoil and financial upheavals of the decade's worldwide depression, more of the comparatively newer Saint-Gaudens coins were sent than the Liberties.

While a large and active trading market exists for $20 Liberties in VF to AU grades, that is not the case with the Saints. Saints in AU condition tend to make up the lower range of actively traded circulated pieces. Like circulated Libs, these AU Saints are usually not certified, but trade raw, thus lending themselves to more efficient shipping and storage in bulk quantities.

While the Saints are more "common" than the Libs, many collectors prefer the Saints because of the attractive design. That design was revived in 1986 when the U.S. Mint started to produce its American Eagle gold bullion coins. Certified Saints in MS-61 to MS-64 are extremely popular and actively traded in quantity. The price difference between the MS-61 and MS-62 might be only a few dollars. The jump from MS-62 to MS-63 is currently around 10 percent, which contrasts with the approximate 30 percent premium for the MS-63 Libs versus the MS-62.

Three Steps to Success

U.S. $20 gold pieces are actively traded safe-haven "insurance policies" against an increasingly dangerous and uncertain world. This is particularly so when they can be bought and sold under three opportune circumstances. The first is when the POM is relatively low. The second is when the premium for the grade you are considering buying is low compared to the next lower grade. The third is when the price of gold is not high enough to materially increase the risk of a substantial price correction.

Both Maurice Rosen and Scott A. Travers believe that the gold coins described in this appendix should constitute no more than a tiny part of your overall holdings. Readers are urged to consult competent financial service professionals and expert coin dealers to determine the suitability, if any, of the coins described herein.

GLOSSARY

abrasion: an acquired mark or nick that mars a coin's surface and lowers its eye appeal.

abrasive: the category of chemicals or substances which, if used on coins, will abrade or scrape away the top layer of metal.

accumulation: a hoard or group of coins being held at a common location.

album: a holder used by collectors to store coins of a series. A useful way of assessing progress in completing a collection.

alloy: a solid solution made by melting two or more metals together. Most U.S. coins are made of alloys, rather than a single metal.

almost: a term often used to describe a coin which is near a higher grade, but isn't that grade.

altered: usually a genuine but common coin that has been tampered with by an unscrupulous person in order to make it resemble a rare coin.

ANA: American Numismatic Association, world's largest coin collector organization, and the former owner of ANACS.

appraisal: professional opinion offered by a dealer. Appraisals are rarely objective because dealers like to buy coins for less than they are worth.

ask: the Ask column of *The Coin Dealer Newsletter*. Refers to "wholesale" prices dealers are asking for particular coins.

attribution: the description and background information given to a coin in a dealer's retail catalog, auction catalog, etc. Does not refer to a grade.

bag-mark: a mark on a coin's surface which has been acquired through contact with another coin or coins banging around inside a Mint-sewn bag.

bid: the Bid column of *The Coin Dealer Newsletter*. Refers to "wholesale" prices dealers are offering to pay for certain coins.

bidder: a person participating as a buyer in an auction or making serious offers to buy a coin or coins in competition with others wanting that same material.

blank: a disc (usually round) on which a coin is to be struck.

Bluesheet: *The Certified Coin Dealer Newsletter* (CCDN), a weekly guide which reports on the "sight-unseen" market for coins graded by grading services. Its bid prices refer to the lowest quality traded for the grade.

book: the list of mail bidders and submitted competitive bids to buy coins at public auction.

bourse: the room where dealers gather to buy and sell rare coins.

branch mint: a coin-producing U.S. Mint facility other than the main mint in Philadelphia.

Breen: *Walter Breen's Complete Encyclopedia of U.S. and Colonial Coins.*

brilliant: a term used to describe the bright, untoned surfaces of certain U.S. coins, especially Proofs.

Brown & Dunn (B&D): *A Guide to the Grading of United States Coins*, by Martin R. Brown and John W. Dunn, a once widely used grading guide with line drawings to illustrate wear.

bullion: uncoined gold or silver in ingots or bars.

business strike: a coin manufactured by the Mint for everyday use.

cabinet friction: a specific type of wear on a coin which has circulated slightly. The term originated in dealers' catalogs years ago when coins were stored in elaborate cabinets with velvet trays. The coins slid about on these trays and developed "cabinet friction" on their highest points.

cameo: usually denotes a contrast between frosted fields and reflective devices.

carbon flecks/spots: usually spots which are not really carbon, but dense areas of toning on a coin's surface. These spots, attributed to "mishandling," are darkened areas resulting from contact with saliva.

cartwheel: a term for a silver dollar, suggesting its large size in relation to other coins.

cataloger: the individual who assigns a grade to a coin or coins in a dealer's catalog (e.g., retail or auction).

CDN: shorthand for *The Coin Dealer Newsletter*, a widely used weekly price guide often called the *Greysheet*.

Choice: a term for a Mint State coin that is better than ordinary but less than "Gem."

circulated: a term for a coin that has been passed from hand to hand and shows evidence of wear.

clad: a type of coin made by the U.S. Mint since 1965 which consists of two outer layers of copper-nickel alloy bonded to a core of pure copper.

commemoratives: special coins issued to mark an important event or honor a person or organization.

Condition-census: the finest existing condition of a given coin. Does not refer to the finest condition ever known or the finest condition possible.

consignor: person whose coins are sold by an auction company.

corrosion: rust or similar unsightly damage on the surface of a coin, usually caused by a chemical reaction.

counterfeit: a fake coin.

cycle: the historical boom-and-bust price performance tendency of the coin market.

denomination: the face value of a coin, such as cent, nickel, or dime.

detraction: an imperfection, either Mint-made or acquired, which detracts from a coin's grade or value or both.

devices: the parts on a coin that stand out, such as the lettering, portrait, and stars.

die: a metal object engraved with a coin's design, used to strike or stamp out coins.

DMPL: shorthand for Deep Mirror Prooflike, a term applied to coins, especially silver dollars, with unusually brilliant, reflective surfaces.

doubled die: term applied to coins with doubling of the letters and date resulting from the die itself having been struck twice in misaligned positions.

edge: a coin's side; the part you touch when you hold a coin properly. This is not to be confused with obverse or reverse.

estimate: dealer's written approximation in his or her auction catalog of what a coin is worth and might sell for at that auction.

exhibit: a display of coins with educational information shown at a coin show and competing for a prize.

eye appeal: a controversial ingredient of coin grading that encompasses a coin's color or quality of toning and strike.

face value: the amount of money a coin represents as a medium of exchange. For example, the face value of a nickel is 5 cents.

fields: the parts of the coin that serve as background and don't stand out.

flip: a pliable, two-pocket coin holder which folds over. The coin is inserted in one pocket; a written description of the coin is inserted in the other pocket.

Gem: a Mint State coin of unusually high quality.

grade: the universal language which coin enthusiasts use to describe what a coin looks like or how much wear and tear it has endured; depends upon level of preservation and overall beauty.

Greysheet: *The Coin Dealer Newsletter (CDN),* a weekly publication essential for successful coin transactions, and the *CDN Monthly Supplement*, the CDN's monthly publication. These are the most relied-upon guides for accurate prices.

hairlines: a patch or patches of light, almost unnoticeable scratches, especially on Proof coins. Usually caused by cleaning.

high relief: a term for a coin on which the design elements stand out above the surface more than usual. High-relief coins typically possess sharp detail, but their high points are exposed and abnormally subject to wear.

impaired Proof: a Proof that has been mishandled, so that its grade is equivalent to that of a circulated business-strike coin.

insert: a sturdy piece of paper with a description of a coin which is inserted into one pocket of a flip-type coin holder.

Judd: a popular reference work written about pattern coins: *United States Pattern, Experimental and Trial Pieces*, by J. Hewitt Judd, M.D. (issued most recently in an edition edited by Q. David Bowers with pricing by Robert L. Hughes). Each pattern is given a "Judd number." These numbers are referred to almost any time a pattern is offered for sale.

junk dealer: a dealer who sells inexpensive and relatively common circulated coins, as well as rolls of Uncirculated recent-issue coins.

Kointain: a trademark and popular name for a transparent, curvilinear triacetate coin capsule that fits snugly around the coin and is used to protect it.

legend: an inscription on a coin.

lettered edge: a term used when letters and/or numbers are inscribed on the side of a coin.

luster: the circular pattern in which a true Uncirculated coin reflects light.

market-maker: a dealer who makes offers to buy certified coins sight-unseen.

Matte Proof: a Proof produced by a process that imparts dull, granular surfaces, sometimes said to have a "sandblast" appearance.

mintage: the number of examples of a given coin produced with the same date at a given mint.

Mint error: a coin with a mistake that occurred during its manufacture. Some collectors collect only Mint errors.

Mint-mark: the letter or letters on a coin indicating where it was minted: No Mint-mark: Philadelphia or West Point; P: Philadelphia; O: New Orleans; CC: Carson City; S: San

Francisco; D: Denver or (on pre-1862 gold coins) Dahlonega; W: West Point; C: Charlotte.

Mint State: the condition of a coin that has not circulated. Mint State coins should not exhibit wear. The terms Mint State and Uncirculated are the same.

motto: an inscription on a coin, such as "Liberty," "In God We Trust," and "E Pluribus Unum."

MS: a shorthand description for "Mint State"

mutilated: a term for a coin that has been damaged or defaced in an obvious way.

national show: a coin convention attended by dealers from throughout the country.

NCI-certified: authenticated and graded by the Numismatic Certification Institute, a division of Heritage Capital Corporation, a coin dealership. The coin should be accompanied by a photo-certificate. NCI no longer actively grades, but its 1985 standard is regarded as a coin-grading benchmark.

NGC-certified: authenticated and graded by the Numismatic Guaranty Corporation of America. The coin should be encapsulated in a tamper-resistant holder.

non-abrasive: the category of chemicals or substances which, if applied to coins, will not remove the top layer of metal. Non-abrasives are usually not harmful to coins.

numismatics: the study of coins, medallic art, and paper money.

obverse: the front or "heads" side of a coin.

off center: a term for a coin struck on a planchet improperly aligned with the dies, so that the design elements aren't centered.

overgrading: describing a coin as being in a higher grade than it actually is.

overpaying: paying more money for a coin than the coin is worth.

overtones: traces of toning colors on a coin that is toned one primary color.

patina: the brownish color that forms on the top layer of metal on copper coins.

pattern: a coin struck by the Mint to see how an experimental design would look if made into a coin.

PCGS-certified: authenticated and graded by the Professional Coin Grading Service. The coin should be encapsulated in a tamper-resistant holder.

periphery: the outermost area of a coin's obverse or reverse. Can be identified by a thin imaginary ring around the obverse or reverse.

Photograde: a grading guide by James F. Ruddy with photographs of coins. Helpful guide to grading circulated coins.

PL: shorthand for "Prooflike," a term applied to a business-strike coin whose brilliant surfaces resemble those of a Proof.

plain edge: a term used when the side of a coin is smooth, not reeded or lettered.

planchet: a blank disc ready to receive impressions from two dies and become a coin.

polyvinylchloride (PVC): a plastic found in many popular coin holders. Destructive to valuable Uncirculated coins.

premium: the amount of money a coin is worth above its face value. This value is set in the rare-coin marketplace.

premium quality (PQ): refers to a coin of one grade which nearly qualifies to be assigned the next highest grade.

preservation: refers to how well a coin has been kept since it was made by the Mint. Careful steps have to be taken by the collector to make sure that coins are meticulously stored and remain well preserved.

prices realized: the list of prices of coins sold in auction and usually available from the auction house within a few weeks after the auction.

Proof: a coin struck by the Mint especially for collectors to save. Proof coins are struck twice on specially polished dies and specially selected planchets to assure a chromium-like brilliance.

Prooflike: a coin made by the Mint for circulation which looks like a proof. A Prooflike coin has similar reflective properties to a Proof.

raw: a coin which has not been certified by a grading service.

Red Book: *A Guide Book of United States Coins*, by Richard S. Yeoman.

reeded edge: a term used when the side of a coin has raised ridges. These were placed on gold and silver coins to discourage removal of metal, and continue to be used on some coins that contain no precious metal.

regional show: a coin convention attended by dealers from a number of nearby states.

registry [illegible] a set of coins assembled for inclusion in the Set Registry program of the P[illegible]oin Grading Service or a similar program of another grading service. (See [illegible]

[illegible] coin struck by the Mint at a later date with dies which suggest that the [illegible]n earlier date.

reverse: the back or "tails" side of a coin.

rims: the raised rings which encircle the obverse and reverse and protect a coin from wear.

rip: a coin bought for considerably below its real value.

roll: in general, a stack of coins of the same denomination, year, and Mint-mark. The number of coins composing a roll is often, but not always, fifty.

series: a collection of an example of each coin date and Mint-mark issued for a specific type coin design.

Sheldon: the late Dr. William Sheldon, author of *Penny Whimsy*, the book about large cents in which the coin-grading scale of 1-to-70 was introduced.

slab: a plastic, tamper-resistant holder in which a coin is sealed.

slider: a lightly circulated coin that appears to be Uncirculated.

SMS: an acronym for "special mint set," a type of coin set sold by the U.S. Mint from 1965 to 1967.

state quarter: one of a series of special Washington quarter dollars issued by the U.S. Mint in its 50-State Quarters Program. The reverse of each coin bears a commemorative design honoring one of the 50 states of the Union.

stick: a term used by mail-order coin dealers. Usually refers to an overpriced and less than desirable coin sold through the mail and not returned for a refund by the buyer.

striations: light patches of a raised scratch-like texture that result from polishing of a die.

strike: the quality of design detail present on a coin after it is minted.

Swiatek & Breen: *The Encyclopedia of United States Silver and Gold Commemorative Coins*, by Anthony Swiatek and Walter Breen.

switch: occurs when a less expensive coin is substituted for a valuable coin by an unscrupulous person.

table: a booth at a coin convention rented by a dealer from which to conduct business.

teletype: any of a number of networks used by dealers to communicate and do business with each other. Although many dealers use the teletype for contacts, these same dealers often confirm terms and negotiate prices over the telephone.

toning: a slow, natural, regular process by which a coin oxidizes over a period of months and years.

Type: an example of a major design of coin (e.g., Barber quarters and Liberty Seated halves). Does not refer to different metals of the same coin type. Sometimes used to refer to variety (e.g., Type I).

Uncirculated: a coin that has never circulated or been spent and, most importantly, has no wear on its highest parts.

underbidder: the person bidding on an auction lot in an unreserved public auction who does not bid high enough to acquire the coin he or she is seeking, but whose bids are second-highest.

undercounting: an unscrupulous practice by which, for example, a "fifty-coin roll" containing only forty-nine coins is sold at the fifty-coin price.

undergrading: describing a coin as being in a lower grade than it actually is in.

vest-pocket dealer: a dealer who goes to coin shows with an inventory of coins in his or her vest pocket. Vest-pocket dealers rarely take tables at coin shows and often deal in coins on a part-time basis.

view: looking at coins to be sold at auction at a set later date. During this presale viewing, prospective buyers have the opportunity to assess a coin's suitability, grade, authenticity, etc.

virtually: a popular term used to gloss over a coin's shortcomings. "Virtually free of scratches" means the coin has scratches.

weak strike: a coin produced without sharp detail; a weakly struck coin may appear worn, but is still considered Mint State if the lack of detail is from the way it was made, not from subsequent use.

wear: the smoothing or abrading of a coin's top layer of metal caused by circulation.

whiz: artificially simulating Mint luster by removing the top layer of a coin's metal with a circular wire brush and/or abrasive chemical.

INDEX

D

E

ABOUT THE AUTHOR

Scott A. Travers ranks as one of the most knowledgeable and influential coin dealers in the world. His name is familiar to readers everywhere as the author of six bestselling books on coins: *One-Minute Coin Expert*, *How to Make Money in Coins Right Now*, *Travers' Rare Coin Investment Strategy*, *Scott Travers' Top 88 Coins Over $100*, *The Insider's Guide to U.S. Coin Values*, and *The Investor's Guide to Coin Trading*. All of them have won awards from the prestigious Numismatic Literary Guild (NLG). In 2002, NLG awarded him its highest bestowable honor, the lifetime achievement Clemy. He was elected vice president (1997-1999) of the American Numismatic Association, a congressionally chartered, nonprofit educational organization. He is contributing editor to *COINage* magazine and a regular contributor to other numismatic periodicals, and has served as a coin valuation consultant to the Federal Trade Commission. His opinions as an expert are often sought by publications such as *Barron's*, *Business Week*, and The *Wall Street Journal*. A frequent guest on radio and television programs, Scott Travers has won awards and gained an impressive reputation not only as a coin expert but also as a forceful consumer advocate for the coin-buying public. He serves as numismatic advisor to a number of major investment funds and has coordinated the liquidation of numerous important coin collections. He is president and member of Scott Travers Rare Coin Galleries, LLC, in New York City.

CONTACT THE AUTHOR

The author welcomes your comments and reports on how well you did following the suggestions given in this book. Although there is no guarantee of an answer, every inquiry will be carefully studied.

Scott A. Travers
Scott Travers Rare Coin Galleries, LLC

P. O. Box 1711, FDR Station
New York, NY 10150-1711
Telephone: 212-535-9135
Facsimile: 212-535-9138
E-mail: travers@pocketchangelottery.com
Internet: www.pocketchangelottery.com